John Anderson

Essays on various subjects relative to the present state of religion

John Anderson

Essays on various subjects relative to the present state of religion

ISBN/EAN: 9783337718817

Printed in Europe, USA, Canada, Australia, Japan

Cover: Foto ©Lupo / pixelio.de

More available books at **www.hansebooks.com**

ESSAYS

ON

VARIOUS SUBJECTS

RELATIVE TO THE

PRESENT STATE OF RELIGION

1. On the Controversy about some BURGESS OATHS.
2. On the SECESSION TESTIMONY.
3. On PUBLIC COVENANTING.
4. On the REVOLUTION SETTLEMENT.
5. On CHURCH COMMUNION.
6. On the Constitution of the ASSOCIATE SYNOD.
7. On ECCLESIASTICAL CENSURES.
8. On the Religious CHARACTER of the TIMES.

By JOHN ANDERSON.

PREFACE.

THE Judicial testimony of the associate presbytery, has now been forty-five years in the hands of the public; and yet it seems to be little attended to or understood. Hence the cold indifference of its professed friends; while others are led by prejudice to an open enmity against it. "The greater part of "your testimony," say many, "consists of facts "with which we are unacquainted, and in which we "cannot conceive ourselves to have any interest. "We never thought Christianity required us to study "the precise meaning of acts of parliament, or the "exactness of the dates of history. Satisfied that "the duties of our station are enough to employ our "whole attention, we leave it to the critics and to "the dealers in controversy, to wrangle about those "insignificant circumstances. In short, we cannot "see the *practical* use of your testimony: shew us "that it contributes to render the espousers of it "more meek, more humble, more self-denied, more "abundant in the love of God and men, and more "free from all the opposite vices, or we shall still "continue to judge it unworthy of our examination." These objections have been kept in eye through the following essays: so that the subjects of them are treated in a practical, rather than in a critical or controversial manner.

Though the writer has endeavoured to consider these subjects without regard to any party or any prejudice; though he wished truth to be the ornament of his page, and was well resolved to follow where-ever evidence led; he will hardly escape the imputation of a blameable attachment to the opinions of *his party*, especially with such readers as have the most obstinate and bigotted predilection for those of *their own*. But it may be asked, whether a writer's principles should be disregarded, because he is so much convinced of the truth and importance of those principles, that he esteems it his happiness to enjoy the fellowship of a church that professes her adherence to them? Mr. Locke's treatise on civil government is materially a defence of the constitution of his own country as it was established at the Revolution: Is it therefore the less valuable? The truth is, to *reject* a religious opinion, merely because it is held by those with whom we are connected, would be no less unreasonable, but far more ill natured and inconsistent than to *receive* it on that account.

THE writer must now leave these Essays to the judgment of the candid reader; or rather he wishes to leave them in his hand, who alone can make them useful to his church; who *hath chosen the foolish things of the world to confound the wise; the weak things of the world, to confound the things that are mighty: the base things of the world, and things which are despised, hath God chosen; yea, and things which are not, to bring to nought the things which are.*

ESSAY I.

Of SOME BURGESS OATHS.

WHEN People are formed into Societies, they always come under obligations, which are either expressed or implied, to be useful to one another. Sometimes these obligations are confirmed by an Oath. Hence when one is admitted member of a Corporation, or obtains the freedom of a city, he is commonly sworn to be faithful to the interests of that City or Corporation.

ONE would naturally expect that the obligations he should have to come under on being admitted into any Society, would be only such as are suitable to the nature of that Society, and to the end for which it was formed: if it were a civil Society, that the obligations would be of a secular kind; or if it were a religious Society, that they would be of a religious kind. But from the great influence which religion is generally acknowledged to have on human affairs, from the pride and animosity of religious parties who are too apt to magnify themselves upon any worldly advantage they have over one another, and from the prevailing disposition of the multitude to mingle religion with their worldly interests, and to make the former subservient to the latter; from these and the like causes it has come about that persons are too often brought under explicit engagements to some profession of religion in order to their admission into a Society of a purely civil nature. Thus in some Burgess Oaths we have the following religious clause, which has been the subject of so much controversy among Seceders: 'I protest before God and your Lordships 'that I profess and allow with my heart the true re-'ligion presently professed within this realm and au-'thorised by the laws thereof, renouncing the Ro-'man religion called Papistry.'

History of the Controversy concerning the Religious Clause in some Burgess Oaths.

In the Year 1744, The Associate Presbytery found it necessary, from the multiplicity of business and from the extent of the Secession, to form itself into a Synod, which was to have three Presbyteries subordinate to it. The Associate Synod met for the first time in the beginning of March 1745.

One of the first things which they entered upon, was, the consideration of a motion for the removal of hindrances to the duty of Covenanting; a motion which immediately brought on the controversy of the religious clause in some Burgess Oaths, that clause being deemed by several members inconsistent with the present state of the Secession Testimony. The views of these members were vehemently opposed, and the debate was carried on at great length in each of the four meetings that were held in 1745.

At last, on the ninth of April in the following year, the Synod came to a decision, by which the

"Swearing of the Religious Clause in some Burgess Oaths, by any under their Inspection, as that clause comes necessarily in this period, to be used and applied, does not agree to the present state of the testimony for religion and reformation, which the Synod, with those under their inspection, are maintaining, and particularly that it does not consist with an entering into the Bond for Renewing our Solemn Covenants: and that therefore those of the Secession cannot further, with safety of conscience and without sin, swear any Burgess Oath with the said Religious Clause; while matters with reference to the profession and settlement of Religion, continue in such circumstances as at present."

This decision was carried by a majority of thirteen against nine.

The thinness of the house and the smallness of the majority have been objected to this decision.

If that thinness or majority could be proved to have been procured by unfair means, such a circumstance would, no doubt, very much diminish the authority of the decision. But since this can hardly be said to have been so much as attempted, (whatever may have been suggested as to the impropriety of the time in which a question of so great importance was brought to a determination) the validity of this decision, as a deed of the Associate Synod, stands unimpeached.

It is necessary to observe that it was not a negative that was opposed to the overture for condemning the religious clause; but only a motion for a delay. Hence one would naturally suppose that several, who were convinced of the unlawfulness of the Burgess Oath, would be led, from the consideration of circumstances, to vote for a delay: And this was actually the case; for we are well assured that some voted for the delay who afterwards acquiesced in the decision. So that the friends of the overture absolutely considered, were a much greater number than they appeared to be from this division.

The Synod met again in September, 1746. Those who had protested against the decision concerning the religious clause of some Burgess Oaths, now thought proper to bring in the question, Whether that decision should be a term of Ministerial and Christian Communion?

A Reader who is unacquainted with the history of this affair, if he has only read the Synod's decision, will be very much surprised at this question, as it seems to insinuate that the decision might stand, and yet the evil of swearing the Burgess Oath never be taken notice of; and that the Synod might find something to be a heinous and publick offence; an offence no less than that of swearing contradictory oaths; and at the same time go into a resolution exempting the offenders from all censure.

This question was of such a nature that the bringing in and vehement pressing of it gave every one just cause to fear an approaching rupture of the Synod. The question, Whether the decision with regard to the religious clause in some Burgess Oaths, was to be a term of Communion? was the same as Whether the protestors against the decision, adhering to the spirit of their protest, were still to be in Communion with the supporters of the decision? that is, Whether there was or was not to be a breach? Let any one judge, then, who were most instrumental in bringing on that mournful event? those who were for such a question, or those who were against it?

It has been often observed, that this was a question in which those who had protested against the Synod's decision, were parties. They would not have been so in the question, Whether the Act should be repealed? that being a question concerning a point of truth and duty, of the same import as Whether the religious clause in some Burgess Oaths were sinful? But this question, Term, or not, of communion? seemed to suppose the condemnatory Act of Synod, and respected the consequence of inattention or opposition to that Act. It was, in effect, evidently the same as if it had been, Whether those who neglected or opposed the Synod's decision, were to be found fault with? Now, let the Reader judge, whether a violent opposer of that decision was a party in such a question.

SEVERAL members pleaded with great force of argument against proceeding any further in the consideration of this question. But others, and, among these some of the most respectable names insisted on it so warmly, that the majority agreed to have it further considered, thinking that, as yet, it would not be expedient to throw it out.

ON the eighth of April 1747, those who had protested against the Synod's decision, again brought in their question in this larger form: "Whether the decision about the religious clause "of some Burgess Oaths, passed by this Synod "in April, 1746, shall now or afterwards be "made a term of Ministerial or Christian Com- "munion; ay and until the making of the "same to be so, shall be referred by way of o- "verture, unto Presbyteries and Kirk-sessions, "in order to their giving their judgment there- "anent: that so there may, in the mean time, "be a friendly dealing among the members of "the Synod with one another, in a way of con- "ference and prayer; in order to their coming, "through the Lord's pity, to see eye to eye in "the matter of the said religious clause."

ANOTHER motion was made at the same time for having the reasons read which those who protested against the Synod's decision, had given in, together with the answers which a committee had prepared. The question was put as to which of these motions should be first considered. A majority of seven votes was in favour of the former, the whole being twenty nine against twenty two. From this resolution fourteen ministers and ten elders dissented.

NEXT day, the friends of the question concerning the Synod's decision being a term of Communion insisting, with great animosity, on having it put without further delay, those on the other side joined in solemn declarations against the Synod going on to vote upon such a question: While the lights, which might have been given to the matter in dispute by hearing the before-mentioned reasons and answers, were suppressed; and while those who were directly parties in the affair, sustained themselves judges.

THESE declarations being made, the impatience of those in the opposition to the Synod's decision, was now so much increased as to admit of no longer delay. The Moderator was required, once and again, to call or to order the calling of the roll. The Moderator made no reply. Nor would the Clerk be prevailed on to call it. The business of voting on this question was now at a stand, had not the boldness of two members come in to help it forward: Mr. John Mac Cara and Mr. Henry Erskine thought proper to take upon them of their own accord, the one to call the roll, the other to mark the votes.

THOSE who voted in favour of the motion (and there were no other voters on this occasion) were in all nine Ministers and eleven Elders, of whom six Ministers and one Elder were directly parties.

AMIDST so affecting a scene, it was necessary that some one should act as Moderator, and maintain the Constitution of the Synod, the present Moderator, in the violence of the tumult, having ceased acting. In this case, it was necessary for those who adhered to the Constitution and the before-mentioned Decision of the Synod, to take measures, as they must have done, if a band of robbers, or the sweep of an irresistible tempest had deprived them of some of their number, and among others, of the Moderator and Clerk.

It is usual in Presbyterial courts for the Moderator of the former meeting to officiate, as occasion requires, for the present Moderator. According to this custom, it was the part of Mr. Thomas Mair to deliver the following declaration.

" Whereas this meeting of Synod have now
" passed a Vote, and made a resolution upon that
" question, which has been insisted upon in oppo-
" sition to a proceeding unto the reasons against
" the sentence of Synod in April 1746, with the
" answers to said Reasons : And considering the
" protestations which have been entered this day,
" concerning that affair ; considering that by the
" foresaid step this meeting of Synod have mate-
" rially dropt the whole Testimony among their
" hands, allowing of, at least for a time, a ma-
" terial abjuration thereof ; and considering that
" besides a considerable number of Elders, the
" majority of Ministers, who are the proper judg-
" es in a controversy of Faith and case of Consci-
" ence, and who could be judges in the present
" controversy, have been all along contending for
" the proper business and duty of the Synod, in
" opposition to the contrary torrent : Therefore
" I Thomas Mair, Minister of the Gospel at Or-
" wel, do hereby declare, and protest, that the
" lawful authority and power of the ASSOCIATE
" SYNOD is devolved upon, and must ly in a con-

"stitute meeting of the forefaid Members, Minifters and Elders, together with any other Members who shall cleave unto them in a way of confessing what sinful steps and compliances they have fallen into on this occasion: As likewise I declare and protest, that the forefaid members ought, in duty to the Lord and his heritage, to take up and exercise the authority and power of the Associate Synod, lawfully and fully devolved upon them as above; and, for this end, to meet to-morrow at ten of the clock forenoon, in Mr Gib's House, that they may regularly enter upon and proceed in the business of the Synod."

Mr. Mair having made this declaration, removed with the twelve other Ministers and ten Elders who had all along maintained a vigorous opposition to the putting of the before-mentioned question. They met next day in Mr Gib's House, and unanimously passed an Act, asserting the Constitution and Rights of the Associate Synod. They afterwards proceeded to inflict Censure on the separating Brethren. The sentence of the greater Excommunication was not passed till nearly two years after the breach. Meanwhile, the controversy of the religious clause in some Burgess Oaths was carried on in a great many publications on both sides.

In the course of the debate, the field of enquiry was gradually enlarged, and several other subjects were handled; such as, the nature of the Church's Testimony, the duty of Public Covenanting, the Scriptural terms of Church Communion, and the object and effect of Church Censures. *A little leaven leaveneth the whole lump.* The cloud that appears at first only a small speck, overspreads in a little while the ample sky. An opinion which was once deemed harmless or of little consequence, has at length been seen to diffuse itself so widely as to give the prevailing tincture to the whole religious system of those who entertained it.

Of the IMPORTANCE *of the* CONTROVERSY *concerning the* RELIGIOUS CLAUSE *in some* BURGESS OATHS.

THE Importance of this controversy is a very natural conclusion from the history of it; considering the characters of those great and good men, who were engaged in it, and who, we may reasonably think, would not have disturbed the peace of the church for a light or trivial matter; considering too, the many important points that have been drawn into this controversy.

But it is a controversy that evidently carries very great importance in itself.

1. It is a controversy about an Oath, which is a solemn appeal to The Most High God, Possessor of heaven and earth, the Searcher of hearts, with regard to a person's truth and sincerity in what he says. If this appeal is either unnecessary, or in favour of any falsehood, it must be taking God's name in vain. The good man is one that *feareth an Oath*, Eccles. ix. 2.

2. This Oath contains a solemn engagement to a religious Profession; even to that which is presently authorised by the laws of the land. Now the glory of God and the good of our own souls, which are incomparably the most important things in the world, are nearly concerned in our profession of religion; for it is written, *With the mouth Confession is made unto Salvation.* It behoves us, therefore, to consider with all possible care, attention and impartiality, what is indeed sworn to in this

Oath, before we either take it, or justify the taking of it. If the religion presently professed and authorised by the laws of the land is wrong, so far wrong that we cannot safely hold Church Communion with those whom these laws acknowledge as the professors of it; engaging to it by oath, would, in that case, be unspeakably dishonouring to God, and prejudicial to our own souls.

3. It is a fact sufficiently known, that the swearing of this Oath has given great offence to many of those whom we must regard as the friends and followers of Christ. But such offence is to be avoided by every lawful mean, as a most dangerous evil. It is an awful word which we have in Matth. xviii. 6. *But whoso shall offend one of these little ones that believe in me, it were better for him that a milstone were hanged about his neck, and that he were cast into the depths of the sea.* Thus our Lord manifests his wonderful tenderness for his people by the guard that he plants around them. Good reason had the apostle to say, 1. Cor. viii. 13. *If meat make my brother offend, I will eat no flesh while the world standeth, lest I make my brother to offend.*

O ye Rulers and Courts of Judicature, whether higher or lower, whether belonging to the Church or the State, beware of thinking it a small matter to offend the Followers of Christ. On this account, the Synod of the Apostles and Elders, at Jerusalem, Acts xv. enjoined the Gentile converts to abstain from blood. Supported by such a precedent, the Associate Synod might well prohibit the Swearing of the Religious Clause of some Burgess Oaths, even supposing that clause, like the use of blood, to be in itself a matter of indifference.

Hence it is improper to speak of the truth on this head as a matter of doubtful disputation in which the Scripture, though the only Rule of our faith and practice, gives no certain direction. The

Bible is the whole Religion of Proteſtants, and ſerves for a lamp to guide their feet in the way of truth and peace with regard to every matter of real importance.

Of the Meaning of the Religious Clause in ſome BURGESS OATHS.

ONE circumſtance that may lead us into the true meaning of it, is the Time in which theſe Oaths were framed; the time of the reformation from Popery. The religious Clauſe would no doubt, be adapted to the ſtate of religion at that time. But it is well known, that in Scotland Proteſtants were then all included in one Church Communion. The original Framers, then, of this religious Clauſe, regarding the ſtate of religion in their own time, cannot reaſonably be ſuppoſed to have intended any other thing in theſe words, " I " profeſs and allow with my heart the true religion " preſently profeſſed within this realm, and autho- " riſed by the laws thereof," than an engagement to continue in that Communion which was deſcribed in the laws. Hence if we would keep to the primary deſign of the Framers of theſe Burgeſs Oaths, we muſt conſider the religious Clauſe as an obligation to that Communion authoriſed by the laws of the land.

If any ſhould aſk, Whether our Forefathers meant, that we ſhould continue in the Communion of the Church by law eſtabliſhed, whatever her corruptions might be? we anſwer, by no means: But theſe Burgeſs Oaths were adapted to times, like their own, of reformation; and not to times of prevailing apoſtacy when the witneſſes of Chriſt are called forth to a Seceſſion from the Communion of the Church established by law. The word *Presently* intimates, that the religious Clause is to be always understood as having a respect to the state of religion at the time in which it is administered; and that it must be taken, or refused accordingly.

It is obvious that the words, "presently professed within this realm, and authorised by the laws of it," are an explication of the general expression, "I profess the true religion." Hence the meaning would have been no other than it is, if the particle *as* had been used after the words *true religion*. Let us try any sentence where, after a general term, words are used by way of explication, and we shall constantly find that inserting this particle does nothing to alter the meaning of the sentence. Thus in the following sentence: Man, being a rational creature, is capable of glorifying and enjoying God: If we put the particle *as* after the word *man*, it gives the sentence a more formal air of precision, but still the meaning is the same. It is true, when the words that are used after a general term are not meant to explain it, but only to point out some accidental circumstance, the inserting of the particle *as* would often be very improper. So in the following sentence: He fought bravely with a sword formerly worn by a coward: Here *as* worn by a coward, would be ridiculous. But nobody supposes that the words in the religions clause, immediately following the general expression, *I profess the true religion*, are of this kind.

It is a received maxim, that every oath should be taken in the sense of the administrator, and in pursuance of his declared design; and that all those to whom he administers it at the same time, should be considered as taking it in the same sense. Hence one should think, that, as the administrator of these Burgess Oaths himself professes the true religion in the way of Communion with the Church authorifed by the laws of the Realm, fo he would naturally expect that thofe who take thefe Oaths, fhould profefs the true religion in the fame way. The practice of the magiftrate may ferve to afcertain the fenfe in which he intends thefe Oaths fhould be taken. Befides, to fuppofe that the Magiftrate, while he adminifters thefe Oaths to all in precifely the fame terms, really means to bring under an engagement to profefs the true religion, fo many in one way, fo many in a different way; fome to be in Communion with the eftablifhed Church, and others to be in a ftate of Seceffion from it; to fuppofe this appears to be altogether abfurd, and deprives thefe Oaths, not only of the fenfe of the adminiftrator, but of any determinate fenfe whatfoever.

PERHAPS fome one will fay, The religious claufe may be underftood of the Profeffion, as diftinguifhed from the finful Practice, of the eftablifhed Church; a profeffion which lies in an acknowledgment of the Scripture as the word of God, of the Confeffion of faith as grounded on the Scriptures, and of Prefbyterial Church government and difcipline.

IT may be obferved, that fuch an explication departs from the plain and obvious defign of the religious Claufe, which is, not to determine the particular points of doctrine or difcipline that the fwearer approves of, but to afcertain the Church Communion to which he belongs. An obligation to Communion in that religion which is defcribed as profeffed within this realm and authorifed by the laws, extends not to every particular contained in that profeffion, or in that authorifing; becaufe fuch an obligation can bind one to no more than what Church Communion itfelf binds one to. But when a perfon holds communion with any Church, it does not neceffarily follow, that he approves of whatever evils he may see in her—and no Church is without her evils—since it is enough for warranting communion with any Church, that she is evidently endeavouring to go on toward perfection, and to keep the word of Christ's patience. Hence it is not necessary to consider the religious Clause as obliging the swearer to all the particular opinions and practices of the Church of Scotland, but to be of her Communion.

But supposing, with the Objector, that the religious Clause contains an obligation to such particulars as are professed within this Realm and authorised by the laws; then, we must consider it as taking in the whole of what is so professed and authorised without making any distinctions, since the religious Clause itself makes none. Upon this supposition, the unfairness of the objector's interpretation of the religious Clause appears, whether we consider the religious profession of the Church of Scotland at present, or what is authorised by law with regard to it.

As for the word *Profession*, though it has been the subject of much refined Criticism, it occurs continually in conversation, and nobody complains of it as hard to be understood. A religious Profession is neither more nor less than a person's or a party's declaration of what is held by that person or party in matters of religion. Hence a conversation becoming the Gospel (considered as what we openly approve of, and consent to observe) is no less a part of our Christian Profession than the articles of our Creed. Hence, too, a corrupt practice in matters of religion,—in the administration, for example, of Church government and discipline, when openly avowed and obstinately persisted in, whatever testimonies are offered against it,—becomes at last, a part of the profession of that Church in which it has place. Thus Crossing in Baptism and Kneeling at the Lord's

Table may justly be said to belong to the Profession of the Church of England. In like manner, those corruptions which have been so long testified against, may now be regarded as belonging to the Profession of the Church of Scotland. If, therefore, we consider the swearer of the religious Clause as engaging to what is professed in that Church, honesty seems, on that supposition,—honesty that never allows us to take an Oath which we cannot take without making some fine distinction not either expressed or plainly implied in the Oath itself, seems to regard him as professing an attachment to the principles and practices which that Church, as represented in her Judicatures, publicly holds.

In like manner, if we consider the religious Clause as implying an approbation of particular things authorised by the laws of the land; then in order to know what is approved of in the religious Clause, we are to have recourse to these Laws only. Nor does the religious Clause warrant us to make any selection of such particulars. Hence no partial enumeration, like that in the objection, of those things with regard to religion that are authorised by the laws of Scotland, can be fairly admitted as an adequate explication of the religious Clause; since other things, as Patronages and the chief magistrate's power of Dissolving the Assemblies of the Church, are as much warranted by law as Presbyterial government. These evils, coming under the description, in the religious Clause, of being presently authorised by the laws of the land, can not be understood as excluded by the general term *true religion* : Because the meaning of the general term must be gathered from the explanatory words that follow it, and not the meaning of these words from the general term. Nor does it hinder these evils from being among the things authorised by the laws, that they are contrary to the Confession of faith, or other standards of the Church no less authorised by the laws ; because we are not to interpret the laws by our ideas of consistency in direct opposition to the letter of them. But supposing this to be the case, it is only setting the laws against one another, and making the religious Clause self-contradictory.

It appears, then, that the difficulty of reconciling the Clause in question to the state and testimony of Seceders, is far from being removed by supposing that it has not a respect to Church Communion, but only to some particular things with regard to religion authorised by the laws of Scotland: Because we must not make any selection of particulars which the Clause itself does not make : Nor will it mend the matter to call the assemblage which we ourselves have made of these particulars, the Constitution of the Church of Scotland, or by any other plausible name whatsoever: For the difficulty still recurs, whether no more is meant by the religious Clause than what we mean by such plausible name?

Some people seem to consider the religious Clause as merely a renunciation of Popery. But it is hard to conceive that these words, *renouncing the Roman religion called Popery*, express the whole design of the religious Clause, and that the rest of it has no further determinate meaning. Is it likely, that the Clause would ever be designed for all indiscriminately, who would renounce the Communion of the Church of Rome, whether Presbyterians or Episcopalians, whether members of the Greek Church or those that are denominated from Martin Luther?

On the whole, we should guard against those who take advantage of the imperfection and ambiguity of language to give a fair colouring to their opinions. " I overheard the other day," says Eugenio to his friend Probus, " some religious people talking together. The conversation happened to turn on a Secession of some Ministers and private Christians, which, they said, was not from the established Church of Scotland itself, but from its corruptions. Is this distinction applicable to the case of those who have withdrawn from the Communion of that establishment?" "In my opinion," says Probus, "it is not, unless departing from the Communion of a Church were the same thing as departing from the Corruptions of a Church. But these two may not only be distinguished in thinking, but they have been separated in fact. In the days of Henry VIII. the Church of England was separated from the communion of the Church of Rome, without being separated from the errors and superstitions of Popery. On the other hand, our Saviour and his disciples were members of the Jewish Church; and yet they separated themselves from its corruptions which were then great and numerous. Degenerate as the times are, we hope there are still some in the communion of the Church of Scotland, who desire to keep themselves from its prevailing evils. How far their conduct is proper, considering the present state of religion in that Church, is another question: But they are aiming at no more than what was attained by many witnesses of Christ in former days, that is, a Secession from the evils of a Church without a Secession from the Church itself."

"Perhaps, Eugenio, the persons you speak of meant some former state of the Church of Scotland. But it is not the use that Candour would make of language, to speak in such terms as lead one think of the Church of Scotland *at present*, when some *former* state of it is meant. Had these people said, The Secession is not from what the church of Scotland was in her purest times, a Critic might possibly have questioned the propriety of the word Secession as here applied, but there would have been no dispute about their meaning."

Of the Unlawfulness of Swearing the Religious Clause in some Burgess Oaths.

ABSTRACTING from the fault that many people find with the Clause in question, as being imposed for the purpose of qualifying persons for enjoying the privileges of free citizens, the swearing of it does not seem unlawful to one who, on solid and scriptural grounds, is so far satisfied with the profession of the true religion which is made by the Church referred to in the Clause, that he chooses to be of her communion.

It may be asked, How a person may safely come under such a general engagement as that in the religious Clause, while many things are allowed in the established Church that he cannot approve of?

As to this we may observe, that it seems agreeable to the word of God, and to the example of his people in past ages, that one may hold Communion with a church—though in many respects blameable, and may profess his adherence to her in the most solemn manner, provided one finds the following circumstances in her case:

First, If there is no call, in Providence, for a Secession from her communion. Those who fear the Lord are attentive to the course of Providence, comparing it as well as their heart and way with the word. Thus they often obtain satisfying light as to the time and manner of setting about particular duties. Though the Old Testament œconomy was, in effect, abolished upon the resurrection of Christ, yet the apostles and other believers did not absolutely forsake the Temple Service, till Providence clearly directed them to do so. But when their freedom from the yoke of the ceremonial law came to be set in the fairest light, when the Gospel was preached to the Gentiles, when the Jews had *filled up their sins,* and when *wrath had come upon them to the uttermost* in the destruction of their City and Temple, no Christian was then ignorant that it was unlawful to associate with the Jews in their form of worship. In like manner, when the love of the truth as it is in Jesus, brought Luther and Calvin and others out of the church of Rome, the faithful found themselves shut up to a secession from her, Providence having raised up and spirited these great men to lead his people out of mystical Babylon. Then was that voice heard from heaven, Rev. xviii. 4. *Come out of her my people, that ye be not partakers of her sins, and that ye receive not of her plagues.* Indeed, we are not to regard providences as the rule of our practice, for the word of Christ is our only rule; but Providences are the means or occasions of our attending to the rule; they often throw light on the rule; and they afford opportunities of putting the rule in practice. It appears then, that there are Providences—and let those who like the men of Issachar, 2 Chron. xii. 32. *have understanding of the times, to know what Israel ought to do,* observe when these providences take place—Providences, which call us to follow the direction of the Lord's word in separating ourselves from obstinately corrupt Churches, and after which it is no longer excuseable to hold communion with such Churches, or to come under any engagements to them, like that in the religious Clause of some Burgess Oaths.

SECONDLY, If there are real evidences that a Church is endeavouring to attain a greater measure of conformity to the law of Christ. An obligation of adherence to the state of religion in a Church that is endeavouring to make progress in reformation, is, in truth, an obligation to strive against every remaining corruption in her: Because so to strive is, in that case, only to espouse her cause; in regard that so far as she is in a reforming state, she is herself faithfully striving against all her own remaining corruptions. Thus we find the saints under the Old Testament, in communion with the Jewish Church, labouring to better her condition. Thus did our forefathers in Scotland, in the periods of our first and second reformation. But when a Church gives abundant evidence that she hates to be reformed; when every mean of reclaiming her serves only to increase her attachment to her idols; when she begins to disallow any plain or faithful testimony against her backsliding course, it becomes, at length, unlawful to continue in her communion, or to come under any such engagement to her as that in the religious Clause of some Burgess Oaths.

THIRDLY, If a Church is not in any stated opposition to a testimony for truth in another Communion. We are not to withdraw ourselves from the enjoyment of the ordinances of Christ in that Church where Providence casts our lot, on account of some —nay, not on account of many corruptions remaining in her, while we know of no other purer Communion that bears testimony against those corruptions. This was the case with the faithful members of the Jewish Church; who, had they forsaken the divine ordinances administered in her, could have enjoyed them no where else. This, too, has been the case of many in the Protestant Churches. But if it sufficiently appears that a Church is carrying on a malignant opposition to a testimony against her corruptions in another and purer Communion, we need not hesitate a moment to pronounce it utterly unlawful to be of her communion, or to come under such an engagement to her as that in the religious Clause of some Burgess Oaths.

On the whole, If Providence calls us out of a corrupt Church, that we may not be partakers of her sins; if she is found irreclaimable after every proper mean has been used for her recovery; if she is so far gone in corruption as to be a declared enemy to the cause of truth in another and purer communion; we ought, in these circumstances, to withdraw from her, and to hold the testimony of Jesus in a separate communion; and, in these circumstances, we cannot, without sin, take any Oath, like the religious Clause in question, obliging us to join in her profession of the true religion: And the sin in this matter, is greatly aggravated, if we have entered into a contrary obligation, like the bond of the Associate Presbytery, to exert ourselves for the support of *a Secession Testimony.*

THE dispute about the sense of this Clause, is much against it. That an Oath may be sworn *in truth, in judgment, and in righteousness*, its meaning should be clear and determinate. An ambiguous Oath has ever a tendency to ensnare, since it may be interpreted in a sense that probably is never once thought of by those who take it. Instead of being for confirmation the end of all strife, an ambiguous Oath is the beginning of strife. As to the religious Clause in question, even those who have written in defence of it, have not been able to settle its meaning with any degree of precision, sometimes seeming to understand it of the true religion in the abstract, sometimes of the true religion as it was settled at the Revolution, and sometimes only of a renunciation of Popery.

WHO can forbear lamentation, when he reflects on the mournful consequences of the dispute about the religious Clause of some Burgess Oaths? A goodly number of professors, gathered out of different parts of the land to the banner of truth, made a noble stand against the corruptions of the times, till that controversy, like some envious blast, rose and scattered them; while the honours of our Lord's Testimony seemed, for a time, to lie prostrate in the dust.

His way, however, *is in the sea, and his path in the great waters, and his footsteps are not known.* In all cases, we should avoid any expressions that favour of a reflection on God's good Providence. Let us believe that, however the breach may be considered as a testimony of the Lord's great displeasure with this generation, yet he who does all things well, who makes darkness light before his Church, and crooked things straight, will over-rule this matter, as he did the cruel jealousy of Joseph's brethren, and as he has done many other death-like events in every age, to the Church's unspeakable advantage: and that his cause shall, at length, shine forth with the more conspicuous lustre for having been a while under clouds.

ESSAY II.

Of the Secession Testimony.

TESTIMONY is a word that frequently occurs in the sacred writings. Sometimes it signifies the whole word of God, as in Isa. viii. 20. *To the law and to the testimony: if they speak not according to this word, it is because there is no light in them.* Sometimes it has a particular reference to God's revelation, which, indeed, comprehends the whole scope and design of the scriptures, as in John iii. 33. *He that receiveth the testimony of Christ hath set to his seal, that God is true.* This is represented with peculiar glory and solemnity, as the testimony of the three persons in the Godhead, 1 John v. 7. *There are three that bear record or testimony in heaven, the Father, the Word, and the Holy Ghost.* Ver. 11. *And this is the record, that God hath given to us eternal life, and this life is in his Son.* Such is God's testimony or declaration of the truth to men.

As the faith of the saints corresponds to the word of the gospel,† so they have their testimony corresponding to God's. Thus we read of their testimony, Rev. vi. 9. *I saw under the altar the souls of them that were slain for the word of God, and for the testimony which they held.* Rev. xii. 11. *And they overcame by the blood of the Lamb, and by the word of their testimony.* Thus the promise which the Father made

† Which is also called, *the faith* in Jude 3. and Rev. ii. 13.

to Chrift, is accomplifhed, Ifa. lix. 21. *My words which I have put in thy mouth, fhall not depart out of thy mouth, or out of the mouth of thy feed, nor out of the mouth of thy feed's feed, faith the Lord, from henceforth and for ever.*

In holding this teftimony, all the true followers of Chrift have communion with him. Chrift is the faithful and true Witnefs, Ifa. lv. 4. *Behold, I have given him for a Witnefs to the people, for a Leader and Commander to the people.* And his people have the fame character, Ifa. xliii. 10. *Ye are my witneffes, faith the Lord, and my fervant whom I have chofen.* It is on account of their fellowfhip with Chrift in adhering to and declaring this teftimony, that the world hates them, and fhews, on every occafion, an irreconcileable enmity againft them, Matth. ix. 22. *Ye fhall be hated of all men for my name's fake;* that is, on account of my teftimony which ye fhall exhibit. Hence this teftimony is called *The word of His patience,* Rev. iii. 10. as it is an occafion of manifefting the long-fuffering of our Lord himfelf toward the men of the world, while he delays to avenge his quarrel with them for their malignant oppofition to it; an occafion, too, of trying and exercifing the patience of thofe who through grace are cleaving to it.

Could men fee the mutual relation that the feveral parts of the teftimony of Chrift bear one to another; could they apprehend the full refult of them all: the luftre of the divine wifdom, holinefs, truth and mercy therein manifefted, would immediately overpower all their objections, and, if it did not bring them heartily to receive the truth, would put them to fhameful and everlafting filence. In which cafe, it feems to be only for the perfection of wickednefs in hell to make a direct oppofition. For this reafon it has always been the policy of Satan and his fervants to fingle out some particular part of Christ's testimony, to consider that part as unconnected with the rest, and then to employ against it all the force which the sophistry of worldly wisdom or the prejudices of a depraved imagination could supply.

When this is the case, the part of Christ's testimony, so attacked, becomes, in a special manner, the testimony of his followers: Their character of witnesses requires that they should then openly avow that part of his testimony; since the proper time for witnesses to confirm the truth by a public deposition, is when the truth is controverted. This part of Christ's testimony is, indeed, *The present Truth*, in which we are to be established, 2 Pet. i. 12. The present Truth has been sometimes one part of the testimony of Jesus, sometimes another. Against the Jews in the apostles' times, it was the truth of Christ's divine mission: In the fourth century, it was the Deity of Christ, and the efficacy of his grace, in opposition to the errors of Arius and Pelagius: In the seventh and eighth centuries, it was the simplicity and spirituality of God's worship in opposition to the idolatrous use of images: During the height of Antichrist's reign, it was the supreme authority of the Scriptures as the ony rule of faith and practice in opposition to unwritten traditions or the commandments of men: Finally, in the last age when the Church of Scotland reformed from Episcopacy, it was the Covenanted Union of *The Iles of the sea*, of Britain and Ireland, in the profession of the doctrine, worship, discipline and government of the Church, as Christ has appointed them in his word. A great body of ministers and people through these Lands, obtained mercy, at that time, to be faithful in holding this testimony; but, alas, what a falling off has there been since the year 1650! *The people have slidden back with a perpetual backsliding.* Providence, however, has never suffered this testimony to be altogether dropt. Some few were always endeavouring in one way or another, to stand forth the assertors of it; till, at length, it assumed its present form of A Secession Testimony.

Of the RISE and PROGRESS of the SECESSION TESTIMONY.

THIS denomination was occasioned in the following manner. In the year 1732, Mr Ebenezer Erskine delivered, before the Synod of Perth and Stirling, a sermon in which he gave a faithful testimony against the corruptions that then prevailed in the Church of Scotland, particularly, against an act that the Assembly had passed the same year giving the election of ministers to Protestant heritors and elders. The Synod judges him censurable for his plain dealing, and appoints him to be rebuked and admonished. Mr. Erskine, holding what he had delivered in his sermon agreeable to the word of God, and to the subordinate standards of the Church of Scotland, protests against the Synod's procedure, and appeals to the General Assembly.

The Assembly confirms the sentence of the Synod, and appoints Mr. Erskine to be immediately rebuked. Mr. William Wilson, Mr. Alexander Moncrief and Mr. James Fisher join Mr. Erskine in protesting against that censure. It is without effect that a Committee deals with these four to withdraw their protest. The Assembly appoints a Commission to proceed in the affair. A Commission of the Assembly is a kind of occasional court composed of so many select members of the Assembly, with powers delegated from that supreme judicature for some particular purpose. Such is the court before which the four are ordered to appear, and to signify that they are sorry for, and retract their protest.

The Commission executes the Assembly's orders with great rigour. Disregarding the defences of the four, not so much as condescending to hear the representations in their favour from several Presbyteries and Kirk-sessions, that deputed court proceeds to suspend them from the exercise of their ministry; and afterward, the suspension being disregarded, to declare them no longer ministers of the Church of Scotland, absolving the people of their respective parishes from every obligation to them in that character. Upon this, the four give in their protestations, intimating that they find themselves under the necessity of making A Secession from the prevailing party in the established Church; declaring themselves, at the same time, zealously attached to the principles of the Church of Scotland according to the word of God, and our national covenants.

The prevailing party, here meant, was made up of those who took the lead in church-matters; and who found means to have always a majority on their side in church-courts.

This was the æra of the Secession in Scotland. The following were at first the grievances which the four ministers with their adherents, chiefly insisted on as grounds of it: The act of Assembly in 1730 forbidding reasons of dissent to be marked in the records of that court: The beforementioned act in 1732 concerning the election of ministers: The settlement of ministers without the consent of the people, especially as these violent settlements were countenanced and promoted by the courts of judicature: The discouragements that were given by these courts to such as refused to submit to the ministry of Intruders: The negligence of these courts as to giving any suitable testimony against erroneous doctrine, or as to using the proper means for hindering the spread of it: In fine, their excess of lenity to such propagators of error as Mr. Simpson and Mr. Campbel*; while they did not scruple to pronounce ministers liable to severe censure for testifying against any particular wrong steps they took; thus, upon the matter, prohibiting them from bearing so much as a doctrinal testimony against public evils.

Thus was the banner of a Secession Testimony set up; nor did the four brethren and those who espoused their cause, think it consistent with

---

* Some of Mr Simson's tenets were, That there is an obscure revelation of God, sufficient for salvation, made even to the heathens, who never hear the word of the gospel; That Adam was not properly the covenant head and representative of his posterity; That there will be no sinning in hell after the day of judgment; That the terms, necessary existence, supreme Deity, and the only true God may, in some sense, be considered as the personal property of the Father, and, of consequence, as not belonging to the Son and the Holy Ghost.

Mr. Campbel held, That the sole motives to virtuous actions are self-love, interest and pleasure; That without revelation, men cannot find out that there is a God; That the laws of nature are, in themselves, sufficient to direct men to happiness; That the apostles do not seem to have had any notion of Christ's divinity at the time of his crucifixion; That it is enthusiasm to look for the guidance of the Spirit in the common affairs of life.

Mr. Simson was only suspended from teaching and preaching. As Mr. Campbel's tenets (such of them as were not quite overlooked) were judged to be only doubtful or too strongly expressed, he was dismissed from the bar of the General Assembly without any censure: and not only so, but his explanation of the mentioned proposition about self-love, That our delight in the glory of God is the chief and only motive of virtuous and religious actions, was adopted as agreeable to the standards of the church.

The disposition, in a church court, to favour the erroneous, will operate, in various ways, to the prejudice of soundness in the faith. The same Assembly in 1720, passed an act condemning several propositions contained in that evangelical treatise, The marrow of modern divinity; among which propositions were these unspeakably precious truths: That the gospel is a deed of gift and grant of Christ to mankind sinners indefinitely; That faith is an appropriation of Christ to one's own self in particular; That believers are wholly set free from the commanding power of the law as a covenant of works.

their duty, to let it fall; notwithstanding all that the Assembly in 1734 did to repair the mischiefs of the year before. It repealed, indeed, the two offensive acts, that in 1734 about excluding reasons of dissent from a place in the minutes of the assembly, and that in 1732 giving the right of election to Protestant heritors and elders: But then it repealed them on this account merely, that they were not made according to former acts with regard to innovations, and were found hurtful to the Church. It likewise, restored the four brethren to the full exercise of the ministry in their respective parishes; because the sentences against them had been attended with disagreeable consequences: The Assembly, however, avoided remarking upon the irregularity or the injustice of those sentences. But the four and those who had joined them, would be satisfied with nothing less than an acknowledgement of these and other evils they complained of, as contrary to the word of God, and as breaches of our national covenants: without that, they did not reckon themselves warranted to drop their Secession Testimony.

Their views of this testimony were gradually enlarged: They saw more and more clearly, that it was their duty to hold it fast, and to exhibit it not only in their doctrine; but also in a judicial way: And for that purpose, they formed themselves into an ecclesiastical court, called The Associate Presbytery; By the authority of which, An Act, declaration and testimony, An Act concerning the doctrine of Grace, and other Judicial Deeds tending to set several controverted truths in a fairer light, were given to the public.

It was the same TESTIMONY, *as to the* MATTER *of it, which had been Held by many in the Communion of the* ESTABLISHED CHURCH, *before the* CRISIS *in which the* SECESSION *took place.*

IT was materially the same testimony in favour of the reformation attained to in the period between 1638 and 1650, which was kept up in one way or another, from the restoration of Charles, till Mr. Ebenezer Erskine was arraigned at the bar of the General Assembly; and which was, at last, exhibited in one view, in the Judicial Testimony published in 1737. It was evidently the same testimony that was held in a state of communion with the established Church of Scotland before the Secession; though, after that event, it was placed in a fairer light, and probably was better understood. The witnesses of Christ would not forsake the communion of that Church, while she allowed them, in her judicatures, in her Synods and Assemblies, to bear a particular testimony, on every proper occasion, against her public apostacy from our covenanted reformation. Mr. Shields's large paper given in to the General Assembly in 1690; The Trust, a sermon delivered in 1721, before the Synod of Merse and Teviotdale by Mr. Wilson of Maxtoun; A Representation and Petition addressed to the General Assembly in 1732, subscribed by upwards of 1500 members of the established Church, which representation has been commonly called, The People's Testimony; these are instances of the freedom and faithfulness which the witnessing Few were enabled to use in the Communion of that Church. But when her opposition to the testimony they held, was so direct, and so violent as no longer to suffer the exercise of such freedom and faithfulness, another way of maintaining their testimony became necessary; the way of Secession from a Church that obstinately refuses to be reclaimed. This necessity occasioned the Secession.

The SECESSION TESTIMONY *is not only for all the Purity of* RELIGION *the* CHURCH *of* SCOTLAND *has already attained, and against all Departures from that Purity; but also for making further Progress in* REFORMATION.

THE Secession Testimony is, in the first place, *A Confession of whatever purity the Church has already attained, whether with regard to doctrine, worship, discipline, or government;* agreeable to the exhortation in Philip. iii. 16. *Nevertheless, whereto we have already attained, let us walk by the same rule, let us mind the same thing;* and to that in Rev. ii. 25. *That which ye have, hold fast till I come.* A Church ought to hold any profession she has made of the truths of Christ; for the greater agreement there is between the word and the profession of any Church, she has the more conformity (while her members are enabled to walk in a manner becoming that profession) to her glorious head. A Church ought carefully to preserve any purity of profession to which the Lord has brought her; since it is one principal end of the erection of every Church, that she should record the instances of his kindness, and *utter abundantly the memory of his great goodness*: And surely it is no small instance of his kindness, that a Church has been brought to a pure profession of the truth.

The Secession Testimony is on the behalf of whatever conformity to the word in doctrine, worship, discipline and government, our Fathers attained; and on the behalf of whatever faithfulness they were enabled to in keeping the Trust committed to them. We are by no means to confine the Testimony to what is mentioned in the first papers that were published by the four brethren, upon their ejection from the establishment. The testimony given in these papers should be considered as carried on in the Judicial Testimony, in the Acknowledgement of sins, and other publications of the Associate Presbytery.

It has been the Lord's usual way (it is agreeable, indeed, to the whole course of Providence) to bring his people by degrees, to the knowledge of the testimony that he has ordained them to go forth and maintain. This was remarkably exemplified in the case of Luther, who taught the doctrine of justification by faith alone, and testified against the Romish Indulgences for some time, before he came to see the evil, enormous as it is, of the Papal usurpation. Providence has wise purposes to serve by this method. Luther's moderation in the beginning of his opposition to the errors and corruptions of Popery (a moderation which rose, in a great measure, from defect of knowledge) led people to examine his doctrines with candour, and prevented the Pope from exerting his whole power toward crushing the first appearances of reformation, till the cause of truth had acquired, by degrees, that strength, that his impotent attempts against it were odious only and ridiculous. It was likewise well ordered for the Secession, that the four brethren did not, in their pleadings with the Assembly, insist on some pieces of reformation for which they afterwards contended; as it was a circumstance that made the rigour of ecclesiastical administration exercised toward them, appear the more unreasonable and oppressive.

The Secession Testimony is frequently, in the publications of the Associate Presbytery, called *A Testimony for the doctrine, worship, discipline, and government of the Church of Scotland*: This must be understood of all the conformity to the word which that Church ever attained; and has a particular respect to the period between 1638 and 1650; the period of our covenanted reformation in which the Lord so remarkably accomplished his promise, *I will give them one heart and one way.*

In the next place, *It is a Testimony against all the opposition that has been made to that reformation; and against every departure from it.* Surely it becomes the friends of Christ to be affected with real sorrow, when they see his enemies *breaking down the carved work* of his house, *at once, with axes and with hammers*; when they see his truths openly denied, and his ordinances despised: And that sorrow will seldom fail to manifest itself in some testimony against the indignities that are done to Christ, and his cause.

Such a testimony is plainly implied in the full and free acknowledgment which the scripture enjoins us to make of our sins; not only of our personal sins, but of the sins of the church or nation that we belong to, of the sins not only of the present, but likewise of former generations, Levit. xxvi. 40, 41, 42. *If they shall confess their iniquity, and the iniquity of their fathers, with their trespass which they trespassed against me, and that also they have walked contrary to me; and that I also have walked contrary unto them, and have brought them into the land of their enemies: if then their uncircumcised heart be humbled, and they then accept the punishment of their iniquity: Then will I remember my covenant.*

It is evident from the history of the church and nation of Israel, that a society continues chargeable with the iniquities for which it has never been brought to any suitable exercise of repentance and humiliation; however long the time may be, since those iniquities were committed. Indeed, neither a society nor a particular person is truly and thoroughly convinced of present evils without an humbling remembrance of the past: for when the Holy Spirit convinces men effectually of sin, he shews them the poisonous nature of past evils in the prevalence of present evils. Thus it is promised in Jer. xvi. 19. that when the Gentiles, convinced of their sin and misery, should come to the Lord from the ends of the earth, they would say, *Surely our fathers have inherited lies, vanity, and things wherein is no profit*: they would see the sin of their fathers in their own. Besides, the same bitter root of a depraved nature is manifested, and God is alike dishonoured, whensoever or by whomsoever sin is committed. In this exercise we are to follow the examples of the saints, Psal. cvi. 6. *We have sinned with our fathers.* Dan. ix. 16. *For our sins, and for the iniquities of our fathers, Jerusalem and thy people are become a reproach to all that are about them.* The ninth chapter of Nehemiah is a noble pattern for the public acknowledgment of sins.

Further, granting what was shewn in the preceding particular, that it is our duty to bear testimony for whatever conformity to the word of God the church has already attained, then it follows of course, that we ought to bear testimony against the departure which is, and has been made from that conformity to the word of God.

AGREEABLY to these truths the Secession Testimony is directed against the whole course of backsliding in the church of Scotland from the rise of the public resolutions toward the end of the year 1650 down to the present times; those resolutions by which many malignants in principle, and many of immoral practice were brought into places of civil and military trust, contrary to some commendable acts of Parliament for the regulating of the admission of persons to such places in subserviency to the reformation of religion. The Testimony we speak of, is against other evils than those which were the immediate occasion of its appearance in the form of a *Secession* Testimony; it is no less against the negligence of our ecclesiastical managers in the Revolution Settlement, than against the restraint laid upon ministerial freedom in 1733. A witness for Christ must be like the builders in Nehemiah's time, who had every man his sword girded by his side, and so builded. He is to seek the edification of the church in the way of opposing vigorously whatever is contrary to it.

IN the third place, it is a testimony *for making progress in reformation*. Every church should attend to the apostle's exhortation in Heb. vi. 1. *Therefore leaving the principles of the doctrine of Christ, let us go on unto perfection.* No church is perfect; but every church ought to give satisfying evidence, that, neither enslaved by prejudices in favour of old customs or opinions, nor yet disposed to palliate or excuse her present corruptions, she is indeed aiming at perfection. As in most instances, the case of particular Christians is parallel to that of the church, it is remarkably so in this instance, according to the apostle's example, Phil. iii. 12. *Not as though I had already attained; or were already perfect: but this one thing I do: forgetting those things which are behind, and reaching forth to those things which are before, I press toward the mark for the prize of the high calling of God in Christ Jesus.* On the other hand, a church that is well satisfied with herself, pluming herself upon the rectitude of her administration, or upon the number and reputation of her members, has good reason to fear that she is like the church of Laodicea, lukewarm, neither cold nor hot.

A CHURCH may be said to be advancing in reformation as far as her attention is fixed singly upon the Lord Jesus as her head, as her refuge and portion, having his word for her rule, his Spirit for her guide, and his glory for her aim ; and therefore renouncing the poor advantages of worldly policy and worldly interest. While the church is in such a state, she will regard the greatest names in the world when set in competition with the name of Christ, as lighter than a straw. For her own name, as far as she is enabled to keep the testimony of Jesus, she will never dare to lay it in the balance with His.

THOUGH the Secession Testimony contains a solemn approbation of all the real reformation that the church of Scotland attained in the period between 1638 and 1650 ; and professes to adopt that reformation, as far as it suits with our present circumstances : Yet the design of the Secession Testimony is not to rest in the attainments of our fathers ; but to make further progress, in the way of having a single regard to the word of God.

THAT the endeavours of the Associate Presbytery and of the Associate Synod have not been altogether wanting in that respect, will be apparent to any one who carefully considers what they have done to explain the evangelical nature of public covenanting, to illustrate the duty of the witnesses of Christ with regard to the civil magistrate, and from time to time as occasion required, to enlarge their testimony in other particulars.

Among the numberless evils of our depraved nature, there is, it must be owned, a capricious fondness of novelty, of something that we have never seen nor heard of before, without regard to intrinsic value or to real usefulness; a ridiculous passion which has been too often gratified under the fair pretences of impartial inquiry and a spirit of improvement, and against which we have need to be very much on our guard. But we hope this evil may be easily known from the sober endeavours of the church of Christ to make progress in the knowledge and profession of the truth, and to cleave more closely to the way of the Lord. Her endeavours toward these ends will always be distinguished in the following respects.

First, The church, in that case, looks to the word of God as the only source, whence she is to derive all her new informations with regard to truth or duty. New pieces of real reformation, whether it be that of particular Christians or that of the church, are always the effect of greater diligence in searching the Scriptures. See an example of this in Neh. xiii. 1. *On that day they read in the book of Moses in the audience of the people; and therein was found written, that the Ammonite and the Moabite should not come into the congregation of God for ever.* We have the consequence of this discovery in ver. 3. *Now it came to pass, when they had heard the law, that they separated from Israel all the mixed multitude.* Thus every proposal of taking a new step in reformation should be either the express words or the necessary consequence of *what is found written;* and being from such a source, it cannot be rejected without an affront to the authority of God interposed in his word. Jealous of the luxuriance of our imaginations; jealous even of our opinions as to what is proper or useful in matters of religion, we should be anxiously careful to keep without wavering to the Scriptures of truth as our only rule of truth and of duty.

SECONDLY, A church that really is making progress in reformation, thankfully acknowledges what measure of conformity to the word she has attained, and sincerely endeavours to hold it fast; agreeably to the charge that our Lord gives to the church in Philadelphia, Rev. iii. 11. *Behold I come quickly; hold fast that which thou hast; that no man take thy crown.* A person cannot be said to be making any progress in the study of holiness, who, when he begins to be diligent in the practice of some duties formerly neglected, grows, at the same time, negligent as to other duties which he was once careful to perform: he forgets, in that case, to hold fast what he had. The same case may easily be supposed with regard to the church.

BESIDES, in all our endeavours after reformation, the Scripture calls us to have regard to the examples and attainments of those who have gone before us. These examples may even contribute to our information as to what we do not know, Song i. 8. *If thou know not, O thou fairest among women, go thy way forth by the footsteps of thy flock; and feed thy kids beside the shepherds tents.* The several parts of divine truth are uniform, consistent, and serve to recommend each other: they are so much of a piece that they are called *one way;* and with regard to the examples of those who have gone before us, they are called the *old way,* Jer. vi. 16. *Thus saith the Lord, stand ye in the ways, and see, and ask for the old paths, where is the good way, and walk therein, and ye shall find rest to your souls.* Our new advances in reformation should be so much of a piece with the examples of the Lord's people in former times, as to be, on the matter, no other than our walking forward in the same old path.

On the whole; the new creature, which is begotten of God with the word of truth, wrestles against whatever is opposite to the word: nay, it never was a question with any man so far as he was a new creature, whether on proper occasions, he should give a faithful testimony against all sin and all error in himself or in others. It is true indeed, believers are not all enlightened alike: one is better acquainted with some parts; another with other parts of truth and duty. Some have made greater, some less proficiency in the knowledge of Christ. In truth, the most eminent saints, while here, are described rather as panting after the knowledge of Christ, than as having actually obtained it. Hear the apostle Paul declare what was his desire and his constant aim, Phil. iii. 10. *That I may know him, and the power of his resurrection, and the fellowship of his sufferings.* The wisest in this respect, acknowledge themselves to be fools: though all true Christians have so much experimental knowledge of Christ as makes them look incessantly to the Lord, that he would grant them a more abundant supply of *the Spirit of wisdom and revelation in the knowledge of Christ.*

ALL this is true; but then it is likewise true, that it is the native disposition of the new creature to cleave to the whole of God's revealed will, and especially to those truths and duties, against which Satan, the world and the flesh make the most violent opposition. Hence we ought to commune with our own hearts, and to examine particularly how we stand affected to such truths and such duties. People may imagine they cordially receive a great deal of God's word, while they secretly wish to be excused from a strict adherence to some part of it, which more evidently strikes against their beloved idols. The heart is very deceitful; it uses every artifice to disguise the true cause of their indifference or opposition to such parts of

God's word, imputing it to the obscurity of the word itself, to the little importance of such a truth or duty, to the circumstances in which divine Providence has placed them, to any thing, in short, rather than to the enmity of the carnal mind against God: a striking verification of what our Lord says in John iii. 20. *Every one that doth evil hateth the light, neither cometh to the light, lest his deeds be reproved.* It is, therefore, a matter of great delicacy and importance in what manner we behave with respect to those points of truth or duty, which meet with peculiar opposition from Satan, the world and the flesh; those points which are, in a particular manner, the testimony of Christ; those points on which the dispute between him and Belial is most doubtful to the eye of carnal sense and reason; those points which above others, occasion both the old and the new nature to manifest themselves; the one by a propensity to neglect and oppose them; the other by a propensity to cleave to them with purpose of heart.

Let us encourage ourselves in the Lord to hold fast the Testimony of Jesus. It is our indispensible duty to do so. This testimony is a sacred trust that the Lord hath committed to us; a banner which he hath given us to display because of the truth. To do so is practicable. The testimony of Christ has been held by multitudes who have gone before us. The hundred forty and four thousand who stood with the Lamb on Mount Sion were a glorious company of witnesses. However weak and unworthy, let us follow them in the strength of the Lord God, making mention of his righteousness, even of his only. From the snares of the world, from the devices of Satan, and which is the worst of all, from our depraved nature we have, no doubt, many and formidable difficulties to encounter in keeping the word of Christ's patience. Worldly wisdom is ever suggesting, that we are never to get over them; and represents the witnesses of Christ as a number of silly fools or desperate madmen. On the other hand, the word of God assures us, that these mountains are a plain before our Zerubbabel and his followers; that the faithful witnesses of Christ shall thresh the mountains and beat them small as chaff; and that in all these things, they are more than conquerors through him that loved them. The wise men of the world are of opinion, that the poor despicable handful of Christ's witnesses will soon be dispersed, and his testimony for such particular truths fall to the ground. But as we are to believe God rather than man, so we are to be verily persuaded, that Christ and the Spirit are always in the church to maintain that standard, and that all the efforts of earth and hell against it, shall serve only to make it appear more glorious, Mat. xxvii. 20. Acts v. 32. Isa. lix. 18. In fine, as it is one of the sweetest comforts to have the testimony of our consciences that we deal faithfully in this matter, so there is not a nobler and more honourable character under heaven, than that of A WITNESS FOR CHRIST.

ESSAY III.

Of the NATURE *of* PUBLIC COVENANTING.

THIS duty is misrepresented in various ways: some decry it as a yoke of bondage contrary to our Christian liberty; others insist that it is not necessary, because we covenant, on the matter, when we partake of Baptism and the Lord's Supper. Perhaps the following observations, if attended to, with a single dependence on the Spirit of truth, may be of use to obviate such prejudices.

COVENANTING has many things in common with other ordinances, that shew it to be equally agreeable as they, to the nature of the gospel-dispensation. There is no duty, which, rightly performed, lies more in the exercise of faith than the duty of covenanting. It is by faith that we lay hold of the new covenant as it stands fast in Christ. But when we avouch the Lord to be our God in covenanting, we solemnly profess to lay hold of the covenant of grace, since he cannot be our God (nor the God of any of fallen mankind) otherwise than according to the covenant of grace. How can we engage to obey the law otherwise than as it is the law of Christ, or as it is made over to us in such great and precious promises as these; *I will put my law in their inward parts, and write it in their hearts: I will put my fear into their hearts, and they shall never depart from me?* So far as persons are suitably excercised in going about the duty of covenanting, they have a real persuasion that they owe their all, their strength for duty, their support and perseverance in it, and the crown of righteousness at the end of their course, to the grace of our Lord Jesus Christ. All our purposes, vows and engagements are only the staff of a broken reed, on which if a man lean, it will go into his hand and pierce it, if they are, at bottom, either more or less than a confident trust that the Lord, through his infinite mercy in Christ, will deal well with us according to his word: one cannot be a true covenanter but as far as he is a true believer.

In social covenanting as in our public prayers, in our public praises, and in our partaking of the Sacraments, there is an open confession of our faith. In all these duties, we stand forth and declare, that we are not ashamed of our confidence, nor of the cause of Christ. In other duties as in prayer, in receiving Baptism or the Lord's Supper, as well as in covenanting, we come under obligations to be the Lord's. In each of these duties, we are strictly bound to abide by his truths and ways: in prayer we call him *Our Father*, and express our desire to follow him as dear children.

In receiving Baptism and the Lord's Supper, we solemnly profess that we ly under infinite obligations to the Lord, as the God whose we are and whom we serve, and who seals to us all the benefits of the new covenant in those ordinances.

It is obvious, that the circumstance of many concurring in one action, is common to covenanting with other gospel ordinances. Both when we go about the duty of covenanting, and when we receive the Lord's Supper, we may justly say, *We being many, are one body.*

Such are the things that social covenanting has in common with other public ordinances.

But we are likewise to observe, that covenanting as it is pointed out to us in the word, has so many things peculiar to it, as shew that, in order to answer the rule that the Lord has given us, it is not enough that we covenant, so far as covenanting is implied in our observing of other divine institutions. These peculiarities lead us to go about covenanting in a distinct and formal manner, as we observe fasting, the Lord's Supper, or any other ordinance of Christ.

By things peculiar to covenanting we do not mean things that are no way implied in other duties; we mean that they have not place in other duties in the same manner as they have place in covenanting: so a person may be said to eat the flesh and drink the blood of the Son of God in reading or hearing the word, in meditating on it; or in prayer; but in these duties they cannot be said to do so sacramentally as in the Lord's Supper.

In the first place, there is necessary in the regular performance of this duty, a formal deed of conveyance wherein we give ourselves to the Lord, corresponding to the gospel which is God's deed of gift and grant of Christ to sinners of mankind. Several circumstances, characterizing a legal deed, are obvious in the examples of covenanting set before us in scripture. One circumstance is a form of words ratified by the consent of all the covenanters, in which they acknowledge the Lord to be their God, and themselves to be his people, binding themselves at the same time, to walk in all the ordinances and commandments of the Lord blameless. Josh. xxiv. 18. *The people said, We will serve the Lord, for he is our God.* They repeat the same again and again ver. 21, and 24. It is added in ver. 25. *So Joshua made a covenant with the people that day, and set them a statute and an ordinance in Shechem.* That a form of words was used is no less apparent in other examples of covenanting, 2 Chron. xv. 12. 13. & xxx. 31. Neh. x. 29, 38,—33. Nor is it unworthy of notice that this form of words is called a covenant, or in the original languages, Berith, and by the Septuagint, ΔΙΑΘΗΚΗ; for whoever is acquainted with Hebrew and Greek, will grant that it is natural to understand these words of a legal deed or constitution.

The Lord is said to make a covenant with us, when he exhibits and makes over to us the covenant of grace, Isa. lv. 3. *I will make an everlasting covenant with you, even the sure mercies of David.* In like manner, we are said to make a covenant with him, when we lay hold of the New Covenant according to that exhibition of it, particularly, when we do it in the most solemn and formal manner, as in the ordinance under our consideration. *It is in mine heart,* said Hezekiah, *to make a covenant with the Lord God of Israel.* Hence the matter of these deeds or instruments that are drawn up for public covenanting, should be no other than an abstract of God's covenant of grace; including indeed, a declaration that every covenanter heartily consents to it. Agreeable to this view of the matter is the promise, Jer. li. 4, 5. *In those days, and in that time, saith the Lord, the children of Israel shall come, they and the children of Judah together, going and weeping: they shall go and seek the Lord their God. They shall ask the way to Zion with their faces thitherward, saying, Come and let us join ourselves to the Lord in a perpetual covenant that shall not be forgotten;* or *the perpetual covenant,* that is, the covenant of grace mentioned in the thirty third chapter of this book, *shall not be forgotten.* In covenanting we join ourselves to the Lord, as the Borrower by a bill or some other legal deed, binds himself to the Lender for the restoration of the loan *. But it is plainly our duty as well as it was that of church members under the Old Testament to join ourselves to the Lord, and to be his people. Whatever primary respect this passage may have had to the return of the Jewish captives from Babylon, there is nothing to hinder us from applying it to ourselves. We are by no means to confine the particular application of the promises to those who were first to have the benefit of them.

In every civilized nation legal deeds are confirmed by witnesses and subscriptions. We have both these in our scripture examples of covenanting, Josh. xxiv. 22. *And Joshua said unto the people, Ye are Witnesses against yourselves, that ye have chosen you the Lord to serve him. And they said we are Witnesses.* Neh. ix. 38. *Because of all this we make a sure covenant and write it, and our princes, levites and priests seal unto it.* Hence covenanting, or our saying in the most express and public manner, I am the Lords, is represented in Isa. xliv. 5. as our *subscribing with the hand unto the Lord, and sirnaming ourselves by the name of Israel.* Our best name by nature is that of sinners; but considered as persons that subscribe with the hand unto the Lord, in this solemn ordinance, we have a new name given us, we are sirnamed the Lord's peculiar people, sought out, and not forsaken: a great encouragement to persons joining in so delightful an exercise.

In order to obviate some objections that are commonly offered against our application of this and some other texts of the Old Testament to the practice of covenanting under the New Testament, two things should be attended to. First, We are never to depart from the literal sense of a text, unless we see it necessary to do so from the context,

---

* This is the exact import of the word in the original, which is rendered, *Let us join ourselves to the Lord.*

from some other scripture truth, or in fine, from the nature of the thing. Secondly, Because several expressions in a sentence are clearly to be understood figuratively, it will not follow, excepting in an allegory such as Ezekiel's vision, the Revelation, or the Song of Solomon, that we must depart from the literal meaning of any other part or expression in that sentence. An allegory is a continued figure, and therefore it is contrary to the nature of it, that one part of it should be understood figuratively, and another literally. But every one knows, that for the sake of elegance and energy, figures are frequently employed in the common language of mankind which for the most part is meant to be understood literally. Hence no one can reasonably be surprized, that in perusing the writings of the prophets, he should continually meet with passages that are to be taken partly literally and partly figuratively. An example will make our meaning plain. Zeph. iii. 9, 10. *I will turn to the people a pure language, that they may all call on the name of the Lord, to serve him with one consent. From beyond the rivers of Ethiopia, my suppliants, even the daughter of my dispersed shall bring mine offering.* Here the expressions *pure language* and *bringing mine offering* are to be understood figuratively; yet it does not follow that the expressions *to serve the Lord, and to call on his name,* are so to be understood. The truth is, the prophets commonly describe the worship of God that was to obtain under the new Testament in terms that are applicable to the forms of worship under the old, which, we know, were partly moral, partly ceremonial. It is obvious, in that case, that the terms which are applicable to what was moral, must be taken literally; while these that are applicable to what was ceremonial, must be taken figuratively. The last chapter of Isaiah and the last of Zechariah are illustrious examples of this observation.

APPLYING these two things to the above-mentioned passage; though it is true that neither the church nor her members are now called Jacob and Israel; why may not a church-member say, *I am the Lord's*, as well under the New Testament as under the Old? Why may he not *subscribe with the hand*, signifying that he desires it to stand on record, that he was a witness for the cause of Christ? Why may he not give the most public and solemn assurance that he is not ashamed of the name, the truths and ordinances of Christ, even as a member of the Jewish church was not ashamed to *call himself by the name of Jacob*, and to *surname himself by the name of Israel?*

In the second place, Vowing to the Lord our God may be considered as one of the peculiarities of covenanting. Vowing, or devoting ourselves and all we have to the Lord may be *implied* in other ordinances; but this is *called* vowing. Our exercises of reading and hearing the word should never be without prayer; yet no body considers prayer as the same thing with reading and hearing the word. In like manner, though we may be considered as making vows in our Baptism or in the communion of the Lord's Supper, we are still to distinguish these ordinances from the ordinance of vowing. We read in Scripture of particular vows by which persons of their own accord, came under obligations with regard to something that was otherwise indifferent. Of this kind were the vow of the Nazarites under the Old Testament, Num. vi. 2, 3, 4, 5, 6. and Paul's vow under the New, Acts xviii. 18. Public covenanting still answers the same purpose as these vows did. In vowing, some particular thing was specified as a sign or evidence of the person's devoting himself to the Lord: Thus Jacob devoted the tenth of his substance to the Lord, avouching him to be his God. In the same manner, when public covenanting is rightly gone about, there is always an explicit engagement to faithfulness in opposing some prevailing evil, or in cleaving to some despised truth or duty, according to our present circumstances, as an evidence and public pledge of our sincerity in giving ourselves to the Lord. Thus in Psal. lxxvi 11. *Vow and pay unto the Lord your God; let all that be round about him bring presents unto him that ought to be feared.* We may consider the former part of the verse as respecting the dedication of ourselves to the Lord, which was implied in every vow under the old Testament; and the latter part as a sign or token of such dedication; which sign or token is varied according to circumstances †.

SWEARING *to the Lord* is undoubtedly a phrase put for Covenanting in the old Testament. But that phrase and *Vowing* are used indifferently for the same thing in Isai. xix. 18, 21.

WHEN Vowing is spoken of, as in the two last mentioned passages, without restriction to any particular thing, or as of perpetual obligation on all the hearers of the word, it is to be understood of Covenanting or devoting ourselves to the Lord; which may be done either by individuals in the closet, or by a number of people jointly and publicly. So we may understand Psal cxxxii. 2. *How David sware unto the Lord, and vowed unto the mighty God of Jacob.*

---

† THIS token, pledge, or whatever other name may be given it, was often under the old Testament, an engagement to something of an indifferent nature, to something which the divine law leaves at the option of persons to do or not to do. Hence it is said in Deut. xxiii. 22. *But if thou shalt forbear to vow, it shall be no sin in thee.* This kind of pledge has been and may be used under the new testament dispensation, as in Paul's vow abovementioned; but it seems more agreeable to the ceremonial nature of the old. That the token or pledge we speak of, may be also an engagement to a much neglected moral duty is clear from the scriptural precepts and examples of Covenanting; which engagement is, indeed, the most suitable to the new Testament dispensation.

G

A THIRD thing that serves to characterife this duty is the formality of an oath, 2 Chron. xv. 24, 25. *And they sware unto the Lord with a loud voice. And all Judah rejoiced at the oath.* The following paffages deferve particular cofideration.

THOU *shalt swear, The Lord liveth in truth, in judgment, and in righteousness ; and the nations shall bless themselves in him, and in him shall they glory,* Jerem. iv. 2. It is true, the Lord is here fpeaking to Ifrael; but not to Ifrael only. Every one who acknowledges, that *whatsoever was written aforetime was written for our learning,* will grant that the firft verfe is to us as well as to Ifrael; and why not the fecond? Befides, the connection between the former and the latter claufe of the verfe leads us to underftand both as applicable to the Gentiles. It is ufual in fcripture to lay down a rule, and then to add a prophecy or promife with refpect to the obedience that fhould be yielded to that rule. See examples in Ifai. xlv. 23, 24. Jerem. iii 14, 15, 16, 22. and various other places. The connection, therefore, between the two members of the verfe; a connection which is alfo hinted by the particle *and* prefixed to the laft; intimates, that the nations were to blefs themfelves and glory in Chrift, profeffing that they did fo with the folemnity of an oath. This rule was complied with in Nehemiah's time; but the completion of the prophecy belongs to the glory of the new Teftament difpenfation.

To indulge a reflection on the beauty of this verfe; it is agreeable to obferve how the prophet having reprefented the matter of Covenanting, fuitably to the circumftances of the ancient Ifraelites, as an adherence to this truth, *The Lord liveth,* in oppofition to the practices of the Nations who worfhipped dead idols; is, of a fudden, rapt into future times, and sees the people of those very nations; sees not merely individuals, but whole states and commonwealths engaging in the duty of Covenanting; the purport of their oath, agreeably to the superior light of the new Testament dispensation being to this effect, That they should bless themselves in the Lord Jesus Christ, and in him should they glory.

IN *that day, shall five cities in the land of Egypt speak the language of Canaan, and swear to the Lord of hosts.* Isa. xix. 18. Agreeably to what is remarked above concerning the style of the prophets, though it is true, that *the language of Canaan, the altar in the midst of the land,* and the *doing sacrifice and oblation to the Lord* are here to be understood figuratively, it does not, therefore, follow, that *swearing to the Lord of hosts* is to be so understood. It is plain, that several other expressions in this passage, are to be taken literally: Such as, *they shall cry unto the Lord because of the oppressors, and he shall send a saviour and a great one to deliver them: And the Lord shall be known to the Egyptians, and the Egytians shall know the Lord in that day: They shall return to the Lord, and he shall be intreated of them.*

IT is agreed on all hands, that the worship of God in his church is here meant, and that the language is such as would apply to the worship of the old Testament. But it was never shewn (hardly indeed ever attempted to be shewn) that swearing to God was a ceremonial institution which was to cease at the death of Christ. It remains, therefore, that we understand it literally of accompanying a pure profession of religion or *Speaking the language of Canaan,* with the solemnity of an oath.

WITH regard to the accomplishment of this prophecy, we are well assured that Christianity was planted in Egypt soon after our Lord's ascenſion. By the conſent of antiquity, Peter and Mark are ſaid to have laboured in propagating the goſpel there. Hiſtory gives us very few particulars concerning the church of Egypt. Here, however, Egypt may be conſidered as repreſenting the Gentile nations in general. Beſides, though this prophecy may, in a meaſure, be already fulfiled, probably the moſt eminent completion of it is yet to come.

I HAVE *ſworn by myſelf, the word is gone out of my mouth in righteouſneſs, and ſhall not return, that unto me every knee ſhall bow, every tongue ſhall ſwear,* Iſa. xl. 23. The univerſal terms, here uſed, may be conſidered as reſpecting the ſubmiſſion of men to the Lord Chriſt; their ſubmiſſion abſtractly taken, without regard to the quality of it, whether willing or conſtrained; that ſubmiſſion, in ſhort, which is the general and final effect aſcertained in theſe words, and in reſpect of which the apoſtle applies the paſſage to the day of judgment when all ſhall be ſeen ſubjected to Chriſt, Rom. xiv. 10, 11. *We ſhall ſtand before the judgment ſeat of Chriſt. For it is written, as I live ſaith the Lord, every knee ſhall bow to me, and every tongue ſhall confeſs to God.* But it is certain, that many paſſages of the old Teſtament are applied in the new, not according to the full comprehenſion of their meaning, but only according to ſome particular part of it. So the ſaying of Iſaiah, *Surely he hath borne our griefs, and carried our ſorrows,* is applied in Matt. viii. 17. to the cures our Lord performed in the days of his fleſh; and that of Zechariah, *They ſhall look on him whom they have pierced,* is applied in John xx. 37. to the piercing of his ſide with a ſpear. Neither of theſe texts, ſurely, can reaſonably be reſtrained to the occaſion on which they are quoted by the evangeliſts. Hence we cannot certainly conclude from the use the apostle in the abovementioned place, makes of this passage, that it is to be confined to that submission alone which shall be given to Christ at the last day. One thing, however, we may learn from the apostle's manner of rendering the words of the prophet; That the swearing here meant, is a confession of Christ's name. But what other swearing than that in public Covenanting, is so properly an explicit confession of Christ's name?

It appears, then, that these phrases *bowing the knee* and *swearing to Christ*, in all the comprehension of their meaning, denote the grateful homage and willing submission which the Lord requires in his word. In which sense the universal terms refer to believers only; for who are the persons of whom it is said, *every tongue shall swear*? They are such as comply with the call, *Look unto me, and be ye saved, all the ends of the earth*. They make a profession of their faith with the solemnity of an oath, each of them saying, *Surely in the LORD* alone *have I righteousness and strength*. In truth, as there are greater or less measures of faith, so the profession of believers may correspond, in a greater or less degree, to the word of God. A profession of faith may be without an oath; but accompanied with an oath, it is more suitable to the manner in which God exhibits to us the covenant of grace. Well may we swear to the Lord for his declarative glory, since he swears to us for the increase of our faith and comfort.

Thus the duty of public Covenanting is characterised by a formal deed of conveyance, by vowing, and by swearing to the Lord.

Though we come under the strongest obligations to be the Lord's in receiving Baptism and the Lord's Supper; yet these ordinances are distinguished in their nature from the ordinance of

Covenanting, vowing or swearing to the Lord. Baptism and the Lord's supper are the public seals which God himself, in condescension to our weakness, puts to the covenant of grace: on the other hand, the duty we speak of is the public seal which according to the precepts and promises of the word, we ourselves put to that sure and well ordered covenant. Faith is *the setting to of our seal that God is true*, John iii. 33. Reader, do that in as express and formal a manner as the church of christ ever did, and you do all that we mean by public covenanting. Baptism and the holy supper are pledges from the Lord himself that He is our God and Father in Christ; but our covenanting is a public pledge, on our part, that we are his willing people.

Perhaps some will say, we cannot give any greater public assurances of our being the Lord's people, than those we give in partaking of Baptism and the Lord's supper.

But the Lord may require other assurances which, though not greater, are of a different kind. If some generous benefactor promises to grant us a very great favour, adding only, that he expects we will render him some piece of service as an evidence of our gratitude; if he also condescends to give us some pledge or token to assure us that he will do as he hath said; our acceptance, no doubt, of such a pledge may justly be construed as a declaration that we believe his word, and desire to make the grateful return. But should he require us to give him before witnesses, some pledges, on our part, of our sincerity in believing his word, and in resolving to make the grateful return; would honesty, in that case, suffer us to refuse such pledges? or would we have the impudence to tell the generous benefactor, that we could see no reason for our giving any other assurance of sincerity than our acceptance of the pledge with which he accompanied his promise? Now, Baptism and the Lord's Supper correspond to the pledge on the part of the generous benefactor; Covenanting corresponds to the assurances which he requires on our part.

It is indeed very commonly said, That Baptism and the Lord's Supper are oaths and vows. The three following things seem to be the principal grounds of that opinion.

1. These ordinances are called Sacraments from the ancient *Sacramentum* or military oath of the Romans. But besides that we are not to regard terms, like this, of men's devising any farther than they are proper to express the meaning of scripture; it is not the only signifiation of the word *Sacramentum*. According to Varus, it was used by civilians for the money which each of the parties in a law-suit laid down in the court: the pledge of the party who gained the cause was restored to him; that of the other was forfeited to the public treasury. In the writings of the Fathers, and in the oldest Latin translations of the new Testament the word *Sacramentum* is used for *a mystery*. There seems to be no impropriety in applying the name in either of these two senses, to the ordinances of Baptism and the Lord's Supper. " Indeed," says a judicious reformer, " it
" is abundantly clear that the ancients, when
" they gave the name *sacramenta* to those ordi-
" nances, had little or no regard to the accepta-
" tion of the word in the classical writers. They
" devised a signification of their own suitable to
" the nature of those divine institutions to which
" they applied the term: with them *Sacraments*
" meant no more than sacred signs or pledges.
" Much the same liberty has been taken with the
" Latin word *fides*; which in the purest writers
" of that language, signifies faithfulness to one's

"promise: however, it is now constantly used by theological writers for a certain persuasion of the truth. By a similar process, the *Sacramentum* which originally signified the obligation of the soldier to his commander, was brought to signify the obligation of the commander to the soldier: for the sacraments are the solemn assurances which the Lord himself gives us, that he will be our God, and that we shall be his people." Agreeable to Calvin's opinion is the definition, in our Shorter Catechism, of the general nature of Baptism and the Lord's Supper: "A Sacrament is a holy ordinance instituted by Christ, wherein by sensible signs Christ and the benefits of the new covenant are represented, sealed and applied to believers."

2. ANOTHER thing that seems to favour this opinion is, the common practice of parents coming under solemn engagements at the Baptism of their children; which are called baptismal engagements, though to Baptism they do not seem to be otherwise necessary than as they evidence the person to be a professing Christian parent whose children have a right to that ordinance. These engagements have their use in their own place; like the law, they are good, if a man use them lawfully; but to consider them as an essential part of Baptism is a very great abuse of them. The Lord says to Abraham concerning Circumcision, *It shall be a token of the covenant between me and you*; and the apostle calls it *A seal of the righteousness of the faith*; but never is it called a vow or an oath. Now Baptism is of the same nature as the ordinance of Circumcision. We are said to be *baptized into Jesus Christ, into his death and burial*, Rom. vi. 3, 4. that is, our partaking of Christ, and of the benefits resulting from his death and burial are sealed to our faith in Baptism. That this is the

true meaning of the abovementioned expressions appears, if we consider that the scope of the apostle in that chapter is to represent the obligations to Gospel-holiness, not those of oaths and vows, but those arising from the principles and privileges of our new state in Christ.

3. But the principal thing that seems to lead persons into the notion, that Baptism and the Lord's supper are oaths and vows, is this, that the strongest obligation to new obedience is implied ‡ in our participation of these ordinances. Our approach in them to the Lord who is *glorious in holiness*, renders it absolutely necessary that we be careful to sanctify ourselves. The language of every partaker should be, "I love him who shews me by these pledges and sensible signs, that he first loved me: and what shall I render to the Lord for all his benefits?" But still our resolutions and engagements are to be distinguished from what is properly our act of receiving Baptism or the Lord's supper; though they are, no doubt, implied in that act, and follow naturally upon it. Nor is any one to look on this as only a nice distinction of little importance; it is the pernicious error of the greatest perverters of the gospel, that the partaking of the Lord's Supper is only our swearing over the elements of bread and wine, that we have a great veneration for the memory of Jesus Christ as a person of unspotted virtue, and that we shall always be careful to imitate his example. On the contrary, we are to hold it fast as a precious truth, That our partaking in

---

‡ It is indeed no small warrant for the distinct observation of any thing that has been observed distinctly by the church of Christ in former times, That the matter of it is implied in some other divine ordinances. For example, if in receiving Baptism and the Lord's Supper, we do materially the same thing which the Israelites did in their public covenanting; why should we scruple to be as distinct and explicit in that matter, as they were? for they too, had other ordinances in which the duty of covenanting was implied.

faith of the Lord's supper is nothing less than the real partaking of a crucified Christ. When we set about the observance of that solemn ordinance, we should seek the holy Spirit to work in us a real perswasion, that as we receive the bread and wine according to Christ's appointment, so we receive Christ himself as made of God unto us wisdom, righteousness, sanctification and redemption. In this ordinance the Lord says, Take ye; and right communicating lies in our taking according to the Lord's command. Thus though it is necessary to observe the harmony and close connection among the ordinances of Christ, it is dangerous to confound one with another: to hold Communicating to be the same as Covenanting favours much of a Socinian error with regard to the Lord's Supper†.

UPON the whole, it appears that covenanting has so much in common with other ordinances of the New Testament as may serve to shew that it is equally suitable as they to the nature of the gospel-dispensation; while, on the other hand, it has so much to distinguish it from other ordinances as may serve to warrant us in observing it distinctly and formally as we do Baptism, the Lord's Supper, fasting and prayer.

FROM the preceding observations we see, that it tends to mislead us in examining the warrants for public Covenanting to consider swearing as the only formality or distinction of that duty. For it has other characteristics than swearing. Giving ourselves to the Lord, and promising an honest adherence to God's word, particularly to such parts of it as meet with the greatest opposition; these two things may be some how con-

---

† THE candid reader will see that the above observations with regard to Baptism and the Lord's supper are not to be understood as determining what is comprehended in these ordinances, but only as respecting the formal nature and distinguishing characteristics of them.

tained in other duties; but it is denied that they characterise them as they do Covenanting. These two things are essential to this duty: but though swearing and subscribing are highly proper and warrantable; we have reason to believe that Covenanting has often been gone about without them. The church's observance of a particular duty is sometimes more sometimes less adequate to the divine rule. It is said of the passover, that before Hezekiah's reign *it had not been kept for a long time in such sort as it was written.*

Of the Character which Persons bear in PUBLIC COVENANTING.

SINCE God, and not man, is the great party with whom immediately we have to do in the Covenanting of which we treat; since it is an avouching of the Lord to be our God; it seems evident, that it is a religious duty to be observed by the Church only; by the Church as a society founded on the covenant of grace‡.

‡ IF it is an advantage inseparable from the general nature of society, that the members of it may enter into a covenant for the preservation or advancement of whatever is the object of their common interest and endeavours; we cannot reasonably suppose the Church of Christ, the noblest society that was ever formed, to be precluded from that advantage. Were church members to covenant on this principle alone, they would be chargeable with no superstition; for in that case, they would be only prosecuting the purposes of the divine command according to which they have been erected into a visible church or *Civitas Dominica*; they would only be making an explicit declaration of what is implied in the formation of every society; in fine, they would only be putting *the social compact* into words, and applying it to a particular case. There would be no parallel between such covenanters and those who use the sign of the cross in baptism, kneel at the Lord's

It is competent to the church only or to her members to go about spiritual duties; and such are all those duties the immediate end of which is something spiritual. The glory of God should, no doubt, be the highest end of all our actions, whether civil or religious. But the end we have most immediately in view, subordinate to the highest, must be according to the nature of our actions; that is, our civil actions must have some worldly or political advantage for their object; and our religious actions must have the good of our own souls and of the Church for their object.

Now what is the immediate end of Covenanting? is it only for the promoting of trade, of manufactures, of agriculture? is it only for making us wealthy at home, or formidable abroad? No; but as Moses expresses it, *that we may walk in the Lord's ways, that we may keep his statutes, and his commandments, and his judgments, and hearken to his voice*; that we may be engaged to follow the Lord fully, and to assist one another in learning the truths and in performing the duties of the word. Though upright Covenanting may be conducive to our temporal happiness, this like the other ways of wisdom being pleasantness and peace; yet the direct and immediate object of covenanting is the advancement of our spiritual interests.

Thus Covenanting being a duty of a spiritu-

---

table, and keep saints' days. These things are neither commanded of God, nor do they necessarily belong to the general nature of any thing that he commands: But when the Lord enjoins Christians to walk together in the fellowship of the gospel, the injunction implieth, as what necessarily follows from the nature of society, that they ought, occasionally, to give one another all proper assurances of their stedfast adherence to the truths and ordinances of Christ. To those, especially, which are at present the most disregarded; such assurances, we mean, as are common to societies of every kind; and surely covenants, oaths and subscriptions were never peculiar to any kind of society.

al nature, it is the business of the church alone, a spiritual society, to set about it: it is the first and most necessary thing in the description of a covenanter, that he is a church-member.

This, however, does not hinder Covenanters from being considered in their civil relations, or from coming under particular and formal engagements to the faithful discharge of the various duties they owe to God and their neighbour as good citizens. Hence a family, a city, a nation, or several nations, jointly acknowledging themselves members of the church of Christ, may go about the duty of Covenanting.

The truth is, church-membership does not destroy civil relations, but consecrates them to the Lord. A person may be considered as husband or wife, as master or servant, as parent or child, both in civil society and in the church, or as the apostle expresses it, *both in the flesh and in the Lord*, Phil. 16. Indeed, the church of Christ knows no such superiority as is the object of worldly ambition, and has no respect of persons. Church-members, however different their situation in life, are all considered as in the same relation to the Lord Jesus Christ; a glorious relation before which all the pre-eminence arising from the distinctions among the men of the world, disappears, like the stars before the rising sun. In the church of Christ the duties of the servant and the subject, are no less honourable than those of the master and the magistrate; because here all the honour lies in conformity to the word of God and a single eye to his glory.

Civil relations, then, being known and acknowledged in the church, it follows that in observing any of the ordinances that Christ hath given to the church, people may be considered as standing in such relations to one another, in those, for example, of a family, of a kingdom, of a commonwealth. So they may be considered in the duty of gospel-humiliation for sin, Zec. xii. 12. *And the Land shall mourn, every family apart.* In the same social capacity, they may avow themselves a part of the kingdom of Christ in the most open explicit manner by the duty of public Covenanting: which seems to be the only adequate sense of Revel. xi. 15. *And the seventh angel sounded; and there were great voices in heaven, saying, The kingdoms of this world are become the kingdoms of our Lord and of his Christ.* Not merely the individuals of those kingdoms, but the kingdoms themselves, or bodies of people considered collectively, are here said to be our Lord's.

COVENANTERS *must* be considered as church-members; but they *may* be considered, too, as members of a civil society. If we regard the act merely of vowing and swearing to the Lord of hosts, Covenanters are to be viewed as church-members only; but if we regard the character or denominations at large, of those who set about this duty, or if we regard the extent of the obligations it brings upon them, then covenanters may be viewed as members both of the church and of civil society.

Of the Obligations come under in PUBLIC COVENANTING.

SINCE this duty is of a spiritual nature the obligations that it brings persons under, are spiritual; and it belongs properly to God and the church to take notice of men's behaviour with regard to thefe obligations. The neglect of this duty, and the breach of the engagements come under in it, are crimes in the fight of God and of the church; but they do not fall under the obfervation of the ftate. They are crimes indeed, which thofe to whom Chrift has committed the keys of church-government and difcipline, are bound to reftrain and chaftife, by admonitions, by rebukes, or by excommunication: but the corporal punifhments of the ftate cannot properly be applied here; for here the ftate has no authority. The word of God and prayer are the great weapons that we fhould diligently make ufe of to check the oppofition to this duty from fatan, the world and the flefh.

We grant, indeed, that the ftate may not only take notice of, and punifh breaches of thefe obligations, when fuch breaches are crimes the cognifance of which belongs to the ftate; but it may go a ftep farther: if the oppofition or contempt with which perfons treat covenanting, as it is gone about in the church at any particular time, be an undeniable fact; the ftate may make ufe of the fact in any cafe where it may ferve as an evidence of a crime the cognifance of which is the province of the ftate. For example, if oppofition to the duty of Covenanting fhould happen to be very generally accompanied with difaffection to the civil government; that oppofition, being an undeniable fact in the cafe of any perfon, might, in that cafe, be admitted as a prefumptive evidence of fuch difaffection; and in that view, might be taken notice of by the ftate.

Of the Extent of these OBLIGATIONS.

WE have endeavoured to shew that the people of any nation, having in their collective capacity become a part of the church of Christ, may in the same capacity, observe the duty of Covenanting. We add, that wherever this is done, there will be, of necessity, some degree of representation; unless we could suppose the individuals of a whole nation to have all, at the same time, ability, inclination and opportunity for joining in this exercise; a supposition absurd enough surely.

There are other cases in which the church admits of representation. Thus when a minister is called to be the pastor of any particular congregation, it is only a part of the members that give their votes for him: the common order of society requires that part to be the majority: The consequence is, that the candidate is declared to be duly elected; the act of those individuals who gave their voices for him is considered as the act of the whole congregation; and accordingly the whole congregation is under the same obligations to regard him in his ministerial character as those individuals. Let us only suppose a nation to be one large congregation, and the parallel between this case and that of national covenanting appears to be very exact.

We have a remarkable instance of a covenant which was binding on a whole nation through successive generations, having been entered into by the representatives of that nation, in the transaction with the Gibeonites wherein Joshua and the princes along with him represented Israel, Josh. ix. 15, 18, 21. The Lord himself confirmed this league, and punished the Israelites for the breach of it upwards of five hundred years afterward, 2 Sam. xxi, 1, 2.*

H

* It may be asked, how the contract with the Gibeonites was binding, notwithstanding the craft they used to obtain it, and the Lord's express command to destroy the Amorites, and to make no league with them?

We answer, If the Gibeonites, in pretending to come from a far country, meant no injury to the Israelites, or if they were willing to make reparation for whatever disadvantage should arise to the Israelites from their deceit; it is agreeable to the candour and simplicity of pure morals to hold the validity of a contract which was unexceptionable in its matter and its end. It is plain, the Gibeonites, instead of doing any injury to the Israelites, had an honest intention to serve them; all they sought was their life; and their life was to be employed in the service of Israel.

It is probable, too, that Joshua went into this contract in pursuance of the divine direction in Deut. xx. 10, 11. A direction which is delivered in general terms without limitation, being indeed a part of the moral law which binds us to the exercise of humanity even in necessary wars. In the issue, the Lord left considerable remains of these nations in the land, to prove the Israelites, and to hinder them from forgetting the art of war, Jud. iii. 1, 2. And Solomon (nor does it appear that herein he ought to have acted otherwise) did not destroy such devoted cities as remained in his days, but laid them under tribute, 1 Kings ix. 21. How then are we to understand the awful injunction to destroy these nations? It respects the manner in which the Israelites were to treat the cities that should reject the offers of peace: It implies too, that they were, in that case, to exercise far greater severity toward the Hittites, the Amorites, the Canaanites, the Perizzites, and the Hivites, than toward other nations: for whatever they might spare of the conquered cities which were very far off from them, they were to save alive nothing that breathed of the cities of these five nations: see Deut. xx. The utter excision in ver. 16. seems to be opposed to the reserve of the women, children and spoil in ver. 14. This view of the matter is agreeable to the conduct of Joshua. The forward, unprovoked attacks of the Canaanitish nations justified and rendered necessary every instance of severity that Joshua practised against them, Josh. xi. 19, 20. Now his conduct may justly be regarded as the best explanation of the divine command.

We will not be surprized at the peremptory manner in which this command of destroying the Canaanites is expressed, when we consider that it is adapted to their peculiar case and

It will perhaps be objected, that this was only in a civil matter; and that from the example of civil superiors representing the people of Israel in this instance, it will hardly follow, that civil character; for the Lord who knows all things, saw their hearts so much hardened, and so fully set in them to do evil, that no clemency, no offers of peace could have any effect upon them.

With regard to the Lord's prohibition of the children of Israel from making any covenant with these nations, it is to be understood according to the reason of it, which is, That such a covenant would be *a snare to them*. A reason which is sometimes contained in the prohibition itself, Exod. xxiii. 32. *Thou shalt make no covenant with them, nor with their Gods*. Indeed it is not conceivable, that the Israelites could enter into a covenant or form any close connection with an idolatrous people without very great danger of being corrupted both in principle and practice. The Israelites were to settle in the territories of the Amorites; therefore the Israelites could not enter into an alliance with the Amorites, unless the latter consented to be of the Israelitish commonwealth: but how could such gross idolators be good members of a commonwealth the whole constitution of which was subservient to the true religion, and in which open and avowed idolatry was a capital crime?

The league with the Gibeonites, then, does not seem to have been contrary to the spirit and design of the mentioned prohibition: for the Gibeonites declared themselves willing to be subject to the laws of the Israelitish commonwealth, when they said to Joshua and the princes, *We are your servants*. It is true, Joshua and the princes were much in the wrong to go so precipitately into this league, *without asking counsel of the Lord*. Church-members are likely to have but little comfort even in a lawful thing, when they neglect to acknowledge the Lord in it. The whole congregation, whether mistaken as to the nature of the league, or offended because the sense of the people had not been taken in the affair, murmured against Joshua and the princes. The Israelitish chiefs, however, shewed, on this occasion, a noble firmness against the clamours of the populace: they were steady to the right, saying, *We have sworn unto them by the Lord God of Israel; now therefore, we may not touch them*: But, added the princes who without fearing, respected the people, and endeavoured to give them all reasonable satisfaction, *let them be hewers of wood and drawers of water to all the congregation*. Thus the religion of an oath was preserved inviolable by sparing the refugees, while by their subjection to perpetual servitude, their falsehood was punished, and the whole congregation of Israel appeased.

The Lord himself confirmed the obligation of this oath in two remarkable instances. One in the encouragement and success which he gave the Israelites against the five kings of the Amorites, who had conspired the destruction of Gibeon, Josh. x. The other in the famine with which in the time of superiors may represent their people in a religious covenant; superiors who have no powers lawfully delegated to them, to act for the people in matters of religion, as they have in civil matters.

It is answered, that with regard to the general nature of an oath, and of the obligations arising from it, there is no imaginable difference between politics and religion. To the members both of church and state an oath *is for confirmation the end of all strife.* While the church and civil society have common imperfections, they must, in many cases, have common remedies. Thus they are both made up of men who may deceive; and therefore the obligation of an oath is necessary in both: they are both made up of men that labour under manifold defects and disorders of body and of mind, besides many inconveniencies and incapacities arising from other circumstances; and therefore representation is

David, he visited Israel for a slaughter Saul had made of the Gibeonites, 2 Sam. xxi. 2.

But perhaps it will be said, That other causes of the famine might be assigned than breach of covenant: the Gibeonites might be innocent, religious people; and Saul might slay them from motives of cruelty and revenge.

Let us then, consider the passage in the second book of Samuel; but let us guard against adding our own conjectures to the sacred history. It is observable, in the first place, that this covenant is represented as the deed of Israel. It is not said that Joshua and the princes, but *the children of Israel had sworn unto them.* But how did it come to be the deed of Israel? Because each individual gave his consent to it? Rather because the legal representatives of the People treated with the Gibeonites in the name of the people. In the next place, the conduct of Saul seems to be set in direct opposition to the oath which Israel had taken to the Gibeonites. It might be asked, Since the Gibeonites were a remnant of the Amorites, the people who were utterly to be cut off, whence was the slaughter of them so grievous a crime? We have reason to look for some answer to such an obvious difficulty in the narration of the punishment inflicted on Israel for that crime. Nothing is intimated in the narration concerning Saul's motives, or concerning the religious character of the Gibeonites. But the opposition between the oath which was sworn to the Gibeonites and Saul's slaughter of them will strike every reader. *The children of Israel had sworn to them,* and directly contrary to that oath, *Saul sought to slay them.*

neceffary in both. Hence the circumftances of an oath and of reprefentation in this tranfaction, are compatible to any kind of fociety among the fons of men.

Though Joshua and the princes were only civil reprefentatives of the people; yet fince they might be known and acknowledged by the church as fuch reprefentatives on account of the duties which in that character they owed to God and to the people; fince we fhould confecrate every civil relation to the Lord, and on proper occafions as the word directs, make ufe of it in his fervice; why would it have been wrong for Joshua and the princes to fet about a plain indifpenfible duty of religion, as they made a covenant with the Gibeonites, in the name of the people; fuppofing Ifrael had been called to the immediate performance of fuch a duty?

But farther, it is clear that fuch reprefentation had place in the examples of Covenanting recorded in fcripture; particularly in the Covenanting that Mofes fpeaks of in Deut. xxix. 14, 15. *Neither with you only do I make this covenant and this oath; but with him that ftandeth here with us this day before the Lord our God, and alfo with him that is not with us this day.* No words could have been more proper than thefe to defcribe the reprefentation we mean, and to fhew that, when the Ifraelites as a nation, entered into a covenant with the Lord their God, every Ifraelite was deeply concerned in that covenant, whether he was, or was not prefent at the tranfaction.

This reprefentation may be confidered with refpect to the prefent generation, and with refpect to pofterity.

As to the prefent generation of any fociety, it is reprefented fufficiently in public Covenanting, if there is evidently a majority agreeing to go about it; if the better part is in that majority;

if there are some of all ranks among the covenanters; as in Nehemiah's time, (ix. 38. and x. 28.) the princes, the priests, the levites, the porters, the singers, the Nethinims subscribed the covenant; in a word, if there is a concurrence of high and low, of rich and poor, that would be deemed sufficient in other instances, to constitute a lawful national deed, or something done by the consent of the nation.

The present generation in any society being sufficiently represented, the representation is extended to posterity. The individuals, it is true, of which the society is made up, are continually changing; so that if it were to be considered as the same society, only while these remained the same, it would follow from the births, the deaths, the emigrations, and other accidents which daily occur, that the society would be a transient thing, which no contracts would bind for a month, for a week, or so much as for one day. But the truth is, while the succession of members goes on under the same denomination, the society, with regard to contracts, is in the same state as an individual; that is, it continues under the obligation of whatever contracts it has entered into, till they be fulfilled, or till some circumstance arise equivalent to what would lawfully free an individual from the obligation of his contract.

How agreeable this is to the common sense of mankind will appear, if we consider that it is never objected to the obligation of any law, or of a treaty with any neighbouring state, that such a law or treaty was made before an individual of the present age had a being. A British magistrate would be ridiculous indeed, if he should offer no other apology for some glaring violations of the *magna charta*, which is deemed the great bulwark of English liberty, than this, That there has not been a person alive for many hundred years past who was present at the making of that charter.

FARTHER still with respect to the obligations of public covenanting, it will be useful to consider not only on whom they are laid; but the matter also, and the ends of them.

IF the matter of these obligations were something in itself indifferent, then the continuance of them would be according to the end of them. This may be illustrated by the case of the Rechabites in Jerem. xxxv. 1—11. The things that Jonadab commanded his children (to dwell in tents and to abstain from wine) were in themselves indifferent; but the temperance and humility which Jonadab's injunction was intended to promote, were so suitable to the situation of the Rechabites, that its obligation continued, in all probability, while they sojourned as strangers among the Israelites. Supposing with most of the Commentators, that this Jonadab was the same whom Jehu invited, in the vanity of his heart, to come and see his zeal for the Lord, the Rechabites at the time when Jeremiah offered them wine, had kept their father's command nearly three hundred years. It is observable, that this whole affair was of a purely civil nature‡, and cannot be supposed to have reference to any religious

---

‡ THESE observances of the Rhecabites are not to be considered as belonging to religious worship; because in the worship of God nothing is acceptable to him but what he himself hath appointed: in that matter, we are to call no man father. Nor can we think that Jonadab's command proceeded from caprice, or was without some weighty reason; for to impose needless rules about matters of indifference is only to lay a snare for the conscience. It is, therefore, likely, Jonadab was led to lay down these regulations for the conduct of his children, from a prudent regard to their situation, and for such ends as the following: That they might not be tempted to quit the pastoral kind of life which the Kenites of whom they were descended, used to lead, 1 Chron. ii. 55. Jud. i. 16. That they might avoid the envy of the Israelites among whom

peculiarity of the old Testament; so that it cannot reasonably be denied that the like instances may have place under the new Testament, or that we, like the Rechabites, may lie under obligations from the commands and covenants of our forefathers.

But since the matter of the obligations of which we treat, belongs to the moral law, they will be perpetual; that is, they will continue to bind the individual till death, and the society till its dissolution. The reason is plain. The obligations of our vows are always from the moral law. They are so, even when restrained to certain times and circumstances; a restraint or limitation which arises wholly from the indifferent nature of those things to which persons or societies bind themselves. But when these are such things as the moral law requires, there is evidently no such restraint or limitation. An example may be given. Suppose a person makes a vow that he will drink no wine for the space of ten months; whence, in that case, is the binding force of his vow? It is from the moral law which forbids us to break our vows. And whence is the continuance of it limited? From the indifferent nature of the thing about which the vow is made; as one may either drink or not drink wine, he may refrain from it either for a shorter or longer space of time, without any breach of the moral law. But suppose one makes a vow to love Christ and his people: in that case, there will be no such restraint or li-

---

they were strangers; for Jethro their great ancestor who, at the invitation of Moses his son in law, Num. x. 29. had joined himself to Israel in the wilderness, was originally of Midian: That, guarding against an over-attachment to the country of Israel, they might be ready to go wherever Providence should call them; In fine, that they might be preserved from the enticements of luxury which unfit men for bearing the hardships of their lot. See a Dissertation of Witsius on this subject.

mitation, the matter of the vow as well as the binding force of it being derived wholly from the moral law.

It is true, the obligations that societies now enter into, will cease with the societies themselves: so that there will be no such obligations in a future state. In the heavenly kingdom, Covenant-obligations, like the command of keeping holy to God one day in seven, honouring our civil superiors, and some other duties of the moral law, will then be lost in the superabounding displays of the divine glory in the face of Jesus Christ.

"But it is very hard," cries Leviculus, "that we should be bound by any covenant, to "a set of religious opinions before we examine "them." Are there any truths, Leviculus, which God requires us to believe? "I hope "you are not so uncharitable as to take me for "an infidel: I believe the truths of the bible "like other Christians." And are you under an obligation to believe these truths? "Yes, "in regard they are the word of God; but—" I beg you to inform me of one or two things more. Does that obligation remain the same, whether you be at the pains to enquire into those truths, or not? "Yes." May persons of ordinary capacity, through the Lord's blessing on their diligent use of the appointed means, attain such a certain knowledge of those truths, as to be able to specify them? "Undoubtedly; for "otherwise these truths could not properly be "said to be revealed to mankind at all; and "surely He whose yoke is easy, will not com- "mand any thing without affording strength for "the performance of it: But the right of pri- "vate judgment—" Stop a moment, Leviculus; consider what you have granted: you are, it seems, under an obligation, independent of all your own inquiry, to believe certain truths which may be specified. Pray suppose now, these truths are actually specified, and laid before you by your parents or others. "What "then?" Why, then you would have a set of truths presented to your view, which you acknowledge yourself bound to believe, whether you take the pains to enquire into them, or not. Suppose, again, you should be laid under covenant obligations to the same set of truths‡, would these, any more than your former obligation, be a bar to impartial inquiry. "Christians differ "so often and so widely among themselves as to "what ought or ought not to pass for truths delivered in the scriptures, that one cannot help "thinking it must be a work of the greatest difficulty to ascertain those truths: hence if I am "laid under the obligations of a covenant specifying a number of things as divine truths, I "may, in reality, be only tyed down to so many "errors." It is an ungrounded apprehension, Leviculus; for it is plain, that covenant-obli-

---

‡ Though no addition can be made to the obligation of the divine law, there may be obligations of another and subordinate kind; such are those of gratitude, of dutiful subjection to our lawful superiors, and those in question, of our oaths and covenants. It is true, these obligations arise out of the obligation of the divine law, and are included in it: for example, the obligations of gratitude belong to the rule of doing to others as we would have them do to us; the obligation of obeying our lawful superiors belongs to the fifth commandment; that of acting consistently with our professions, to the ninth; and that of our oath or covenant, to the third. Thus if one is under all these obligations to pray for his neighbours, and to seek their good; the sin of neglecting to do so will be agravated by the additional breach of the fifth, ninth and third commandments. Hence the falsehood of this proposition, That an oath does not lay us under a new obligation to any thing which the law of God previously requires of us. The law of God binds us to declare the truth when we have a call in providence; but no one will say, it is, therefore, needless for a court of judicature to swear witnesses. The direct contrary to the above mentioned proposition, is the truth; which is, That in every case wherein we are under a primary obligation from God's law, we may, as occasions require, come under the subordinate obligation of an oath.

gations to any thing as a divine truth, can have no place, unless there is a previous obligation to it from the word of God. The former never can be larger in their comprehension than the latter. With regard to the difficulty you mention, we have ourselves alone to blame for it: It is not any obscurity or ambiguity in the bible; but our own pride, passion, prejudice, heart-enmity, and our neglecting to look to the Lord the Spirit without whose illumination we cannot reap the least saving advantage by searching the scriptures; these are the things which render us unable to determine what particular truths the Lord is, at any time, calling us to profess, or what duties to practise; these are the things from which have sprung all the animosities and divisions of the religious world. It is, however, our unfailing comfort, that so great is the salvation which Christ hath procured for his people, and so effectual the aids of the Holy Spirit who dictated the word, and who remains in the Church unto the end of the world, that the Church, endeavouring singly to keep the Lord's way, may warrantably seek, and confidently hope to obtain the most certain and determinate knowledge of whatever truths and duties Providence calls her, in a particular manner, to hold fast and maintain; and truths and duties, thus known, are of all things the fittest to become the matter of an oath, the obligation of which extends to posterity. "But is there, indeed, "no reason to apprehend, that these obligations "may hinder people from seeking those religi- "ous principles in the bible which are specified "in their covenant?" No more, Leviculus, will these obligations hinder people from attending to the word, than a profession of adherence to the faith and worship of any particular church, with which we communicate; no more (however man's corrupted nature may abuse these obligations as it does every thing) than a most ready reception of the apostles' word hindered the Bereans from *searching the scriptures daily whether these things were so*, Acts xvii. 11.; no more, in fine, than one's engagement to do any thing exactly according to a certain rule, will make him utterly neglect that rule: for indeed it is the very first obligation that our covenanting lays us under, *to search the scriptures*; and our regard to the other obligations will be only in proportion to the regard which we have to this. The truth is, without a diligent and impartial inquiry after the divine warrant in the scripture of the truths and duties that are specified in our covenanting, we can have no due esteem of such truths and duties; we cannot see the propriety of our engagement to them; nor will we cleave to them so stedfastly and resolutely, as is necessary for prosecuting the ends of Covenanting.

BEFORE we quit this part of our subject, it is necessary to observe, that the awful threatnings of the scripture against covenant-breaking shew us how sacred these obligations are in God's account. Such are these threatnings: Lev. xxvi. 25. *I will bring a sword upon you, that shall avenge the quarrel of my covenant.* Hos. viii. 1. *Set the trumpet to thy mouth: he shall come as an eagle against the house of the Lord, because they have transgressed my covenant, and trespassed against my law.* Covenant-breaking was the ruin of Israel, 2 Kings xviii. 12. and of Judah, Jerem. xxxiv. 18, 19, 20. If God resented so dreadfully the violation of an oath which the king of Judah had taken to Nebuchadnezzar, though it was extorted from him by force, Ezek. xvii. 12——21. how much more will he resent the violation of an oath taken to himself? It is chiefly on account of the perfidy of the Israelites that they are so often charged with spiritual adultery, as in Jerem. iii. Ezek. xvi. and xxiii. When we put these examples from ourselves, as if they had no reference to any thing besides the breach of Israel's covenant; we are the dupes of that common artifice of the deceitful heart, to shift the reproofs and calls of the word, on pretence that they are not directed to us.

O ye Churches and nations, that have entered into covenant with the Lord, know for certain, that it will be your security, your honour, your happiness to keep the sacred obligation. You have infinitely more to fear from a breach of your faith with heaven, than from the bold attempts of the most formidable enemy on earth. But have you already forgotten the Lord's covenant? or do you remember only to turn it into ridicule? You have then almost filled the measure of your iniquity; and the time is near for the Lord to make some striking manifestation of himself, as *the God who keepeth covenant for ever.* Hear, while he graciously calls you back to himself; *Turn, O backsliding children, saith the Lord, for I am married unto you.* But if you harden your necks against reproof, he says to you, *Behold, ye despisers, and wonder, and perish.*

Of the PECULIAR ENDS of this duty.

WE have already seen that the proper end of Public covenanting, as being a religious duty, is our spiritual profit, or the good of our souls. We may now inquire, what sort of spiritual profit our Public Covenanting tends to promote, or what are the ends which, in some measure, distinguish it from the other duties of religion.

PUBLIC Covenanting seems to have the two

Of Public Covenanting.

following things for the more peculiar, the more direct and immediate ends of it.

The firſt is, *That we may appear, in the moſt avowed and determinate manner, as the Lord's people; with reſpect to thoſe particular points of truth and duty, to which eſpecially, the Lord (by permitting at any time, men's violent oppoſition, or by other providential circumſtances) calls us to adhere.* If the exigencies of the prince require a vigorous aſſiſtance, if his life, his crown, or his honour is in any hazard, how proper and neceſſary is it for his ſubjects, to give him the moſt public aſſurances of their loyalty and affection to him, and of their diſpoſition to ſerve him? In like manner, the Covenanting of which we treat, is a moſt ſolemn teſtimony, that our reſolution of cleaving to the Lord in ſuch a particular truth or duty, is fixed, and free from allowed heſitation. Thus the covenanters in Jehoiada's time declared themſelves the Lord's people as adhering to his pure worſhip in oppoſition to the worſhip of Baal. Thus too, the Macedonians *gave their own ſelves to the Lord*, teſtifying in that ſolemn manner, their willingneſs to ſupply the neceſſities of the poor ſaints, the duty to which they were then eſpecially called. Church-members, in their covenanted adherence to particular truths and duties, ſtand conſpicuous *with the Lamb on mount Sion, having his Father's name written in their foreheads.*

The other peculiar end of this ordinance is, *To beget and increaſe mutual confidence among the followers of Chriſt, with reſpect to the contributing of their endeavours toward the maintenance of any particular truth or duty.* Each individual of an army acts with greater chearfulneſs againſt an enemy, when he is aſſured by the military oath that his fellow-ſoldiers are voluntarily engaged in the ſame cauſe. So it is a great encouragement to an honeſt heart in contending against particular evils and particular enemies of our Lord's kingdom, to see fellow-professors binding themselves, by oath, to oppose the same evils and enemies.

It is not meant, that these ends are not promoted by the social observance of other duties; for they are undoubtedly some of the principal ends of our public attendance on the word, sacraments and prayer. Nor is it meant, that these are the only ends of Covenanting: in common with other ordinances, it tends to the edification of the church, by confirming and establishing persons in the way of duty; by increasing their faith, love, repentance and new obedience; by glorifying the Lord before the world. But Covenanting has a peculiar fitness to ascertain our present adherence to any particular point of truth or duty, to increase the unanimity of the Lord's people, and their confidence in one another, with respect to the resolution of striving together for that point of truth or duty. So the peculiar ends of the Lord's Supper (whatever other ends, generally speaking, it may answer) are these two; to shew the Lord's death till he come, and to confirm our faith in a crucified Christ as the nourishment of our souls.

These two ends of Public Covenanting are directly opposite to the two great points which the devil is chiefly intent upon in order to support his kingdom among professed Christians. One of which points is this: When he cannot bring persons to be open enemies to the cause and kingdom of the Lord Christ, to keep them in ignorance as to what the apostle Peter calls *the present truth*; or, at least, to hold them so wavering and irresolute with regard to it, that it may remain doubtful to others, and even to themselves, whether, in that respect, they are, or are not on Christ's side. Nothing is a greater eye-sore to satan than an ordinance, which tends to put that matter out of question, and which, by directing our aims to some particular part, will, through God's blessing, make us act, with greater steadiness and with greater effect, against the whole of Satan's kingdom.

The other great point that Satan labours is to sow discord among brethren. Brethren *dwelling together in unity*, delightful as the ointment of perfume used under the law in the consecration of the priesthood, refreshing and causing spiritual fruitfulness, like the descending dews, is a kind of heaven upon earth, and excites, in a peculiar manner, the resentment of hell. When the Lord gives his people *one heart and one way* according to his promise; when they can simply confide in one another; in short, when they have much of a spirit of Public Covenanting, which is, in other words, a spirit of unanimity; then their opposition to Satan's kingdom is most effectual.

Such being the peculiar ends of Public Covenanting, why should we wonder that the malice of satan and his instruments operates, with remarkable keenness, against this ordinance?

Of the Occasion *of Public Covenanting.*

THIS is no stated duty, like the observation of the sabbath, or like morning and evening worship in the closet or the family: it is an occasional duty, like fasting. Hence it is necessary to inquire, at what time, or on what occasions we ought, in this manner, to give our own selves to the Lord.

The proper time for the practice of an occasional duty is this: When Providential circumstances, to which the scriptural grounds and reasons of the duty are applicable, open the way for the performance of it. Thus if the Lord bestows a remarkable mercy upon any person or people, the way is then opened for the exercise of occasional thanksgiving upon the scriptural ground of it, that is, our obligation to give suitable evidences of our gratitude for the Lord's kindness.

The Providential circumstances which give occasion to the performance of such duties, admit of an endless variety: but the grounds and reasons of them are fixed and determined by the word of God. Hence it is that widely different circumstances may warantably occasion the performance of the same duty: the abuse of prosperity, and the ravages of war or of the plague, may, with equal reason, be the occasions of national or family fasting. Hence, too, it is not necessary to warrant us in imitating a scriptural example of an occasional duty, that our providential circumstances should be precisely the same as those mentioned in the example: it is enough, if it appears from our Providential circumstances, that we have the same grounds and reasons for performing the duty, which they had whose performance of it is in scripture recorded with approbation.

Every one will allow the truth of these observations as applied to public fasting; and why should we not allow the truth of them as applied to public Covenanting? Are not fasting and Covenanting very nearly connected? Do not engagements to be the Lord's, and to obey his commands, engagements either more or less explicit, follow necessarily upon sincere confession of, and godly sorrow for sin? If the latter proceeds upon evangelical principles, so will the former. We may as well enter into our engagements jointly and publicly, as make our confession in that manner. If our acknowledgment *that we have done iniquity*, is open and explicit, our engagement, *that we will do iniquity no more*, ought to be equally so. Now, we never imagine, that it is unwarrantable to imitate a Scriptural example of public fasting, when we have manifold grounds for it, on this account merely, that we are not precisely in the same outward circumstances as those mentioned in such a part of the sacred history. In this case, it is always allowed, that when Providential circumstances, however different in themselves, suggest the same reasons for fasting, the call to that exercise, is the same.

Suppose it should be enquired, whether we ought, at present, to imitate the example of Public fasting in Ezra ix.? In order to determine the question, not only would we have to consider, whether, like the people of Israel, the priests and Levites at that time, we are guilty of connecting ourselves by marriage with the profane part of the world? It would be necessary to examine farther, whether we have cause to acknowledge with Ezra, *That our iniquities are increased over our heads, and our trespass is grown up unto the heavens?* This would surely be enough to warrant our imitation of Ezra's fast, even supposing we could not find any thing in our case, like the circumstance of the Israelites intermarrying with the heathens around them.

In like manner, if we would know, whether, in our present circumstances, we ought to imitate the example of public Covenanting recorded in the book of Nehemiah; the question would not be, whether, like the Jews at that time, we are just come out of a state of captivity, and are still under the dominion of an heathen prince? But the point necessary to be known, would be this: whether our circumstances furnish us with the same reasons for co-venanting which the circumstances of the Jews then furnished them with? whether our sins, the tokens of God's displeasure on account of them, our hazard, in any instance, of backsliding from the way of the Lord; whether these and other things plead as much for public Covenanting in our case, as they pleaded for it in the case of the church in the days of Nehemiah?

FARTHER, if we never deem ourselves to have an opportunity of imitating a scriptural example of any religious duty, till our circumstances in Providence, coincide with all the circumstances in that example, we may live to the age of Methusaleh, without ever having such an opportunity. Nay, there is one circumstance that, under the Mosaic œconomy, attended the public observance of occasional duties, which is never to occur again: the circumstance was, that one visible immediate communion in the ordinances of God's worship, appeared then to comprehend the whole church of Christ upon earth. But how absurd is it to suppose that we are enjoined to imitate examples, which we never can have an opportunity of imitating! or that our obedience to one of the plainest precepts of the word, such as this, *Vow and pay unto the Lord your God*, should be confined to such imitation! To avoid the absurdity, it seems necessary to admit the following observation: That Providential circumstances are connected with the practice of public Covenanting, or of any other occasional duty, in these respects only; as opening the way for it, as suggesting motives to it, or as making the ends of it necessary for the help of church-members in the path of duty.

ON the other hand, it is absurd and superstitious to regard Providential circumstances as, of themselves and for their own sakes, warranting the performance of any duty. Such a capricious connection between the events of Scripture-history and certain religious duties, gave rise to Christmass, to Lent, to Easter, and to many other uninstituted observances by which professed Christians have deviated from the simplicity of New Testament worship. They gratified their taste for novelties in religion by annexing, as in the instances now mentioned, certain duties to certain times, places and other circumstances: at first, they took both the circumstances and the duties out of the Bible; only the connection was appointed by themselves: afterward, they proceeded farther; they added new duties and new circumstances of their own invention. Thus superstition was carried by degrees to that enormous height at which we find it in the church of Rome. But we do not mean to dwell on this remark, though it is no great digression from the subject of our present inquiry.

It may be farther observed, that neither the precepts nor the promises of the word concerning public Covenanting, mention any particular set of providential circumstances as marking the season of this duty, Psal. lxxvi. 11. *Vow and pay unto the Lord your God.* Rom. xii. 1. *I beseech you by the mercies of God, that ye present your bodies a living sacrifice, holy and acceptable to God which is your reasonable service.* Isai. xix. 18. *In that day, shall five cities in the land of Egypt, speak the language of Canaan, and swear to the Lord of hosts.* verse 21. *They shall vow a vow unto the Lord, and shall perform it.*

With regard to the last of these passages, it is observable that the season of Covenanting is pointed out by the expression *in that day*; by which (as will easily appear from the consideration of the whole passage, in which *altars, sacrifices* and *oblations to the Lord,* which under the

K

Mosaic dispensation, were allowed to be at Jerusalem only, are foretold to be in Egypt) is undoubtedly meant the day of the New Testament-dispensation, intimating that the frequency and the evangelical manner of public Covenanting, were, among other things, to be the distinguishing glory of the New Testament-dispensation.

AGAIN, in the following comfortable promise, the exercise of Covenanting is connected, not with any outward circumstances which fall under the observation of the carnal eye, but with a rich effusion of the Holy Ghost, whom the world neither sees nor knows, Isai. xliv. 3, 5. *I will pour waters upon the thirsty; and floods upon the dry ground. And then One shall say, I am the Lord's; and he* (for so we may read the words) *shall call himself by the name of Jacob, and he shall subscribe with the hand, and surname himself by the name of Israel.* Thus the general concurrence of church-members in the duty of Gospel-humiliation, is connected with the gift of the Spirit in that remarkable promise, Zech. xii. 10. *I will pour upon the house of David, and upon the inhabitants of Jerusalem, the Spirit of grace and of supplications, and they shall look upon me whom they have pierced, and they shall mourn for him.* We should learn from these promises, (which, blessed be God! have often been remarkably verified in the experience of his people) to set forward in the duties of Gospel-humiliation and Covenanting in the faith of the Holy Spirit being poured out upon us: for it is the Lord's usual manner of dealing with his people agreeably to the order of the new Covenant, to give the Holy Spirit in his remarkably strengthening, enlightening and comforting influences, neither while they carelessly neglect their duty; nor yet, in any respect or in any degree, (as the legal pride of the heart will suggest) on account of the performance of their duty; but rather while they are honeftly endeavouring to go forward in it. Hence the prophet Ifaiah fays, *Thou meeteft him that rejoiceth, and worketh righteoufnefs, thofe that remember thee in thy ways.* Hence, too, the Holy Ghoft is faid to be given *to them that afk him,* Luke xi. 13. and *to them that obey him,* Acts v. 32. Thus the Lord honours his own inftitutions and his own way; not indeed, for our fakes, but for his own name's fake.

PERHAPS it will be faid, if it be our duty to effay covenanting, whenever our Providential circumftances afford motives and incitements to it, why was it fo feldom practifed by the Ifraelites? One fhould think, the prevalence of iniquity, the danger of feduction from the path of duty, and alarming evidences of the Lord's difpleafure (had thefe been deemed fufficient reafons for Covenanting) would have led the church of Ifrael to covenant in the days of the Judges as well as in the days of Jofhua; in the reign of Jehofhaphat as well as in that of Afa.

IN anfwer to this it may, in the firft place, be obferved, that we cannot reafonably fuppofe that all the inftances of the Covenanting of the Jewifh church, are exprefly mentioned in the hiftory of the Old Teftament; a hiftory which is very fuccinct; recording rather the revolutions of the church than the feries of her tranfactions. There is, however, hardly any other occafional duty of which we have more frequent examples, than of Covenanting. One may produce out of the Old Teftament as many examples of public Covenanting as of public occafional Fafting or Thankfgiving. We have no account of any public Covenanting in David's time; and yet we cannot prove that there was none, or that he does not refer to it when he fays, *I have sworn, and I will perform it, that I will keep thy righteous judgments.*

WHEN the examples of any duty in Scripture are obviously sufficient for our direction with regard to the grounds, the reasons, and the manner of performing that duty, it is but a poor excuse for the neglect of it, that it is not exemplified so often or in such places of the bible as we think proper.

BUT farther in answer to the objection, we grant, that in times of prevailing corruption and apostacy from the Lord; nay, even when the church of Israel was considerably reformed, this and other particular duties might be greatly neglected: as we know, Jehoshaphat, Hezekiah, and other good kings, though they did much toward the reformation of Israel, suffered the high places to remain untouched. When the Lord reproves his professing people for their obstinacy in departing from him, the reproof implies their neglect of this duty; because their public Covenanting was no other than an explicit avowal of their resolution to return to the Lord; a resolution which could hardly be deemed upright and sincere, while they refused to make such an open avowal of it.

IF it be asked, why the neglect of Covenanting is never expresly mentioned among the other sins of the Israelites? We answer, That as Covenanting was not so much one particular duty, as the proper appointed means of returning to the Lord in the observance of all the duties incumbent on them; so the neglect of Covenanting was not so much one particular sin as an obstinate persisting to depart from the Lord in all their sins. Hence we may very well understand the neglect of Covenanting to be meant by such general expressions as these; *forsaking the Lord, rebelling against him, refusing to hearken to his voice.*

If it should be said, that Covenanting may be proper, when the body of the nation is willing, as the body of Israel were, to concur in it: but how are a few persons of a Christian country, warranted to distinguish themselves from their fellow-christians by public Covenanting? The answer is obvious from the foregoing observations. The reasons for the duty of Covenanting, as they may be gathered from the dispensations of Providence compared with the directions of the word, may not only warrant, but urge us to essay the performance of the duty, however great the multitudes that despise it. These reasons are our warrant and our call to it; and not merely the coincidence between our circumstances and those of the examples in Scripture.

In the abovementioned passage of Isai. xix. it is foretold, That *five cities of the land of Egypt* shall not be ashamed of the singularity of *swearing to the Lord of hosts*. In antient Egypt there were, according to Herodotus, no less than twenty thousand cities. Undoubtedly five cities were but a small part of so large and flourishing a kingdom. It is plain, that the few who feel their obligation from God's authority to the practice of this duty, are by no means to forbear it, because the many refuse to concur in it. We are as little to follow a multitude in omitting to do good as in doing evil.

Those who join in Public Covenanting should, no doubt, be unanimous among themselves, like the Jewish Covenanters in Nehem. x. in shewing a suitable zeal for reformation, such unanimity being no more than the import of their covenanting. But supposing many others to be against the principal ends of it, those who sincerely seek the advancement of these ends ought, by no means, to omit it on that account.

But what if those who refuse to join with us in public Covenanting, are, in other respects, more faithful and active in reformation than ourselves? Why then, in these respects, let us prefer them to ourselves; let us love and esteem them; let us encourage them; let us imitate them. But allowing them to be equal to the apostle Paul in the labours of love and zeal for the cause of Christ, it is at our utmost peril, if we follow them in matters of religion, any farther than they follow Christ. In these matters it should be our single aim to have the approbation of Christ: but it cannot be shewn, that He will admit our great respect for the piety and the different opinions of eminent men, as a sufficient excuse for our omission of a duty which his word calls us to observe, as in other respects suitable to our Providential circumstances: and it behoves us to have our reasons for omitting, as well as our reasons for practising an occasional duty from no less authority than that of *the law and the testimony*: in both we have much need to *cease from our own wisdom*.

A Person who, in singleness of heart, is *seeking of the Lord a right way*, may find very scriptural motives and incitements to this duty in those very considerations by which many would excuse themselves from taking any trouble about it. Such a one will say: "This duty
"is opposed by the civil magistrate, by the
"greater part of the nation, and even by some of
"those who, I hope, are, in the main, fearers
"of the Lord. But this, I am well persuaded,
"is an ordinance of the Lord Christ; and the
"more numerous and the more respectable they
"are who oppose it, I desire, through grace, to
"be the more stedfast in cleaving to it, and the
"more ready to embrace any opportunity of put-
"ting it in practice. I ought to rejoice at such
"an occasion of testifying my love to the Lord
"Jesus, and of shewing, that my regard to the
"honour of his name, which is so deeply con-

"cerned in each of his inſtitutions, prevails over every inferior conſideration."

But farther, it may be objected, that if two parties, equally active in reformation, and equally tenacious of their reſpective peculiar tenets, ſhould both ſet about public Covenanting, each party would take its own tenets into its covenant, and conſequently the covenant of the one party would be contradictory to that of the other: thus by their covenanting, inſtead of helping, they would hinder the endeavours of one another toward reformation.

We anſwer, if neither the peculiar tenets of the one party, nor thoſe of the other, are truths of God's word, then they ſhould not be inſiſted on as matters of great importance: an oſtentatious profeſſion of them is a grievous ſin, diſhonouring God, and hindering the peace of the church. But thoſe of both parties who deſire to drop ſuch *matters of doubtful diſputation*, ought not, for the bigotry of the reſt, to be hindered from *joining themſelves to the Lord*, and to one another, in ſocial covenanting.

But ſo far as the diſtinguiſhing principles of of either party are truths of God's word, they are to be held faſt; and let the reputation of ſuch as oppoſe them be, otherwiſe, ever ſo great or ever ſo unqueſtionable; yet in reſpect of their oppoſition to theſe truths, and ſo far as they carry it, they ſhew themſelves to be real enemies of reformation *; ſpecious perhaps, but

---

* We are not to give up an important truth, becauſe thoſe who deny it, are engaged in the ſame cauſe with us in reſpect of many other important truths. Independents join with us in teſtifying againſt the impoſition of ceremonies in the church of England; the church of England, in teſtifying againſt the Papiſts; and the Papiſts themſelves, in teſtifying againſt Deiſts and Arians. Indeed, we have rather a nearer connexion with the firſt than with the ſecond, and a connexion incomparably nearer with the ſecond than with the third, according

so much the more ensnaring. Church-members may engage by solemn covenant, to contend for any particular truth of God's word, with so much the more propriety, that it is called *one of their peculiar tenets*, that is, a tenet which is almost universally neglected and opposed; because it is more especially when that is the case with any divine truth, that we are called on to avow and to promote our joint adherence to it by our public Covenanting.

ALL that we do or can engage to in Covenanting is an adherence to the truths and duties of God's word. Hence the covenanting of one society of professing Christians, so far as it is right or attended with any real obligation, must be perfectly agreeable to the covenanting of other societies.

IN matters of fact, an honest man will not deliberately assert any thing but what he could swear to, if such confirmation were necessary: much less should we profess any thing as a part of the true religion, unless we receive it so heartily and sincerely as a truth or duty of God's word, that, on a proper call, we could without hesitation, confirm that profession by the solemnity of an oath.

CONTRADICTORY professions defeat their own ends no less than contradictory covenants defeat theirs. Indeed, there do not seem to be any consequences of the latter which do not, in some degree, attend the former: a truth which is obvious enough, when one considers that public Covenanting is only a very solemn and explicit manner of declaring our Christian profession.

---

to the measure of truth which they hold in common with us. But whatever is the degree of our connexion with them, we are not, on that account, to drop our testimony against Independency, Episcopacy or Popery.

ALL we contend for on this head, may be summed up in these three particulars.

FIRST, It seems plain from the preceding observations, that whenever the proper grounds and reasons of Covenanting are applicable to our circumstances in Providence, we have, then, a sufficient call to the practice of this duty.

SECONDLY, Though we can hardly suppose the church, while on earth, to be any considerable time without some call to this duty ‡; yet there are particular seasons in which, from Providential circumstances, the call appears to be more urgent than at other times; for it must be still more urgent, as our sins, our temptations, and the signs of the Lord's displeasure with us, increase and grow more alarming.

THIRDLY, As we are never to be deterred from any thing which we clearly perceive to be our duty by the fear of what may follow upon it, so with regard to the consequences of such a resolute adherence to the path of duty, it should be our only care to make the word of God in opposition to the dictates of carnal sense and reason, the ground and measure of our expectations. Carnal sense and reason are continually suggesting, that a strict and explicit cleaving to the

---

‡ HENCE it is that several of the circumstances which have been specified as marking the season of public Covenanting, are circumstances inseparable from the earthly condition of the church of Christ. Such are the two following: *First*, Returning to the Lord after much backsliding from him; but surely that is the church's exercise in her best times; and her duty in the worst: *Secondly*, Being in manifest danger from enemies; but when was the true church, or when will she be without such danger? Never till she have no more occasion to watch or to fight. The truth is, it will be hard to imagine a situation of the church militant in which social covenanting would be altogether unwarrantable; and yet there are undoubtedly times in which the church discerns the Lord's call to this duty more clearly and with less disagreement among her members than at other times.

truths of God will ruin the peace of the church. On the contrary, faith holds it the only way to to preserve the church's unity; because it is the truth dwelling in the saints that makes them *love one another with a pure heart fervently.* See to this purpose the first two verses of the second epistle of John. Hence the more fully, constantly, powerfully, and evidently the truth dwells in church-members, so much the more will they love one another. Hence it is that the manifestation of the truth dwelling in believers by their profession and their practice, are the great means of encouraging and strengthening one another in the Christian course: their practice and profession ought, on that account, to be single and explicit; the ambiguity or doubtfulness of either in any case, being a hindrance to edification. Let the ends we propose in covenanting and our prospect of attaining them be according to this principle; and we will not be apt to let slip an opportunity, when Providence affords it, of joining with our fellow church-members in so profitable an exercise.

Of the HISTORY *of Public Covenanting.*

BY the history of Covenanting we do not mean only a series of instances wherein the members of particular churches formally lifted up their hands and swore allegiance to the Lord Christ. We consider it as vastly more comprehensive. It includes, in the first place, all the instances of church-members declaring, as Providence offered occasions, their adherence to some particular truths and duties of religion. When they were not ashamed in the presence of their enemies to avow the relation they stood in to the Lord as their God, and their fixed resolution to serve him; when they acknowledged their own sins, and engaged particularly to the contrary duties; or when, upon some particular evidences of the Lord's displeasure with them, they entered into a mutual agreement to return to the Lord; in all these cases, we consider church-members as real covenanters.

In the next place, It includes every instance of church-members explicitly declaring their adherence to particular revelations of the covenant of grace, or to any particular truth or duty contained in those revelations. We consider every explicit profession of faith in the promises of that covenant, whether these promises were first made known to Adam and Eve, to Noah, or the prophets, as really and to all intents the very covenanting for which we plead: and in the same light we may regard the resolutions they expressed, of obeying the particular divine commands which accompanied those promises.

In fine, the history of Public Covenanting shews us how the church's profession of confidence in the Lord and of obedience to him, came, by degrees, to be more express and formal. As in dictating the holy scriptures, God made use of the language of men; and in the different ages in which the several parts of the scriptures were given to the church, he still made use of that language which was most generally understood in the places where the church then subsisted: hence the Old Testament was written in Hebrew, and the New in Greek. In like manner, the forms which the Lord directed his people to use in Covenanting, were such as mankind had already begun to employ in civil transactions: it was when oaths and subscriptions became the usual confirmations of public deeds, that the church was warranted to make use of them in social covenanting. As during the long period of time between Moses who began, and the apostle John who closed the cannon of scripture, the improvements of human society were gradually advancing; so the Lord condescended not only to render them subservient to the instruction of the church in the metaphors, similies and parables of the word; but likewise to preserve a striking resemblance of many of them in those ordinances which he appointed for the church's edification. But this will never warrant any to introduce the usages of worldly kingdoms or commonwealths into the church of Christ, of their own accord. We are not to be bold and presumptuous, because our Lord is condescending. It is his authority alone that lays us under an obligation to observe all the ordinances that ought, at any time, to have place in the church; the resemblance of them to human affairs serves only to make the obligation more easy and more suitable to our nature and situation.

PUBLIC Covenanting has always a particular and immediate reference to the present state of religion: indeed, for church-members to join in covenanting, what is it other than to avow in the most solemn and the most determinate manner, whatever conformity to the Lord's will and word the church has already attained? Hence the history of this duty in the different periods of the church cannot be understood without attending to the state of religion in those periods.

THE truth of the following observation will be illustrated in the history of Covenanting: That positive institutions are observed in the greatest purity and perfection on the appointment of them: the after observation is more likely to be defective than the first. We have reason to think, that the ordinance of the Passover was hardly ever kept with so exact an attention to all the circumstances mentioned in the words of institution, as in that night wherein the destroyer of the first-born went through the land of Egypt. The case is quite the reverse with respect to what we call moral duties, or those which we are necessarily led to infer from the nature and perfections of God, from our relation to Him as our God and Redeemer, and from our relation to one another in him. Such duties, while the church is in an infant state, while her knowledge and other attainments are small, will be found to be but imperfectly understood, and of course imperfectly and indistinctly practised. But as the church advances toward maturity, grows in grace, and knows more of the Lord and of her relation to him; her knowledge of moral duties enlarges and becomes more distinct, and her practice of those duties more adequate to the rule. Thus with regard to public Covenanting, how various the degrees of distinctness and of conformity to the rule in the manner of going about it, from the time of Enos when *men began to call upon the name of the Lord* to *the sealing of the covenant* in the days of Nehemiah?

Of the church's Profession from Adam to Abraham.

THE church of Christ was at first built upon the revelation of the covenant of grace in that illustrious promise, Gen. ii. 15. *I will put enmity between thee and the woman, between thy seed and her seed: it shall bruise thy head, and thou shalt bruise its heel.* The history of the church, in this period, consists of a very few particulars. There seem to have been hardly any other societies for the stated worship of God, than families; the father or head of each family being the prieſt of it. Hence we may eaſily conceive their manner of worſhipping the Lord to have been very ſimple: nor can we reaſonably expect to find church-members at this early time, obſerving any religious duty of a public nature, with all the diſtinctneſs and formality which attended the obſervance of it afterward.

We may be ſure, however, that the church held faſt the word of grace that the Lord had given her, and that ſhe profeſſed her faith with ſuch formality as the meaſure of revelation ſhe was favoured with, and the circumſtances of her lot rendered neceſſary. Abel adhered to the truth of the promiſe concerning the ſeed of the woman; and gave ſuch explicit teſtimonies, ſuch open aſſurances of that adherence in oppoſition to the unbelief, pride, envy and hypocriſy of Cain, that Cain was filled with rage, and killed his brother. The teſtimony of the church was then what it is now, and what it always will be, a torment to the ſeed of the ſerpent. But what aſſurances did Abel give Cain of his adherence to the promiſe? We read of one only; but that was ſuch as may be deemed equivalent to all the formalities of Public Covenanting in the more advanced ſtate of eccleſiaſtical and of civil ſociety: *Abel brought of the firſtlings of his flock and of the fat thereof: And the Lord had reſpect unto Abel and to his offering.* Thus that faithful martyr teſtified his adherence to the truth. As for writings, oaths and ſubſcriptions, they could as little have been underſtood, before theſe or other legal ſecurities were in uſe, as a lnaguage which never had been heard.

We have a deſcriptive hint concerning the ſtate of the church at the birth of Enos upwards of one hundred years after the death of Abel. Then, it is ſaid, *began men to call on the name of the Lord.* Some, indeed, have rendered the text, *Then began men to curse the name of the Lord.* But this interpretation is far from being so natural, since the name of the Lord had been profaned by Cain and his impious posterity long before: On the contrary, the account in the same passage, of Seth and Enos, who as witnesses for the truth, were in opposition to the Cainites, leads us naturally to consider the expression as having a respect to the worship of God. So that this text points out a remarkable æra of reformation in the church. Probably several families then agreed to call on the Lord; or to call themselves by a name that served to denote their holy profession, and to distinguish them from the profane race of Cain: such a name we have in Gen. vi. 2. where the descendents of Seth, who then made up the visible church, are called, *The sons of God.* The latter explication is from the marginal reading of our translation, *Then began men to call themselves by the name of the Lord.*

THE remarkably gracious revelation that Noah was favoured with immediately after the flood, was such as could not suitably be received without explicit engagements to be the Lord's. Then it was that the Lord first gave the name *Covenant* to the declaration of his saving grace and kindness toward sinners of mankind; a name indeed full of consolation, sweetly intimating the Lord's condescension, love and faithfulness. This covenant consists of absolutely free promises; it is not suspended on any conditions whatever to be performed by us; the gradual accomplishment and the final result of this covenant are no less than the revelation of it, from the sovereign authority, grace and faithfulness of God. Hence we must beware of supposing that God's covenant, like men's covenants with one another, owes its effect to the compliance of the parties to whom it is proposed. If the faith of God's elect is necessary in order to our enjoying of the benefits of the new covenant; the reason is, that faith is among the first of these benefits according to the order in which divine wisdom sees fit to communicate them, for that noble grace is no less made over and secured to us in the promises of the covenant than the benefits which follow it. On this occasion, the Lord appointed *his bow in the cloud* to be a sign of his covenant. It seems to be partly on account of this appointment that the Lord here calls his gracious constitution a covenant: for every covenant among men is accompanied with some sign, memorial, seal or pledge. The Lord's promise would naturally be considered as a covenant, when a visible sign was annexed to it. *This is the token of the covenant*: as if the Lord had said, As surely as you behold the rainbow, so surely will I fulfil every promise I have made.

It is true, that temporal benefits only are here expresly mentioned; and the rainbow is the sign of a temporal benefit. But it was the general nature of the Old Testament dispensation to make use of earthly things for shadowing forth heavenly and spiritual things, Heb. x. 1. As the Lord, in his providential bounty, grants to man freely the use of the brute creatures, security against the return of the deluge, the agreeable vicissitude of the seasons, of day and night; so in his kindness toward us through Jesus Christ, he gives us all the saving benefits of the new covenant. All mankind partake of these outward favours; but it is the peculiar happiness of those who by faith set to their seal that God's covenant is true, that they consider these temporal benefits as promised blessings of God's covenant, as shadows and tokens of something better, and in a word, as certainly connected (we mean as they have place in the covenant of grace, not as they are dispensed in common Providence) with all the blessings of grace and glory. Isai. liv. 9, 10. may be regarded as the very best comment on the Lord's covenant with Noah: *For this is as the waters of Noah unto me: for as I have sworn, that the waters of Noah should no more go over the earth; so have I sworn that I would not be wroth with thee, nor rebuke thee. The mountains shall depart, and the hills shall be removed; but my kindness shall not depart from thee, neither shall the covenant of my peace be removed, saith the Lord that hath mercy on thee.* This way of considering the works of creation and providence renders the Christian's contemplation of them both delightful and improving, serving to exercise faith as well as the natural understanding.

THIS everlasting covenant (that covenant the only proper condition of which is the blood of Christ, Heb. xiii. 20.) is, indeed, said *to be between God and every living creature of all flesh that is upon the earth.* These universal expressions are used to signify, that all the creatures, rational and irrational, are included in the covenant with respect to their subserviency to the great spiritual designs of it: though many of them, considered in any other respect, may properly be said to have neither lot nor part in that matter. There seems to be likewise a reference to the extent of the gospel dispensation, which was to become greater and greater till it should extend as far as the goodness of Providence in *giving rain and fruitful seasons, filling men's hearts with food and gladness.* In this respect Isaiah says (xl. 5.) *The glory of the Lord shall be revealed, and all flesh shall see it together.*

THE way in which Noah entered into this covenant was the same as that in which we enter into the covenant of grace still; it was by faith in the sacrifice of Christ. Had it not been for that sacrifice, the Lord would never have said to Noah, (what he now says, indeed, to every sinner that hears the gospel) *I will make with you an everlasting covenant.* That Noah exercised faith in the sacrifice of Christ appears from his burnt offerings; in consequence of which it is said, *the Lord smelled a sweet savour,* or *a favour of rest.* In what? in Noah's burnt offerings? Rather in the sacrifice of Christ typified by these burnt offerings, Ephes. v. 2. *He gave himself for us an offering and a sacrifice of a sweet smelling savour.* Smelling, in this manner, a favour of rest, the Lord revealed himself as establishing his covenant with Noah, and with his seed after him.

Along with so gracious a revelation of the *everlasting covenant* †, the Lord gave Noah a variety of precepts; precepts which seem to be stated in direct opposition to the rapine, violence and impurity which prevailed among mankind before the flood. When God's law has been remarkably transgressed in any particular manner, he would have our obedience to his law conspicuous in opposition chiefly, to that manner of transgressing it.

Though the Holy Ghost has not given us any particular account of the way in which the several members of Noah's family expressed their adherence to that revelation which the Lord had given them; yet as this revelation plainly called for a suitable profession of their faith and obedience, so we have no reason to doubt tha Noah who was a *just man and perfect in his generation,* would require them to make that profession with

---

† This epithet is given to the Covenant of grace in various other places, as in 2 Sam. xxiii. 5. Isa. lv. 3. Jerem: xxxii. 40. Heb. xiii. 20. This covenant is everlasting in opposition to the covenant of works; the representing head of which, the first Adam, being in honour, continued not; but the last Adam the head of this covenant, continues a quickening Spirit for ever. It is The Everlasting Covenant; there is no other covenant for our eternal salvation.

such formality and solemnity as might serve to impress their minds with a just sense of their obligations to the Lord who had so graciously revealed himself in his covenant with Noah.

Of the Church's Profession from Abraham to Moses.

IN course of time, mankind being again greatly corrupted, the pure profession of the truth, as taught by Noah, was almost universally forsaken. Hitherto the church had been scattered here and there among mankind: her members were connected with one another by worshipping the same God, and by walking according to the same rule; but not formally as yet, by any other outward ties than such as are necessary in civil life, in families, or in a neighbouring situation. But now the Lord having determined to restore the purity of his truths and institutions, saw fit in gracious sovereignty, to call Abraham out of Ur of the Chaldees, in order that he might fix his church as a visible society, separated from the rest of the world, in the family of that patriarch, upon the ground of a new revelation of the covenant of grace, a revelation clearer still and more particular than that which had been made to Noah.

THE church of God, from its beginning, was a society of the same nature as it is at this day; it was always made up of persons called out of the world, not according to their works, but according to the sovereign purpose and free grace of God. The family out of which Abraham was taken was no better, no less grossly idolatrous, than the rest of that degenerate world out of which he was called, Josh. xxiv. 2. *And Joshua said unto all the people, Thus saith the Lord God of Israel, your fathers dwelt on the other side of the flood in old time, even Terah the father of Nahor: and they served other gods.* Whatever may be found in the fabulous legends of the Jewish writers, or among the conjectures favourable to human pride, of our modern advocates for Arminian free will, the scripture says not a syllable of the virtue or integrity of Abraham before his calling; nay, from this passage we are led to think he was, like the rest of his father's house, a gross idolator; for it is plainly the scope of the passage to shew that the Lord's choice of the Israelites was not from a regard to any deserving qualifications that he found in them or in their fathers when he called them to be his peculiar people, but purely from his grace and sovereign good-pleasure.

WHEN the Lord called Abraham *out of his country, and from his kindred,* he revealed to him his covenant, in which an infinitely nobler inheritance was made over to him than any he had left. In this revelation of the covenant of grace, three remarkable things were secured to Abraham. In the first place, His own personal interest in the Lord as his God: As when the Lord says, *I will bless thee; and thou shalt be a blessing. Fear not, Abram, I am thy shield and exceeding great reward.* In the second place, It was secured to him, that the seed of the woman who was to bruise the head of the serpent, should descend from him according to the flesh: *In thy seed shall all the families of the earth be blessed.* Thirdly, The spiritual privileges of his posterity were secured: It was promised, that in his family exclusively almost of all others, the Lord would preserve his church till the Saviour should come; that the Lord would give to those of his descendents among whom he should preserve the true religion, the land of Canaan, where they were to *dwell alone, and were not to be reckoned among the nations. I will establish my covenant between me and thee, and thy seed after thee, in their generations, for an everlasting covenant; to be a God unto thee, and to thy seed after thee. And I will give unto thee, and to thy seed after thee, the land wherein thou art a stranger, all the land of Canaan for an everlasting possession; and I will be their God.*

This covenant, like Noah's, was confirmed by a sign or seal, Gen. xvii. 11. *Ye shall circumcise the flesh of your foreskin, and it shall be a token of the covenant between me and you.* Rom. iv. 11. *Abraham received the sign of circumcision a seal of the righteousness of the faith which he had being yet uncircumcised.* This seal was of such a nature, that while the Lord's grant of it to Abraham and his children, was a pledge and assurance of the promised blessings of the covenant, their participation of it was an evidence of their faith and obedience; for it was not merely, like the rainbow, a sign to be contemplated, but an appointment to be observed. *This is my covenant, which ye shall keep between me and you, and thy seed after thee: Every manchild among you shall be circumcised.* By this new circumstance which did not attend any former revelation of the covenant, it seems to have been the Lord's gracious design to teach the Israelites in a sensible and striking manner, that he wanted every one of his professing people to intermeddle in the covenant, taking the Lord for his God in particular; and that they were to set about every piece of obedience to the divine law, as they were to observe circumcision, in the way of laying hold of God's Covenant. We have the same circumstance serving the same ends in the sacraments of the new Testament.

This covenant of promise was the great charter of the church from Abraham to the coming of Christ. The revelations of the covenant of grace which were afterward made to Isaac, to

Jacob, to Moses, to David and the other prophets who spoke in the name of the Lord, had constantly a reference to this revelation made to Abraham. Hence the covenant of grace is often mentioned as the truth which the Lord spake to Abraham and to his seed. Hence the apostle calls it in Gal. iii. 14. *the blessing of Abraham*; in ver. 16. *the promises that were made to Abraham and to his seed*; in ver. 17. *the covenant which was confirmed by God in Christ*; and frequently is it called *The Promise*, by way of eminence, ver. 19, 22, 29. Acts ii. 39. In short, this revelation of God's everlasting covenant to Abraham was the ground on which the church of Israel was built; and the tenure by which she held all her peculiar priveleges.

WHILE the Lord was thus revealing himself to Abraham as his own God, as God almighty, or alsufficient to supply his needs, he enjoined him, at the same time, to exprefs his gratitude in a course of new obedience, Gen. xvii. 1. *Walk before me, and be thou perfect*. The Lord who knows the heart, represents what Abraham ought, as what Abraham would be enabled, to do with respect to the instruction of his family, Gen. xviii. 19. *For I know him, that he will command his children and his houshold after him, and they shall keep the way of the Lord to do justice and judgment; that the Lord may bring upon Abraham that which he hath spoken of him.*

As to Abraham's profession of faith in this revelation of the everlasting covenant, and of his obedience to these precepts, we have, at least, several instructive hints. In Gen. xii. 8. it is said, that *he built an altar to the Lord between Bethel and Ai, and called upon the name of the Lord*; openly professing, no doubt ‡, that he

---

‡ It is universally allowed, says Dr. Owen in Theolog. lib. 4. cap. 1. that under the general description of calling on the name of the Lord, the whole of his external worship, not excepting even sacrifices, is comprehended.

was not ashamed of his confidence in the word of the Lord.

ABRAHAM's very solemn address to the king of Sodom concerning the division of the spoils they had taken, undoubtedly contained in it a declaration of his adherence to the Lord as his own God in virtue of the everlasting covenant, Gen. xiv. 22. *And Abram said to the king of Sodom, I have lift up mine hand unto the Lord, the most high God, the possessor of heaven and earth, that I will not take from thee a thread, even to a shoe-latchet.* Two things are obvious, and seem to be intended by the Holy Ghost in recording this declaration of Abraham. One is, that the patriarch descibes the divine Being to whom he swore, in the same terms as Melchizedec had use in blessing him; *Blessed be Abram of the most high God, possessor of heaven and earth.* The same terms repeated in the same passage, lead us to think that Melchisedec and Abram had the same object in view. But it was undoubtedly the God who made the covenant with Abram, God in Christ, in whose name that memorable blessing was pronounced. The other thing is, that this oath appears to have been of the nature of a vow. It was not to the king of Sodom that Abram lifted up his hand, but to the Lord: Abram, in order to shew that what he had done in his late atchievement against the kings, did not proceed from any selfish or interested views, but from a single regard to the glory of his God, had pledged himself to the Lord, that he would not touch the spoils. The king of Sodom was so far from being the party to whom the oath was made, that it is not said, he was so much as a witness of it.

WE have a very plain and explicit profession of Abraham's faith in his instructions to the eldest servant of his houshold with respect to the affair of taking a wife to his son Isaac: *The*

Lord God of heaven who took me from my father's house, and from the land of my kindred, and who spoke unto me, and who sware unto me, saying, Unto thy seed will I give this land, he shall send his angel before thee. This declaration plainly implies that he gloried in his covenant-relation to the Lord, as a satisfying security for all the blessings of grace and providence †.

We may consider the signs or memorials which the patriarchs left behind them wherever they journeyed, memorials of the Lord's kindness to them, and of their obligations to him; as so many professions or testimonies of their faith and obedience. Of this kind were these; the grove that Abraham planted in Beersheba, and the altar that he built in the land of Moriah; the pillar that Jacob erected at Bethel; the name Peniel which he gave to one place, and Mahanaim the name which he gave to another. In these times of simplicity, stones were set up, altars and heaps were made, trees were planted, names were given to places, in order to perpetuate the memory of particular actions or events: these were the first public records; these the histories of the patriarchal age.

† To the above observations concerning Abraham we may add, that it is not a singular opinion to consider that patriarch as a covenanter. Mr. Pemble may be admitted as an unexceptionable sample of our old Protestant divines. "After "that men," says that judicious writer in his treatise of Justification, "had now almost forgot God's promise and their "own duty, and idolatry had crept into these families wherein "by succession the church of God had continued, God calls "forth Abraham from amongst his idolatrous kindred, and "with him renews that former promise in form of a league "and covenant, confirmed by word and solemn ceremonies. "God on one side, promising to be the God of Abraham and "of his seed; Abraham, for his part, believing the promise, "and accepting the condition of obedience," or coming under engagements, "to walk before God in uprightness." The word Condition is used here and by many writers, not in a proper sense, but only to signify the indispensible necessity of obedience according to the order of the new covenant.

THE revelation of the covenant of promise, which the Lord made to Abraham, was afterward renewed to Isaac, Gen. xxvi. 24. and to Jacob, Gen. xxviii. 12, 13, 14, 15. Each of these new revelations had an express reference to former revelations, particularly to Abraham's covenant.

IT was immediately after a new revelation of the covenant of grace that Jacob made his remarkable vow: *Jacob vowed a vow, saying, since God will be with me, and will keep me in this way that I go, and will give me bread to eat, and raiment to put on; since I shall come again to my father's house in peace; and since the Lord will be my God: therefore, this stone which I have set up for a pillar shall be God's house: and of all which thou shalt give me, I will surely give the tenth unto thee.* Here we have a profession of faith in the Lord's promise, and grounded on the promise, a resolution of doing something to evidence his grateful sense of the divine grace and mercy; and both these under the solemn form of a vow. This example is very instructive: it shews us, that in vowing to the Lord, it is not enough that we come under a general obligation to believe the Lord's revelation of the new covenant, and to persevere in a course of new obedience; we should likewise come under such particular obligations according to circumstances, as may evidence the sincerity of our general profession to follow the Lord. Jacob here specifies several things; as first, his confidence in the favour of Providence with regard to the success of his journey: Secondly, his consecration of the stone he had set up for a pillar, to be God's house: Thirdly, his promise to give the Lord the tenth of all he should possess.

JACOB shewed his zeal for the pure profession of the true religion in the exhortation he delivered to his family, when he was about to go up to Bethel: *Then Jacob said unto his houshold, and to all that were with him, Put away the strange gods that are among you, and be clean, and change your garments. And let us arise, and go up to Bethel; and I will make there an altar unto God, who answered me in the day of my distress, and was with me in the way that I went.*

In this exhortation, the godly patriarch's aim, is evidently to prevail on his family to cleave more resolutely to the Lord, to his worship and service, and to avow such adherence more explicitly, than they had ever done before.

The success that attended Jacob's exhortation was remarkable: *They gave unto Jacob all the strange Gods which were in their hand, and all their ear-rings which were in their ears: and Jacob hid them under the oak which was by Shechem.* What the members of Jacob's family did on this occasion, gave an evidence of their disposition to follow the Lord; an evidence which, considering their circumstances, was equally satisfying as oaths and formal declarations would be, in other circumstances.

The blessings that Jacob pronounced upon his children, foretelling not only their outward lot, but how the true religion should be preserved among them, till the coming of Shiloh, may be considered as belonging to the church's profession in that age, and would, no doubt, be accordingly held fast by every true church-member. *The testimony of Jesus is the spirit of prophecy.* Prophecy, indeed, seemed to characterise the Old Testament dispensation; as the fulfilment of prophecy characterises the new.

To the examples we have given in this period, we may add that of Job. He was probably contemporary with Isaac and Jacob: it is almost certain, that he lived before the written law, and before the Lord's limitation of his visible church to the people of Israel, since in the whole book of Job, there is not a single reference or allusion either to that law or to that peculiar people. It is clear, that this eminent person was far from thinking it improper to bind himself by solemn oath to the performance of particular duties. He does so, or narrates that he had done so, as a testimony to his friends of his integrity, and as a mean of confirming himself in the ways of wisdom, chap. xxvii. 2, 3, 4. *As God liveth, who hath taken away my judgment, and the Almighty who hath vexed my soul; all the while my breath is in me, and the spirit is in my nostrils; my lips shall not speak wickedness, nor my tongue utter deceit.* Chap. xxx. 1. *I made a covenant with mine eyes; why then should I think upon a maid?*

Of the Revelation which the Lord gave to the Church by Moses.

THE church's profession was placed in a still fairer light by the ministry of Moses. Of a sudden she was raised from the lowest and basest condition of Egyptian slavery to a degree of beauty and glory she had never attained before. So wonderful was the divine interposition by which the children of Israel were brought out of the house of bondage, and their church-state rendered more conspicuous, that it is often mentioned as one of the most glorious manifestations of JEHOVAH's arm, and may well be considered as a proper emblem of the Lord's kindness in bringing us out of a state of nature into a state of grace.

The Lord declares that it was upon the footing of the covenant of grace, as it had been revealed to Abraham, to Isaac, and to Jacob, that he did such wonderful things for his people, Exodus ii. 24. *God heard their groaning, and God remembered his covenant with Abraham, with Isaac, and with Jacob.* And iii. 16. *Say unto the elders of Israel*, (this is the divine commission to Moses) *The Lord God of your fathers, the God of Abraham, of Isaac, and of Jacob appeared unto me.* Hence it is apparent, that the legation of Moses was indeed, an administration of the covenant of grace.

It is true, this legation is often called *The giving of the law*, John i. 17. Gal. iii. 17. and iv. 24. The reason of this is, neither that there were no precepts delivered to the church before Moses, nor yet that the promises of the new covenant were neglected by Moses: for it is evident, that in the patriarchal age, the church was instructed in the law of God as the rule of duty; and we meet with many great and precious promises, many abstracts of the everlasting covenant, in the writings of Moses: But the true reason is, that the exhibition of the law serves to characterise the Mosaic revelation, being the larger and more conspicuous part of it: nay, so much did the law prevail in the outward form or appearance of this dispensation, that the whole covenant of promise was delineated in a system of ceremonial institutions, and the figures and shadows of good things to come were enjoined on the Israelites as rules of practice. Thus God's revelation of the new covenant to Abraham is called *The giving of the promise;* not that there were no promises given to the church before Abraham; or that the divine revelation to Abraham consisted of promises only without any precepts; but because the promise was more largely and more clearly revealed to him than it ever had been before.

How the Law given by Moses is to be considered.

THE Lord's revelation of the law by the hand of Moses is, in scripture, plainly represented to us in these two lights.

1. It was a revelation of the law as a covenant of works, or a condition of life, demonstrative of the majesty, authority and holiness of the most high God. Hence the apostle says, *the covenant from the mount Sinai gendereth to bondage.* Hence the tremenduous circumstances that attended the promulgation of the law, Exod. xix. 16,—20. and xx. 18. This was not an useless pomp; the design of it was to convince the Israelites of their absolute need of the promise, and of a mediator between God and them. From the day that the Lord had sent Moses to the children of Israel, he had still been dealing with them upon the ground of his gracious promise to Abraham, to Isaac, and to Jacob, and he wanted the Israelites to deal with him upon the same ground. At the beginning, indeed, of this transaction, forgetful of the plague of their own hearts, and much under the dominion of legal pride, they seemed presumptuously ready, without regarding the promise, to deal with God as a lawgiver only, engaging to obey all his commands, Exod. xix. 7, 8. *And Moses came and called for the elders of the people, and laid before their faces all these words which the Lord commanded him. And all the people answered together, and said, All that the*

Lord hath spoken we will do. But the Lord having given them an awful and magnificent display of his glorious majesty and holiness, they or such at least, as were brought to fall in with the gracious design of that amazing transaction, found themselves under a necessity of fleeing to the free promise in which their fathers hoped, and to a mediator between God and them; for, says the apostle, Heb. xii. 19. *When they heard the voice of words, they intreated that the word should not be spoken to them any more:* they saw, that it was impossible for them to deal with God immediately as a lawgiver: hence they intreated Moses to interpose between God and them, Exod. xx. 19. *And they said unto Moses, Speak thou with us and we will hear: But let not God speak with us lest we die.* The Lord, indeed, commanded the Israelites to receive the law; but by no means as a covenant of works, or a condition of life; for to receive it in that view would have been to act as if the promise made to Abraham had been annulled and invain; while by such receiving of the law is meant the considering of our personal obedience to it as a condition the performance of which is necessary to ensure the enjoyment of blessings from the Lord: but if the Israelites had considered their obedience to the law in this light, they would, on the matter, have denied, that the promise made to Abraham was a sufficient security for these blessings; or, in other words, they would have held the promise to be disannulled. The truth is, the Lord gave them a revelation of himself, according to the covenant of works, as a consuming fire; that, like the cherubim and flaming sword that turned every way, it might be a mean of dissuading them from every attempt to seek salvation in the way of that covenant. The law, then, was so far from disannulling the promise that had been made to Abraham 430 years before, that it was given in such a manner as to be a powerful incitement to the faith of that unchangeable promise. The thunders, the lightenings, the blackness and darkness and tempest, and all the display that was given on this occasion, of Jehovah as glorious in holiness, and of terrible majesty, might have served to shew the Israelites, that though they were now to receive a more complete system of laws * than their fathers possessed, yet they were to put as little trust in their own obedience for their justification and acceptance with God, as their fathers did ; and that they, like their fathers, were still to have access to the Lord and to receive every blessing at his hand, on the single ground of his merciful, free and absolute promise.

3. It was a revelation of the rule according to which the Israelites were to walk, and by which they were to evidence themselves to be the Lord's peculiar people. The display of the divine majesty and authority, which was intended to drive them from the law as a covenant of works, or as it was inconsistent with the promise made to Abraham, served at the same time, to bind them to an universal obedience to the law as a rule of life, agreeable to that free and gracious promise ; a promise which every believing Israelite regarded as a sufficient security not only for his pardon and acceptance with God, but likewise for whatever was necessary to the acceptable performance of duty. While the believing Israelite saw the rule of his conduct in the law, he saw his own conformity to that rule, (more or less clearly indeed, according to the measure of his faith) abundantly secured in the promise ; and that conformity to the rule still proved, in the issue, to be steady or wavering, ac-

* Vain man is prone to think that he needs no more to qualify him for the performance of duty than to be informed of it ; tho' that information has frequently no other effect than to irritate and inflame his corruptions.

cording to his faith in the promise: because faith is the appointed way in which we experience the benefit of the promise.

Of the Nature of the various Precepts given by Moses.

VARIOUS laws had formerly been given to Adam, to Noah, to Abraham, and had been handed down by oral tradition from generation to generation. But now the Lord's will as to the right manner of worshipping and serving him, being revealed anew, that it might be no more subject to the uncertainty of oral tradition, was committed to writing. So ample was this written word, including all the revelations of the covenant of grace which the Lord had given to the patriarchs, that the church had no need of any new institution, or of any new doctrine, till Shiloh came, the great prophet whom the Lord was to raise up like unto Moses.

OF the laws given by Moses to the children of Israel, some regarded only the relation between God and them as individuals; while others, besides that, regarded likewise their relation to one another in society. Their relation to one another in society was of two kinds. The first was peculiar to themselves, as the church of the living God, separated from the rest of the world to preserve the pure profession of religion. The laws, regulating the conduct of the Israelites in this relation, were all those with respect to the public worship, the discipline and the government of the church. Some of these being shadows of good things to come, and a kind of emblematical predictions of the Lord Christ, were abolished upon the fulfilment of them in him: Others are of perpetual obligation, the grounds and the ends of them being perpetual. The former are called ceremonial laws, the latter moral.

The second kind of relation to one another, was common to the Israelites with the rest of mankind, that of civil society. The laws regulating the conduct of the Israelites in this relation, are usually called *The Judicial laws.* Some of these had such respect to the peculiar circumstances of the Israelitish commonwealth, that they can hardly be applied with propriety, in the government of any other state: Such are the laws with respect to the division of the lands, with respect to the succession to inheritances, and various others. But some of them, plainly founded on the principles of equity, are of universal obligation in civil society: such are the laws of retaliation in judging between man and man, of punishing murder with death, of offering peace on reasonable terms before we make war on any nation. The spirit of some of their laws is binding upon other nations, though not the form. Thus it is not necessary, that every country should have ten cities of refuge; but it is necessary, that the criminal laws of every country should distinguish between man-slaughter and murder.

As all the laws of Moses, so in particular these political institutions were delivered to Israel not immediately considered as a civil society, but to Israel considered as the church of the living and true God. The whole of that revelation of the Lord's will of which these political institutions are a part, was given to the church, to that people to whom the Lord says, (what he could never be considered as saying to any people viewed merely as a civil society) *I am the Lord thy God.* It is to the church alone that the Lord reveals himself in so gracious a manner. The truth is, these political institutions were to shew how the Israelites, or church-members under the Mosaic dispensation, were to behave in civil society, a situation common to them with the rest of mankind; and to shew what constitution and order in their commonwealth would be subservient to the good of the church, and to the sanctification of church-members, assuring them at the same time, that his particular providence would be always present to them, and would often work miracles to promote that subserviency.

Of the Jewish State.

THE children of Israel residing in the land of Egypt, were members of the Egyptian state. They were not called, in that situation, to attempt altering the constitution and laws of the state, in order to serve the church: their duty was only to abstain from every thing inconsistent with the character of church-members, while they were to make conscience of obedience to the lawful commands of Pharaoh and subordinate rulers. But when the Lord brought them out of the house of bondage, and formed them into an independent state, it is reasonable to expect that the constitution and laws of that state would be subordinated to the good of the church.

The laws of the Jewish state afford, in this respect, an example for our imitation. If ever it falls to the share of church-members to frame the laws of a state, they undoubtedly ought so to frame these laws as to promote, in every reasonable and peaceable way, the true interest, that is, the purity of the church. Such legislators would be workers together with God, who manages the whole

Of Public Covenanting.

kingdom of providence in subserviency to the church's good.

This subserviency, being injoined by their laws, appeared afterward in the following circumstances: in the subjects of the commonwealth being, for the most part, church members, descendents of Jacob; in the name of Israel being common to the church and the commonwealth; in the active part that their civil magistrates took in the reformation of the church.

But notwithstanding this subserviency, we are by no means to consider the Jewish state as partaking of the nature of the church; but rather as one of the kingdoms of this world, as our Lord plainly intimated when he said, *My kingdom is not of this world*, in answer to the accusation, that he had pretended to be king of the Jews, John xviii. 35, 36. Christ came to change the dispensation of the church, but by no means, (as the carnal Jews might imagine in their fond expectations of a Messiah attended with worldly pomp and grandeur) to change the forms of civil government.

As all the church-members to whom the political institutions of Moses were immediately delivered, belonged to the Jewish commonwealth, so we need not wonder to find these institutions peculiarly suited to the situation of that commonwealth. But as they are an important part of that revelation which the Lord has given not to the Jews only, but to his whole church scattered over the face of the earth, and which by means of the church is exhibited to all mankind, they are binding by divine authority upon every state, so far as they are suitable to its constitution; so far as they rise necessarily out of the general principles of equity; so far as they may be requisite to secure that which ought to be the great and important end of all the restraints that men suffer from laws and forms of government, the enjoyment of the sweets of liberty; and, I dare not forbear adding, so far as they are subservient to the good of the church, according to the dispensation of grace and of providence, whatever it may be, that she is under.

To suppose that the Lord was to the Hebrew commonwealth instead of a visible chief magistrate, seems to be at variance with fact: for after Moses, by the advice of Jethro, had settled the mode of civil government among the Israelites, they never were without magistrates both supreme and subordinate. It is remarkable that the counsel of Jethro, upon which the civil constitution of Israel was formed, was not communicated as an immediate revelation from God, but as the native dictates of that common sense of justice and of order which is the foundation of all the civil government in the world.

It is true, when the men of Israel desired Gideon to take upon him the government of their state, offering to make it hereditary in his family, he generously refused the offer, saying, *The Lord shall rule over you,* Judg. viii. 22, 23. Intimating that they were to be ruled, not by the will of one man, but by the laws which they had received from God himself; nor was their government to be administered by one man, but in the manner of a republic, by their judges and elders, with the consent of the people. Considered as a church, the Lord ruled over them; and Gideon would not have them acknowledge any other monarch. In like manner, when the Israelites desired a king in the days of Samuel, the Lord said to the prophet, *They have not rejected thee; but they have rejected me, that I should not reign over them.* They may be said to have rejected the Lord that he should not reign over them, if, having lost sight of the spiritual glory and beauty of the Lord's kingly authority over them as his church, they ceased to delight in it, affecting rather the worldly grandeur of the nations around them, that were governed by kings. They may be said to have rejected the Lord on this occasion, if they neglected to acknowledge him, or to ask counsel of him in taking so important a step as that of changing the mode of their civil government. In this respect, the Lord says, speaking of this very matter, Hosea viii. 6. *They have set up kings, but not by me: they have made princes, and I knew it not.* They may be said to have rejected the Lord's kingly authority over them, if they were either wanting in the respect that was due to Samuel as a civil judge, or deaf to the messages that he brought them from the Lord as a prophet. Something of this kind seems to be implied in the Lord's saying that they had not rejected Samuel only.

We may take notice of a fact which strongly implies that the Hebrew state as to its intrinsic nature, whatever extraordinary circumstances attended the administration of it, was a mere worldly society formed and conducted upon the maxims of human policy. The fact is, that the reasons the elders of Israel gave to Samuel for the resolution they had taken of setting up the monarchical form of government, were no immediate revelations from heaven, but considerations of ordinary prudence. —1 Samuel viii. 5. *They said unto him, Behold, thou art old, and thy sons walk not in thy ways: now make us a king like all the nations.* Considering that the question here, was not merely concerning a step in the public administration, but it was concerning a change in the internal constitution of the government: considering that the elders representing the children of Israel, being gathered together, exercised a right of deliberating, and making a resolution on that question; considering, in fine, that the Israelites do not seem to have been wrong in taking upon them to exercise such a right, as it is reasonable to think the Lord allowed it in granting their desire; though he blamed them for their motives or their manner of exercising that right; for thefe reafons, we are led by this example, to regard the Hebrew commonwealth as of the fame internal nature, proceeding upon the fame political principles, as other civil focieties.

WE need not be furprized, that in the hiftory of the Ifraelites, we have a train of fuch extraordinary interpofitions of Providence in the conduct of their civil affairs, as we have no example of in any authentic hiftories of other nations. They had a circumftance in their cafe which never was in the cafe of any nation fince the refurrection of Chrift, and never will be till his fecond coming; the members of the Jewifh commonwealth, from Mofes to the coming of Chrift, made up very nearly the whole vifible church of God upon earth. The prefervation of the true religion was the great end for which this commonwealth was erected. Though that ought to be one principal end of the erection of every commonwealth wherever the true religion is known, yet fince the Jewifh commonwealth was diftinguifhed, in that refpect, from all the contemporary ftates and kingdoms in the world, we need not wonder to find it the diftinguifhed care of providence.

ONCE more, let us confider the civil conftitution of Ifrael as one of thofe temporal benefits, which the Lord had freely promifed to his church long before that conftitution exifted, and which he beftowed upon church-members according to his word. We cannot reafonably fuppofe that this circumftance would alter the nature of fuch a temporal benefit, more than the nature of a fruitful foil; that it would turn either the one or the other into a fpiritual blefling; or make it quite a different thing in the land of Ifrael from what it was in any other country. Surely a civil conftitution is a temporal benefit, whether in Judea, in Greece, or in Italy. We acknowledge, indeed, that this circumstance, namely, that the civil constitution of Israel was a promised blessing of the covenant which the Lord made with Abraham, had two remarkable effects. The first is, frequent interpositions of Heaven for the defence or the improvement of that constitution; as in the Lord's designation of some of their kings, in his destruction of their enemies, in the counsel that he gave them with respect to perplexed and intricate cases. But indeed the care of that special providence that watched continually over the church of Israel and over each of her members, was no less about other temporal benefits than about their civil government. The fruitfulness of their lands, for example, depended on the former and the latter rain: they were successful or otherwise in their undertakings, they were afflicted or comforted in their outward lot, according to the regard they had to the Lord and his law. Though God's dealing with his church in this manner, seems to have characterised, in some measure, the old Testament dispensation; yet it was not peculiar to that dispensation: the promise of the good things of this life, is often repeated in the new Testament: Matt. v. 5. *Blessed are the meek, for they shall inherit the earth.* Eph. vi. 2, 3. *Honour thy father and thy mother, that it may be well with thee; and that thou mayest live long on the earth.* 1 Cor. iii. 22. *Things present or things to come; all are yours.* 1 Tim. iv 8 *Godliness is profitable to all things, having the promise of the life that now is, and of that which is to come.* 1 Pet. iii. 10. *He that will live long, and see good days, let him refrain his tongue from evil, and his lips that they speak no guile.* Though we are by no means to judge of the Lord's love or hatred by any thing that is seen; yet we have reason from scripture and experience to assert that the Lord, as well under the new as under the old Testament, takes occasion, in the course of his adorable providence, to shew his pleasure in his people's aims at obedience, and his anger for presumptuous breaches of his law, Amos iii. 2. *You only have I known of all the families of the earth; therefore I will punish you for your iniquities.* 1 Cor. xi. 30. *For this cause* (for partaking of the Lord's supper unworthily) *many are weak and sickly among you, and many sleep.* Not that the Lord deals with his people according to the rules of merit and demerit; but he carries on his moral government of the world, by thus, in some measure, marking the difference between right and wrong: by this method too, he teaches his people the exceeding hatefulness of sin, and how much they owe to Christ their Saviour, upon whom was the chastisement of their peace; he teaches them that wisdom's ways are pleasantness and peace, and leads them to pray with Jabez, *Keep me from evil that it may not grieve me.*

The second effect arising from the civil constitution of the Israelites being among the temporal benefits made over to them by promise, is, That the church was warranted to consider it as a type or shadow of something better to come. Thus Jerusalem on earth typified the Jerusalem which is above: and several persons who made a figure in the state, were types of Christ, such as Samson, David, Solomon, Zerubbabel, and others. But this was a particular consideration of the state, for the use of the church only; which did not in the least affect the internal nature of the state. For example, David was a type of Christ in respect of his government of the Israelites. Yet this did not hinder his government from being in itself of the same political nature as that of other kings. In a word, whenever we speak of the Jewish state being typical, we do not speak of its internal nature, but only of a certain light in which it was appointed to be considered by the church for her edification.

In order to clear the Jewish law against idolators from the charge of intolerance, it has been said, that the government of the Jewish state was the peculiar, immediate government of God, and (which no mere man may do) he enforced his laws by whatever penalties he pleased. But, besides that the notion of God's immediate government of the Jewish state considered abstractly from the church, appears to be utterly ungrounded, this account of the matter is very unsatisfying in other respects. Intolerance is a breach of the moral law, being contrary to the clearest dictates of justice and humanity; and therefore must be perpetually evil; equally so under the old as under the new Testament dispensation: so that it is not conceivable that the Lord would give a place to any thing *really* intolerant among the laws of the Jewish state. It should be likewise observed, that the crime, in question, is no less than an open avowed breach of the first commandment of the moral law, a commandment of the same obligation at all times, and on all persons; and that the reasons assigned in this law for stoning the idolator, are all of a moral nature, equally suitable to all nations and to all ages. Deut. xiii. 10. *And thou shalt stone him with stones that he die; because he hath sought to thrust thee away from the Lord thy God, which brought thee out of the land of Egypt, from the house of bondage. And all Israel shall hear, and fear, and shall do no more any such wickedness as is among you.* The whole law, as was observed before, was given to the church of Israel, and therefore when the Lord is directing her members how to behave in the state, he still denominates himself the Lord their God, who had done wonders of mercy for them. Thus it is common in the new Testament to exhort and encourage persons to the duties of civil life from the consideration of their obligations to God in Christ. Servants are to obey their masters according to the flesh, as those who have to serve the Lord Christ, Col. iii. 22, 23, 24. Consider the reasons of this law in such an evangelical light, and the force of them is not diminished, but greatly increased under the new Testament dispensation. Or consider them as applicable only to the state of the Israelites: in this view the import of them is, that the good providence of God had laid them under unspeakable obligations; having delivered them from slavery, formed them into a commonwealth, and countenanced them in all their journeys: therefore they were by no means to allow any to seduce the members of the commonwealth from the acknowledgment of the true God. Surely gratitude to Providence is equally due from all states and kingdoms at all times.

Perhaps it would be better to deny that any real intolerance or persecution is favoured by this law. It is intolerance or persecution to hinder a person from living quietly, because he is known to entertain some opinion different from these generally received in the country; even though his *nostrum* has no tendency to disturb the peace of society. But the evil condemned by this law is not, in general, opinions different from these received among the Jews; it is idolatry, a practice which implies a denial of God even according to the notions of his attributes and providence which men have from the light of nature. A gross idolator would deprive civil society of almost all the advantages that it receives from the belief of God. Farther, the criminal, in this case, is described not only as having idolatrous opinions, but as doing all he can to propagate them, persuading those whom he converses with, not only to receive such opinions, but to put them openly in practice. Besides, the Israelites were distinguished, in respect of idolatry, from all the nations around them; so that an idolator or one who said, Let us go after other gods, might serve as a descriptive name of an enemy to the Ifraelitifh commonwealth. If we regard the execution of this law, the only perfons we read of being put to death for idolatry, were guilty of other crimes; and an impartial enquiry into their character and conduct would fhew them to have been equally enemies to the church and the ftate of Ifrael; fuch were queen Athaliah and Baal's priefts. We cannot argue from this law againft idolatry, that there was no toleration among the Ifraelites, more than we could argue from the penal ftatutes againft Popery before the late repeal of them, that there was no toleration in Britain; though it is an undeniable fact, that there never was an age or country in which a greater freedom of religious opinions has been enjoyed than in Britain fince the glorious revolution. We do not read of any being forced to conform to the ceremonial inftitutions of the Jewifh church. Strangers were permitted to live among the Ifraelites, and they were commanded to be kind to ftrangers; there is not a fyllable about compelling fuch guefts to conform to the religious profeffion of the Jews. Jofhua and the princes entered into a league with the Gibeonites, without once requiring the Gibeonites to conform to their church. As to the penalty of cutting off, under which many of the ceremonial inftitutions are enjoined, the beft interpreters underftand it of church-cenfure. Upon the whole, we cannot conceive that the Ifraelites, the moft enlightened people then on the face of the earth, were againft toleration, or that they did not know that the church was a voluntary fociety, and that perfons could never become church-members otherwife than by free and deliberate choice. As it is undoubtedly the will of God that the kingdoms of men fhould be fubfervient to the church of Chrift; the toleration we mean is a toleration confiftent with the diligent endeavours of the ftate to difcourage errors in religion, and to promote the truths of Chrift, by all means compatible with the security and liberty of every honest member of civil society on the one hand, and on the other with the free and independent nature of the church as a kingdom not of this world. That persecution is none of these means is too obvious to need any proof.

Of the Jewish Church.

SUCH was the commonwealth of Israel. Let us now turn our attention on the church to which the whole Mosaic revelation was made, to which the Lord declared, *I am the Lord thy God*, and the members of which, agreeably to that declaration, *avouched the Lord to be their God*.

THE church of Christ under the Mosaic œconomy, as far as she was conformable to the pattern shewn in the mount, was indeed a spiritual and heavenly society. Though she was less perfect, from her carnal ordinances and her worldly sanctuary, than the new Testament church, yet she was of the same spiritual and heavenly nature. The church had always a respect to Christ alone as her head, to his word as her only rule, and to a future state of glory as her perfection. The government of the church is the true Theocracy. Besides a God in Christ, Zion never had, and never will have a sovereign in whom her children are to be joyful, Psal. cxlix. 2. The language of the church under every dispensation is that of the spouse, *Cause me to hear thy voice; until the day break, and the shadows flee away; turn, my beloved, and be thou like a roe or a young hart upon the mountains of Bether.*

GENTLE as the government is of the church's head and lawgiver, he is a most absolute monarch; and it is infinitely proper that he should be so, since in him are hid all the treasures of wisdom and knowledge: he has varied his manner of governing the church as his infinite wisdom hath seen fit. He orders it so, that his church grows to maturity by degrees, and he varies his mode of administration according to the several stages of that growth. The patriarchal age was the infancy of the church; under the Mosaic dispensation, though she was considerably grown, yet she was still in childhood under tutors and governors; but under the new Testament, compared to what she was under former dispensations, she is arrived at maturity. The spiritual nature of the church, and the alone sovereignty of Christ over her, though not so conspicuous in some of these periods as in others of them, were in reality always the same.

From these observations it is apparent, that the church of Israel was distinct from the state. The church was grounded upon the Lord's revelation of the covenant of grace; the state, upon those principles of justice and humanity which are, in a great measure, the foundation of all the civil societies among mankind. The former was of a spiritual, the latter of a worldly nature. The end of the one is heavenly, that of the other, earthly happiness. As church-members, the Israelites never owed subjection to any as their king besides the Lord Christ; but as members of the state, they owed subjection, in all lawful commands, to a succession of civil magistrates, who were sometimes good sometimes evil, at one period professing the true religion, at another heathens and propagators of abominable idolatry. The administration of the state was placed in the hands of kings, of judges, or the heads of tribes; the administration of the church in the hands of prophets, priests, Levites and scribes. The judicatories of the state were different from those of the church, Deuter. xvii. 8, 9. *If there arise a matter too hard for thee in judgment,——then shalt thou arise, and get thee* *into the place which the Lord thy God shall choose: and thou shalt come unto the priests the Levites*, that is, to the ecclesiastical judicature, *and unto the judge*, or civil magistrate, *who shall be in those days and enquire; and they shall shew thee the sentence of judgment.* Much light is given to this passage by another in 2 Chron. xix. 8, 11. *Moreover, in Jerusalem did Jehoshaphat set of the Levites and of the priests, and of the chief of the fathers of Israel, for the judgment of the Lord and for controversies.* It seems to be meant here, that the judgment of the Lord should belong *to the Levites and the priests;* but that controversies between man and man should be decided by such as were *of the chief of the fathers.* This is agreeable to the royal instructions, ver. 11. *And behold, Amaziah the chief priest is over you in all matters of the Lord; and Zebadiah the son of Ishmael, the ruler of the house of Judah for all the kings matters.* The matters of the Lord, the head of the church, may well signify matters of religion; the matters of the king, the head of the state, may well signify affairs relating to civil life. The regulations of the state, as we have seen, were different from the ordinances of the church. Among the latter was national covenanting *.

---

* The foregoing observations are offered on the nature of the church and the state of Israel, because much of the cavilling in the controversial writings against the duty of Public Covenanting proceeds upon strange misrepresentations of that church and of that state; because right views of these are very conducive toward a profitable reading of the old Testament; and because of late it seems to have grown fashionable to represent the church and state of Israel in such a light as to render almost all the approved examples of both the one and the other improper for our imitation, and consequently to deprive us of the benefit of a great part of the old Testament.

At the same time, it must be owned, that such an enquiry does not seem necessary in order to establish the morality of Covenanting. An adversary to this duty gains nothing by declaiming about the typical state and the mere earthly ceremonial church of Israel; unless he can go so far as to assert, That the one was so thoroughly typical, and the other so thoroughly ceremonial, that all they did and all they were commanded to do was nothing but mere type and ceremony, which we have nothing to do with.

Of the Engagement to duties which the children of Israel entered into at Sinai.

WE have considered the revelation which the Lord gave to Israel by the hand of Moses; a revelation that contained a repetition of the promise made to Abraham, together with a compleat system of laws regulating the conduct of that peculiar people both in the church and in the state. We are now to take notice of the manner in which they expressed their submission and adherence to that revelation; which manner is called their covenanting with the Lord, or their avouching of him to be their God.

The awful and rigorous manifestation of the law as a covenant of works, convinced the trembling Israelites, that it was not for them to deal with God absolutely as a lawgiver, Deut. v. 24, 25, 26, 27. *And ye said, Behold the Lord our God hath shewed us his glory and his greatness, and we have heard his voice out of the midst of the fire: we have seen this day that God doth talk with man, and he liveth. Now therefore why should we die? for this great fire will consume us. If we hear the voice of the Lord our God any more, then we shall die. For who is there of all flesh that hath heard the voice of the living God speaking out of the midst of the fire, as we have, and lived?* (A confession this, that they were utterly unable to deal with God for themselves, much like that of David, *Enter not into judgment with thy servant; for in thy sight shall no flesh living be justified.*) *Go thou near,* added the people, *and hear all that the Lord our God shall say; and speak thou unto us all that the Lord our God shall speak unto thee; and we will hear and do.*

In thele words, besides a renunnciation of the covenant of works, we may obferve, that the Ifraelites avow their intereſt in God according to the promife, ſtill calling him, in the language of faith, THE LORD OUR GOD; that they defire a Mediator to deal with God on their behalf; and in the way of taking the Lord for their God, they promife, (not indeed with that legal pride and foolifh forwardneſs which attended their former engagement, Exod. xix. 8. but with fuch modeſty and caution as manifeſted an humbling fenfe of their own weakneſs and finfulneſs, they promife) to yield a willing obedience, faying, *We will hear and do.* The obedience they engage to is the obedience of faith: they were in the firſt place, to hear, that is, to believe; for fo the word is ufed in Ifai. lv. 3. *Hear, and your foul fball live.* Gal. iii. 2. *Received ye the fpirit by the works of the law, or by the hearing of faith* ‡. Thus the engagement of the Ifraelites correfponded to God's declaration of the ten commandments; the latter beginning with a revelation of the Lord as their God and Redeemer, the former with a believing acceptance of that revelation.

The Lord teſtifies his approbation of the people's engagement, Deut. v. 28. *And the Lord heard the voice of your words, when ye fpake unto me; and the Lord faid unto me, I have heard the voice of the words of this people, which they have fpoken unto thee: they have well faid all that they have fpoken,* that is, in fleeing to the promife of the covenant of grace, in defiring a mediator, and engaging to receive the law at his mouth. *O that there were fuch an heart in them!* We need not doubt that the Lord ſtill takes notice, in a gracious manner, of our effays toward the performance of the duty of covenanting. Applying to this fub-

---

‡ See Mr. Boſton's notes on the Marrow of modern divinity, chap. 2. fect. 2.

ject, what the apostle says of prayer, 1 John v. '14. *This is the confidence that we have in him, that if we enter into covenant with the Lord as our God in Christ, according to his will, he heareth us,* and accepts of the weakest, if honest, endeavours.

Who are they now, that know and acknowledge the Lord to be their God? Who are they that deal with God through a Mediator? Who are they that avow their obedience to the law, as in the hand of a Mediator? Whose character do all these things mark? The character of the Israelites in the church, or in the state? In the church undoubtedly.

Hear how the Lord himself represents this covenant between himself and Israel. Speaking to Israel, he says, *Thou hast avouched the Lord this day to be thy God, and to walk in his ways, and to keep his statutes, and his commandments, and judgments, and to hearken to his voice. And the Lord hath avouched thee this day to be his peculiar people, as he hath promised thee, and that thou shouldst keep all his commandments.*

This was a covenant of gratitude and thankfulness. It was by no means the import of it, that the children of Israel consented to yield obedience to the law of Moses as the condition upon which they were to inherit the land of Canaan. A covenant of that import, would have been a covenant of works by which the reward would have been reckoned not of grace, but of debt: a covenant of that legal import, would have made the free and absolute promise to Abraham, of no effect. But, says the apostle, *the covenant that was confirmed before of God in Christ, the law which was four hundred and thirty years after, cannot disannul, that it should make the promise of no effect.* The promise of the land of Canaan to the Israelites and the promise of eternal life, are alike in this respect; that both are absolutely free and unconditional,

Gen. xv. 18. *The Lord made a covenant with Abram, saying, Unto thy seed will I give this land* No condition is mentioned to be performed either by Abram, or by his seed. The Israelites were to come to the enjoyment of the land of Canaan by the same means, by which a poor sinner comes to the enjoyment of eternal life, that is, by believing the promise of God in Christ, or accepting heartily of his free gift. Hence the unbelief of many of the Israelites hindered them from seeing the good land, Heb. iii. 19. *We see that they could not enter in because of unbelief.*

WITH respect then, to the land of Canaan, what may we suppose to have been the exercise of a believing Israelite in the covenanting at Horeb? He would, in the first place, believe, on the single ground of the divine promise, that the Lord would not fail to put his people in possession of the good land; and then he would say, Since the Lord is my God, a promising and promise-performing God, I profess my faith in him, and avow my desire and resolution, in the strength of his promise, to express my gratitude and thankfulness to my God and Redeemer by a chearful obedience to all his commands. Such is the import of the exercise of which Moses said to the Israelites, *Ye have avouched the Lord to be your God, to walk in his ways.*

NOR is it any real objection to this view of Israel's covenanting, that the outward dispensations of Providence toward them, were according to the regard they had to their covenant with the Lord; that they were to eat the good of the land, if they were willing and obedient; and that, if they were otherwise, the Lord would send a sword to avenge the quarrel of his covenant. We are, by no means, to think, because the Lord chastises his people for their disobedience by depriving them of worldly, or even of spiritual comforts, that their obedience, is the condition or tenure on which they enjoy these comforts. The supposition is contrary to the nature of the everlasting covenant; by which believers receive all the blessings of time and eternity, as the gift of free and sovereign grace: nor can any work they do, or any quality they possess, add in the least degree, to the right which the great and precious promises of the covenant, give them to those blessings. This was the case under the Old Testament no less than under the New. Moses assures us that it was so with regard to the grant of the land of Canaan to the Israelites, Deut, ix. 3. *Not for thy righteousness, nor for the uprightness of thine heart, dost thou go in to possess the land: but for the wickedness of these nations* THE LORD THY GOD *doth drive them out from before thee; and that he may perform the word which the Lord sware unto thy fathers, Abraham, Isaac, and Jacob.* The Lord dealt with the people of these nations as moral agents according to the demerit of their crimes; but he dealt with the Israelites as church-members according to the gracious promises of the everlasting covenant.

WITH regard, indeed, to the time and the manner in which he is to bestow the spiritual or temporal blessings he hath promised, we must acknowledge that he hath reserved them in his own hand. One thing, however, is clear, that the established ORDER of the covenant for the accomplishment of the promises is such as tends most eminently, to shew forth the glory of God's wisdom, power, holiness, mercy and faithfulness. Hence that beautiful order requires, that spiritual comforts, not excluding those of our outward lot, should attend a diligent course of obedience, and that the witholding of such comforts should correct the children of God for their iniquity. The promise of the covenant in Psalm lxxxix. 30. 31, 32. belongs to the new as well as to the old dispenfation: *If his children forsake my law, and walk not in my judgments; if they break not my statutes, and keep not my commandments; then will I visit their transgressions with the rod, and their iniquity with stripes.* This order is visible to an attentive observer in the Lord's dealings toward every body of professing Christians. Several of the promises and the threatenings in the epistles to the seven churches of Asia as plainly respected their outward church-state, as ever any promises or any threatenings, did that of Israel. Indeed it must be acknowledged, that in the Lord's providential conduct toward particular churches, *clouds and darkness are often round about him.* But under what dispensation did he fail to exercise the faith and patience of his people by such providential conduct? It has freqently been the language of the church, both under the old and new testament, *Verily, thou art a God that hidest thyself, O God of Israel the Saviour.*

Though the circumstance of the Israelites lifting up their hands and formally swearing is not mentioned in the account of this transaction, yet their Covenanting is called their *entering into the Lord's oath*, Deut. xxix. 12. Accordingly they afterward used that form in the renewing of their covenant.

We only observe farther with respect to this transaction, that it makes an æra in the history of the church of Israel, not less remarkable than that of the giving of the promise to Abraham. As the latter was the *Magna Charta*, the great charter of all their privileges; so the former was always afterward the *Jus et Norma*, the standard and example of all their professions of faith and obedience.

How the Israelites renewed their Covenant.

SO great was the stubbornness of the Israelites, and so frequent the relapses of that people into idolatry, that their history is a continued display of man's depraved nature. Here we may see, as in a glass, that the best outward means and the purest dispensation of ordinances are, in themselves, utterly insufficient to make us turn or cleave to the Lord; and that we, every moment, stand in absolute need of his grace and Spirit to uphold us. Here, too, we often see him interposing in amazing sovereignty, to stop a course of backsliding among his people, and to make them return to himself in the most explicit manner, according to his command, Deut. vi. 13. *Thou shalt fear the Lord thy God, and serve him, and shalt swear by his name.* Chap. x. 20. *Thou shalt fear the Lord thy God: him shalt thou serve, and to him shalt thou cleave, and swear by his name.* We need not scruple to understand this *swearing* of a public declaration, upon oath, of their adherence to the Lord, since the connection and the manifest intention of these precepts, lead us to such an interpretation; since the phrase is used to denote a character of his professing people, by which they were distinguished from the rest of the world, Zeph. i. 4, 5. *I will cut off them that—— swear by the Lord, and that swear by Malcham,* that is, both professors and profane; and, especially, since the meaning of the precept is delineated in the approved example of the Old Testament church.

When Moses delivered that perswasive repetition of the law which we have in the book of Deuteronomy, the Israelites entered anew into their covenant with the Lord, Chap. xxix. 1. *These are the words of the covenant which the Lord commanded Moses to make with the children of Israel in the land of Moab, beside the covenant which he made with them in Horeb.* This example of the Israelites renewing their covenant in obedience to the Lord's immediate command, was for the imitation of the church till the end of time; that command being a divine warrant for the exercise of renewing covenant with the Lord; a divine warrant, not only to the Israelites, but to the church of Christ in after-times; since the duty, as hath been shewn, is of such a nature, that it is equally competent to the church under the old Testament and under the New. It was, no doubt, peculiarly proper for the Israelites to set about the renovation of their covenant at this time. It was a suitable conclusion to the ministry of Moses. It was a suitable preparation for their entrance into the promised land.

These two eminent chiefs of Israel, he who brought them out of Egypt, and he who brought them into Canaan, chiefs whose ruling passion, next to the love of God, was the love of their people, were both desirous, before they left the earthly house of this tabernacle, to see those over whom they had exercised so much fatherly care, renew their covenant with the Lord; expecting, no doubt, among other precious fruits which, through the Lord's blessing, would attend this exercise, that it would be a mean of establishing the Israelites in the way of the Lord.

Grown old, and ready to drop, like a shock of corn, Joshua gathered all the tribes of Israel to Shechem, and called for the elders of Israel, and and for their judges, and for their officers; and they presented themselves before God, Josh. xxiv. On that day, it is said, *Joshua made a covenant with the people, and set them an ordinance in She-*

them. Besides what we took notice of before in this transaction, the two following things are remarkable. The first is, an accommodation of their engagement to present circumstances. In their covenanting at Sinai, they acknowledged the Lord who brought them out of the land of Egypt and out of the house of bondage; but now they acknowledge him as the Lord who *drave out from before them all the people, even the Amorites who dwelt in the land.* The other thing is, that they were in great danger of miscarrying in the duty, from self-confidence, and from ignorance of the plague of their own heart. Hence Joshua *said unto the people, Ye cannot serve the Lord; he is a holy God: he is a jealous God; he will not forgive your transgression, nor your sins.* We should never set about the performance of any duty without a heart-affecting remembrance of God's infinite holiness and of his infinite indignation against sin; a remembrance tending, through the efficacy of the Holy Ghost, to produce a frame of mind equally opposite to the deceit of the heart harbouring or disguising some beloved idol, and to the legality of the heart disposing us to lean on our own righteousness or on our own strength. That many of the Israelites then attained such a suitable frame of mind, is highly probable from the happy consequences of this transaction: for it is written, *Israrael served the Lord all the days of Joshua, and all the days of the elders that overlived Joshua, and that had known all the works of the Lord, which he had done for Israel*

How the Israelites renewed their covenant under their Kings.

THE whole Jewish commonwealth was formed with the greatest subserviency to the good of the church. Their kings, their judges, the heads of their tribes were obliged by their connection with the church, to regard her welfare in the administration of the state. David and several others were very useful to the church in two respects; the one peculiar to the Old Testament dispensation, the other may have place under the new also.

First, Some of their kings and judges were useful in a way peculiar to the time of the Old Testament; in regard that they were not only magistrates in the state; but they were in the church, prophets, inspired writers, and types of Christ; such were Moses, Samuel, David. Hence it is of importance to distinguish what is recorded of them in the one character, from what is recorded of them in the other. When Samuel anointed David to be king of Israel, he acted not as a political ruler, but as a prophet having an extraordinary commission from the head of the church for that purpose. The covenant of royalty was made with David not as a civil magistrate merely, but as a church-member and one of the most eminent types of Christ *.

* Perhaps it may be questioned, whether all the kings of Israel were, properly, types of Christ. The princes, indeed, of David's line were types of Christ in respect of the covenant of royalty: but how does it appear that this circumstance had any effect toward either the increase or diminution of the kingly power? We beg leave to repeat a truth which seems to have been little attended to; which is, That the circumstance of persons, places or things being types of Christ, neither arose from, nor affected the intrinsic nature of such persons, places or things; it was only a certain consideration of them for the

SECONDLY, Several of their kings and judges were useful to the church in a way in which all magistrates who have an opportunity of being themselves church-members, ought to be useful to her. Thus David assisted at bringing the ark from Kirjath-jearim; Solomon built the temple; Hezekiah and Josiah stirred up the people to reformation, and appointed the passover to be kept. We add (what is the subject of the following observations) that several of them used their influence and authority in exciting their subjects to renew their covenant with the Lord.

LET us consider how the church of Israel went about this duty in the reign of Asa, 2 Chron. xv. The people were stirred up and encouraged to it by a message from the Lord. *And the Spirit of God came upon Azariah the son of Oded. And he went out to meet Asa, and said unto him, Hear ye me, Asa and all Judah and Benjamin, the Lord is with you, while ye be with him; and if ye seek him, he will be found of you; but if ye forsake him, he will forsake you. Now for a long season Israel hath been without the true God, and without a teaching priest, and without law. But when they in their trouble did turn unto the Lord God of Israel, and sought him, he was found of them. Be ye strong, therefore, and let not not your hands be weak; for your work shall be rewarded.* In compliance with so seasonable an exhortation, various pieces of reformation were begun and carried on. *When Asa heard these words, and the prophecy of Oded the prophet, he took courage, and put away the abominable idols out of all the land of Judah and Benjamin, and out of the cities which he had taken from Mount Ephraim,*

---

use of the church, without which it had no existence. Hence considering the Jewish state abstractly, one may say, There were no types of Christ in it at all. The typical consideration of the kings was equally different from the civil consideration of them, as the ceremonial was from the judicial law.

and renewed the altar of the Lord that was before the porch of the Lord. And he gathered all Judah and Benjamin, and the strangers with them out of Ephraim and Manasseh, and out of Simeon. The influence which Asa here used in making the people concur in the work of God, was not a mere exertion of his civil authority which did not extend to the strangers out of Ephraim and Manasseh, and out of Simeon; it seems to have been much more the influence of his example and exhortations. Hence their concurrence is described as in the highest degree, voluntary and cheerful: *So they gathered themselves together at Jerusalem. And they offered unto the Lord in that day, of the spoil which they had brought, seven hundred oxen and seven thousand sheep.* They set about Covenanting as a mean of confirming and establishing the degree of reformation they had attained, and as a mean of advancing and carrying it forward: *They entered into a covenant to seek the Lord God of their fathers;* relying on the promises made to their fathers, and recognising the engagements of their fathers; in both which respects he might be called *the God of their fathers;* for as the Lord had shewn by his promise that he was not ashamed to be called their God; so in their covenant of duty they were not ashamed to avouch openly, that the Lord was their God.

We may observe an accommodation of their engagements to the circumstances of the church at that time. The ten tribes had fallen into idolatry in worshipping the calves that Jeroboam had set up at Dan and Bethel; and therefore the followers of the true God profess their stedfast adherence to his law concerning the punishment of idolators in the thirteenth chapter of Deuteronomy; engaging, *that whosoever would not seek the Lord God of Israel, should be put to death, whether small or great, whether man or woman.* They did not think it enough to covenant, that they would observe the law of Moses in general; but they pointed out that precept, which was then most remarkably transgressed, as a precept to which in a particular manner, they vowed adherence. The manner in which the Israelites were led forward to covenanting, and the happy effects of it, should powerfully recommend the duty to our serious regard: *They sware unto the Lord with a loud voice, and with shouting, and with trumpets, and with cornets. And all Judah rejoiced at the oath; for they had sworn with all their heart, and sought him with the whole desire; and he was found of them: And the Lord gave them rest round about.* On the whole, it is plain that the several circumstances we have taken notice of in this piece of sacred history; such as, complying with the calls of word and providence; beginning reformation; engaging to carry it on when begun; avowing an adherence to particular precepts of God's law in opposition to particular prevailing evils; binding themselves by oath to be the Lord's; performing religious duties cheerfully and with the whole heart; all these are for our imitation, being plainly of a moral nature, and as compatible with the New as with the Old Testament dispensation.

The next instance that occurs, of the Israelites renewing their covenant with the Lord, was at the coronation of Jehoash the son of Ahaziah. 2 Kings xi. 17. *And Jehoiada made a covenant between the Lord and the king and the people: between the king and the people. And all the people of the land went into the house of Baal, and brake it down; his altars and his images brake they in pieces throughly, and slew Mattan the priest of Baal before the altar: and the priest appointed officers over the house of the Lord.*

A good church-member will always be a good citizen. Hence our measures for the better security of our property and political freedom will not

not the lefs but the more effectual for being attended with suitable endeavours for the reformation of the church. Jehoida, as became a true lover of his country, had been very inftrumental in bringing about that happy revolution by which the people were delivered from the tyranny of Athaliah. And as became an office-bearer in the houfe of God, he fet about the reformation of the church, encouraging the people to renew their covenant with the Lord. Jehoiada, in the firft place, made a covenant between the Lord the head of the church on the one fide, and the king with the people, one the other. It is plain, that the king and the people were in this tranfaction, confidered as church-members: for they covenanted to be the Lord's people, that is, *the Lord's peculiar treafure, a kingdom of priefts, an holy nation:* There never was, nor ever fhall be a fociety to which thefe characters belong, unlefs it is one founded on the covenant of grace: But the fociety that ftands alone upon this foundation is the church. Hence it was only in virtue of the priefthood, and of that minifterial authority which the Lord grants to fome for the edification of the church, that Jehoiada could adminifter this covenant.

BESIDES this religious covenant, a political one between the fovereign and the fubject is diftinctly mentioned: a circumftance which intimates that the former was not regarded in a political, but in a fpiritual light.

THE havoc which the people made of Baal's trumpery, and the flaughter of his priefts, fhew us what particular public evil their covenant with the Lord had been exprefly levelled againft.

SOMETIMES, when divine providence is bringing a people, at once, both to a purer profeffion of the true religion, and to the enjoyment of civil liberty, an individual, like Mr Calvin of Geneva, or like the great Gustavus, the deliverer of Sweden, is honoured with great authority and with great usefulness both in the church and in the state. As a patriot, Jehoiada rids his country of a tyrant, gives the crown to the rightful heir, and and administers an oath obliging both king and subject to the duties, they mutually owe one another. As a priest, he carries on the reformation of the church, stirs up her members to renew their covenant with the Lord, and appoints 'officers over the house of the Lord. However, it was seldom, only indeed on sudden emergencies or in very difficult situations, that a priest had occasion to act in a political capacity. It does not appear, that it was lawful for any of the tribe of Levi, *which the Lord had separated to bear the ark of the covenant of the Lord, to stand before the Lord to minister unto him, and to bless in his name*, more than it is lawful for ministers of the Gospel, under the New Testament dispensation, to entangle themselves unnecessarily in the affairs of this life, or to bear any ordinary stated office or employment of a political nature.

We have another instance of covenanting in Hezekiah's time. 2 Chron. xxix. 4———15. *He brought in the priests, and the Levites, and gathered them together into the east street, and said unto them, Hear me, ye Levites, sanctify now yourselves, and sanctify the house of the Lord God of your fathers, and carry forth the filthiness out of the holy place. For our fathers have trespassed, and done that which was evil in the eyes of the Lord our God, and have forsaken him.———Wherefore the wrath of the Lord was upon Judah and Jerusalem, and he hath delivered them to trouble.———Now it is in mine heart to make a covenant with the Lord God of Israel, that his fierce wrath may turn away from us. My sons, be not now negligent: for the Lord hath chosen you to stand before him, to serve him, and that you should minister to him and burn incense. Then the Levites arose——and they gathered their brethren, and sanctified themselves, and came according to the commandment of the king by the word of the Lord, to cleanse the house of the Lord*

WHILE Hezekiah is exhorting the priests and Levites to set about the reformation of the church, he declares that, for his part, *it was in his heart to make a covenant with the Lord God of Israel.* The active part that Hezekiah and Josiah took in carrying on covenanting work, leads us to enquire, what is meant by the kings of Judah appointing, or causing particular ordinances of the church to be observed.

PROBABLY it will throw much light on the subject, to observe, that these kings acted not merely as political rulers, but likewise as church-members, and some of them as under the immediate influence of the Spirit of prophecy.

As church-members, they might stir up the office-bearers of the church by an holy example, by admonitions, by reproofs. What should hinder Hezekiah considered as a church member of eminent gifts and graces, from addressing the priests and Levites in these words, *My sons, be not now negligent, for the Lord hath chosen you?* What should hinder him, in the same honourable character, from declaring, that, for his part, it was now in his heart, that he should no longer neglect the duty of public covenanting, but along with any that chose to join with him, should set about it without any delay? In this character, too, Jehoshaphat, fearing a threatened calamity, and setting himself to seek the Lord, might stir up fellow church-members to fasting and humiliation, pointing out the calls of word and providence to that exercise.

As bearing, in some instances, the extraordinary character of prophets, they might deliver to the church an immediate meſſage from God, and enjoin what they delivered by divine authority. Solomon, undoubtedly, acted as a prophet in his dedication of the temple. Nor have we any reaſon to doubt that it was under the infallible guidance of inſpiration, that Jehoſhaphat poured forth that remarkable prayer, 2 Chron. xx. 6,——13. Hezekiah, too, ſeems to have ſpoken here to the prieſts and Levites, as he was *moved by the Holy Ghoſt.* Hence this *commandment of the king* is ſaid to be *by the words of the Lord.* Now, the ſtate, as ſuch, has nothing to do with this character: it belongs to the church, 1 Corinth. xii. 28. *God ſet ſome in the church—prophets.*

FARTHER, the kingly authority was in Judah (what indeed it ought to be in every nation under heaven, where the Lord hath erected a viſible church for himſelf) ſubſervient to the good of the church, as far as two diſtinct, independent powers in friendly alliance, may, conſiſtently with their independence, be ſubſervient to one another*: hence the kingly authority in Judah might do much to forward the duty of covenanting. The

---

* IT is not meant, that every civil power ſhould, like the firſt Chriſtian emperor of Rome, heap worldly riches and honours upon eccleſiaſtical officers; or that the clergy, as in Popiſh countries, ſhould be exempted from the juriſdiction of civil courts of judicature, or from bearing equally with their fellow-ſubjects the burdens of the civil government: and leaſt of all is it meant, that the magiſtrate ſhould yield to them, or allow them to poſſeſs, any power or authority whatſoever over the bodies, the liberty or the property of men. But we hold it to be the duty of the magiſtrate to labour, all he can, to promote the purity of goſpel ordinances, and ſecure to church-members the undiſturbed and peaceable enjoyment of them. If the ſpiritual nature of the church were duly attended to, one ſhould think, there might be a more ſincere and permanent amity, and a more conſtant intercourſe of friendly offices between the church and a particular ſtate, than ever can have place between two independent civil powers; becauſe the ſame individuals may, at the ſame time, be good members both of the church and of the ſtate; and becauſe while the church, paying no regard to worldly wealth, power and preferment, keeps up the character of a truly ſpiritual ſociety, there can be no rivalſhip between her and a civil ſtate.

king might issue proclamations, in which, as a church-member sollicitous for the reformation of religion, he might communicate his sentiments and counsel on that subject, to fellow church-members. It seems difficult to prove that there was any thing more than this, in Jehoshaphat's proclamation of a fast. By the giving or the withholding of such favours as are not due to any individuals on the single consideration of their being members of the state, by that influence which the splendor of royalty has over mankind, and which makes the example or instructions of a king be universally regarded, he may, humanly speaking, do more than other church-members, to engage his people in the practice of any particular duty such as Covenanting. This, and not the application of outward force and violence, seems to be meant by Josiah's *causing all that were present in Jerusalem and Benjamin, to stand to the covenant.* As it is, in the nature of things, one of the grossest absurdities to speak of forcing persons to be church-members, it was never lawful, either under the Old or under the New Testament, to enjoin public Covenanting, an ordinance of the church, under civil penalties.

With regard to this instance of Covenanting, we may observe that Hezekiah wanted the Israelites to set about it in the way of acknowledging,

---

It must be acknowledged indeed, that considering, on the one hand, the exorbitant incroachments of the Romish church on the civil powers of Europe; and considering, on the other hand, that our old reformers, who held the magistrate to be *Custos utriusque tabulæ quod attinet ad externum*, the guardian, with respect to external order, of the first as well as of the second table of the law, seem to have sometimes allowed the Protestant princes too much power of modelling the discipline and government of the church at pleasure; on these accounts, it is necessary that church and state should be constantly watching against the incroachments of each on the other; and that, in all their proceedings with regard to one another, they should be careful to keep within the sphere of duty marked out for them severally in the word.

not only their own sin, but likewise the sin of their fathers, *Our fathers have trespassed.* The people of God ought to do so, in opposition to the men of the world, who, instead of making any such acknowledgment, think themselves authorized by custom and prescription, to do whatever their fathers were wont to do, and to hand down to posterity as well the vices as the virtues which they have received from their predecessors.

FARTHER, Hezekiah meant that this Covenanting should have a reference to what was then the present situation of the Israelites. They were under particular tokens of the divine displeasure: Therefore, says Hezekiah, *it is in my heart to make a covenant with the Lord God of Israel, that his fierce wrath may turn away from us.* In the words *with the Lord God of Israel*, he intimates that he meant to recognise his own and his people's covenant-relation to the Lord. No exercise could be more proper amidst the awful signs of God's wrath.

THE last of the kings of Judah in whose reign the Lord's covenant is recorded to have been solemnly renewed, is Josiah, 2 Kings xxiii. *And the king sent, and they gathered unto him all the elders of Judah and of Jerusalem. And the king went up into the house of the Lord, and all the men of Judah and all the inhabitants of Jerusalem with him, and the priests and prophets, and all the people both small and great: and he read in their ears all the words of the book of the covenant which was found in the house of the Lord. And the king stood by a pillar, and made a covenant before the Lord, to walk after the Lord, and to keep his commandments and his testimonies and his statutes, to perform the words of this covenant, that were written in this book, and and all the people stood to the covenant.* 2 Chron. xxxiv. *Then the king sent, and gathered together all the elders of Judah, and Jerusalem. And the king went up into the house of the Lord, and all the men of Judah amd the inhabitants of Jerusalem, and the priests, and the Levites, and all the people both small and great: and he read in their ears all the words of the book of the covenant which was found in the house of the Lord. And the king stood in his place, and made a covenant before the Lord, to walk after the Lord, and to keep his commandments and his statutes with all his heart and with all his soul, to perform the words of the covenant which are written in this book. And he caused all that were present in Jerusalem and Benjamin to stand. And the inhabitants of Jerusalem did according to the covenant of God, the God of their fathers.*

At this time, the call to the duty of covenanting was very urgent. The grounds of the Lord's controversy with the land had been greatly increased by the wickedness of the preceding reign. The Lord had put it into the heart of Josiah to attempt a national reformation. Several Providential circumstances concurred to favour his design: such as, Hilkiah's finding a copy of the law of the Lord; the king's alarming apprehensions from the perusal of it; the message of Huldah the prophetess from the Lord to Josiah. When *the set time* for the revival of true religion is come, it is instructive to observe how a variety of occurrences, and the designs of men whose views are the farthest imaginable from any such thing, conspire to hasten that revival. Here is much of God to be seen.

On this occasion, the young prince is all activity. Having assembled the people, he uses the same means to awaken them to a sense of their sin and danger, whereby he had himself been awakened: he reads the law of the Lord to them. And then standing conspicuous amidst the congregation, he is the first to enter into covenant with the

Lord, inviting his people to come into the same sacred engagement.

Whatever influence the king used, we must not conclude, that the people were compelled by civil pains, to enter into the covenant. We have no reason to doubt, that Josiah well understood that Covenanting was a mere farce, and by no means the duty which the Lord requires, unless it was altogether voluntary.

Josiah was, indeed, young and unexperienced: he knew and loved the Lord; and the ardour of his zeal might carry him farther than a phlegmatic casuist, coolly pondering the matter in his closet, would allow to be prudent. On the other hand, we justly suspect, that the bulk of the people went into the covenant to gratify their king and in compliance with the times. Wherefore they are charged with gross hypocrisy in this matter. Jerem. iii. 10. *Yet for all this her treacherous sister Judah hath not turned unto me with the whole heart, but feignedly, saith the Lord.* On this account, it is not said of the covenanters in Josiah's time, as of those in the time of Asa, that *they entered into the covenant with all their heart and with all their soul.* And probably for the same reason, it is said of the former, but not of the latter, that *the king caused them to stand; and that he made them serve the Lord their God.*

These words, *To walk after the Lord, and to keep his commandments, and his testimonies and his statutes with all the heart and with all the soul, to perform the words of the covenant which are written in this book,* seem to have been a part of the instrument, or form of the oath into which the people entered; as we have them both in the book of kings and in the book of chronicles without any other variation than this; that the words, *with all the heart and with all the soul,* are mentioned in the one as the words of the king, and in the other as the words of the people along with him.

The univerſality of the obedience here promiſed, is intimated in the various terms, *commandments, teſtimonies, ſtatutes:* the ſincerity of the dedication that they here make of themſelves, is declared in the expreſſions, *with all the heart and with all the ſoul.* Thus we ſee, this covenant was framed in direct oppoſition to the evaſions of hypocriſy which then prevailed among the Iſraelites.

The covenant that the church entered into at this time, was not abſolutely a new covenant: it was the covenant *of the God of their fathers;* it was therefore a renovation of the Lord's covenant.

Our Lord takes care to preſerve the purity of his ordinances, even when, comparatively, little divine efficacy ſeems to attend them, and few reap ſpiritual and ſaving profit by them*. That was probably much the caſe with the covenanting in Joſiah's time. Upon the death of that amiable prince, the bloſſoms of public reformation ſoon diſappeared, and hardly any good fruits of their covenanting were to be found. Like the dog returning to his vomit, they returned to the old courſe of ſinning, and perſiſted obſtinately in it; till the fierceneſs of the Lord's anger brought on the ruin of their city and their temple, and the captivity of their nation for ſeventy years.

---

* A consideration both alarming and comfortable: alarming, when we conſider how many abuſe ordinances to the foſtering of their pride, of their legality and ſecurity: but comfortable, when we reflect, that the benefit of ſuch purity is not confined to the preſent time, but extends to poſterity, and is very uſeful to the church in the obſervation of the ſame ordinances in all after ages.

Of the Public Covenanting in the time of Ezra and Nehemiah.

DURING the Babylonish captivity, the Lord continued to take care of the Israelites as his church. He softened the rigour of their exile by his word and Spirit, by the ministry of the prophets, and by the hopes of a return to their native country. He dealt well with them according to his word; *Thou shalt go to Babylon, there shalt thou be delivered: there the Lord shall redeem thee from the hand of thine enemies.*

BEFORE the captivity, the hopes of the reformation of the Israelites were utterly lost; in regard that their obstinate apostacy from the Lord was so great and so general; and in regard that the faithful few could not have a church communion separated from that of a corrupt majority, the administration of their public ordinances being appropriated, by a positive command of God, to one place, and to the priesthood of one family. But after the captivity, the same people, purified in the furnace of affliction, were encouraged by their prophets, particularly by Haggai and Zechariah, to set about a public reformation: Accordingly, the princes, the priests, all ranks of men concurring cheerfully in the good work, the conformity of the church to the divine rule was, in this period, carried much farther than it had been even under the best of their kings.

WE cannot forbear taking notice of an instance that shews how far these reformers were freed from a slavish regard to custom; an attachment, which is commonly a great bar to reformation. The instance is recorded in Nehem. 13, 14, 15. *They found it written in the law which the Lord had commanded by Moses, that the children of*

Israel should dwell in booths in the feast of the seventh month, or of tabernacles. Now that appointment had been overlooked from the days of Joshuah the son of Nun to that day. But the reformers in Nehemiah's time, convinced that it was their duty to supply the defects, as well as to perserve the attainments of their fathers, found themselves shut up to conform their practice to God's word alone, and to keep the feast of tabernacles in booths. As this was a public evidence of their single regard to the authority and honour of God, so it was accompanied with much comfort: for *there was very great gladness.*

Hence we may learn, that we should not be discouraged from the practice of public Covenanting, because it has been much neglected, and few examples of it occur in the history of the church since the coming of Christ. Here we see the Israelites going forward in the performance of a duty for which they had not the shadow of a precedent for nearly a thousand years back. We should readily embrace an opportunity of this kind to shew the singleness of our regard to the rule of God's word.

But to come to our purpose, we shall proceed to consider the examples of Covenanting in this memorable period of reformation.

The first passage we take notice of, is in Ezra x. 2, 3, 4, 5. *And Shecaniah the son of Jehiel, one of the sons of Elam answered and said unto Ezra, We have trespassed against our God, and have taken strange wives of the people of the land; yet now there is hope in Israel concerning this thing. Now therefore let us make a covenant with our God, to put away all the wives, and such as are born of them according to the counsel of my Lord, and of those that tremble at the commandment of our God, and let it be done according to law. Arise: for the matter belongeth to thee; we also will be with thee: be of good cou-*

rage, and do it. Then arose Ezra, and made the chief priests, the Levites, and all Israel to swear, they would do according to this word: and they sware.

PUBLIC Covenanting, we have said, is always to be gone about with an express reference to some particular point of truth or duty, of sin or error, concerning which our present circumstances call us to bear testimony: so the covenanting here, is pointed against the unlawful marriages of the Israelites with the people of the land, and mingling the holy seed with strangers. If people are heartily resolved on the extirpation of any particular evil, they will not be backward to join in covenanting against it. We have reason to fear that much of the opposition which persons make to this ordinance, proceeds from the deceitfulness of the heart, which still retains, perhaps unnoticed, a secret hankering after some evil or another, of which, in covenanting, they would have to make a solemn renunciation.

CHURCH-MEMBERS ought to embrace the opportunities that offer, of stirring up and encouraging the officers of the church to the duties of their station. The Collossians are exhorted to say to Archippus, *Take heed to the ministry which thou hast received of the Lord, that thou fulfil it.* Shecaniah here, sets us an example of this duty. Shecaniah was a chief of the fathers, Ezra viii. 3. an eminent member of the commonwealth, and as we may conclude from what is here recorded of him, a most valuable member of the church. Having shewn Ezra that the proper course in their situation was, to make a covenant with the Lord as their God, he adds that Ezra ought to exert himself in that matter, as the management of it, belonged, in a special manner, to him: for Covenanting being an ordinance of the church, it lay upon him as an office-bearer of the church, a priest and scribe, to point out to the people the present call to that duty, to give them an opportunity of joining in it, and to preside in the administration of it.

It is agreeable to observe how church and state concurred, at this time, in carrying on the work of God. *They made a proclamation throughout Judah and Jerusalem, unto all the children of the captivity, that they should gather themselves together unto Jerusalem; and that whosoever would not come within three days, according to the counsel of the princes and the elders, all his substance should be forfeited, and himself separated from the congregation of those that had been carried away.* As the regulation of marriages was a part of the civil police, so it was proper enough for the princes and elders to command the attendance of the people at Jerusalem, in order to an inquiry, who had, or had not taken strange wives. Nor can their right of annexing the penalty of the confiscation of goods to so reasonable a command, be disputed. The civil penalty, according to the obvious meaning of the words, was not intended against refusing to swear the covenant, but against wilful absence from the assembly of the people at Jerusalem.

Besides, it was plainly the duty of ecclesiastical office-bearers to excommunicate all open enemies and despisers of the reformation, which was now begun; and all might justly be accounted such who disregarded the command of the princes and elders. Hence the proclamation bore, that whosoever did not come within three days, according to the counsel of the princes and the elders, was to incur not only the forfeiture of his goods, but likewise excommunication. It was the same crime that was to be punished as prejudicial to the state, and censured as a scandal to the church.

The next passage is in Nehem. ix. 38. and x. 1, 28,—31. *And because of all this, we make a sure covenant, and write it; and our princes, Levites and priests seal unto it. Now those that sealed were Nehemiah,* &c. *And the rest of the people, the priests, the porters, the singers, the Nethinims, and all they that had separated themselves from the people of the lands unto the law of God, their wives, their sons and their daughters, every one having knowledge, and having understanding: They clave to their brethren, their nobles, and entered into a curse and into an oath, to walk in God's law, which was given by Moses the servant of God, and to observe and do all the commandments of the Lord our God, and his judgments and his statutes: and that we would not give our daughters unto the people of the land, nor take their daughters for our sons. And if the people of the land bring ware or any victuals on the sabbath day to sell, we would not buy of them on the sabbath day, or on the holy day: and that we would leave the seventh year, and the exaction of every debt.*

A REMEMBRANCE of the covenant at Sinai seems to be implied in the mention here made of the Lord's law as given by Moses; an expression which could hardly fail of bringing to their mind the consent of their fathers to that law; and the obligation which that consent brought upon their posterity.

It is probable, too, that they were not unmindful of the engagements, which, by the counsel of Ezra, they had entered into about ten or twelve years before. Indeed, some reference to it seems to be intimated in their promise, *that they would not give their daughters to the people of the land, nor take the daughters of those people to their sons.*

THEY covenanted not only against present, but also against former evils. You ask, how they did so? They acknowledged the sins of their fathers, they expressed their sorrow for them, they promised, thro' grace, to forsake them. *Because of all this*, say they, on account of all the particular evils and circumstances we have mentioned, *we make a sure covenant, and write it.*

FARTHER, they engaged, in the most explicit manner, to those duties which were peculiarly suitable to their circumstances at that time. Hence they entered into an oath that they would not marry with the people of the land; that they would not buy on the sabbath, the wares or victuals which the people of the land might bring to them on that holy day; that they would leave the seventh year and the exaction of every debt. Why are these things specified? Are they greater evils in themselves than other transgressions of God's law which are not mentioned here? By no means; but they were evils which prevailed at that time; evils into which the children of Israel had already fallen, and were in danger of relapsing. It appears indeed, from all the preceding instances of Covenanting, that there is hardly any thing that so uniformly characterises it, as an express reference to some truth or duty, in adhering to which we are likely from our present circumstances, to meet with the greatest opposition.

THE leading men of the State having subscribed the covenant, the people followed their example; *they clave to their brethren*; an expression which intimates the particular tendency of this duty to unite church-members in the matter about which they covenant. For it is only in the way of *giving them one heart and one way* according to the promise, Jerem. xxxii. 39. that the Lord ever brings them to yield themselves to him in covenanting.

BEFORE we leave this passage, we should observe, who were admitted into this covenant: we say, admitted into it; for we have no ground to believe that any were *forced* into it. In the first place, they were persons of all the different ranks

Of PUBLIC COVENANTING.

in society; princes, priests, Levites, porters, Nethinims. Hence the people of Israel may be said to have been properly represented in this transaction. In the second place, they were persons that made a credible profession as church-members. They were such as had *sparated themselves from the people of the land unto the law of God; every one having knowledge and having understanding.* We know not a juster account than this, of the qualifications necessary in church-members.

Of the Use which we ought to make of the Old Testament.

SOME will ask, To what purpose is the survey we have taken of the various instances of Covenanting under the old Testament? Has not the old Testament or Covenant given place to the new? Has not Christ plainly declared in the new Testament what ordinances he will have his church observe? Why then look so much into the old, for the warrants of a duty of the new Testament-church?

To all declamation of this kind, which we are daily hearing from the enemies of covenanting, we offer the following reply.

THE old Testament is a necessary part of that written word which we are commanded to search, and which *makes us wise unto salvation, being profitable for doctrine, for reproof, for correction and instruction in righteousness.* No one, therefore, is to be blamed for having regard to the Old Testament as the rule of their duty.

IT is true, many things that were practised by the antient Israelites, are now no more incumbent on church-members. Yet even these things are still to be attended to, and received as the word of God. We ought to acquiesce in the connection which the Lord appointed between the circumstances of the church under the Old Testament and the observation of the ceremonial law, as well as in the connection between our own circumstances and our partaking of Baptism and the Lord's supper. The submission of the heart to God's authority in his law is one thing; the expressing of that submission in our outward actions, is another thing. The former ought to be constant and invariable, extending also to the whole of God's law, Psal. cxix. 128. *I esteem all thy precepts concerning all things to be right.* The latter is of necessity occasional and partial, as circumstances require and opportunities occur. We are to reverence the Lord's authority as it was interposed in the ceremonial institutions, though we have no occasion, like the antient Jews, to put them in practice. Besides, our faith and love, our esteem and veneration should be exercised with respect to whatever the Lord reveals, of his conduct toward the church, the one body of which every Christian is a member. We ought to observe with holy admiration, how the building of mercy began, and how it gradually advanced. Some regulations were observed in the first stages of the building, which afterward became unnecessary; but the greater and more important part of them is continued from the beginning to the end. The whole is eminently the work of infinite mercy, power, wisdom and faithfulness, Psal. lxxxix. 2 *Mercy shall be built up for ever: thy faithfulness shalt thou establish in the very heavens.* If we have a higher station in that building, than the old Testament saints had, we are by no means to despise their inferior station: to which indeed, according to the appointed order of the building, we owe the superior advantages of our own situation. To that purpose is the apostle's caveat, Rom. xi. 18. *Boast not against the branches: but if thou boast, thou bearest not the root, but the root thee.* Nor should it be here forgotten, that, as we observed before, many of the laws of Moses are still obligatory upon us as to their spirit and ultimate design, though not as to their form. The same holds true of Old Testament examples. So that *whatsoever was written afore-time, was written for our learning, that we, through faith and patience of the scriptures, might have hope.*

But the authority of the Old Testament binds us to regard not only the spirit, but likewise the letter and form of many of its precepts and examples. It will hardly be disputed, that whatever was the duty of antient Israel, is so far still the duty of Christians as it had no necessary relation to the peculiarities of their church or of their state, or as it may be practised by any church or state without impropriety or inconsistency with the advantages of the new Testament dispensation. And then we are, by no means, to depart from the letter or form of any precept of God's law, if he has not himself given us any intimation that we may depart from it. Hence if the form of a duty is the same in the new Testament as in the old, we may conclude, that the form as well as the spirit of it, is obligatory upon us. Hence, too, if a duty, with respect to the spirit of it, is plainly enjoined in the new Testament, without any change, either expressed or implied, of the form or manner in which it was practised under the Old Testament, we may safely conclude, that with regard to such a duty, we are not allowed to deviate from the form prescribed by the divine authority of the old Testament.

But some appear to be of opinion that the precepts and examples of of the Old Testament repeated or referred to in the New, derive their authority and obligation upon us from that repetition or that reference.

So far is this opinion from being true that, in some respects, the authority of the new Testament rests upon the authority of the old, as its foundation: not that the new is less immediately from God than the old; their origin and intrinsic excellence are equally divine: but with regard to order and connection, the one is to the other, as the higher parts of a building are to the lower. The new Testament continually establishes the authority of the old, and builds upon it. The history of the new Testament answers to the prophecies of the old. As to the doctrines of the new Testament, our Lord and his apostles constantly referred their hearers to the old, affirming that they said *no other things than what Moses and the prophets had said before.* Our Saviour and his apostles proposed many examples to the imitation of their hearers, as obligatory upon them by the authority alone of the old Testament. So our Lord defended the conduct of his disciples in plucking and eating the ears of corn on the sabbath, from the example of David, Matt. xii. 3, 4, 5. So the apostles encourage us to faith, to patience and prayer from the examples of Abraham, of Job and Elias, Rom. iv. Jam. v. 11, 17, 18. The phrase *It is written*, which commonly in the new Testament denotes divine authority, is applied to the history of the old, Gal. iv. 22. Indeed hardly any thing would appear more unreasonable to an impartial reader of the new Testament than to suppose, that, when the penmen of it repeated a precept or referred to an example of the old Testament, they meant to give something a divine authority and obligation, which, otherwise, it would not have had.

For a great part of the first century, the old Testament was all the written word that Christians were in possession of; and yet they were enjoined to take heed to that word, and commended for searching the scriptures daily, 1 Pet. i. 19. Acts

xvii. 11. *The Bereans were more noble than those of Thessalonica.* But in what respect were they noble? in setting aside the authority of the old Testament? Quite the reverse; it consisted in manifesting so high a regard to the authority of the old Testament, that they would not receive even the doctrine of the apostles, without examining, whether it was, or was not, agreeable to that divine record. It is plain, therefore, that the first Christians subjected their hearts and consciences to the old Testament as much as ever the Jews did. And why should not we do the same? Were church-members loosed from their obligation to submit to the authority of the old Testament as soon as all the books of the new Testament were published? By no means. The obligation was constituted by God himself, and none but he could loose them from it; and that he never did. Nay, they were more obliged than ever to read and study the old Testament, when the Lord, in the new, had drawn aside the vail, and had placed the great things of his law in the most glorious point of view.

The authority, therefore, of the old Testament being, in itself, superiour to objection, we are bound to obey the precepts and to imitate the examples of it, even such of them as we cannot find expresly repeated in the new Testament. So we are obliged by the authority of the old Testament, to abstain from marrying within the prohibited degrees of consanguinity; to swear to the truth when we are called before a lawful magistrate; to spare the life of one chargeable with accidental manslaughter; to have the seal of the covenant administered to our children: and yet not one of these precepts is to be found expresly repeated in the New Testament. In the same manner, the history of the old Testament comprehending a period of nearly four thousand years, contains a vast variety of characters and situations unnoticed in the new Testament, which are highly proper for our imitation. We are not more bound to imitate the patience of Job which is mentioned, than the victorious chastity of Joseph and the faithful friendship between David and Jonathan, which are not mentioned, in the new Testament.

Besides, with respect to those situations which are common to both the old and new Testaments, the duty of the church in some of them is much more fully exemplified in the old. The new Testament, indeed, gives us some account of the public proceedings of the churches planted by the apostles, of those in Jerusalem, in Antioch, in Ephesus: but these accounts are very short; it is plain, they were never intended to be the only standard of the duty of God's people in a visible church-state to the exclusion of the various useful examples of their duty in that capacity which the more copious, particular and long-continued history of the old Testament supplies. In the new Testament, we have hardly any more than a view of a particular church during the stay of an apostle in it, which was sometimes but one day, and seldom longer than a few weeks: but in the old, we see the church of Israel passing through a great variety of conditions, sometimes in prosperity sometimes in adversity; sometimes excited to reformation, sometimes seduced to idolatry by the civil magistrate or by her own office-bearers; sometimes lively and zealous in the observation of divine ordinances, and sometimes grown lukewarm, carnal and secure. Hence we need not be surprized to find some duties incumbent on church members in their joint capacity, more clearly exemplified in the old Testament than in the new; since in that long succession of circumstances and situations which are recorded of the Jewish church, we cannot, in reason, suppose but that there must have been occasions for the regular performance of whatsoever the Lord requires of a people in their church-capacity: But so extensive an exemplication of such duties is not to be expected in the period of about thirty years after our Saviour's ascension; the period to which the history of the new Testament is confined.

On the whole, nothing is more absurd than attempting to raise our esteem of one part of revelation at the expense of another. A believing submission of heart is due to all that God says. It is undeniable, that we have more of the great and precious promises of the everlasting covenant, and more precepts and examples with respect to the duties of civil and of sacred society, in the old, than we have in the new Testament. The new Testament constantly in all its histories, in its rules and exhortations, in its doctrines and reasonings confirms the authority of the old: So that if a duty is plainly injoined in the old Testament, and is not altered or annulled in the new, we need not scruple to go forward in the practice of such a duty upon the authority alone of the former.

Of the characteristics of the New Testament Dispensation.

"NEW Testament dispensation!" cries one: "ay, our divines are very shy of using the "scripture expression on this subject. It is called "in scripture the new covenant; as much distinct "indeed, from the old as heaven and earth. Do "our divines think they express the thing better "than the Spirit of God, who knew best the fit- "test words?

There is no occasion for such an outcry against our divines, if they mean no more by *the dispensation of the covenant of grace*, than what is frequently meant in scripture by the word *covenant*. All that our divines intend is, A manner of declaring or exhibiting the covenant of grace. Indeed the word which we render *covenant*, is sometimes used to signify that secret eternal transaction among the persons of the Godhead which is called *the council of peace*; as in Psal. lxxxix. 3. *I have made a covenant with my chosen.* Luke xxii 29. *I appoint,* or *covenant, to you as my Father hath appointed, or covenanted, to me, a kingdom.* That appointment of the Father must be understood of of the covenant between him and the Son from eternity; for all God's appointments are eternal. So the word may be taken in Hebr. xiii. 20. *The blood of the covenant.* Such passages are sufficient to justify our divines in terming the counsel of the three persons of the Godhead with regard to the salvation of sinners, a covenant of grace. At the same time, it must be acknowledged that both the Greek word rendered *covenant* and the Hebrew corresponding to it, are much more frequently to be taken for *a revelation of the covenant of grace.* So we are to understand the Lord's covenant with Abraham, with Isaac, and with Jacob; so we are to understand the words in the institution of the Lord's Supper, *This is the cup of the new Testament in my blood.* So in Heb ix 15,———20. the word is constantly to be understood of *a testamentary deed*, that is, a declaration of our Lord's will concerning our deliverance from sin, confirmed by his death. Now, that is all our divines mean by a dispensation of the covenant of grace.

It is plain, therefore, that the word *covenant*, when it is used in scripture with respect to God's appointed way of saving sinners, has two significations: First, it signifies the council of peace, which was among the persons of the Godhead from eternity: Secondly, the revelation of that council of peace to the church *at sundry times and in divers manners.*

Our divines have expressed the last of these senses by the phrase *Dispensation of the covenant of grace*; both because it is evidently agreeable to the meaning of the Spirit of God; and because the English word *covenant* has not such a variety of acceptations as the original word. Our translators, for that reason, have rendered the Greek substantive noun sometimes *covenant*, sometimes *testament*, and the verb of the same derivation, *appointing*.

It is commonly observed, that, in scripture, a thing is often said to be or take place when it is only manifested: So God is said to *dwell between the cherubims*, that is, he continually manifests himself there. So when it is said in John vii. 38. *The Spirit was not yet*, it means that the manifestation or abundant out-pouring of the Spirit was not yet. Nor is this manner of expression without reason, since the manifestation of a thing gives it a kind of being with respect to those to whom it is manifested. We have reason to believe the Holy Ghost never uses this manner of expression but with peculiar propriety. In the epistle to the Hebrews, for example, it was highly proper for the Apostle to use the word *covenant* for the *revelation of the covenant in Christ*, because the Jews against whom the apostle is there disputing, took up with the shadows in opposition to the substance; they were not only enemies to the new Testament-revelation of the covenant of grace; but in the legal pride of their zeal for antiquated ceremonies, they shewed much enmity to the spiritual nature and gracious design of that covenant itself.

Adventuring, therefore, to follow our divines in the use of the phrase *new Testament dispensation*, we have now to consider the characteristics of this dispensation; in order to know whether those characteristics be inconsistent with that Public Covenanting which we have seen the church under the Old Testament, practising so often to her spiritual profit.

In the first place, it is the distinguishing glory of the new Testament dispensation, that it reveals the Saviour as already come. Faith's plea under the old Testament was, *Thou wilt perform the truth to Jacob, and the mercy to Abraham, which thou hast sworn unto our fathers from the days of old.* But under the new Testament, faith's plea is, *Thou hast raised up an horn of salvation, and performed the mercy promised to the fathers.*

At the coming of our Lord Jesus Christ, the church obtained a nearer and fuller view of the covenant of grace. She saw the condition of it fulfiled in his obedience unto the death: She saw the promises of it all yea and amen in him: She saw him as her great prophet, taking off the vail that had been spread over spiritual things, and causing her to behold them, *with open face*: She saw him as her king *meek and having salvation; exalted to give repentance and the forgiveness of sins.* The new Testament is called *the ministration of righteousness that excels in glory.* The beginning of the epistle to the Hebrews is never to be omitted on this subject: *God who at sundry times and in divers manners spake unto the fathers, hath in these last days spoken unto us by his Son.* Surely it was necessary that the superior excellence of the new Testament revelation should be some way suitable to so glorious an event as that of the Son of God appearing in our nature and dwelling among us. That excellence, however, was not in the matter, but in the manner of the revelation: the doctrines, the precious promises and the moral precepts that God hath spoken to us by his Son, are the very same which he had spoken before *by the prophets, at sundry times and in divers manners.*

Among those various manners in which God instructed his church under the Old Testament, were, the appointment of sacrifices, the Levitical priesthood, circumcision, typical persons and places, external purifications, and all the other observances of the ceremonial law. These were shadows of good things to come; they only signified that Christ had not as yet *put away sin by the sacrifice of himself*. Now, it is evident, that Christ being already come, such institutions would, of themselves, wax old and unprofitable. They were like a herald who has no more to do after the arrival of the personage whose approach he proclaimed. They were like the pictures of plants and flowers, which the student of Botany makes use of, till he procure specimens of the plants and flowers themselves.

As to the state, the new Testament required no alterations, excepting in a few instances; such as, the distinctions among the tribes, the law with regard to the cities of refuge, the prohibiting of intercourse with lepers or others that were ceremonially unclean: Regulations, which, under the Old Testament, served as a fence to the ceremonial law as it was distinguished from the moral; and prevented the clashing of the church with the state. To prevent that ought still to be carefully studied, wherever the same people are members of the church and of the state. But the ceremonial institutions having obtained their end in the death of Christ, there is no more occasion for the fence of them. As to the intrinsic nature of civil government, and the immediate end of it, which is, the good of civil society, the New Testament made no alterations.

It is evident, then, that covenanting does not come under the description either of the ceremonial or of the judicial law. It is not a ceremonial institution; because it has nothing in its nature, that necessarily refers to the coming of Christ as a future event: avouching the Lord to be our God by solemn oath says not whether Christ is, or is not come. Nor does it belong to the judicial law. Nobody, it is presumed, will maintain, that it is now unlawful for the members of a political body to enter into an association for the preservation of their civil and religious liberties, and to confirm it by oaths and subscriptions: the public covenanting, under the Old Testament, if we could consider it in a political view merely, would have been the same, in effect, with such an association. On this supposition, public Covenanting must have belonged, not to that part of the judicial law which respected the peculiar circumstances of the Jews, but to that part of it which is remaining in force. But the truth is, it could not belong to the Judicial law; because, as has been shewn, it was always an ordinance of the church.

Farther, as the New Testament has taken away the occasion of the church's observation of the ceremonial law, so it has introduced some positive institutions of its own; such as baptism, the Lord's supper, and we may add, the change of the sabbath from the seventh to the first day of the week. Positive institutions are useful for preserving lively impressions on the minds of church-members, of the Divine authority of their King and Head; and therefore a few are appointed in the New Testament: and but a few, because simplicity and spirituality were to characterise the worship of the New Testament. In this sense, it is acknowledged, Covenanting is by no means, an ordinance of the New Testament; because it is of a moral nature, and equally binding under every dispensation

With regard to moral duties, the New Testament corrects the gross mistakes concerning them, which, in our Saviour's time, prevailed among church-members; it gives further instructions as to the occasions and spiritual manner of performing many of them: and the illustrious display that it makes, of the everlasting covenant in Christ crucified, sets the motives and encouragements to the practice of them in the strongest light. The privileges of our new state in Christ are continually set forth in all their glory and fulness in order to engage us to the study of holiness. Hence Covenanting, like other moral duties, is now to be gone about in the way of avowing those privileges, and proceeding upon them, rather more explicitly than was usual under the Old Testament.

Another glorious characteristic of the New Testament dispensation is the unlimited extension of the kingdom of Christ among the Gentiles. Christ's visible kingdom was no longer confined to Israel according to the flesh: no longer a national, it now became a catholic church. Nations might still be received into the church; and might still, under that denomination, be acknowledged as belonging to her: But then as she allows no respect of persons, she allows as little of nations. In the New Testament church, Jew and Greek, circumcision and uncircumcision, Barbarian, Scythian, bond and free, are all on the level. In this church, the honourable distinctions, the power, the authority of civil societies have no place; for though chuch-members ought to be in all dutiful subjection to these, they must not acknowledge them as belonging to the church; as either limiting, enlarging, or any way affecting the peculiar duties or the peculiar privileges of the church. To be thus spiritual and independent was, indeed, the property of the church, even under the Old Testament; but the New set this property in a fairer and more conspicuous point of view: and what had been the privilege of one nation was then extended to many. So that though the church of Christ cannot now be described as merely a national church; yet many national churches may belong to her, and may acknowledge that they do so, in as open, explicit and solemn a manner, as ever ancient Israel did: which acknowledgement is, in truth, the national Covenanting we contend for.

T

Thus the coming of Christ, with regard to the effects it produced on the church, was like some remarkable incident in the history of a state, which brings about so great a revolution, that, though materially the civil constitution remains the same, almost every part of the administration takes on a new appearance, and the general course of government bears obviously another character.

That Public Covenanting is still the duty of the Church, appears from the moral nature of it, and from particular precepts of the New Testament.

WE hope, it will be granted, that our obligations to any thing, if they are deducible from the nature of God, and from the relations we bear to him and to one another, continue, while those relations continue. When we consider that God is infinitely excellent, that we owe our all to his goodness, and that we never can sufficiently acknowledge our obligations to him; surely, it will not then appear unreasonable to bind ourselves to his service by what the universal sense of mankind holds to be, in all cases civil and sacred, the strongest of ties; that is, by the religion of an oath. On this subject let us hear Arrian representing the sentiments of Epictetus. "God and 'your guardian angel,' says the moral philosopher, "are always present to observe your behaviour: "But think you they need light for that purpose? "Indeed, they do not need it. To this all see- "ing God you should swear allegiance as the sol- "diers do to Cesar. The soldiers who receive "their wages from Cesar, swear that they will ne- "ver prefer any thing to his interest. And will "you not swear to God whose bounty is incom- "parably greater than Cesar's ? or having sworn "will you not keep your oath? But what should you swear? Undoubtedly this: that you will never be disobedient to him, nor find fault with any of his dispensations, nor behave improperly under them; in fine, that you will always be ready to do and suffer whatever is necessary." Such were the noble sentiments of a poor heathen.

As we have much weakness both of a natural and of a moral kind; we have occasion continually for one another's help: and in particular cases, if we expect the help of others, we naturally desire to be fully assured of it. The desire is reasonable; for without such assurance, we cannot properly avail ourselves of their help, nor act in concert with them. Hence according to that rule of our conduct in society, *Do to others whatsoever ye would have them do to you,* those who mutually expect assistance from one another, ought to give and receive assurances of that assistance; assurances proportioned in degree, to the importance of the matter wherein assistance is required. If it be a matter of the utmost importance, such as the glory of God and our own salvation are concerned in; then a very great assurance, even that of a solemn oath, is highly proper. Such an assurance is Public Covenanting. It is reasonable, that we swear allegiance to the most high God, the Possessor of heaven and earth: not that He needs any such profession; but that we may suitably testify to others the homage that we owe him. Our call to do so will be the greater, if much rebellion and contempt of his law appear among those around us. Now, swearing in this manner, is all we mean by our public Covenanting.

It has been objected to the morality of Covenanting, "That men are not led, as they generally are with respect to moral duties, to agree in the approbation of it; many christians of different denominations utterly rejecting it."

All men have, indeed, a general sense of right and wrong: but as our ignorance of God's law is a branch of the corruption of our nature, that sense of right and wrong is very insufficient for our direction in many instances of moral duty. Hence the apostle says in Rom. vii. 7. *I had not known sin for I had not known lust, except the law had said, Thou shalt not covet.* The atrocious wickedness of the Gentile world proceeded from their ignorance of God and of pure morality, Ephes. iv. 18, 19. Because the innate sense of right and wrong informs us of many moral duties, it does not follow, that it informs us of all. No moral duty is clearer than this, that we ought to believe whatever God reveals; and yet how few professed Christians feel any uneasiness from the moral sense for not believing what themselves acknowledge to be the word of God. As our natural sense of right and wrong is very defective, so it is very weak and easily perverted. How can we otherwise account for the shocking barbarities that so generally prevailed in the heathen world; such as selling children for slaves, exposing them to wild beasts, murdering their enemies in cold blood, and human sacrifices? Many gross immoralities are mentioned by the polite authors of Greece and Rome as what were commonly practised by their countrymen without reproach. Conscience has been strangely perverted even in good men. We have no reason to think that the Patriarchs felt any remorse for the crime of Poligamy.

That men in their present state of depravation have a natural sense of *all* moral duties, is an assertion altogether unworthy of any one who acknowledges that he needs the scriptures to be a *light to his feet and a lamp to his path.* It is an undoubted fact, that, in manifold instances, men are insensible of moral obligation; especially with regard to sins of omission against the first table of the moral law: for example, the omission of secret prayer, of family-worship, of personal fasting.

After all, it may be asked, Whether a natural sense of the duty of covenanting does not lead the generality of Christians to consider several other duties, such as receiving the sacraments, as equivalent to it? And the consciences of those who, after having been fully acquainted with what has been offered in support of covenanting, have yet despised and rejected it, can best tell, whether they have not found it a very hard task to evade the evidence attending it, and to stifle the convictions that rose naturally in their minds, of its divine warrant and perpetual obligation.

We may lay it down as an established maxim, that it is not the uncertain opinion of any denomination of men, whether Papists or Protestants, whether Calvinists or Arminians, whether Presbyterians or Episcopalians; but right reason and the word of God, that are the true tests by which we may try and know, whether any thing is a moral duty, or not. To give divine worship to a very exalted creature; to worship God in ways not appointed in his word; to play at games of chance; to refuse obedience to the lawful commands of such a government as ours in Britain; to reject the observation of the Sabbath as a day which is no less holy to the Lord under the New Testament, than it was under Old; to countenance the intertainments of the stage; in fine, to propagate error under a mistaken apprehension of its being truth: these and many other things, defended by different denominations of Christians, are justly considered by others as contrary to the moral law, and matter of deep humiliation before the Lord. So that public Covenanting is far from being the only moral duty which is controverted among professed Christians. When there is little of the practice of God's law, and much indifference to that sound doctrine which is according to godliness, it is well known that speculative errors with regard to almost all the branches of morality will, in course, very soon prevail. Sinful practices put people upon devising sinful opinions to defend them.

But it is not only from the nature of the thing, that our obligation to public Covenanting is apparent. However clearly any thing may seem to be founded in reason, and however strongly we may be bound to it in that respect; yet in our application and appropriation of such a thing to the use of the church, the authority of Christ, as the church's only head, king and lawgiver, is chiefly to be regarded and acknowledged. Thus we are to perform the duties of natural religion, we are to pray and sing praise, because the Lord Christ hath appointed us. It is only as far as any observance is authorised by his word of appointment, that we have ground to look for his gracious presence and his efficacious blessing to attend it. We have seen that the authority of Christ bound the church under the Old Testament to the practice of Covenanting: for then as well as now, Christ was the leader and lawgiver of the church, Exod. xxiii. 20, 21. We hope it is evident, too, that Covenanting was by no means abrogated, like the shadows of the ceremonial law, at the death of Christ. But that is not all. Our Lord has been pleased to repeat the command in his new Testament.

To this purpose is Matt. v. 33. *Ye have heard, that it hath been said by them of old time, Thou shalt perform unto the Lord thine oaths.* It is evident with respect to this and other precepts of the old Testament repeated in our Lord's sermon on the mount, that he not only explains them in order to vindicate them from the corrupt glosses of the Pharisees; but enjoins them anew upon his people: So that we cannot reasonably doubt that this commandment belongs to the law of Christ as given to the New Testament church. Our Lord seems not here to repeat the words of any particular text of the Old Testament; but rather to give the sense of several texts, such as Exod. xx. 7. *Thou shalt not take the name of the Lord thy God invain; for the Lord will not hold him guiltless that taketh his name invain.* Deut. x. 21. *Thou shalt fear the Lord thy God: him shalt thou serve, and to him shalt thou cleave, and swear by his name.* Deut. xxiii. 21. *When thou shalt vow a vow unto the Lord, thou shalt not slack to pay it.* Hence we may gather that more is meant by this command, than merely that what we swear *by* the Lord is binding on us: it means, too, that we should swear *to* him; so much being plainly implied in *performing* oaths to the Lord; so much being expresly required in the parallel texts of the old Testament.

Our obligation to covenanting is plainly implied in several commands and exhortations of the new Testament. In covenanting, *we present our bodies a living sacrifice to God, holy and acceptable, which is our reasonable service,* according to Rom. xii. 1, 2. Surely there is no duty so adequate to the import of presenting ourselves a living sacrifice to God, even with respect to our *bodies,* not in secret only, but before the world, as public covenanting; which not only in common with other duties, but with regard to its distinguishing characteristic, is *the giving of our own selves to the Lord;* and the avouching of him to be our God. Again, we are called *to stand fast in the faith; to stand fast in one spirit, with one mind, striving together for the faith of the gospel; to hold fast the profession of our faith without wavering,* 1 Corinth. xvi. 13. Phil. i. 27. Heb. x. 23. These exhortations having been primarily directed to several churches in their collective capacity, are to be complied with not only in a personal, but in a social way. These exhortations bind us to the use of all such means compatible with our circumstances, as have ever been found profitable to the church of God for promoting her stedfastness in the faith. These exhortations oblige us not only to be, but to appear stedfast in the faith; oblige us to give every proper assurance both to fellow-church-members and to the world, that we are unanimously so; oblige us, in fine, to be as open and explicit in declaring our engagements to stedfastness as the church ever was in any former period ; the general nature of engagements being the same in every period ; and the duty of openly declaring ourselves for the Lord Christ alone, and of binding ourselves to him in the most solemn manner, being no less reasonable and necessary under the New Testament than under the Old. These and the like passages of the New Testament being considered in this manner, afford arguments for Covenanting which its adversaries will never be able to invalidate ; encouragements to the practice of it which its friends can never sufficiently improve.

Of Examples of Covenanting in the New Testament.

OUR Lord has not contented himself, like most of those who have taken upon them to give laws to the states and kingdoms of this world, with publishing a dry collection of precepts accompanied only with severe threatenings against the disobedient. He proposes his laws in the most winning and persuasive manner. To engage our attention, he uses all the variety, all the plainness, all the force and elevation, which human language and human nature can admit of. But why does our Lord so much more than other lawgivers, to render his laws easy and agreeable to his subjects? Has he less authority than other lawgivers? No, but infinitely more: *He is the blessed and only potentate.* His authority is, at once, the most righteous and the most absolute. Various, however, and important are the ends of that rational and condescending manner in which the Lord Christ makes his laws known to mankind. One is obvious: That the obedience and subjection of his people may proceed from an inward principle of love; because all the external obedience and subjection, proceeding from slavish principles; such obedience and subjection as men who know not the heart must often be satisfied with; are utterly rejected in the kingdom of Christ. Now the various ways in which our Lord addresses us in his word, *his precept upon precept, his line upon line, here a little and there a little,* are the most proper means, through the Spirit, of begeting and increasing the principle of love which is at the bottom of all acceptable obedience to his laws.

One of those *divers manners* in which the Lord's word shews wonderful condescension to our weakness, is instruction by examples. Knowing our frames, he has adapted his word to one of the most powerful principles of our constitution, the principle of imitation. When we see others going before us in any duty, we think the difficulty and the danger grow less: Those who lead the way seem to invite us to follow them: Of course, we wish to be like or equal to them. Besides, the new nature has a peculiar suitableness, as indeed to every part of the written word, so particularly to the examples of it. Believers are still members of the same mystical body of Christ as the saints recorded in scripture; they have the same head, the same Spirit, the same faith, the same inheritance. No wonder, then, that the examples of Abraham, of David, of Peter and of Paul are still dear to believers, and congenial to their heart.

There is great reason to think, that examples are to be found in God's word contained in the scriptures of the Old and New Testament, of all the duties that the divine law requires either of individuals or of societies: The more comprehensive duties indeed, such as fortitude in resisting temptation, zeal for the glory of God, concern for the welfare of the church, are more fully and expresly exemplified: but other duties which are included in and easily deduced from these are, some of them, not so expresly exemplified. Such is the duty of refusing to endanger the loss of one's life in a duel, for no other reason than the folly of another who wants to run that hazard. We cannot say, there is an example of such refusal in the whole Bible; but then the implication of it in multitudes of examples that shew the value we ought to put upon our own life, and that of others, makes the duty as clear as an express example of it would do.

We have shewn that Public Covenanting was abundantly exemplified under the Old Testament. We shall now offer some observations on the examples of the New Testament.

To begin with the example of Christ; we observe, that though he magnified the law by a divinely glorious obedience on all occasions; yet it is no way necessary, nay, from the endless variety of circumstances which daily occur, it is absurd to suppose, that he was in every particular situation wherein any of his followers may be. It is often their duty to act as civil magistrates, or as members of a court of judicature; characters that our Lord never assumed. So he had no call to the duty of public covenanting; a duty which is competent to a visible church alone. Though our Lord testified against the corruptions of the Jewish church, yet as he continued to attend regularly on her ordinances, he never did any thing that interfered with her public administrations. Hence if the Jewish church had then returned to the Lord in the way of covenanting, as every one must allow they might warrantably have done, our Saviour, though he could not have covenanted like church members, who as having been personally chargeable with sin, were returning to the Lord, would at least have countenanced them in the exercise.

It may be asked, how we are to regard the example of Christ, in circumstances or situations wherein we know not that he ever acted?

In the first place, we may always imitate him in his regard to the whole will of God. In the second place, we should consider whether we may not observe, in the life of Christ, some exemplification of a duty like what is incumbent upon us, of the same kind, or equivalent to it. We do not read that he ever gave money to the poor; but he gave hearing to the deaf, sight to the blind, salvation to the miserable captives of sin and Satan. We do not find that he engaged in a particular worldly calling; but we are certain, that he never ceased to promote the welfare of society; for *he always went about doing good.* In the same manner, though he never joined with the church in public covenanting, we see him in every circumstance of his life, bearing a public and particular testimony to the truth. Though a simple affirmation from him whose name is THE TRUTH, was enough to command the assent of every reasonable creature; yet he often accompanied what he affirmed with the most solemn asseverations. Of that kind was his frequent repetition of the word, *Verily.* When the high priest adjured him to tell, whether he was the Christ the Son of God; he answered in the most pointed manner, I AM, or THOU HAST SAID. The solemn assurance that he gives us, in Matth. v. 18. is little, if at all, inferior to an oath: *Verily I say unto you, till heaven and earth pass, one jot or tittle shall in no wise pass till all be fulfilled.* The good confession that he witnessed before Pontius Pilate was of the same public, particularizing, and ascertaining nature as our covenanting, John xviii. 37.

Nor should it be forgotten here that our Lord covenanted with his eternal Father. The love which he manifested in his fulfilment of that covenant is proposed to our imitation, and so in some measure may his covenanting itself; especially, as he compares the Father's transacting with him to his transacting with us, Luke xxii. 29. He covenanted to obey as a bond servant, that we might covenant to regard him, and to follow him as dear children. The truth is, our covenanting derives its name, its nature, and all its usefulness from its conformity to that everlasting covenant.

The history of the New Testament is concise. Continued only to about the thirtieth year after our Lord's ascension, it informs us, how successfully the apostles preached the gospel; how the hand of the Lord was with them when they had no less, but, for the most part, far greater outward difficulties to struggle with than any of their successors have; and how the power of the Lord was revealed in the planting of the first churches among the Gentiles. But we have not a regular history of any one of those churches for any considerable course of time. A few select particulars only of their proceedings which infinite wisdom saw necessary to complete the rule of our faith and practice, are left on record. Why should we wonder that public covenanting is not found among such particulars, since the precepts and examples on this head in the Old Testament, were clear, were full, were easy to be applied to the use of the New Testament church?

We have, however, a remarkable hint concerning the covenanting of the Macedonians which must not be overlooked. It is in the eighth chapter of the second epistle to the Corinthians, where the apostle having spoken of the liberal contribution of the Macedonians for the relief of their poor brethren in Judea, adds, *And this they did not as we hoped, but first gave their ownselves to the Lord, and to us by the will of God.*

The opinion of a late ingenious writer on covenanting, that there is an Ellipsis in the latter part of the verse, seems reasonable. In the fourth verse, the Macedonians are said to have used much importunity with Paul and his fellow-labourers to accept of what they had contributed toward the assistance of their poor brethren; *to receive the gift, and take upon them the fellowship of the ministring to the saints.* The verse under consideration shews in what manner they proceeded to deliver their contribution to the apostles. It is observed, that *they first gave their ownselves to the Lord;* and then followed their giving to the apostles: what was given to the apostles, as we cannot reasonably suppose it to be any thing else than their contribution for the poor saints, is easily supplied from the former verse. This way of understanding the passage is the more reasonable, that we cannot suppose the Macedonians would, in the most natural sense of the words, *give themselves to the apostles*, who were not lords of their faith but helpers of their joy: nor do we read in any other place of churches *giving themselves* to the apostles.

It is a remarkable circumstance, that the Macedonians, on this occasion, did more than the apostle and his brethren expected. This cannot be understood of their profession of Christianity, because they had made that some time before; nor of their participation of the sacraments, because that was common in all the churches; nor of the abundance of their liberality, which the apostle celebrates in verse second, and from which the act of giving their ownselves to the Lord is plainly distinguished; nor, lastly, of their frame and disposition of mind in contributing to the help of their brethren, because it is mentioned as a particular action equally distinct, and equally open to observation as that of their contributing toward the relief of the poor saints; for they first gave their ownselves to the Lord, and then their contribution to the apostles.

It is observable, too, that the phrase, *They gave their ownselves to the Lord,* corresponds exactly to the various periphrases by which the duty of covenanting is expressed in the Old Testament; such as *avouching the Lord to be our God, joining ourselves to the Lord, making a covenant that we shall be the Lord's people, and saying we are the Lord's*. Though we are, no doubt, *to yield ourselves to the Lord* in every duty, yet we do not recollect, that there is a duty besides covenanting, to the performance of which, the above mentioned expressions or any equivalent to them, are so constantly and uniformly applied.

But how comes it about, may some say, that we never find the apostle giving the Corinthians any directions with regard to covenanting?

We answer, that the apostolic approbation was a sufficient intimation of the duty of the Corinthians. Besides with regard to the warrant and the manner of covenanting, the Corinthians had the same authority and directions of the Old Testament which the Macedonians had had: for as there were manifold duties enjoined in the Old Testament, which Christians had no ground to consider as abrogated by the New Testament; so those who searched the scriptures diligently, and sought the aid of the Spirit of truth, might set forward in the practice of such duties without any new recommendation of them.

It appears to have been a circumstance that did much to render the conduct of the Macedonians in this matter beyond expectation praise-worthy, that they were led from an attentive regard to the written word as their only rule, *to give themselves to the Lord*, without waiting for any oral recommendation of the duty from the apostles. In this, no doubt Paul rejoiced, as a nurse does to see the unexpected but successful attempt of her child to walk alone.

We need not ask, why the apostle does not insist upon covenanting as upon the duty of contributing to the relief of poor saints; since it is plainly, the principal design of the apostle in this place to inforce the practice of the latter as what the present dispensations of providence were calling for; whereas it is but transiently or by the way that he takes notice of the former. How often do the inspired writers expatiate and enlarge on some duties because of their suitableness to a particular occasion; not that other duties which they only mention, are of less obligation; but in order to impress us in a lively manner with the importance and necessity of attending to the present calls of providence?

Of the Period between the Close of the Cannon of Scripture and the Reformation from Popery.

THE examples we have hitherto treated of, taken from the Old and New Testament, are obligatory in themselves as a necessary part of the only rule of our faith and practice. These we are now to produce have no such authority. They are examples that we are bound to imitate as far as they are agreeable to the word of God; no farther. They are to be recognised, because it is necessary to hold fast what the church has already attained; because, too, it should encourage church members to the practice of any duty, when they learn that in the case of those who have gone before them, it has met with many remarkable tokens of Heaven's regard and acceptance.

Even in the first century many abominable errors, such as the blasphemies of Ebion and of Cerinthus against the divinity of Christ, sprung up and troubled the church. It is generally allowed, that the apostle John had these blasphemies in his eye, when he wrote his gospel: and is it not reasonable to suppose that the Christians at that time, would give one another explicit assurances that they were to abide by the testimony of John, and that they were of one mind and of one judgment, particularly as to the Godhead and eternal Sonship of Christ? Though we cannot find that they observed all the formalities of covenanting which the church has warrantably used at other times, yet so far as their open declarations and apologies served to ascertain their joint agreement with respect to any matter of profession or of practice, so far in reality were they covenanters.

We may take notice of a well known passage in the 97th of the 10th book of Pliny's Epistles. He writes the Emperor Trajan concerning those who had been prevailed on to renounce Christianity, that even such constantly averred, that all their crime was, that they usually met on an appointed day before the dawn, that they sung an hymn to Christ as to God, that they bound themselves by oath, not as the heathens alledged, to any thing that was wicked, but to abstain from theft, from robbery, from adultery, from violating their promise, and from unfaithfulness to their trust.* Pliny writes this, not as a report, but as the confession of the Christians themselves; a circumstance which leads us to consider it as a literal account of facts.

The Creeds and Confessions of the antient churches may be called solemn covenants, in regard they expressed the consent or agreement of the true church in certain articles of belief, or in certain rules of practice; articles and rules which were pointed in the most direct manner, against particular errors and particular evil practices. When the antient Christians publicly gave their assent, as we have reason to believe they did frequently, to those Creeds and Confessions, their doing so, was in reality public covenanting. ‡

---

* *Seque sacramento non in scelus aliquod obstringere, sed ne furta, ne latrocinia, ne fidem fallerent, ne depositum appellati abnegarent.*

‡ "It was a commendable custom," says Witsius, "of the Christian church to require of every grown person a public declaration of his faith, before his admission to baptism. Afterward, the children of Christians were usually presented before the bishop or pastor, in order to make the same declaration. For

So early as the beginning of the second century, what is commonly called the Creed of the apostles (because it is a summary of the apostles, doctrine) appears to have been made use of, as a test for distinguishing the lovers of true Christianity from hereticks.

In covenanting it is not enough that we enter into such bonds as the church has gone into in former periods: it is necessary that we form a new bond suited to our present circumstances. So the antient churches framed new creeds and confessions as new heresies rose. The truth of our Saviour's deity was plainly asserted in the apostle's Creed in these words, *I believe in Jesus Christ his* (the eternal Father's) *only Son, our Lord.* But Paulus Samosatenus and others attempted to overturn the scriptural doctrine of the Deity of Christ by new opinions about the constitution of his person, confounding the properties of the two natures. This occasioned the drawing up of the Creed which bears the following title: *A determination of the bishops assembled in the Synod at Antioch concerning the incarnation of the word of God, Son of*

X

"they were incapable at the time of their baptism, being then in their infancy, of giving the church that solemn and public testimony of their adherence to her faith, it was judged necessary that as soon as they had passed the period of childhood, they should be brought by the parents before the bishop who might examine them according to the catechism or form of sound words then in use. Hence the church of Rome derived her pretended sacrament of confirmation. The brethren of Bohemia, too, imitated this ancient custom: Among them, the parents presented their children at twelve years of age, to the pastor of the church, that the children might make a public profession of their faith, and that it might appear whether the parents had performed their engagements which they had come under at the baptism of their children. A similar practice obtains in the church of England. It is indeed a pity but it were likewise customary in our own churches, to make those whom we admit to the sacred communion, profess the Lord in the most explicit manner before the whole church: Those who refuse, on this or the other vain pretence, to make such a profession even before the eldership or privately to the pastor, would do well to remember what our Lord has denounced against such as are ashamed of his word." *Exercitat. De fide Salvifica.*

the Father; and that Synod's determination with regard to Paulus Samosatenus. The Creed itself begins in this manner: "We acknowledge our Lord Jesus "Christ who according to the Spirit was begotten "of the Father before time, but according to the "flesh was born of the virgin in the last days; be- "ing one person consisting of the heavenly divinity "and of human flesh." After a variety of consi- derations serving to distinguish between the two na- tures in the person of Christ, the conclusion is to the following purpose: "By the above distinctions and "explications we do not mean any division of that "one undivided person; but only to shew that there "is no confusion of the distinguishing properties of "of the flesh and of the eternal word; at the same "time that we hold what regards the undivided uni- "on of the two natures."

Toward the beginning of the fourth century, Arius made a new attack upon the scriptural doctrine of the trinity. He indeed allowed the Son to be in some sense God: but then he denied that he was co- essential or co-eternal with the Father. It was his great maxim, ην ποτε, οτι ουκ ην. The church was not contented, upon this occasion, with the assertion of our Saviour's Deity in former creeds. Something pointed against the novelties of the Arian heresy was requisite. Hence the council of Nice in Bythinia, consisting of members sent from all parts of the Chris- tian world, agreed (though neither the bishop of Rome nor his legate were there to procure such a- greement) upon a new creed, condemning the er- rors of Arius, and asserting the contrary truths. "We believe," says that venerable council, "in one "God Father Almighty, Maker of all things visible "and invisible: And in one Lord Jesus Christ, "the Son of God, the only begotten of the Father, "that is, of the substance of the Father, God of "God, light of light, true God of true God; be-

" gotten, not made; of the same substance with the
" Father; by whom all things were made, both in
" heaven and on earth; who for us men and for
" our salvation descended, was incarnate, became
" man, suffered, rose on the third day, went up in-
" to the heavens, and is to come to judge the living
" and the dead. And we believe in the Holy Ghost.
" But as to those who say, that there was a time
" when the Son of God did not exist, that he was
" not before his birth, that he was made of nothing,
" that he is of another substance or essence than the
" Father, or that he is created, or that he is subject
" to modification or change; the catholic and apos-
" tolic church holds them accursed."

SOME of the artifices that are used in our own times, to prejudice people against the forms that have been found necessary in going about covenanting, are only a repetition of the artifices which some of the more subtle and refined Arians employed to draw the unwary from the doctrine of the Nicene Creed. The credit of so scriptural a testimony to the truth being much established by a council held in the year 359 at Ariminum in Italy, the Arians finding it impracticable to set it aside altogether, had recourse to another expedient. They tried to render such terms in the Creed as were pointed the most directly against the Arian opinions odious and detestable to the people. Valens and Ursacius, two leaders of the party, pretended an uncommon zeal for the peace and unity of the church: " Ay," said they, " the peace and unity of the church might
" easily be restored, were it not for two or three
" hard words," such as, *essence, consubstantial*, and *subsistence*. " These same hard words," continued the artful haranguers; " do much harm, as they are
" an occasion of stumbling to the weak and ignor-
" ant who cannot understand them: and why should
" we think it necessary to retain them, since they are

" not to be found in the Bible? Let us hold the
" doctrine of the Bible; and let us drop the obnoxi-
" ous terms."* By so specious pretences they sub-
verted the faith of many.

About twenty years after the Council at Arminium, another was held at Constantinople. The immediate occasion of it was the heresy which Macedonius bishop of Constantinople had newly broached denying the deity of the Holy Ghost. This council framed a new Confession of the church's faith as a proper way of repelling the new attack that was now made upon it. The first part of that Confession or Creed is a repetition of the Nicene; a circumstance that shewed how careful the Council was to hold fast what the church had attained. The latter part again, is a scriptural assertion of the truth pointed expresly against the error of Macedonius. " We believe," says the Council in the name of the church, " in the
" Holy Ghost, the Lord, the quickner, who pro-
" ceedeth from the Father, who is worshipped and
" glorified with the Father and the Son, who spoke
" by the prophets."

Various other Creeds might be produced; particularly, that of Athanasius, which is a fuller exhibition of the church's faith in opposition to the above mentioned and various other errors: but what we have said may serve to shew how analogous they were to the form of words used in covenanting.

How far the subscriptions to the Emperor Zeno's Henoticon or epistle recommending unity †, resembled public covenanting, the reader may judge from the following account of it. This epistle was published in the year 470, when the church was much distracted by the errors of Nestorius, on the one hand, who held the two natures of Christ to be two persons,

---

* Forbesii Instruct. Hist. lib. i. Cap. 2. § 7.

‡ See a Copy of the Epistle taken from Evagrius, Forbesii Inst. Histor. Lib. iii. Cap. 10.

and of Eutyches, on the other, who, confounding the perperties of the two natures, held them to be one. The Emperor in this epistle confirms several of the Creeds and Confessions of the church, and condemns the contrary errors. Toward the close he expresses himself to this effect: " Sensible that neither the or-
" thodox churches any where, nor the godly priests
" set over them, nor our empire have received or
" do receive any creed or article of faith, in the way
" of relinquishing the holy doctrine we have men-
" tioned concerning the trinity and the person of
" Christ; we have declared ourselves one with the
" orthodox churches as to that doctrine. We have
" written these things, not that we mean to bring
" any thing new into the faith of the church, but
" that we may give you full assurance of our adhe-
" rence to sound doctrine." Here the Emperor professes himself a church-member, declaring himself one with the holy bishops and people to whom he addresses his epistle. He specifies particular truths which he approves, and particular errors which he condemns. He gives his fellow-church members the fullest assurance of his attachment to sound doctrine. The orthodox generally subscribed this epistle. What meant that subscription? Surely, that the subscriber gave his fellow-church-members the like assurances, as the Emperor had done, of his unfeigned stedfastness in the faith, and of his opposition to the mentioned errors. The analogy of such subscription to public covenanting is worthy of observation.

Some objections might be made to this epistle, and perhaps more to the character and views of Zeno. Considered however as an effort to unite Christians in the defence of the truth, the epistle is highly commendable. An eminent writer of ecclesiastical history, indeed, charges the Emperor with favouring the Eutychian heresy. But in this epistle, though the Council of Chalcedon is not named, the confounding of the two natures in the person of Christ is as expresly condemned as the dividing of them: Eutyches is branded as a heretic no less than Nestorius.

In the sixth and following centuries the Papal tyranny was advancing to its height. Hence the church of Christ, with respect to the purity both of her faith and her practice, was brought into retirement and obscurity. The church, as she is represented in the 12th chapter of the Revelation, began to sojourn in the wilderness. Yet in this period, dark and dismal as it continued till the dawn of the reformation, we have several instances of the Lord raising up eminent men to bear testimony to the truth; Chalemagne, for example, toward the close of the eighth century, who wrote so well against the idolatrous use of images; and Berengarius who made so vigorous a stand against the doctrine of transubstantiation. We see noble examples of meekness, of patience, of humility, of self-denial, of unshaken fortitude and persevering faithfulness in maintaining the cause of Christ, of the efficacy of divine truth, and of the constraining influence of the love of Christ, in what is handed down to us concerning the Wickliffites and Lollards in England, and concerning the Hussites, the brethren and sisters (as they were called) in Bohemia. But we can hardly expect to find any distinct and formal examples of public covenanting, (a duty almost impracticable, but in an organized and regular state of the church) among the Waldenses, the Wickliffites, or the brethren of Bohemia, *who feared continually every day because of the oppressor who was ready to destroy.* While the church was in a poor captive condition at Babylon, she could not well either sing the songs of Zion, or go about public covenanting.

Of several of the Reformed Churches.

WHOEVER considers the state of Europe at the beginning of the sixteenth century; how deeply men were sunk in ignorance and superstition; how firmly the Papal dominion was established; how it had found means to spread its roots through all the temporal and eternal concerns of mankind; how artfully the Popish religion suited itself to the taste of depraved human nature; whoever duly considers these and other circumstances, will readily acknowledge, that the reformation from Popery was nearly as difficult as the reformation from Paganism had been; and that Erasmus, humanly speaking, had some reason to say, that Luther undertook what the apostles themselves would hardly have undertaken. But it was the Lord's doing, and it was wondrous in our eyes.

As the first reformers had many difficulties to overcome, as they had crafty and powerful enemies on every side, it was necessary for them to act as one body, and to use the proper means of preserving their union, and of ascertaining it in such a manner as would beget sincere confidence among themselves. It was one of the most obvious of these means to enter into a league or covenant. Accordingly the Smalcaldic league was concluded soon after Luther had shaken off the yoke of papal authority, and declared his full and final separation from Antichrist. The occasion of that solemn engagement was as follows.

THE Emperor Charles the fifth, a prince of unbounded ambition, set himself to check the progress of reformation, and to hinder the spreading of that pure doctrine, which now seemed a novelty by reason of the long continued custom and prescription which the grossest corruptions had obtained. The Emperor's resentment against Luther did not proceed from any great regard he had for the Pope: against whom in the year 1527, he carried his victorious arms to the city of Rome itself: Rome was taken, was plundered; the pope and his cardinals being forced to suffer all the contumely and ill usage that military insolence is accustomed to exercise.* Charles indeed opposed the proceedings of Luther, only because he was afraid that the religious factions at home would hinder him from the prosecution of his great designs of conquest, and of empire abroad.

IN a diet or meeting of the Germanic princes held at Worms in the year 1521, after Luther had been teased in vain to retract the doctrine he had propagated in his writings; no other argument having been used for his conviction, even according to the account of Maimbourg the Jesuit, than this; that his doctrine had been condemned by Councils, particularly, by that of Constance; the Emperor caused an edict to be read to the diet, in which he expressed his resolution to support the religion which he had received from the emperors and the kings his predecessors, and which a poor apostate monk † was endeavouring to overturn: he then declared Luther a schismatick and a heretic whom it was unlawful to receive or protect.

THOUGH a diet held at Spires about five years after, averawed on the one hand, by the growing

---

* Maimbourg in the second book of his history of Lutheranism, gives a very pathetic account of this sack of Rome. An emblem, we hope, of the final ruin that still awaits the mother of harlots and abominations of the earth.

† Un miserable Moine apostat. The kings and great men of the world have always been offended at the cross of Christ. Herod and Charles the fifth were of the same mind. The one set the master, the other the servant at nought. Maimbourg Hist. Du Lutheranisme.

strength of the reformers, and afraid on the other, of the Turkish arms now threatening the empire, seemed to allow every one the free exercise of religion, till a general or at least a national council should be called to determine the differences about religion: yet the diet at the same place in the year 1529, made a new decree confirming the above mentioned edict of Worms; ordaining that the princes, while they waited the calling of a general council, should endeavour the re establishment of the ancient religion, wherever the new had obtained; that the Mass should not be abolished, nor the Catholicks (for so the Papists call themselves) hindered from the free exercise of their religion; that none of those Catholicks should be allowed to profess Luther's religion; that the Sacramentarians (so the followers of Zuinglius and Carolstad were called) should be banished the empire; and in fine, that ministers should no where be allowed to preach the gospel, otherwise than according to the received opinions of the church of Rome. John the Elector of Saxony, George marquis of Brandenburg, the two dukes of Lunenburg, the landgrave of Hesse, the prince of Anhalt, and the deputies from fourteen cities of the Empire, protested against the determination of the diet, as being intended to put an entire stop to the reformation. From this time the reformers, on account of that solemn protestation, were called PROTESTANTS.

In the following year, a diet of the empire was held at Augsburg, in which the Protestant princes laid before the Emperor a confession of their faith, which Melanchton is said to have drawn up in the softest terms. This representation of the reformed religion is commonly known by the name of the Augsburg Confession. The Protestants however, gained nothing. The diet was concluded with a decree, that the Catholic or Popish religion alone should be exercised all over the empire: forbidding all ranks of persons, under severe penalties, to change any thing, in the doctrine, in the usages and ceremonies of the church, till it should be otherwise ordained by a council.

The Protestants alarmed by a such decree, were apprehensive that the Emperor, and his brother Ferdinand, and the rest of the Popish princes who had been present at the diet, would unite their arms to crush the reformation. On that account, the protestant princes assembled at Smalcald in the territory of the Landgrave of Hesse, in order to deliberate on the measures which their situation required. It was here that they entered unanimously into a solemn league that they would exert themselves to the utmost in the defence of one another against all that should trouble them in the exercise of their Evangelical religion. They solicited the cities of the empire which had embraced the reformed religion to come into their covenant; and the most part of the cities came into it.

Should it be said, that the Smalcaldic league was merely of a political nature, and therefore, not an example of the covenanting for which we plead: we answer, that there were at least two things in it, which may lead us to consider it as a religious covenant. One is, that those who joined in this league plainly declared their agreement in several particular points of truth and duty, as being the testimony of Christ in their day. This is plain from their unanimous approbation of the Augsburg Confession, from the details of religious grievances which they laid before several diets of the Empire, and from their engagement to defend the Evangelical religion as opposed to the corruptions of Popery. The other thing is, that they declared their adherence to those points as what they were warranted and required to hold by the authority of God's word. This appeared not only from the tenor of the league, but from all their petitions and remonstrances to Charles or to the council of the Empire, and from their answers to the declarations of the Pope's legate; in which they constantly appealed to the scripture as the only standard by which they could ever consent to have their tenets tried and examined. We cannot conclude this league to have been merely political, because it may be viewed as a prudential measure necessary for their political safety; in regard that it is often our true interest even in this world to cleave to the Lord in the way of duty; nor is it necessary to view it as merely political, because those who joined in it, engaged to use external means of preserving themselves and their states; since the use of such means, as a duty of God's word, might be engaged to in any religious exercise. Though this league was professedly gone into from a regard to God's authority, with a single eye to his glory, for the preservation and advancement of the Evangelical religion, to suppose that nothing more was meant than to forward political views, and to promote a worldly interest, is a reproach which one would never expect to hear from any who have a sincere regard for the character of those reformers.

Our Reformers from Popery took every opportunity of shewing how sensible they were of the propriety of entering into bonds for securing mutual confidence both in the profession of the truth, and in their opposition to the common enemy. Hence the concordate which Bucer and Melanchton drew up with a view to settle the differences between Luther and Oecolampadius concerning the sacrament. Hence, too, the following transaction between Calvin and the church of Zurich. It had been reported that Calvin's doctrine with respect to the Lord's Supper, differed from what was taught by the ministers of that church. Calvin, desiring to leave no room for suspicion on that head, goes to Zurich and converses on the subject with the ministers there. The result of their conversation was a formula or confession of faith drawn up by Calvin and Bullinger, one of the ministers of Zurich; which confession was approved afterward by the churches of Switzerland, and of Rhetia.* "By this bond," says Melchior Adams in his life of Bullinger, "not "only these churches were united more closely; but "many good men even in other places were the more "established in the profession of the truth."

BESIDES, the necessity of such religious bonds is acknowledged in the custom which has prevailed universally among the Protestant churches, of requiring their members to subscribe their several confessions of faith. Some have complained of this custom as incroaching on the right of private judgment. But it has been sufficiently vindicated on the same principle on which we plead for public covenanting; which principle is, that some such method of ascertaining our religious persuasion to one another, is absolutely necessary to an union of our endeavours in support of any particular points of truth or duty.

A CHURCH declares her public judgment in her Confessions and Covenants. And for a person to become a member of that church is to profess an agreement between his private judgment, and her public judgment: So far then as there is such agreement, he is to be accounted a member of that church; no farther. Hence it appears that we no more offend against private judgment, in subscribing the confessions and covenants, than in being avowed members of the reformed churches.

THE seven United Provinces have shewn their sense of the advantages of public covenanting. They entered into a solemn confederacy in defence of their liberty and of the Protestant religion against Philip II. and supported that confederacy with a vigour, a perseverance and success, which will be remembered for ever, as an encouragement to a generous people, in struggling for those rights and privileges, which

---

* Rhetia the country of the Grisons on the Alps, near the Hyrcinian forrest.

being the gift of heaven, are never to be surrendered to any prince, or pope, or prelate.

AFTERWARD, when the provinces were very much distracted by the controversy with the Arminians, and nearly involved in the horrors of a civil war, the Synod of Dort was held. Divines were invited to that assembly, not only from the United Provinces, but also from Britain, from the Palatinate, from Brandenburg, from Hesse, from Embden, and several other places. Various were the advantages which rose from the Synod of Dort. The Calvinist doctrine in opposition to the Arminians, was clearly ascertained: the union of the adherents to that evangelical doctrine, was greatly promoted, not only in the seven provinces, but in every Protestant country. In these provinces, particularly, the Calvinists being strengthened and encouraged, their adversaries found themselves unable to carry on their designs against them, and civil discord began to subside. The shifts and artifices by which the Arminians used to disguise their tenets being now fully laid open by the Synod, and those who defended its decisions, many of the Arminians became votaries of Socinianism, and all of them were seen verging to that blasphemous extreme. So beneficial is the unanimous, and unequivocal appearance of church-members on the side of truth and duty.

THE Protestants in France, too, found it necessary to enter into such engagements. In the former part of the last century, which was the time of their greatest purity and faithfulness, the oath of union was sworn and subscribed by all the deputies of the reformed churches of France assembled in the National Synod at Privas, in Vivaretz. "We have," say they, " in the name of all our churches, and for their
" their good, and for the service of their Majesties,
" sworn and protested, and we do swear and protest,
" (promising also our utmost endeavour that these
" very self same protestations shall be ratified in and

" by all our provinces) to remain inseparably united
" and conjoined in that Confession of Faith of the
" reformed churches of this kingdom read in this
" Synod, approved and ratified by every one of us,
" swearing not only in our own name, but also in the
" respective names of all the churches of our pro-
" vinces which have deputed us unto the Synod,
" that we will live and die in it. As also we protest,
" in our own and their names, to keep inviolably
" that ecclesiastical discipline established in the re-
" formed churches of this kingdom, and to see its
" cannons observed for the better government of
" these our churches, and the reformation of life
" and manners: acknowledging that it is most a-
" greeable to God's holy word, whose authority is
" supreme."*

INDEED, there are none of the Protestant churches, that have not entered into oaths and covenants,
either more or less explicit, to cleave to the Lord in
the profession of the reformed religion.

Of the rise and progress of Public Covenanting in Scotland.

THE influence of the ambitious and bigoted house of Lorrain, was a chief obstacle to the reformation in Scotland. After the death of James the fifth, his Queen Dowager, who was of that Popish family, having got the administration of the government into her hands, was at length brought wholly under the direction of her French relations, and was led by their counsels into a series of measures as contrary to civil liberty and public faith as to the true religion. Hence our reformers had to contend for their political rights, as well as for the gospel and the pure worship of God: Hence both the

---

* Quick's Synodicon, Acts of the Synod of Privs, Chap. iii.

Of Public Covenanting.

good of the nation and of the church are evidently meant in the various covenants which we are going to mention.

It was in the year 1557, that the friends of the reformation, among whom were several of high rank, first entered into a common bond. In this bond they " promise to apply themselves to forward and esta- " blish the most blessed word of God and his con- " gregation; to have faithful ministers to minister " Christ's gospel and sacraments to his people. Un- " to the holy word," say they, " and congregation " we do join us; and so do forsake and renounce " the congregation of Satan, with all the superstiti- " ous abominations and idolatry thereof."

From this time the Protestants went under the name of the Congregation.

A memorable incident in 1559, hastened on the Reformation. Much people in Perth having embraced the reformed religion, were desirous of being better instructed in it by the faithful preachers of the word. One day as the people were just come from hearing the famous Mr. John Knox, who had been setting before them the heinousness of Popish idolatry, a priest, in contempt of such doctrine, invited them to witness the celebration of the Mass. A boy observing the priest cried out; " Shall we " suffer the practice of that idolatry which the word " of God so plainly condemns?" The enraged priest struck the boy. The former having so much forgotten the dignity of his character, the latter seemed at liberty to disregard it, and threw a stone at him. Mean time, the resentment of the people who were looking on, was raised to the highest pitch by the impudence of the Popish idolator. They flew to pull down his altar, and to lay all its gaudy ornaments in the dust. After that, they proceeded to destroy other monuments of idolatry.

Suppose these buildings to have had as much elegant design and masterly execution as the noblest e-

difices of antient Grece: Suppose too, that the people had so much knowledge of architecture, and correctness of taste as would have been necessary to make them set a just value on such works; yet after all, considering that they had been the haunts of lewdness, of the grossest superstition and idolatry; considering that their pomp and splendor had been used as a mean of diverting the poor people's attention from the simplicity of God's word; of leading them to take up with outward shew instead of spiritual worship; and consequently, of detaining them in that ignorance by which their souls were ruined; considering these circumstances, we need not wonder at the zeal of our forefathers to destroy the structures which they now saw had been subservient to such mischievous purposes, however valuable they might have been as works of art. "Men's consci-
"ences," says Mr. Knox, "were so beaten with the
"word, that they had no respect to their own par-
"ticular profit, but only to abolish idolatry, the pla-
"ces and monuments thereof."

The Queen regent, pretended the greatest resentment for the loss of so many fine buildings; but in reality was grieved that her schemes, or rather those of the house of Lorrain, were likely to be ruined by the rapid progress of the reformation.

She vowed revenge; and sent against Perth Monsieur D'Oysel with some troops which had lately come over from France. That commander having approached within a few miles of the town, had intelligence of such numbers coming in daily to the assistance of the inhabitants, that he thought it was by no means adviseable to make an attack. A treaty was set on foot. The Queen regent, as the situation of her affairs required, gave her promise, that the people should not be molested for what they had done in destroying the religious houses; that they should be allowed the free exercise of their religion; and that she should withdraw the French soldiers immediately. But the Lords of the Congregation suspecting these promises, and fearing the dangers they were still exposed to, entered into a second covenant at Perth, the last day of May, in the year 1559; and bound themselves anew "to endeavour the putting "away of all things that dishonour God's name; "and that they will not spare labours, goods, sub- "stances, and lives, in maintaining the liberty of "the whole congregation and every member of it."

The fears of the Queen regent's insincerity were but too well grounded. As soon as she had entered the town, her Frenchmen discharged their musquets; the son of Patrick Murray, a zealous member of the congregation, was killed. When the Queen heard of his death, she made a reply, which does no great honour to her feelings: "It is a pity it was not the "father; but such is the will of fortune."* Contrary to the article of treaty about withdrawing her troops, she left in the town a number of mercenaries to re-establish the Romish superstition, and to overawe the reformers. When it was represented to her, that this was a breach of the treaty, she replied that the article on that head related to French soldiers only. But the Protestants insisting, that those were to be reckoned French soldiers who were in French pay, she told them plainly, that the performance of promises was not to be exacted of princes with too much rigour: That no faith was to be kept with heretics: "Nay," added our Catholic heroine, "had "I as fair a pretext for the deed, I would not leave "an individual of the heretical tribe, either his for- "tune or his life." Her conduct proved too well her adherence to these maxims.

Z

---

* According to Mr. Knox, a little before her death, the French troops having killed a number of the Scots and English in a skirmish at the siege of Leith, took the dead bodies and with the stupid wantonness of cruelty, laid them out, as public spectacles, upon the walls. "Charming sight," said the Queen regent as she beheld them, "were all the fields between Edinburgh and Leith covered "with the same tapestry!"

SOME time afterwards, at St. Andrews she made a truce with the Lords of the congregation which was to continue for eight days; in which time she was to draw her soldiers to the other side of the Forth; and to send Commissioners to St. Andrew's, in order to treat with the Congregation concerning a peace. She withdrew the soldiers; but sent no Commissioners.

AFTER various changes in the Queen regent's affairs, at last on the 24th day July, she thought proper to agree with the Lords of the congregation, that as, on the one hand, the Protestants should have the free exercise of their religion, and no military force should be kept at Edinburgh; so, on the other hand, the Papists should not be molested on account of religion; the priests should be allowed to receive their dues, as usual, from the people; and no one should attempt pulling down any more churches, monastries, or other buildings consecrated to the purposes of the Popish religion.

As the Lords of the congregation had still nothing to expect, but that the Queen regent would seize the first opportunity that offered itself, to destroy them and their adherents; so they entered into a new bond suitable to their circumstances, for mutual defence, and for the maintainance of the true religion. In this they engage, that none of them should correspond with the Queen Dowager, either by letters or by word of mouth, without the knowledge and consent of the rest; and that as soon as a letter should come from her to any one of them, he should not delay to acquaint them all with it: a necessary engagement on account of the underhand methods that were taken to separate them from one another. This bond was subscribed at Stirling on the first day of August, in the year 1559.

THE Queen regent, sometimes on one pretence, sometimes on another, continued to harass the congregation. Having fortified Leith, she distressed the whole country round by her French soldiers, who never ceased making excursions and plundering wherever they came. The Protestants called in the English to their assistance. The Frenchmen were besieged in Leith by the confederate army of the Scots and English amounting to about 8000. Mr. Knox hints that the French were 4000.

While the siege was carried on with various success, the nobility, the barons, and gentlemen professing Christ Jesus in Scotland, and several others that joined with them for expelling the French, entered into another covenant for reformation, called the last bond, at Leith. In this bond they promise, as formerly, to set forward, all they can, the reformation of religion, to hasten the expulsion of the French whom they call strangers and oppressors of their liberty; to regard the common cause as the cause of every one of them in particular; and the cause of every one, being lawful and honest, as the cause of them all in general.‡ This bond was subscribed on the 27th of April in the year 1560.

The nation continued to groan under Popish tyranny, and under the oppression of a foreign military force, till the death of the Queen regent; which happened in the 9th day of June in the year 1560.

After the death of the Queen regent, all parties, English, Scots, and French, were desirous of putting an end to the war. Accordingly, a peace was concluded soon after; and the French and English armies quitted Scotland. The parliament was immediately assembled to enquire into the state of the nation, and to take the necessary measures both with respect to religion, and with respect to the se-

---

‡ A sentiment which shews that our Reformers had the justest views of the nature and perfection of society, and of the obligations arising from it. The words here used, are perhaps the best definition, any where to be met with, of that social liberty which ought to be so dear to every state and to every church.

curity of their civil rights. A fuller parliament perhaps never met in Scotland. The subjects to be canvassed on this occasion, and the objects to be secured were in the highest degree interesting to all ranks of men; and therefore no wonder, that hardly a baron who had the least claim to a seat, was absent.

THE attention of the parliament was called to the consideration of religion by a petition from the Protestants. The petition being considered, the parliament appointed the ministers and the barons to draw up articles of the doctrine, which they resolved to maintain, and which they wished the parliament to establish. That the ministers and barons cheerfully executed; and within four days laid before the parliament, the sum of Christian doctrine, commonly called, the Scots Confession of Faith. It was immediately approved and ratified. Two acts were likewise passed in favour of the reformed religion; the one forbidding the celebration of the Mass; the other abolishing the Pope's authority in Scotland. Some objected to the validity of what was done by this parliament; because the Queen was not present, nor any one to represent her, but in vain; for the readiness of the people to receive its acts, shewed that it had the general consent of the nation; which might well supply the place of the Queen's approbation in her absence. It is preposterous to confine the generous efforts of a people toward establishing a system of liberty, to those rules and forms which are applicable only to a settled state of society.

THUS was the Protestant religion established in Scotland, when Mary, upon the death of her husband, Francis II. came to the throne. In the beginning of her reign moderation seemed to prevail in her administration: and though she continued to have the Popish worship in her own chappel, she forbore persecuting the professors of the reformed religion, nor did she hinder them from avowing openly their endeavours to propagate the truth. But in 1569 she began to alter her conduct; and guided by the house of Guise, she was thought to have designed a mischief to the Protestant Interest; when holy providence which over-rules the wickedness of men to the good of his people, ordered it so that the assassination of Mary's favourite Rizio, the murder of Darnly whom she had advanced to share the royalty with her only eighteen months before, and her infamous marriage a very short time after to the Earl of Bothwell, the supposed murderer of her husband, falling out, occasioned the loss of all her influence and authority, and put it out of her power to hurt the church of God.

AFTERWARD Mary, while a prisoner in the castle of Lochleven, was forced to subscribe a deed, resigning her crown and kingdom to her son, and committing the administration during his minority, to the Earl of Murray. Encouraged by the example and authority of the good regent, as the Earl was generally called, the reformation was carried on without interruption. The church had her assemblies every year; order and government were established agreeable to the simplicity of the New Testament; the ministers of the word shewed a becoming firmness and freedom in bearing testimony for the truth, and in reproving sin. In a word, shedding light and comfort among her friends, and terror among her enemies, she began to *to look forth fair as the moon, clear as the sun, and terrible as an army with banners.*

IN the year 1680 and 1681, the greater part of the nation and those of the highest rank having embraced the reformed religion, the way was prepared for national covenanting. It cannot be denied that a father may bring his family, as Jonadab did the Rechabites, under obligations to any thing lawful, that is, which is consistent with their duty, and with the liberty and welfare of society. This obligation on the Rechabites from Jonadab's command, was not owing to the peculiar dispensation of religion under the Old Testament; for, dwelling in tents and abstinence from wine, were things of a purely civil nature, and had no reference to the then state of the church. But why should we insist; since we are daily witnesses of parents bringing obligations upon their children in the ordinance of baptism; obligations, too, which are materially the same with those of the covenants and confessions of the Protestant churches? Why, then, may not the greater and better part of a nation do with regard to the whole, what every Christian parent is allowed to do with regard to his children?

POPULAR discontents should seldom be quite overlooked by those in authority; both because they are generally founded in truth, and because the measures that may be necessary for the removal of them, often prove in other respects, the most beneficial. James who was now about sixteen years of age had taken a fondness for a young nobleman whom he had created Earl of Lennox: but the nobleman was a Papist. In order to satisfy the people who could not bear to see the king lavish his favours upon an enemy of the reformed religion, Lennox made a public and solemn recantation of Popery in one of the churches of Edinburgh. But the jealousies of the people were revived by a prevailing report that the Pope had granted dispensations to his votaries to say or subscribe any thing, however heretical; provided they were still attached in their hearts to the Papal interest. James understanding that, ordered one of his preachers to compose a short Confession of Faith in opposition to Popery, and particularly, to the above mentioned dispensations. Then was the National Covenant written; and soon after publicly sworn and subscribed by the king, and by his court and council. Eager to imitate the royal example, and obedient to the direction of the Assembly in 1581, all ranks of people flocked to the taking of the Covenant.

This national covenanting was peculiarly seasonable; as, at that time, the most confiderable of the Popish powers were generally known to have entered into a league for the extirpation of the Protestant religion.

James had a strong aversion for Presbyterian government as being altogether unfavourable to the great object of his pursuit, absolute power; for experience tells us that presbytery and civil liberty must always go hand in hand. Hence he laboured to bring into the church a set of bishops, whom he might consider as his own creatures and obsequious dependents. Though the reformation was retarded by this circumstance; yet the assembly in the year 1592, having agreed upon the plan of church government by Kirk-sessions, Presbyteries, Synods and General Assemblies, obtained the establishment of it by an act of Parliament. Indeed the church continued to make some progress in reformation, till toward the end of the year 1596. In this period we have two instances more of Scotland giving herself to the Lord in solemn covenanting.

The Lord having delivered our land with an outstretched arm from a Spanish Armada and other threatening dangers, our fathers expressed their gratitude to him who was their Saviour in the time of trouble, by renewing the National Covenant in 1590, subscribing along with it a general bond for the preservation of the Protestant religion and of the King's Majesty.

A rumour in 1596, of great war-like preparations which Philip of Spain was said to be making, filled the nation with apprehensions of an invasion. At the same time, the partial regard that James shewed to some Papists of the greatest rank and influence, led many to fear the designs of the Popish party at home. The Assembly therefore having taken the state of the kingdom into consideration, appointed a day of public fasting: it proved a day much to be remembered for a plentiful out-pouring of the Holy Spirit, leading ministers, nobles, and burgesses to lament after the Lord, to acknowledge with many tears the breach of former engagements, and to enter anew into their solemn covenant with the Lord. This covenanting was conducted by the church alone without any mandate of king or of parliament.

But after this, the scene began to be changed. James's king-craft, his flattery, and his tampering with the consciences of men prevailed to turn many aside from a strict adherence to the purity of our Lord's institutions.

As on the one hand, a tame submission to a single instance of usurpation, however small it may seem, will only serve to allure an ambitious prince to attempt farther usurpations; so on the other hand, when ministers or other church-members fall into that snare which the fear of man bringeth, it is often long before they recover themselves out of it. Long indeed, and lamentable was the following train of incroachments on that freedom that Christ has given to his church, and on the simplicity and spirituality of that divine worship which he has appointed in his word.

James's first attempt was to restrain the freedom of ministers in testifying publicly against his own sinful practices: an intimation that he resolved from that time to suffer no controul in the pursuit of his schemes from the reproofs of God's word. Toward the close of the year 1596, he required the ministers (threatening them with the loss of their stipends, if they refused) to subscribe a bond acknowledging him the sovereign judge of treasonable or seditious expressions in their sermons. Though many had the faithfulness to resist the temptation, yet there were not a few who complied.

In the next place, he found means to have packed assemblies, in which all was carried according to his own heart. In one of these he got it ordained, that ministers should not meet for the exercise of church government and discipline without his consent.

Again, he held out a very taking bait: he pretended it was a great loss to the church that she had no minister to represent her in parliament; to offer her petitions, and to see that no measure should be taken to her prejudice. The proposal for having some ministers chosen for that purpose was quickly passed into a law, and approved of by one of James's own assemblies. To the clergymen who by this law sate and voted in parliament, the king afterward gave the title of Bishops.

He laboured to give them the power, too. A little after his accession to the throne of England, they were made constant Moderators in Synods and Presbyteries: but they became formidable indeed, when the two Arch-bishops of Glasgow and St. Andrew's were each of them, with some nobles and gentlemen, authorised to hold a court of high commission, and to excommunicate fine, and imprison all whose religious principles or manners were offensive to them. Episcopacy having tried all its trimming foothing arts in vain, now began to shake the dreadful dart of persecution.

At length James carried his point so far, that his own absolute power in the church, and, which was entirely subservient to it, the power of the bishops were secured both by acts of parliament and by the oaths which ministers were required to take at their ordination.

Farther still: he attempted to introduce a number of superstitious ceremonies, under the colour of an Assembly's appointment: The Assembly we mean, was at Perth in 1618; the members being mostly the King's creatures, and Spotiswood Arch-bishop of Glasgow the Moderator. Such was the meeting wherein were passed the famous five articles with regard to kneeling at the Lord's Supper, private communicating, private baptism, confirmation of children, and the observation of holy days. These articles were afterwards ratified by an act of parliament.

Thus far had James advanced in the scheme of establishing Episcopacy and arbitrary government in Scotland; when Charles succeeding to the crown, entered fully into his father's views, and prosecuted them with all the enthusiasm of a superstitious bigot.

By the time that Charles ascended the throne, the pretence of introducing innovations by the consent of General Assemblies was grown quite obsolete and thread-bare. All men saw that the king modelled these assemblies, and directed their proceedings in a manner contrary to the rights and the liberty of the church: so that their acts were disregarded as of no force nor authority.* Charles therefore found it an useless expedient; and full of the grandeur and universal efficacy of his prerogative, he deemed it unnecessary.

The following instance of his behaviour toward the parliament of Scotland deserves our notice. While he was in Scotland in the year 1633, having called the parliament, he brought in two bills; one declaring his Majesty's Sovereign authority over all estates, persons, and causes whatsoever; and that the power of prescribing an habit to church-men should reside in him and his successors for ever: the other for the confirmation of all the acts and statutes that had been made before with regard to the church.

---

* That many Presbyteries, as well as particular ministers, expressly disowned the authority and constitution of the several pretended Assemblies in this period, is sufficiently demonstrated in Mr. Wilson's Defence, chapter iii. § 3.

Of Public Covenanting.

The members declared that so far as the first of the bills respected his Majesty's prerogative, they agreed to it; but they dissented from what was added about the apparel of church-men; as they apprehended it might open the way for introducing the surplice. But Charles would admit of no distinctions. "I must "have your yes," said he, "or your no to the "whole bill." The question being put, he marked the votes with his own hand. The clerk having counted them, declared that it was carried in the affirmative. "That we deny," cried some of the members. His Majesty then interposed, saying; "The clerk's declaration shall stand, unless one of "you will come to the bar, and at the peril of his "life, accuse me of falsifying the record of parlia- "ment." The truth is, it was carried in the negative, thirteen lords and the majority of the commons voting against it. Charles's treatment of the parliament would perhaps have passed unnoticed in the dark ages of ignorance and superstition; but by this time men had acquired too enlarged ideas of their natural rights and liberties, to suffer any flagrant violation of them without resentment.

Afterward, he began to impose what he thought proper upon the church without troubling himself about the consent of parliament.

He first sent down to Scotland a book of canons, commanding all arch-bishops, bishops, and others exercising ecclesiastical jurisdiction, to see them punctually observed. These canons were designed to overturn altogether the Presbyterian constitution, and to form the church of Scotland entirely upon the model of the English church.

The next point he laboured was to bring the church of Scotland to make use of a public liturgy or book of common prayer; the same as that used in England with a very few alterations. This roused the people effectually. While the accustomed forms of worship were used in their public assemblies every Lord's day, the bulk of them were not so sensible of the deviations from the Presbyterian order and from the liberty of the church in courts of judicature which they seldom have occasion to witness. But the case was altered indeed, when instead of that simple manner of worship by which they had been edified, they were every Sunday (for so the Sabbath was called in the Liturgy) to have the same dull unvaried repetition of morning and evening prayer, of litanies, collects, lessons, confessions, absolutions, responses, amens, creeds, and pater nosters. The clergy, therefore, no sooner offered to make use of the King's Book of Common Prayer, than the populace took the alarm; all was uproar and confusion. The discontents which some how or other had been smothered for about forty years past, now broke forth all of a sudden into an irresistible flame.

This tumult of the common people, which the better sort of the Presbyterians much disapproved of,* was followed by a firm and persevering but regular and deliberate opposition to the court-measures. A great many of the first rank joined in petitioning his Majesty for a redress of grievances; particularly, that he would not insist upon the use of the service book in Scotland, till he received farther information of the matter. This humble supplication was answered in the beginning of the year 1638 by Charles's proclamation; wherein he takes it upon himself to vindicate the imposing of the liturgy, and discharges the meetings of the nobility and gentry, under the pain of treason. After such a proclamation it was found necessary to take more decisive measures for carrying on the intended work of reformation. The noblemen, the gentry, the burgesses, the ministers met in several rooms.† They resolved upon renew-

* "These unhappy and ungodly violences," says Principal Baillie in one of his letters, "hurt our good cause."

† These were called TABLES.

ing the National Covenant. Without delay a writing was made out for that purpose. The writing consisted of three parts. The first was a copy of the national covenant: the next was a list of the various acts of parliament in favour of the reformation: the third was an accommodation of the covenant to the present circumstances, containing a disapprobation of the government of the church by diocesan bishops, and an engagement against the practice of the ceremonies which the court was now seeking to introduce into the worship of God. Such was the covenant so generally sworn and subscribed by all ranks in 1638. The subscription was begun in February, and spread in a very short time all over the kingdom. The people swore the covenant in most parishes with remarkable emotions, with many prayers and tears, all professing repentance and godly sorrow for their sins, especially for their breach of covenant with the Lord, in suffering the purity of his ordinances to be tainted by prelatical innovations.

Those who were witnesses of this covenanting, testified, that " the desire it wrought in the hearts " of his people approved it to be a special mean of " God's appointment for reclaiming the nation to " himself.

Here civil pains did nothing. The ministers who administred the covenant used no other arguments to persuade persons to take it, than such as were drawn from God's words. Nay, so far were the ministers from desiring to force any into their covenant, that they refused to admit some to that privilege.‡

The general truth, that it is lawful to bind ourselves by oath to maintain our profession of religion

---

‡ See Bailie's Letters, Vol. 1st, Page 66. Speaking of the subscription of the Covenant at Glasgow, he says; " All among us in" cline to subscribe.—With many sigh a and tear by all that people " the oath was made.—The Forsythes have subscribed, and almost " all who refused before. Some they will not have their hands."

as agreeable to the word of God, seems to have been allowed by all parties at that time. Hence the writings of that period in defence of the covenant appear always to take this principle for granted; and are for the most part taken up in vindicating the things engaged to in the covenant.

HENCE too, the King on his part, proposed that the people should subscribe the National Covenant with a bond expressing their loyalty to him. This subscription was generally refused; some, however, by the marquis of Hamiltoun, were prevailed on to subscribe.

THE design of the King's covenant, as they called it, was to secure the office of diocesan bishops in Scotland; for, said the marquis, it must now be understood as it was by those who took it in 1581, when Episcopacy was in the church. But yet the greater part even of those who yielded to his solicitations, denied that they considered themselves as under any obligation from the National Covenant to favour Episcopacy. So vain was Charles's attempt to force the National Covenant into the service of his Bishops.

IN November 1638, met the famous assembly at Glasgow, the marquis of Hamiltoun being present as the king's commissioner. That assembly abolished the office of diocesan bishops, and the articles of Perth; annulled all the assemblies that had been held since James's accession to the throne of England; restored and improved the plan of order and discipline which had been agreed upon in the time of John Knox; and overturned at once the whole fabric of Episcopal hierarchy, and of ceremonies which both James and Charles had laboured so long and so zealously to build.

THIS assembly gave a memorable testimony to the freedom and independency of the church by continuing to sit, after the Commissioner in the

King's n me had declared it difolved; a circumftance which, however many doubts and apprehenfions it occafioned to fome at that time, will reflect honour on the honefty and faithfulnefs of the members to the lateft pofterity.

WHEN the affembly's humble fupplication was read to his Majefty, he anfwered: " They have bro-
" ken my head; and now they offer to put on my
" cowl."

SOON after he exacted from the Scotfmen at court an oath, renouncing the Affembly and the Covenant; an oath in which they likewife promifed the King all the affiftance in their power againft their countrymen. And then he erected his royal ftandard at York, to which all the nobles and gentry of England were commanded to repair in order to oppofe the Scots, who were falfly reprefented as about to invade England. The Covenanters were now declared rebels, and nothing but war was thought proper for them.

IN the profecution of the war, Charles was very unfuccefsful; his mercenary troops were lukewarm in his caufe; the people of England, now beginning to be animated with the opening profpects of civil and religious liberty, were, many of them, ready to take part with the Scots. They all murmured at a war undertaken without money to carry it on, and without the confent of Parliament.

ON the contrary, the army of the Covenanters was wonderfully encouraged, believing that they were engaged in the Lord's caufe, and that his hand was with them. And with them it remarkably was, for the Lord is near to all them that call upon him. In the hiftory of mankind there is hardly to be found an example of foldiers being fo diligent in the pure worfhip of God as the armed Covenanters were on this occafion. One who had the leaft real tafte for the exercifes of religion would have been refrefhed to have heard morning and evening in the tents through the camp, the delightful sound of some singing Psalms, some praying, and some reading the Scriptures. True religion is no enemy, like enthusiasm or superstition, to prudent counsel or undaunted valour. The Covenanters used all the proper means of defence with vigour and success: Large sums of money were raised; sufficient quantities of arms were provided; men were regularly inlisted and disciplined; the chief command was given to General Lesly, a man of unquestioned ability in military affairs; while the inferior officers were, many of them, such as had acquired experience and reputation under the great Gustavus Adolphus of Sweden. In short, the Covenanters were so firmly united, and took their measures so justly, that Charles after having in vain attempted by a fair pretence of peace to deceive them into a security that might have rendered them an easy prey to his designs, found it necessary at last, to treat with them in earnest. This treaty was begun at Rippon in the year 1640, just after the Scots had taken Newcastle. He had often declared the Covenanters rebels and traitors; but now he thought fit to acknowledge them before the Parliament of England (for he had now called a parliament) to be his good subjects, to whom he had sent his great seal, and with whom he wished to have a perfect agreement. The truth is, the members of that august assembly, inclined many of them to favour the cause of the Scots from the beginning; but now, quite charmed with their brave resistance, could not forbear murmuring even before the king himself, at the least reproachful word uttered against the Scots. A presage of the Union into which they and the Parliament of England soon after entered; an union in the cause of religion and liberty.

In the summer of 1641, the king having found the English Parliament so refractory, made a visit to Scotland. Having resolved, if possible, to win upon the affections of the Scots, he was now become all goodness, and gave them whatever they asked. He approved their proceedings in opposing the Book of Canons, the Liturgy, and the five articles of Perth. The bond against innovations and all the acts of the Scots Parliament in favour of our covenanted reformation now received the royal assent: which gave them all the legal confirmation which they were capable of receiving.

Observations on the National Covenanting in Scotland.

LIBERIUS represents the Covenanters as "a tumultuous combination inflamed with bigotry for religious trifles, and without any reasonable object." With regard to the approbrious name of tumultuous combination, the history of the Covenanters will enable the reader to judge how unjustly it is here applied. The popular insurrections are out of the question, since the Covenanters themselves never offered to justify them either to the king or to their fellow subjects; though they may sometimes have observed, that Providence over-ruled such insurrections (as it frequently over-rules the greatest disorders) to the most valuable purposes. To call a set of men of whom the leading part was highly distinguished in rank, in education, in the love of religion and of their country, a tumultuous combination, while it is not shewn that they acted contrary to the principles of equity; to call such a set of patriots by so reproachful an appellation, from the circumstance meerly of their being in opposition to the king, is a base partiality which none will excuse but those whose ignorance of the rights of mankind fits them to receive the slavish doctrines of passive obedience and non-resistance.

As to the reasonableness and importance of their object, if *Liberius* reckons nothing a solid or substantial possession but fine houses, well-cultivated lands, or some other kinds of external wealth; if he knows no satisfaction besides corporeal gratifications; if he cannot discern a reality in any thing beyond the sephere of his five senses; if Liberius is such a brute in human shape, * it must be owned that the matters our fathers contended for with respect to religion, never can appear to him other than mere trifles, unworthy the least attention. But some there are who know with the highest degree of certainty, that all their true happiness lies in communion with that God who made and who redeemed them, who supports the life of their bodies and of their souls. They are certain, that God's word and ordinances are the means of that communion; just as our food and raiment are the means of preserving the life and health of our bodies. Hence nothing is more reasonable than for such persons to contend earnestly for the purity of God's word and ordinances as the only appointed outward means, in this life, of attaining communion with God. Christians know that it is the life and consolation of their souls to behold the glory of God in the face of Jesus Christ. But God's word and ordinances are the glass through which they behold that glory; and can we wonder at their zeal for the purity of the glass which is the medium of such desirable contemplation? or can we blame them for refusing to have it sullied with the dirt of human inventions? Farther, those who are spiritual (we mean such as have the Spirit of Christ, for others are none of Christ's) discern a spiritual beauty and glory in the genuine institutions of Christ, entirely different from the beauty and glory of the most ingenious devices of men: The latter are adapted to the carnal eye of the natural man who cannot so much as apprehend the former; for *he receiveth not the things*

---

* Psal. xlix. 12. *He is like the beasts that perish.*

of the Spirit of God, they are foolishness to him, neither can he know them. Hence the manifest tendency of human devices in religious worship to turn away the attention and affections from God's ordinances. Besides, the honour of our Lord's name is deeply concerned in the manner in which we worship him. To pretend worshipping him by means which he has not appointed, is to offer him an indignity which the most pious intentions will never excuse. But there are some to whom the honour of Christ as the king and head of his church is dear above all things. In fine, our fore fathers well knew that one deviation from the rule of God's word leads to another, and that to a third, and so onward to a total apostacy like that of the Romish church. If you admit one thing into the worship or government of the church, which is not mentioned in the word of God, another thing will soon occur that claims a place on the foot of tradition, of ancient custom, of supposed use and ornament. Hence it was a godly jealousy of our fathers that led them so vigorously to oppose the first appearances of unscriptural rites and ceremonies of religion breaking in among them. If Liberius and his admirers reply, that this is the language of fanatics; we may ask, what should we say to a set of blind men who disbelieving the testimony of others concerning the beauty of colours, should agree together for their mutual comfort to call people that see fanatics?

That our ancestors regarded the duty of public covenanting as an ordinance of the church is evident with respect to the National Covenant, from the immediate end of it, the reformation of religion; from the manner in which our divines wrote in defence of it, still representing it as a covenant with God and not with man only; from its administration by ministers on the Lord's day, or on days of solemn humiliation; and especially from the matter of it; in which we may take notice of the following particulars.

In the beginning of it we have these remarkable words strongly expressive of the profession that our fathers made of receiving the truth as it is in Jesus with faith and love: "We believe with our hearts, "confess with our mouths, subscribe with our hands, "and constantly affirm before God and the whole "world, that this only is the true Christian faith and "religion, pleasing God and bringing salvation to "man, which now is by the mercy of God, reveal- "ed to the world by the preaching of the blessed "evangel;—to which we willingly agree in our con- "sciences in all points as to God's undoubted truth "and verity grounded only upon his written word."

In the next place, our ancestors go on to specify the Popish errors which they solemnly renounced. In the present age the common people do not understand many of the terms here used. But we are to consider that church-members had occasion at that time to be much better versed in the Popish controversy, than they are now. It was only a few years before that they had themselves been practising the evils here abjured. Besides, they had been accustomed to hear their ministers, laying open and refuting the errors of Popery almost every Lord's day. The confessions of faith too, and the religious treatises written at that time were, for the most part, taken up in exposing the abominations of Popery. Even in our own times, professors can give some account of the manifold sectaries which at present infest the church. And may we not suppose our forefathers (while yet far from that indifference to the concerns of religion which hath seized on this generation) to have been much better acquainted with that which was almost the only species of false religion against which they had then to contend?

Some think it strange that our forefathers should have mentioned the decrees made at Trent in a bond which the common people were to subscribe. But it should be remembered that the Council of Trent was then a reigning subject of conversation, and as much in people's mouths as the Congress in America is now. We have reason to believe the Protestant ministers would give their people all the information about that council which was necessary for maintaining a testimony against it: They would shew them that whatever the Popish party might pretend, or whatever some of the well-meaning bishops that attended it might look for, the real design of that council was for the ruin of the Protestant cause, and for the confirmation of the errors and abominations of Antichrist. Such a testimony was absolutely necessary at that time, in regard that the Papists were continually boasting of their pretended general council, comparing it with the most venerable councils of antiquity; insisting that its decree ought to be held as binding upon all Christians; and charging the Protestants with inexcusable obstinacy, because they would not submit to those decrees. It was therefore, at that time a necessary branch of the testimony of Protestants, to abjure the authority of the Council of Trent.

FARTHER, That our ancestors meant that persons should take the National Covenant as church-members, is clear from the evangelical character which the Covenanters bear. They are persons "whose "God is the Lord: they are not moved with any "worldly respect, but are perswaded only in their "conscience; through the knowledge and love of "God's true religion imprinted in their hearts by "the Holy Spirit." It is only in the character of believers, or of those who partake of Christ and all his saving benefits, that we can give ourselves to the Lord in a covenant of duties: and surely it well becomes believers and partakers of Christ to use these words. At that time, there were no disputes among Protestants about the nature of faith. They unanimously held, in opposition to the general doubtsome faith of the Papists, that it is an application of

Chrift and his benefits to ourfelves in particular; among which benefits is *the imprinting of the knowledge and love of the true religion by the Holy Spirit*. It is true, carnal men could not confiftently fwear the National Covenant: nor can they confiftently pray or receive the facraments: for thefe and indeed every ordinance of the church of Chrift muft be obferved in the way of depending on Chrift as the Lord our righteoufnefs and ftrength; a dependence to which natural men are abfolute ftrangers. The truth is, if we are to reprobate a religious duty, only becaufe a deceived heart will be fo abfurd as to draw falfe conclufions about the ftate of perfons before God from the profeffion that they neceffarily make in fuch a duty, what would follow? For the beautiful fyftem of Chriftian duties and ordinances we would be prefented with an univerfal blank.

The Covenanters promife to abide by this profeffion all the days of their lives, as they would not endanger " both foul and body in the day of God's " fearful judgment." Some fuch imprecation is expreffed or implied in all oaths. It is highly proper here, not that Covenanters were to entertain a flavifh fear of hell; but becaufe the ground they here profefs to ftand upon is the only ground of our falvation; becaufe they might affure themfelves that the Lord would enable them according to his word to perform their vows; and laftly, becaufe it expreffes the defire and refolution to walk in the Lord's way, with which honeft Covenanters ought to be animated.

Hiftory

History of the Solemn League and Covenant of the three Nations.

THE manner of carrying on the reformation in England was very different from what it was in Scotland. In Scotland we have seen it advancing from the people to the prince; in England it proceeded or seemed to proceed in a contrary direction, from the prince to the people: a circumstance from which many important consequences followed. In England the reformation increased the king's prerogative; in Scotland the reformation limited the prerogative. In England, as the reformed church received her model in a great measure from the king; so the external administration of her government was left almost wholly in his hands: but the church of Scotland absolutely refused to acknowledge the will of any mortal, however exalted in rank, either with regard to her constitution, or with regard to the administration of her government. Scotland prosecuting more fully the spirit of the reformation, admitted nothing in religion, but upon the authority of God's word alone. England, stopping short in the middle of her career, chose a religion conformable to ancient customs, to the opinions of the fathers, and to the dictates of an earthly head. Hence the surplice, the ceremonies, the liturgy and the hierarchy: in all these the church of England favours rank of Popery.

From the beginning of the reformation there were many godly persons who complained of these things as greatly symbolizing with Antichrist, and as leading the people away from that simple and spiritual worship that God has appointed in his word. It is well known how much the pious and faithful Bishop Hooper was against wearing the Surplice, calling it the Pope's Livery.

Queen Elisabeth, though celebrated as protectress of the reformed religion, used all her policy to increase the power of the crown in matters of religion. When princes want a religion that may prove subservient to their worldly grandeur, they always find the religion of the Bible too plain and simple for their purpose. Hence Elizabeth insisted so rigorously on the observance of a few ceremonies and glaring ornaments that were contrived to captivate the senses and imagination. Her successors James and Charles insisted no less rigorously.

Elisabeth's injunctions and persecution seemed to lessen the number of the non-conformists: but those of James and his son only increased it. How did this come about? The talents of the two princes for government were perhaps inferior to those of the Queen. But that was not all: As the knowledge of religion and liberty was daily gaining ground among the people, they grew more and more impatient of any arbitrary exercise of the royal prerogative, either with respect to religion or with respect to their civil rights. They would no more be treated like children; they rose to a more manly and vigorous use of their understanding. They began to bring every thing, even the mandates of the monarch, to the test of reason and of the scriptures. They shewed themselves to be men and to be Christians by choosing to obey God rather than man. At that time they did not embrace the truths of religion, as matters of speculation merely; but so much did they *receive the love of those truths*, that they were ready to do and suffer every thing for preserving the purity of them. Hence very soon after the meeting of the last parliament of Charles I, commonly called the Long Parliament, the general voice of the people of England appeared to be for the removal of Episcopacy and unscriptural ceremonies, root and branch; a fact which cannot be denied when one considers what petitions to that purpose subscribed by so many thousands were presented to the parliament; how popular the long parliament was in all its proceedings against Episcopacy; and what a poor figure they made who followed the fortunes of the king, and who composed his pretended parliament at Oxford; a poor figure indeed, compared to the legal representatives of the nation seconded as they were, by the joint efforts of their constituents. Charles must have been odious to the generality of his Protestant subjects, before he could have been forced into a measure so highly disgusting to them, as that of calling in the Irish Papists to his help, a short time after that dreadful massacre, and while their hands were still reeking with protestant blood.

The war between the king and the parliament fills some of the most interesting pages of history: the one contending for arbitrary power in civil government, and also for Episcopacy and ceremonies in the church; the other for freedom from every semblance of despotism in the state, and from every human imposition in matters of religion. The success of this, as of most other wars, was various. In the year 1643, the affairs of the parliament appeared to be verging toward ruin, when the resolution was taken of sending commissioners to invite the Scots to espouse their cause. These commissioners * arrived at Leith on the seventh day of August. Having appeared before the General Assembly which was then waiting to receive them, they presented a declaration of both houses of parliament, shewing the parliament's care of reforming religion; their desire of having some members of the assembly to assist their divines who

---

* Their names were Sir William Armin, Sir Henry Vane, Mr. Hatcher and Mr. Darley; with two ministers, Mr. Marshal and Mr. Nye.

were now sitting at Westminster; and in fine, their extreme need of help in their present deplorable condition.

Some time before, the Scots had sent commissioners to the king at Oxford to offer their mediation between him and the parliament; but the offer was rejected, and the persons of their commissioners treated, by those about him with all manner of contumely. Afterward he wrote to the Estates of Scotland discharging them to meddle in the affairs of England. Nothing could be more impolitic than the king's harsh and arbitrary treatment of the Scots at this time. It lost him their affections entirely, and determined them to accept the invitation of the English Parliament.

Hence it was that the before-mentioned commissioners from England, met with the kindest reception both from the assembly and from the estates. Some indeed were still for holding a middle course between the king and the English Parliament. But the reasoning of the eloquent Lord Warristoun placed the vanity of that opinion in so strong a light that it was very soon relinquished; and harmony in the resolution of assisting the English Parliament ensued. But still the mode or manner of their union with the parliament was a subject of debate. The English Commissioners proposed at first a civil league only: but the Assembly and the Estates insisted on having a religious covenant. The English Commissioners at length agreed to the latter; only they laboured to keep the door open in England to Independency; a reserve which no consideration could bring the Scots to approve. At last, two or three in private agreed with the English Commissioners upon a draught of that which was afterward called, " The Solemn League and Covenant." This proved satisfying to all. The three committees from the Estates, from the General Assembly, and from the Parliament of England, gave an assent to it, than which nothing could be more unanimous. When it came before the assembly one can hardly imagine a more affecting scene than it was to see the tears of pity and of joy that were shed by so many grave, wise and aged men on that occasion. Persons who had a real concern for the glory of Christ, were transported with the prospect of the three kingdoms (where civil discord had raged for many years, and where horrid war was continuing to mark her progress with ruin and with blood) uniting at such a time in the Lord Christ as their common head, and declaring themselves his willing subjects. Language is unable to express the gladness that arises in the heart of the Christian on seeing the enlargement of our Lord's kingdom; a gladness far greater than that of worldly men when their corn and their wine are increased. All the Presbyteries, the Universities and Parishes through Scotland were appointed to have a copy of this Covenant to be subscribed by their members: an appointment which was observed very universally; the Covenant being taken in this and the following year, every where through the nation.

WITH no less readiness and alacrity was the Covenant received at London. The divines at Westminster, the Lords and Commons assembled in Parliament approved of it as soon as it was laid before them; and in a few weeks after, solemnly swore and subscribed it with great joy and many tears. The Parliament having ordained the Covenant to be sworn by all ranks through England, multitudes took it, rejoicing at the oath of God. The House of Commons ordered the Solemn League and Covenant to be read publicly in every church and congregation on every day of humiliation which was then once in the month. By the same authority every congregation was obliged to have a copy of the Covenant printed on a fair letter, hung up in a proper place within the church. Many of these copies remained till the Restoration. In short it seems to be one of the cleareſt facts of hiſtory, that in England the better ſort and the generality of all ranks went into the Solemn League and Covenant.

About the ſame time, it was ſworn by the generality of thoſe in Ireland who took part with the Engliſh Parliament; which we have reaſon to think, were the greater part of the Proteſtants: for the countenance the king had giving to the Iriſh Papiſts, his accepting of three hundred thouſand pounds and other aſſiſtance from thoſe bloody men, had alienated the hearts of the Proteſtants from his cauſe and party.

It was not long that the reformation prevailed in England. The Weſtminſter Aſſembly indeed, framed an excellent Confeſſion of Faith and Larger and Shorter Catechiſms. But the affairs of the nation were in ſuch confuſion, that nothing could be firmly eſtabliſhed. Preſbyterian church order was introduced; but the parliament that protected and that nouriſhed it, were ſoon overpowered by the independent and ſectarian party; who, having beheaded their Sovereign, cruſhed it before it had time to take root. For nearly ten years after, while Cromwell's arms were renowned and reſpected abroad, all was uſurpation and diſorder, eſpecially in religion, at home. Cromwel having uſurped the ſupreme authority in the ſtate; his example and his unbounded toleration having leſſened men's reſpect for public office in general, the land was filled with preachers without any regular call, and with prophets who ran unſent. Theſe popular haranguers whoſe qualifications were impudence unreſtrained by any degree of modeſty, and wild imagination undirected by any degree of judgment, who knew neither *what they ſaid*, *nor whereof they affirmed*, broached a vaſt number of new opinions more abſurd and more monſtrous than the hereſy of the Gnoſtics, or any other that ever diſturbed the Chriſtian church.

Of Public Covenanting. 233

WHILE Sectarianism was thus overspreading England, the Scots renewed again the Solemn League and Covenant, as a mean of preserving them from the evils of the times. They renewed it in the way of acknowledging the breaches of it, and solemnly engaging to the duties opposite to those breaches. They did so in almost all the congregations of Scotland in December, 1648, with such a solemnity, and with such a mixture of joy and sorrow as became people entering into covenant with the Lord. They did so according to an act of the commission of the General Assembly for renewing the Solemn League and Covenant: which act of the commission was unanimously and heartily approved in a subsequent act of the Committee of the Estates of Parliament; a beautiful order constantly observed in the reformation of Scotland, the resolutions of the church going before, and the approbation of the state following. There is nothing in either of these acts like a disposition to force people into the covenant; not a syllable about fining or subjecting the refusers of the covenant to any sort of bodily punishment. On the contrary, the act of the commission cautions ministers against admitting to the renovation or subscription of the covenant, such persons as were excluded by some directions the commission had given on that head.

In January following, the covenant was renewed by the Parliament of Scotland. The General Assembly that met in July, 1649, ratified all the Commission had done in directing the manner of renewing the covenant.

The National Covenant and the Solemn League were both sworn by Charles II. when the Scots admitted him to the throne of his ancestors. One Mr. Douglas preached before the solemn transaction at Scoon: he shewed with great plainness and faithfulness the danger of breaking the Covenant; assuring the young king that the miseries of his family had been all procured by his grandfather's breach of that solemn engagement.

THUS the covenanting of our fathers received all the confirmation that the highest authority of the nation could give it, as well as all the legal obligation which could arise from the general consent of a free people.

ABOUT this time, many of the Irish Protestants renewed the Solemn League and Covenant. The Presbytery of Bangor in the year 1649 declared that they and others had renewed the covenant. A representation which was read in the several congregations of Irish Presbyterians, against the proceedings of the sectarian party with Charles I. avows the Solemn League as their Covenant. In the year 1662, no less than fifty nine ministers, zealous covenanters in the Synod of Bellimenoch, refused to conform to Episcopacy; a striking proof that the number of Irish Covenanters had been very considerable. *

BEFORE we conclude our account of this period, we would offer a remark which as it is founded in the most undeniable facts, so it serves greatly to recommend the practice of public covenanting. It is this; that the zeal of our fathers for the Covenants National and Solemn League was joined with a proportional concern for the purity of all the other institutions of Christ; for strictness of morals; for

* See Cox's History, Vol. II. page 177, 189, &c. The Christian loyalty of the Presbyterians, particularly in Ulster since their settlement by King James. Acts of Assembly page 151, 190, 191, 214, 217. See the facts collected from these authorities by Mr. Brown in his Letters on Toleration and the obligation of our Covenants, page 139, 140, 141, 142. Yet it must be owned, that whatever took place among the inhabitants of particular Counties, as in Ulster where the preaching of the gospel by Mr. Livingston, Mr. Blair and others, was very successful; yet as to the Irish in general, the greater part of them, being still either Papists or Episcopals, were enemies to the work of God. So that the Associate Synod had reason to say, in the Paragraph relating to Ireland added to the Acknowledgment of Sins, "The Covenanted Reformation "got very little footing and entertainment in that land, but the "truth and purity of gospel ordinances were generally neglected."

true liberty civil and religious; in short, for all that is amiable or praise worthy among mankind. This concern was manifested in the commendable acts of the General Assembly and of the Parliament; in the due execution of the laws for the suppression of vice and for the encouragement of virtue and religion; and in the godly and unblemished lives of the most zealous and stedfast covenanters. And no wonder that it was so, since in all this they did no more than endeavour to prosecute the ends of our solemn covenants; the noblest ends that a reasonable creature can have in view. Nay, the truth of this remark derives confirmation even from the reproachful epithets their enemies have commonly thought proper to give them: They have been called Puritans, because they professed to regard the pure word of God as their only rule; Fanatics for the fervency and frequency of their devotions; gloomy and morose for the severity of their morals; and in fine, hypocrites, that while their enemies could see nothing to blame in their outward deportment, they might give full scope to fancy in supposing them guilty in secret of whatever crimes they pleased.

After the year 1648, the disputes ran high about the admission of persons to places of public trust, who were known to be disaffected to our covenanted reformation. Even many excellent men were for the admission of them; being apprehensive that the exclusion of all such would divide their countrymen from one another; would deprive them of the service of some whose abilities they could not be well without; and in short would so weaken them that they would be unable to support the opposition they were maintaining against the sectaries: Plausible reasoning indeed, but then *it favoured not the things of God, but the things that are of men.* How often has the great enemy of the church made use of worldly policy and the fear of man to spoil the fairest beginnings of reformation! Let history tell the fatal success of the stratagem.

SINFUL measures, though directed by the most consummate political wisdom that we can suppose capable of suggesting them, however conducive sometimes they may appear to the interest of civil society, are always contrary both in themselves and in their consequences, to the welfare of the church of Christ. Those who were averse from our covenanted reformation being once admitted to have a share in the management of public affairs, gathered strength insensibly, and became in a few years the prevailing party. Hence it was, that when Charles II. began to overturn the whole covenanted reformation, and and to set up Episcopacy again, he found little or no opposition from those who took the lead in public affairs. When the motion was proposed in the Parliament of Scotland in 1661, for annulling all the parliaments which had given any civil sanction to the General Assembly at Glasgow in 1638 or any after assembly, or which had ratified the Solemn League and Covenant and Presbyterian church-government; when this motion was made and carried, there were scarcely forty members that appeared against it.

THE Solemn League and Covenant being declared unlawful, what cruelties were exercised in the course of this and the following reigns to make the people renounce their engagements to be the Lord's, nobody is ignorant. The generality complied, in one respect or another, with the impositions of government. A few, however, continued to keep the testimony of Jesus; and *they loved not their lives unto the death.*

THOUGH our martyrs of this period may in a general way be said to have suffered for Christ's alone headship over the church, and for her independency on the kingdoms of this world; yet the obligation of our covenants (in which these were included) was the leading point for which they suffered. It was this principally that enraged their persecutors against them: On this they insisted much in all their testimonies; still representing the other things they mentioned as what the whole nation was bound to by solemn covenant. The persecution proceeded upon the act of parliament declaring the covenants in themselves unlawful oaths; by which act the taking as well as the imposing of the covenants is made treasonable as "being against the fundamental laws and "liberties of the kingdoms." Hence people were not persecuted, at least not unto death, or according to law, for being Presbyterians merely, but for being Covenanters.

Observations on the taking of the Solemn League and Covenant.

THE characters of those who were actors in the covenanting of the last century have been much reproached in order to disprove the lawfulness and obligation of our Covenants. Henry Vane it is said, and the rest of the English commissioners had no other intention in agreeing to the proposal of a covenant for the reformation of religion than to flatter a religious people whose friendship was then become necessary to the English Parliament.

THIS objection might be sufficiently answered by observing, that however we may judge of the characters of particular persons by the views and motives (so far as we know them) with which they perform any duty, the nature of the duty itself must be discovered by other means. A wicked man will sometimes do an action which is materially good and commendable. Here we judge the matter of the action to be good ‡ in opposition to the general charac-

---

‡ "Works done by unregenerate men may, for the matter of "them, be things which God commands, and of good use both to "themselves and others."—*Westminster Conf. Chap. xxvi. Sect. 7.*

ter of the man who does it, on account of its conformity to the law of God, the only rule of duty. In like manner, we are to examine how far the covenanting of our ancestors was conformable to the word of God; how far it was a public acknowledgment of the Lord as our God; how far it was an engagement to cleave to his truths and ways; how far, in fine, it tended to the glory of God and the good of the church: so far and no farther ought we to approve of it; so far should we consider ourselves as having covenanted in the loins of our fathers; so far in the account of God's word, the vow of our fathers is ours, and we are as much bound as they were, to pay that vow to the Lord. If our fathers went about public covenanting as a religious duty in a manner agreeable to the word of God, it is absurd in that case, to suppose that the political views of any that joined in it, would change its whole nature and render it a merely political transaction. After all, it is not remembered that there is any proof of the charge implied in the objection, to hinder us from considering it as a base aspersion on the memory of our ancestors.

That the Scots were more ready to assist the English, when they saw them engaged in the same covenant of religion and reformation with themselves, is true: But it does not follow that the covenanting of the English was "a mere political stratagem." We cannot always judge with any degree of certainty of the nature or moral quality of actions from the occasions or consequences of them. Suppose a very wicked person, having occasion for the friendship of a good man, forsakes his vices and engages in a virtuous course of life; from the circumstance alone of his needing at such a time the friendship of the good man, we could not certainly conclude all his reformation to be mere pretence.

Why should we blame either the English or the Scots for what they did in this matter? What did the Scots do to deserve our censure? Why, when the English desired their assistance, they put the English in mind of their obligations to the God of heaven, and advised them to perform a scriptural duty; a duty which was peculiarly calculated to promote zeal and unanimity in the cause wherein they were then engaged. And what did the English Parliament do to deserve our censure? They did what was plainly their duty: they complied with the Christian admonitions of the Scots; a compliance which far from being blameable, was worthy of great commendation; for a society as well as an individual *that hearkeneth unto counsel, is wise,* Prov. xii. 15.

We may farther observe, that in subordination to the glory of God and the good of the church, it was by no means unlawful in framing such a league to have regard to the political welfare of both nations. The scripture proposes our temporal welfare as an encouragement to religious duties, Deut. xii. 6, 7. Matth. v. 5. James v. 14,—18. 1 Pet. iii. 10, 11. 1 Cor. xi. 30. Our temporal welfare then may well be a subordinate motive to the practice of a religious duty: and our ancestors were by no means blameable for having an eye in their covenanting to the preservation of their civil rights and liberties. Indeed, this duty had a tendency, from the very nature of it, to better the political state of these nations. They were much divided: The covenant was for uniting them to one another in the Lord. They were much weakened by civil broils and other calamities: the immediate design of the covenant was to strengthen them by restoring mutual confidence, by exciting all ranks to the duties of their respective stations, by recognising that relation to the Lord as their God which is the glory and the strength of any nation.

In the present age, we think ourselves vastly more enlightened than our fathers. But posterity may be of a contrary opinion. Our fathers contended earnestly for the rights of the church, and the royal prerogatives of Jesus against the incroachments of princes and of prelates: but the present generation seems to have practically given up some of the most essential rights of the church, either in compliance with the civil magistrate, or in conformity to the fashionable opinions that make the system of outward order, government and discipline which Christ hath prescribed unto the church, a mere thing of wax, varying continually to worldly interest, to aspiring ambition, to popular humour. We have reason to fear, that when the Lord comes to build up Zion and appear in his glory, our boasted superiour lights as to the nature of Christ's kingdom will be found to have been, in a great measure, darkness; and the most part of the present generation will be discovered to have been destitute of the real practical knowledge of the glory, the excellency and purity of the church of Christ: while the zeal and faithfulness of our worthy ancestors, cleared from every malicious aspersion and misrepresentation, shall shine forth with distinguished lustre to the utter confusion of Zion's enemies, but to the abundant consolation of her children.

It has been said, that the Lord gave testimony to the public covenanting of our ancestors by remarkable effusions of the Holy Spirit. In order to obviate some objections that have been made to so comfortable an evidence in favour of public covenanting, we should take notice of the following circumstances.

First, In 1648, the Lord's people were led to set about public covenanting by a memorable outpouring of the Spirit of grace and supplication; which was continued and increased in that solemn work, agreeably to Isa. xliv. 3, 4, 5. where covenanting is promised as a consequence of the Spirit being given. Much leaven of corruption may remain in church-members amidst the largest communications of the

the Spirit with which the militant church is favoured; but never did the Spirit introduce any of that leaven, or countenance the introduction of it. *Secondly*, The sanctification of the Lord's people was very sensibly advanced in and by their public covenanting. We must distinguish between those remains of sin and error which may be in those who experience the saving work of the Spirit, and those divine truths and ordinances which are the proper means of beginning and carrying on the saving work. Sanctification was never promoted by the Popish ceremonies retained in the church of England, nor by the carnal fancies about consubstantiation held by the Lutheran churches; though, no doubt, many saints have been, and we hope still are in those communions. But the Lord's gracious presence was eminently with his people in the very act of public covenanting, bringinging them to godly sorrow for sin, filling their hearts with love to Christ and to one another in him: and those who were witnesses of it testified, that "the desire of true knowledge "wrought by it in the hearts of the people approved "it to be a special mean appointed by God for re-"claiming the nation to himself." It is well known that it was when gospel-ordinances in general, were signally accompanied with the demonstration of the Spirit and with power, that church-members were led forward to join in public covenanting. The more zealous that Christians were for covenanting they were generally the more lively and spiritual in other duties. But the reverse of all that, is true with regard to will-worship and the commandments of men; which are *lies, vanity, and things wherein is no profit*. *Thirdly*, That effusion of the Spirit which our fathers experienced when they were enabled to give themselves to the Lord in a covenant of duty, had permanent effects on the hearts and lives of church-members. Multitudes of these Covenanters to the day of their death continued thanking the Lord for his kindness in that ordinance, and having a conversation every way becoming the gospel of Christ. Nay, the Lord was pleased very soon to put his own work to the trial, by the furious persecution which he permitted soon after to break forth, and to rage for about the space of twenty-eight years. Then was the fine gold of a testimony for the duty of covenanting tried and brought to the light: a testimony which the witnesses held in so rational and scriptural manner that their adversaries with all their malice, were unable to gainsay or resist it: and the witnesses sealed it with their blood. Thus what the Lord wrought for our fathers by the outpouring of the Spirit which attended covenanting-work, was altogether unlike the impressions of Enthusiasm, which are wont to pass away like a land flood. *Fourthly*, In consequence of the effusion of the Spirit that we speak of, the Lord's people had very clear views of the scripture warrants for covenanting; so clear that rather than deny it, they chose to part with all they had, and even with life itself. It is hard to suppose that sincere Christians could ever pretend to see clearly any mere invention or commandment of men to be (what our fathers professed they clearly saw public covenanting to be) an ordinance which God hath expresly appointed in his word. It is true, charity obliges us to look upon many who have written in defence of the unscriptural ceremonies used in the church of England, as good men and eminently useful in their day. Yet it deserves our consideration, that the best and most judicious of those writers, such as Dr. Stillingfleet, have considered them as in themselves matters of indifference, tho' venerable for their antiquity. Nay some Presbyterian divines have abundantly confuted the Episcopalians by collecting passages from their own eminent writers. But the ministers and other church-members of the last age who obtained mercy of the Lord to be faithful, our martyrs particularly, were of one mind, of one judgment, of one full assurance with regard to the warrantableness and perpetual obligation of our covenants, as grounded on the word of God. "I do "judge" said Mr. Rutherford a little before his death, " and in my conscience believe, that no pow- " er on earth can absolve and liberate the people of " God from the bonds and sacred ties of the oath of " God." "I do bear witness," said Mr. James Guthry in his last testimony, " to the National Co- " venant of Scotland, and to the Solemn League and " Covenant of the three nations: these sacred solemn " oaths of God, I believe, can be loosed or dispen- " sed with by no person or party or power upon " earth; but are still binding upon these kingdoms, " and will be hereafter for ever, and are ratified and " sealed by the conversion of many a thousand souls, " since our entering thereinto." So likewise said all our martyrs.

It is objected, that our forefathers were as much for the use of civil penalties in matters of religion as for the duty of covenanting.

That they did not sufficiently guard against all appearance of such use of civil penalties is granted; but that they held it as explicitly and unanimously as the duty of covenanting, is utterly denied. No one wrote or spoke more against the Independent notions (which, to be sure, were very loose and indigested notions) of toleration than Mr. Rutherford; and yet hear how Mr. Rutherford laments, instead of defending, the use of civil penalties in matters of religion: " Our work in public," says he, " was " too much in sequestration of Estates, in fining and " imprisoning, more than in a compassionate mourn- " fulness of spirit toward those whom we saw oppose " the work of God."* The proceedings which occa-

---

* See his Testimony subjoined to his Letters. Mr. Wilson, in his Defence, doubts whether this paper be Mr. Rutherford's; as it did not come out till 1713; and was neither signed by Mr. Rutherford, nor attested by any of his acquaintance: yet that very candid and judicious writer seems to approve of what is here said as pointing at 1650 and the following years.——Mr. Wilson's Defence of the Reformation, Chap. 4. Sect. 5.

sioned this complaint were after the year 1649, when the reformation was going to decay. We do not remember to have met with a syllable in any of the testimonies of our martyrs in favour of the opinion, that a religious profession is to be inforced by civil penalties. We are certain that it is never laid down, like the obligations of our covenants, as a distinct head for which any of them suffered. It is, therefore, a vile reproach that shall be wiped away by him who will effectually stop the mouth of those that speak lies, to represent the testimony of our worthy forefathers as no less for the use of civil pains in matters of religion, than for the obligation of our covenants. They were silent of the former; but for the latter they witnessed uniformly even unto death.

We are to distinguish between the testimony of our martyrs and the reasoning they used in support of it: a distinction that is made use of in every cause that comes before a court of justice. Their testimony consisted in the precious truths of God's word; but their reasonings belonged to their imperfect manner of defending those truths. They had clear, spiritual, scriptural views of the several heads of their testimony: But we dare not say, that all their apologies were free of mistakes; some of the reasons, for example, which they assigned for casting off the magistrates authority we may allow, if taken singly and alone, to have been insufficient. They were men of like passions as ourselves; and we are to regard some of their reasonings as rather dictated by their feelings than by their settled judgment. But out of weakness they were made strong: they were enabled to confirm the obligation of our covenants, and all the other heads of their testimony by such a strength of argument as none of their adversaries have been able to invalidate.

Nor are we to deem lightly of the testimony of martyrs. So far as the grounds and manner of their suffering are conformable to the precepts, prophecies and examples of the word, their martyrdom is an evidence in favour of the doctrine for which they suffer. When we see men remarkable for their uniform regard to all the truths, laws and ordinances of Christ as they are laid down in his word; when we see them evidencing, on all occasions, the greatest aversion to every appearance of making their own will, the will of others, or any thing indeed besides the scriptures of truth the rule of their conduct and religious profession; when we see manifold consistent, scriptural evidences that they have the special supports of the Spirit of God under their sufferings; we cannot persuade ourselves that heaven would bring about all this, only to put a seal to falsehood; or while the general tenor of their conduct and profession is uniformly agreeable to the word, that the matter which is a principal object of their consideration, and of their incessant prayers, and on account of which they are led under the good hand of God to lay down their lives, should, alone, be contrary to the word; and that this should be the case, not merely of one or two individuals whom we may suppose to have been of a temper peculiarly susceptible of enthusiastical impressions, but that it should be the case of multitudes of various dispositions and turns of mind, multitudes who having been sober and regular in their lives, were remarkable for composure and firmness of mind, and for sobriety in all their words and behaviour amidst the studied provocations of their enemies, and when meeting death in its most shocking forms. These things are so conspicuous in the history of the witnesses for our covenanted reformation as must for ever distinguish and set them above a comparison with the most celebrated Popish zealot or Quakerish enthusiast.

We do not mean to consider the example or sufferings of our martyrs as the ground of our belief, that public covenanting is God's ordinance; the word of God is the only ground of our belief. We only mean to shew that this is exactly like the other truths and institutions of Christ in the effects it has upon those who receive the love of it. It is an argument from analogy.

It is a common objection to the obligation of our covenants, that they were enjoined under civil penalties. But besides that it is a Protestant principle in opposition to Jesuitical equivocation, to hold the obligation of an oath, even when persons are compelled to take it, if it be otherwise lawful and proper; besides that a circumstance of this kind, cannot reasonably be supposed sufficient to take away the validity of a divine ordinance; though we grant that probably there was too much reason for Mr. Rutherford's lamentation which we have mentioned, and that sometimes civil penalties were too much employed in pressing people to take the covenants; yet a tolerable degree of candour in perusing the history of our ancestors would lead us to excuse, or at least to extenuate their fault, when it appears that the generality of the refusers of the covenants were their professed enemies both in church and state: we do not find that any refused the National Covenant who were hearty friends to the reformed religion; or the Solemn League either, except those who laboured all they could, to disappoint the generous efforts of the Long Parliament in favour of liberty and of reformation.

Though the Parliament of England enjoined the taking of the Solemn League and Covenant under civil penalties, it does not follow that the covenant was not taken voluntarily; because were we to admit such a consequence, there could be no voluntary or willing obedience to any law human or divine. Besides we know that a spirit of zeal for religion was the ruling character of those times; so that we have reason to think people were generally persuaded to take the covenant, rather by the arguments which the ministers of the gospel (who administered that solemn oath) held forth from the word of God, than by any threatening of confiscation in the act of parliament. A farther evidence of this is, that we hear of no measures being taken for putting the penalty in execution. Add to all these circumstances, the many accounts we have of particular persons, parishes and large assemblies willingly and chearfully going into the covenant.

It is objected, that the disputes between the Presbyterians and the Independents both in the Long Parliament and in the Westminster Assembly shewed the former to be enemies of toleration. Now it was the Presbyterians that set on foot and carried on the subscription of the covenant.

We answer, that if we duly considered the toleration which the Independents pleaded for, we would be thankful that the Presbyterians did not give into it. The Independent was a positive toleration; a toleration which is no less contrary than persecution itself to the liberal principle on which we plead for a negative, that is, the only reasonable toleration. The principle we mean is this; that it does not belong to the civil magistrate to judge authoritatively in matters of religion. No doubt, he ought to encourage what he takes to be the true religion; nay, his authority may be employed to ratify the spiritual judgments, so far as he approves them, of that church which he reckons the true one: Such ratification may be considered as binding upon all that are willing members of that church, while they continue so. But such ratification should have no more effect with regard to others, than to hinder them from giving the church or her members any molestation in observing the spiritual judgments that are so ratified. Such is the rational foundation on which negative toleration stands. On the contrary, the independent authoritative toleration supposes that the magistrate, having established one religion as the true, is to take cognisance of other religions; and having determined them to be false and wrong, is however, to tolerate, or rather to countenance them under the very consideration of their being false and wrong religions. According to the Independent scheme of toleration, therefore, the civil rulers as such, are to judge in matters of religion, and to oblige all their subjects, and not only those of one communion, to acquiesce in their judgment; which judgment and obligation are both of them contrary to the above mentioned principle.

While we thus condemn the loose notions of the Independents, we dare not say that our Presbyterian divines steered always clear of narrow and intolerant principles. However, were the matter searched to the bottom, we hope that making proper allowances for too strong expressions which it is difficult to avoid in controversy; and for the variety of civil and religious concernments which were so much blended together in the cause they were engaged in against the abettors of Charles's arbitrary measures, they will be found to have been, at the bottom, as much enemies to persecution as any of our own times.

So much for the objections against our covenants taken from the character and ruling principles of our ancestors. We would now offer a few observations that may obviate some exceptions which are commonly taken to the articles of the Solemn League and Covenant. It has been objected concerning the whole matter of this covenant, that it is so various and intricate that the bulk of the common people who entered into it, could not be supposed to understand it.

But it is evident that an oath is not to be blamed, because persons may swear it rashly and ignorantly. Full well is an oath accommodated to the understandings of those who are desired to enter into it, if the terms have so much precision as not to be ambiguous; and so much clearness that any person of ordinary capacity, in the due use of the means he has access to, may come at the meaning of them. But the terms of the Solemn League and Covenant are neither hard nor ambiguous. The hardest are the names of the ecclesiastical officers in the Episcopal communion: and, why will some say, are we obliged to acquaint ourselves with all the branches of Prelacy? We should be acquainted with public evils, so far as the knowledge of them is necessary for the keeping of ourselves unspotted from them, that we may not be partakers of them; as is necessary in order to the exercise of gospel mourning and humiliation for them as grounds of God's controversy with the land; as is necessary in order to our testifying against them for the glory of God, and for the benefit of our fellow men. On these accounts, a great part of God's word is taken up in pointing out public evils. On these accounts, we should study to understand the terms alluded to in the Solemn League and Covenant.

Whoever is in the least acquainted with the history of this period, knows that the public attention was then much engaged by the various branches of Prelacy: So that it is reasonable to suppose the several orders of the Episcopal hierarchy and other things relating to that controversy were better understood among the people than they are now.

But is it actually true that I do not so understand the things mentioned in an oath as to be able to swear it falsely, till I have considered these things in all the lights wherein they can be considered, till I am able to explain each of them fully, and to solve all the doubts and difficulties that may be raised about them? For example, supposing I had a call in providence to assure the public by an oath of my loyalty to the British government, and supposing the words *British Government* to be in the form of the oath, would it be unlawful for me to swear it, till I comprehended fully the nature and maxims of that government; till I understood how exactly the three branches of the Legislature were balanced together; how privilege and prerogative went hand in hand; and in fine how easily every objection might be answered against the commonly received opinion, that it is the best constituted government in the known world? Suppose I were called to swear that I remember I was in my usual state of health at such a particular time; would it be wrong for me to take an oath to that purpose with the word *health* in it; unless I could give an account of all the parts external and internal of my corporeal frame; unless I could tell of the solids and of the fluids; of the veins, arteries, nerves, muscles, tendons, glands; of the motion of the heart and of the lungs; of the chyle, the blood, and some mysterious thing they call the animal spirits; and in short, unless the word health suggested to me all the ideas which it ever suggested to a Sydenham or a Boerhave? If this is the case, I may turn Quaker when I please with regard to oaths; for it is impossible that ever in this world an oath can be devised that is not far beyond the reach of my understanding. Such is the egregious trifling which some have tried to pass upon the world for sober solid reasoning against our covenants. The truth is, one understands the things mentioned in an oath sufficiently for the purpose of swearing that oath, if his knowledge of them answer the intention of the administrator. One may take an oath of loyalty to the British government, though he knows no more of the British government than that he lives securely under it, enjoying his liberty and his property. In like manner, one may take an oath renouncing Popery, Prelacy and Arminianism; if he only knows a few of the tenets to which those names are commonly appropriated, and is convinced in his conscience that the tenets are contrary to the word of God. The divine truths opposite to Popery, Prelacy and Arminianism are such as every Christian ought to be acquainted with as contained in the holy scriptures: and surely it requires very little historical knowledge to convince him that there is something contrary to those truths in the religious opinions that go under the above-mentioned names. The truth is a good and honest heart (that is the new heart which God hath promised) is unspeakably more necessary for the right performance of this duty, than much of what passes among men for knowledge and penetration.

Some have objected to the obligations in the Solemn League with regard to the state: The Covenanters, for example, engaged to preserve the rights and privileges of parliament; while, say they, these rights and privileges were not sufficiently ascertained.

So say some of our modern historians who, it seems, with all their parade of learning and improvement can trace the civil liberty of Britons no farther back than the Long Parliament: thus representing that parliament as the author of the greatest of political blessings (beyond their intention surely; for otherwise they cast the vilest reproaches upon that parliament) whereas we have reason to believe that a moderate acquaintance with the records of our native country would convince us that the Long Parliament only endeavoured to correct abuses, to clear away the rust which the constitution had gathered in length of time, and to settle the ancient liberty of the people on a firm foundation. Farther, several of the rights of parliament, such as that of granting the people's money, were then considered as clearly ascertained. After all, this may be taken, in a general sense, as an engagement to maintain the rights of the subject against the incroachments of the crown; an engagement no way unbecoming the Christian; since the love of liberty is the love of human happiness, and wherever it has flourished, has been seen to lead every active and social virtue in its train.

It is true, the people of Britain entered into the Solemn League and covenant at a time when they were struggling for their civil rights and privileges: they looked upon public covenanting as a suitable mean of promoting unanimity in the common cause. In like manner, any providence or any situation may be a mean or occasion of stirring up a person or people to any other religious duty, or spiritual exercise which that providence or that situation may call for. Hence it is that so much of the Covenant relates to the state of the body politic. But that circumstance does nothing to make it a mere political constitution. We may lawfully take our secular concerns into prayer or any other religious duty without lessening the spirituality of the exercise. The Holy Ghost enjoins us to do so; *Acknowledge the Lord in all thy ways.* Surely as we may pray to be enabled, so we may come under engagements, to be faithful to the Lord, and to one another in him in our civil as well as in our religious transactions. The Christian character should be kept up in the market as well as in the church, in the parliament as well as in the assembly of divines. He is as far from behaving like a Christian who barters the liberties of a nation for places and pensions, as he who seeks the advancement of Popery or of Arianism.

In the sixth article of the Solemn League and Covenant our ancestors " engage to endeavour the dis-
" covery of all such as were incendiaries, malig-
" nants, or evil instruments, by hindering the refor-
" mation of religion, dividing the king from his
" people, or one of the kingdoms from another, or
" making any faction or parties among the people
" contrary to the League and Covenant." This has been complained of as contrary to the right of private judgment.

The general design of the article seems to be included in the duty which the apostle exhorts us to in Rom. xvi. 17. *Now, I beseech you brethren, mark them who cause divisions and offences, contrary to the doctrine which ye have learned; and avoid them.* It is undoubtedly our duty to discover the real character and designs, as far as we know them, of every enemy either to the church or the state. Such discovery is always necessary for the welfare, and sometimes for preserving the very being of society. It is necessary that every member of a society and his actions, as far as they affect the public interest, should appear in their true colours and without any disguise, to the end that the society may know its friends from its foes: And that is what our ancestors, in this article, promised their endeavours to bring about.

It is added, as the end of such discovery, that incendiaries, malignants, and evil instruments, behaving in the manner before-mentioned, " might be " brought to trial, and receive condign punishment, " as the degree of their offences shall require or de- " serve." Since the crimes here mentioned, such as dividing the king from his people, or one kingdom from another, were punishable by the laws of the land, the obvious meaning of this is, that Covenanters by making such discovery were to promote the due execution of the laws; a motive that ought to have great weight with every one, whether he is considered as a member of the church or of the state. No society can exist without laws; and the usefulness of laws depends upon the execution of them.

It seems indeed to be the intention of this article, that the real enemies to that reformation in church and state of which covenanters bound themselves to seek the advancement, might be discovered; that individuals who came under the description of such enemies should be taken notice of; that the civil powers should forbear shewing them any particular favour or countenance; and that if their enmity broke forth into the commission of crimes punishable by law, they should be punished accordingly. But how does this infringe the right of private judgment? Surely the right of private judgment is not a right to lay plots for defeating a people's virtuous endeavours to promote religion and the public welfare.

AFTER all, when we contend for the lawfulness of our covenants, and for the obligation of them on posterity, we do not mean that the form of words our ancestors made use of, is above all exception, or absolutely without a fault; for that would be to put it on a level with the inspired writings. The point we aimed at is made good, if it appears from the form of words in question, that our ancestors practised the duty of covenanting agreeably to the rule of the word, that they avouched the Lord to be their God, and engaged to walk in his ways and to keep his commandments; if it appears that they made some advances in reformation, and that they bound themselves and their posterity to hold fast what they had attained, and to carry on the good work which was begun: things which we hope are abundantly clear from the survey we have taken of our covenanting periods. We do not consider the Covenants, Creeds, and Confessions of the church as any other than the imperfect, though honest and faithful endeavours of church members who have led the way to us in keeping the word of Christ's patience. If it is the manifest scope and tendency of any article of a covenant, of a creed, or of a confession to hold fast something of truth and duty in opposition to the malignity of sin and error, we are, by no means, to drop such an article for the sake merely of inadvertent expressions,

———Quas aut incuria fudit,
Aut humana parum cavit natura.

ON the whole, whether we consider the matter of our covenants, the manner in which our ancestors entered into them, or the concurrence of all ranks in the transaction, we can find no solid reason to doubt of their obligation upon us. Nor ought we to overlook the evidences in the course of providence that the Lord has a controversy with these lands for their breach of covenant with him. Besides all that ministers and others have been lead to testify on that head, we have been reproved by famine, particularly a little after the revolution; by remarkable burnings in Edinburgh and London where our covenants had been publicly burnt; by wars not only abroad, but also at home in the two rebellions in favour of a popish Pretender; and, which ought to alarm us more than all these, by the dreadful progress of spiritual judgments. The aspect of providence is growing every day more gloomy: Our Colonies have deserted us; our other allies are about to do the same. Alas, we are justly forsaken by our friends, because we have forsaken the Lord and his covenant. Amidst all these things, the generation is growing more careless and secure. A sense of God and of duty is wearing off men's minds. As we have cast off the obligations of our covenants, so we are losing by degrees even the advantages arising to civil society from religious obligation in general: charters, in which the public faith of the nation is pledged, have been too little regarded; oaths, particularly those to the state, are looked upon as mere forms, and in some cases the breach of them has been apologized for as consistent with virtue and with honour; men having got almost entirely free from the restraints of conscience and regard to a future state, are growing blind even to their present interest, and seem to be hurrying fast away to personal and political destruction in the impetuous current of luxury and dissipation. And if the land at last become desolate, the following passage of scripture will be exactly applicable to our case: Deut. xxviii. 34, 35. *All the nations shall say, Wherefore hath the Lord done this unto this land? What meaneth the heat of this great anger? Then men shall say, Because they have forsaken the covenant of the Lord God of their fathers, which he made with them when he brought them forth out of the land of Egypt.*

Of the Public Covenanting in the Secession.

THE established church of Scotland having neglected several opportunities of setting about this necessary duty, are going on to this day in a course of backsliding and corruption. Those in the Secession aiming at the revival of religion, endeavoured to guard against that neglect; and remembering how much the Lord had blessed and countenanced the practice of public covenanting for furthering the reformation in the days of our fathers, resolved to state themselves as witnesses for Christ in the way of giving themselves publicly to him in that duty. Accordingly the Associate Presbytery agreed upon a bond and an acknowledgment of sins; having both of them a particular reference to the sins and errors of our own times. The Presbytery found it their duty to call and beseech all sorts of persons through the land, and particularly those in communion with them, to turn from sin to the Lord, and with their whole heart, to renew their covenant engagements to the most High God.

THE ministers of the Secession led the way in this work. In December 1743, the four brethren who were first thrust out of the Establishment, with eleven others, publicly swore and subscribed the bond at Stirling before a numerous congregation. In March following, five more entered into that solemn engagement at Falkirk. The example of the ministers was followed by the people in two or three congregations soon after. But the breach among the members of the Associate Synod occasioned some interruption of the good work. After that severe trial, such as held fast the Secession testimony have been gradually coming into the bond for the renovation of our covenants.

This renovation confists chiefly in the three following things; in acknowledging the obligation of our covenants, in confessing the breaches of them, and in a particular application of our covenants to the prefent circumftances.

In the firft place, we acknowledge the obligation of our Covenants National and Solemn League; agreeably to thefe words in the before-mentioned bond: "In regard we are taught by the word of "God, and bound by our Covenants National and "Solemn League." We have already taken notice that fuch an acknowledgment of the continuing obligation of the covenant which the Ifraelites entered into at Sinai, is evident in the after inftances of their covenanting. One principal end of our public covenanting, which is to hold faft what the church has attained, requires this acknowledgment. Befides, the refpect that our covenanting has to that of our fathers is neceffary as an acknowledgment and approbation of the refpect which their covenanting had to us. Nor indeed, while the renewing of our covenants is difregarded, can there be any adequate or fuitable approbation of them, efpecially by thofe who profefs to teftify againft the corruptions of the times and to fet forward in reformation. Our anceftors made fuch a profeffion in the way of public covenanting. Surely then to fhew the fincerity of the commendations we beftow upon their covenanting, we fhould make the fame profeffion in the fame way. Befides, when our anceftors brought their children under fuch obligations to be the Lord's people, they meant that their children fhould likewife willingly and chearfully take the fame obligations upon themfelves.

Secondly, When we join in the bond for the renovation of our covenants, we confefs the breaches of thofe facred engagements; breaches of them not only in the present but in the former generations. This is implied in the following words of the bond: "By the Lord's grace we shall, according to our several stations, places and callings, contend and and testify against all contrary evils, errors and corruptions; particularly, Popery, Prelacy, Deism, Arianism, Arminianism, and every error subversive of the doctrine of grace; as also, Independency, Latitudinarian tenets, and the other evils named in the above confession of sins."

We have already spoken of confessing our own and the iniquities of our fathers: a duty which cannot be denied by any one who believes what *was written afore time to have been written for our learning.* But whoever truly confesses those iniquities, sorrowing for them in a godly manner, will not be backward to resolve and engage, through grace, to forsake them. When the poor sinner sees the lothsomeness of his idols, he says of course, *What have I to do any more with idols?* Thus having endeavoured to make an honest confession of our own and the iniquities of our fathers, we proceed in the bond, to declare our resolution and engagement, through grace to forsake those iniquities. And who that knows what the scriptural exercise is of acknowledging sin, and of turning from it, will blame any set of people for binding themselves to forsake the evils they have confessed?

But with regard to the sins of our fathers, it is pretended, that we have not so much certainty of them as is necessary in order either to a suitable confession of them, or a suitable engagement against them.

We may answer by observing that we have manifold examples in scripture of the saints proceeding upon human testimony as to matters of fact, in the performance of religious duties. Psal. xliv. 1, 2, 3. Psal. lxxviii. 3,———8. We read in 2 Sam. xv. 31. that *one told David, saying Achitophel is among the conspira-*

tors. David had nothing for the truth of this fact but human testimony, Was David then to be hindered from praying about the treachery of a friend, because he was not yet an eye-witness of it? Let his conduct say how he would have relished such an opinion. It follows in the same verse, *And David said, O Lord, I pray thee, turn the counsel of Achitophel into foolishness.*

The British people are for ever bound to thank the Lord for their deliverance from heathen darkness and from popish idolatry, for the defeat of the Spanish Armada, for the happy discovery of the gunpowder plot, for the revolution, and for many other merciful interpositions of a wonder working providence. We hope no one will say, that we may neglect the duty of thanksgiving for these things, on this pretence merely, that we have no other way of coming at the knowledge of them than by human testimony. And yet the knowledge of the mercies, for which we give thanks is equally necessary as the knowledge of the sins which we confess. So when an Israelitish parent informed his children, according to the divine command, how the Lord brought their fathers out of Egypt, Exod. xii. 26, 27. and how miraculously he opened a way for them through the Jordan, Joshua iv. 6, 7. it was evidently the duty of the children to give so much credit to their parents, testimony as was necessary in order to the religious exercises that corresponded with that naration.

It is objected, that the example of the Israelites in this matter, is not parallel to the point in hand, because the facts they commemorated were such as had been engrossed into the inspired volumes.

We answer, Surely the duty of remembering past instances of the Lord's kindness is the same to us, as it was to the Israelites; and considering the superior advantages of the New Testament dispensation, the motives and incitements to such a grateful remembrance are no less, but much greater to us than they were to them. With regard to the circumstance of the facts commemorated being a part of the inspired history, it is not mentioned in the passages referred to, as necessary to the acceptable observance of this duty. Nay, in Josh. iv. 6, 7. the Israelites are commanded to make use of the twelve stones which were set up as a memorial of their passage through the Jordan, and which were the histories of those times; histories no more infallible than our own. Besides, we are not to be hindered from imitating the Israelites in their thankful remembrance of the Lord's mercies, because in their case it was attended with the extraordinary circumstance of those mercies being recorded by inspiration. Surely we may imitate Daniel's confession and prayer for the deliverance of his people, though his exercise, too, was attended with the extraordinary circumstance of the prophecy limiting the continuance of the Babylonish captivity to seventy years. Indeed almost all the examples in the Bible have circumstances of this kind. In fine, as was shewn with respect to the occasions of covenanting, it is by no means necessary to our imitation of a scripture-example, that *our* circumstances and *those* of that example be precisely the same. But to return to our subject ;

Our praying for Christian brethren at a distance, and communicating to their necessities, necessarily proceed upon human testimony. Indeed without proceeding upon it, there can be little, if any, visible church fellowship. A propensity to receive the testimony of one another is a necessary part of our constitution which is not rooted out by the sanctification of the Spirit, but only directed to the glory of God and to our own good. The God of peace sanctifies us wholly in our spirit, and soul and body. This propensity, then, may be subservient to the duties of religion.

And surely if the church may proceed in religious duties upon human testimony at all, she may upon the facts enumerated in the acknowledgment of sins. Let us confider what fort of facts they are. Are they facts of a private nature, to be found only in fome private memoirs? Far otherwife; they are all of the moft public nature; generally known among all ranks of people at the time they happened; ftanding uncontradicted in the hiftories of our public affairs; attefted, many of them, by acts of the civil legiflature or of church judicatures; and feveral of them remembered by many yet in life. It is now about forty years fince the relation of thefe facts in the Judicial Teftimony and the Acknowledgment of Sins has been lying open to the fulleft examination, and to this day thofe who have fhewn the greateft inclination to detract from the reputation of thofe papers, have not been able to detect a fingle falfehood in them.

Various are the attacks that have been made upon the Acknowledgment of fins. Some have carpped at the manner in which feveral of the facts are therein reprefented; though the amount of all their criticifms, if duly confidered, will be found to be no no more than this; that they confidered the facts in another light, and put another conftruction upon them, than the framers of the Acknowledgment of Sins had done.

Others again, have alledged, that it is not eafily underftood, and that the common people in the Seceffion are fworn againft evils of which they are ignorant. Perfons are, no doubt, liable to ignorance, unbelief and treachery of heart in covenanting as well as in other duties. But if minifters are careful to obferve the charge which the Lord as really gives them as he gave it to the prophet Ezekiel, xxi. 2. *Son of man, caufe Jerufalem to know her abominations:* and xx. 4. *Son of man, caufe them to know the abominations of their fathers:* and if the people are actually in earneftto underftand the Acknowledgment of Sins; if they are dilligent in the use of means, not trusting to their own understanding, but relying with the whole heart on the guidance and direction of the enlightening Spirit, there will be as few ignorant Covenanters as ignorant communicants. We can only add, that those who in their writings have so severely reflected on the Bond and the Acknowledgment of Sins as deficient in perspicuity or precision, (for that seems to be the meaning of their declamation about people's swearing to what they do not understand) ought to have specified the obscure and ambiguous passages. The bulk of this generation seems to be of a very contrary opinion: It is their great offence that the Bond and the Acknowledgment of Sins are too plain, too pointed, and too particular.

Some parts of the Acknowledgment of Sins have been grievously misrepresented. An example shall be given. One passage of it has been said to maintain that what is commonly called *Cambuslang Work* was all a delusion and the work of the devil. But no such assertion is to be found in the Acknowledgment of sins. Indeed so far as that work led those people to lay stress upon bodily commotions, swoonings, convulsions, sudden terrors and joys, and imaginary ideas of Christ as man, taking these things for marks of conversion; so far may we justly deem Satan transforming himself into an angel of light to have been the principal agent in that work; especially considering their lax and unscriptural notions about the government and discipline of the church, and about the duty of witnessing for the cause and royal prerogatives of our Lord; notions which Whitefield the great promoter of that work gloried in, and by which his adherents were distinguished.

But the Associate Presbytery never meant to determine the fact; whether the truths of God's word then delivered at Cambuslang or elsewhere, were or were not effectual to the conviction and conversion of sinners. *The word of God is not bound,* whether it may have come from the lips of Whitefield a Methodift haranguer, or of * Flechier eloquent popifh prieft.

THIRDLY, In the renewing of our covenants, there is neceffarily a particular application of them to our own circumftances. As it would be the groffeft abfurdity to fuppofe that the covenants of our fathers bind us to regulate our conduct or our teftimony for the truth according to their circumftances and not according to our own; fo our bond, being an explanation of what our covenants oblige us to at prefent, is with obvious propriety adopted to our own circumftances.

THUS while we folemnly declare our confent to the obligations that were laid upon us in the loins of our fathers, we likewife for our own part, avouch the Lord to be our God, engaging to do the duties of our own fituation, of our feveral places and callings. It is not enough that we approve of the covenanting of our forefathers: the Lord requires us according to the calls of providence, no lefs than he required them, to enter into covenant with him; to vow and pay to him.

SOME have complained of the act of the Affociate Prefbytery by which oppofers, contemners, and flighters of covenanting are debarred from fealing ordinances in the Seceffion. The principle of this act is this: That no perfon ought to be admitted to the fellowfhip of a particular church, who adheres obftinately to fome opinion or practice inconfiftent with the obfervation of any thing which that church, as fuch, knows and acknowledges to be an ordinance of Chrift. This principle we propofe to confider and vindicate more fully afterward. At prefent, we only obferve that without holding this principle, one

---

* In the Sermons of Monfieur Flechier, we have not only many beautiful models of eloquence, but feveral pertinent illuftrations of divine truths.

cannot conceive how the immediate end of church-fellowship, which is to be helpful to one another in observing whatsoever Christ hath commanded us, can be gained; since, without holding this principle, our fellowship may be as much with those that hinder as with those that further our observation of his ordinances.

The occasion of covenanting is the same still as when it was begun by the Associate Presbytery, Which occasion is this: That while the bulk of the three nations have openly cast off the covenant which our fathers entered into with the Lord, a few in a state of Secession from the established churches, bearing the character of witnesses for Christ, have declared, with the solemnity of a public oath, their adherence to that covenant, or deed of conveyance of themselves and their posterity to the Lord. The opportunity is continued for others to declare their adherence to the covenant in the same way. Accordingly from year to year some are offering themselves for that purpose, and appearing under the banner of a sworn and subscribed testimony against the breaches of our covenants, and against the prevailing neglect and contempt of public covenanting.

Still there is no outward appearance of its becoming national. Few in number, poor and despised are the people that have as yet engaged in it. The body of these lands disregard their endeavours. But it is a comfortable token for good that the Lord does not mean to give up his claim to the isles of the sea, that he is putting it into the hearts of considerable numbers to recognise and maintain that claim. This is one of the most comfortable signs of our times: And if the Lord give them one heart and one way, and enable them to honesty in adhering to the word of their testimony, we may have good hope through grace, that they shall overcome by the blood of the Lamb; and that they shall be the means of beginning a revival of our covenanted reformation which will increase till it overspread the land; which will exceed the former in purity, in spirituality and in the plentiful effusion of the Holy Ghost; and which will send the favour of Christ and the glories of his kingdom over all the inhabited world. *Thus the Lord shall cause them that come of Jacob to take root: Israel shall blossom and bud, and fill the face of the world with fruit.*

ESSAY IV.

Of the State of the Church of Scotland immediately after the Revolution.

MANY and various were the advantages arising to Britain, from that wonderful interposition of Providence by which the Prince of Orange was raised to the throne: Liberty was established on a firmer basis: We were secured against the introduction of Popery: Scotland, in particular, was relieved from the yoke of Episcopacy, and saw that beautiful order, in some measure, restored, which Christ has appointed in his church. There was, then, a precious opportunity of returning to the Lord; but it was mournfully neglected. Both church and state were in a great trespass.

WITH regard to the state, it was wrong that the Prince of Orange was admitted to the throne without being required to give any proper evidences of his adherence to our covenanted reformation; or to make the support of it a condition of his government: for though this was not necessary to constitute such a relation between him and the British people, as rendered him a chief magistrate intitled to their obedience in things lawful; ‡ that relation, being in itself,

---

‡ Church-members are not to refuse a dutiful subjection to magistrates, or to neglect praying for them, because they are not such as they would themselves have chosen. The Lord's people are for the most part poor, afflicted pilgrims, and have seldom any considerable share in the modelling of governments, or in the administration of them: Hence they have commonly no more to expect from them than the preservation of their outward peace. Agreeably to this, the apostle enjoins us to *pray for kings and all in authority that we may lead quiet and peaceable lives under them in all godliness and honesty.*

justly held valid, whenever it is constituted with any suitable regard to the consent of the people, or to the immediate end of magistracy, the welfare of civil society; yet it was a great evil, that these nations neglected to acknowledge the Lord in this matter, paying little attention to his glory or to the good of his church; so that the Lord might say of us, *They have set up kings, but not by me, they have made princes, but I knew it not.*

It was a neglect not only of religion, but of the common rights of justice and humanity; that there was no public inquiry with respect to the innocent blood that had been shed on religious accounts, nor any punishment inflicted for the shedding of it. The witnesses of Christ were indeed relieved from the horrors of persecution; but their oppressors, and some who had imbrued their hands in the blood of their brethren, were suffered to live undisturbed, and several of them advanced to places of trust and dignity.

But not to insist on these things, we proceed to consider the evils in the establishment of religion.

In the first place, The State discovered an absolute disregard of all that was done on the behalf of our covenanted reformation in the period between 1638 and 1650. Our rulers took no particular notice of the laws then made with respect to religion. Nay, the acts rescissory (by which the parliaments of that period and all they did, were annulled) are still in force among the laws of Scotland. It is true, Presbytery was established. But that might be done without regard to the above-mentioned period; since Presbytery had been ratified by government long before in the year 1592, (a ratification which is indeed referred to in the act of settlement) and since it was established not as a part of the covenanted uniformity of the three nations, but only as most agreeable to the inclinations of the people in Scotland, they having reformed from Popery by Presbytery. It is plain, that they did not mean to shew any regard to Presbytery as opposite to Prelacy, or in other words, as it was established in the second reformation; but only as opposite to Popery, that is, as it was established in the first reformation. It is true, the rulers likewise ratified the Confession of Faith; but this they did without taking notice of any former ratification of it: they only called it, *The public and avowed Confession of the church:* " meaning no more," as a judicious writer observes, " than the confession " of the church diffusive of Presbyterians, come out " of the furnace of persecution, who were then be- " ginning to recover, and be acknowledged in a na- " tional church-state." Remarkable is the difference between the act of the Scots Parliament approving the Confession of Faith in 1649, and the act that parliament approving it in 1690. The former ratifies it as having been before approved by an act of the General Assembly, and as presented to them by the commissioners of that assembly: But the latter ordains it to be the confession of the church of Scotland without any regard to her preceding acts or her present application. The former ratifies not only the Confession and Catechisms, but also the acts of Assembly approving them as a part of the covenanted uniformity in the three kingdoms; whereas the latter ratifies the Confession of Faith only.

It may farther be observed, that we have no reason to consider particulars not expressed by the legislature, as belonging to the legal settlement of religion, on the footing, merely, of such general declarations as the following: " That their Majesties with " advice and consent of three estates, revive, ratify, " and perpetually confirm all laws, statutes and acts " of parliament made against Popery and Papists, and " for the maintainance of the true reformed Protes- " tant religion, and for the true church of Christ " within this kingdom." General clauses of this kind in the introduction to an act of parliament are not intended to add any particulars to those mentioned in the act itself; for that would suppose that the framers of the act had purposely made it vague and indeterminate: Such clauses are only meant to recommend the law or act in which they are used from the general nature and tendency of it. Thus in the present case, the legislature represents the legal settlement of religion at the Revolution as a ratification of all former laws in favour of the Protestant religion and the kingdom of Christ: but how far it is so, we are still to judge from the particulars that are specified in the act of settlement itself.

The parliament of Scotland at the Revolution, did nothing to vindicate the parliaments held in the period between 1640 and 1649, from the unjust aspersions which had been, and still continued to be cast upon them; but on the contrary concurred with the other branches of the legislature in the establishment of Episcopacy in England and Ireland; an establishment as directly contrary to our covenanted reformation as any of the proceedings of Charles II. This establishment was confirmed by the incorporating union. The Scottish Parliament's settlement of religion at the revolution, and its union with England may explain each other: for as we are not, without an evident necessity; and by no means on account of some general expressions in the preamble of an act, to consider the parliament as contradicting itself; so we may venture to affirm, that no more in the settlement of religion at the revolution than in the incorporating union with England, did the Parliament of Scotland mean to vindicate the parliamentary proceedings in the above-mentioned period or to revive our covenanted uniformity and reformation.

But for proof of this point, we need not insist upon the meaning of a particular act of parliament: Whatever approbation our rulers since the revolution, have given to our reformation from Popery in the period between 1560, and 1596; whatever abhorrence they have expressed of the persecutions in the reigns of the two brothers, as contrary to humanity and civil liberty; we have no sufficient reason to believe that the sense of the legislature concerning the national proceedings in our covenanting period, has been any other since the revolution, than it was when the acts rescissory were passed. Are not those national proceedings constantly traduced as the proceedings of rebellion and fanaticism? Have not our governours, since the revolution as well as before it, countenanced such a representation of them? Do not the proceedings of parliament and the general practice of our courts of judicature since the revolution, shew that the legislature still considers the parliaments held between 1648 and 1649 with all their acts, as null and void? No member of parliament, either lord or common, is ever heard pleading upon any thing then transacted as an unexceptionable precedent. No court of justice will ground a single decision upon a parliamentary deed of that period. The acts of Charles II. however opposite, some of them, to the principles of the revolution, are in full force and in daily use, while the acts of our covenanting times, so perfectly agreeable to those principles, are expunged and forgotten. Besides, it was plainly against our covenanting period, that the oaths of allegiance and fidelity were imposed instead and in exclusion of all other oaths and declarations of allegiance, not excepting those religious covenants by which we lie under the most solemn obligations to be subject to lawful authority.* If we consider the neglect of this period in a political light, we have reason to lament that our fathers did not profit, as they might have profited, by the endeavours of some of the most upright and enlightened patriots that ever adorned our country, to secure to themselves and posterity the enjoyment of civil liberty. But considered in a religious light, the evil was unspeakably worse. It was

---

* See the last article of the Claim of Rights, and the second Act of the first session of King William and Queen Mary's first parliament.

the blackest ingratitude to the Lord, that we were no way concerned to remember the years of the right hand of the Most High: Surely this forgetfulness is one principal ground of the Lord's controversy with these lands; surely it is wrong to palliate or excuse it.

SECONDLY, The State then discovered a disposition to encroach upon the liberty and independency of the church. The barons and commissioners from the royal burghs, assembled in parliament, determined, by their own sole authority, what religious system the church was to receive as her public and avowed confession of faith: they fixed on the Westminster Confession of Faith without recurring to any former deeds of the church; particularly without referring to the act of assembly in 1647: an important act as it guards against any conclusions that might be drawn from the second article of the thirty-first chapter of that Confession, to the prejudice of the church's intrinsic power. The act restrains what is there said of the magistrate's right of calling synods and assemblies to the case of *kirks not settled or constituted in point of government*. Hence on the head of the magistrate's power of calling church-courts, the confession of faith ratified by the parliament at the Revolution was a different confession from that which the church of Scotland had received in her purest times; it was less explicite on the above-mentioned article and more liable to misconstruction. Thus the State arrogated to itself a power of judging what it was proper for the church to receive as articles of belief.

IT was another instance of the magistrates disposition to encroach on the province of the church, that he interposed his authority to procure admission into the church for those who, before the revolution, had been of the Episcopal persuasion. His Majesty ordered, " that neither the assembly nor any com-
" mission, nor any church meeting should meddle in
" any process or business with respect to the purging

"out of the Episcopal ministers." This was a plain infringement of the church's liberty as to the exercise of her discipline.

Besides, by the act in 1592, according to which Presbytery was settled at the Revolution, the king or his commissioner, being present at the general assemblies of the church, is to appoint the time and place of their meeting: nay, the act seems to give the king or his commissioner the sole power in this matter, not so much as hinting the concurrence of the assembly itself: "Providing," says the act, "that the king's majesty or his commissioner be present at ilk general assembly before the dissolving thereof, nominate and appoint time and place when and where the next general assembly shall be holden."

Thus the church is deprived of an important part of that liberty wherewith Christ has made her free, with regard to the meeting of his courts in his name. It is obvious, that this unlimited power of fixing the time and place for the meetings of the General Assembly, might be so exercised as to deprive the church of nearly all the advantages arising from that court. And it is well known how this power was exercised after the Revolution, particularly in dissolving the assembly in 1692, and in adjourning its meetings from that time, till 1694. So the form of the commission granted every year to the nobleman who represents his majesty at the assembly is said to run in this manner; "seeing by our decree an assembly is met at such a time. This must sound harshly in the ears of those who have been accustomed to consider synods and assemblies as courts of Christ the alone head of the church, and as not subject to any other than the decrees of Christ.

Other evidences might be produced of this disposition, in the civil power, to encroach on the liberty of the church; standing evidences, many of them, which every one has occasion to witness. For example, acts have been passed obliging ministers, on pain of ecclesiastical censures, of suspension and deprivation, to take certain oaths, such as those of abjuration and allegiance; or perhaps to read, on the Lord's day, certain papers; such as that concerning the death of Captain John Porteous. To the same purpose, we might take notice of the public fasts and thanksgivings appointed from time to time, by the sole authority of the civil magistrate.

Thus our State is chargeable with these two evils: with the utter neglect of the reformation attained to by our fathers; and with manifesting a disposition to encroach on the liberty of the church. The State has been either quite inattentive to the concerns of religion, Jer. ii. 33. *Can a maid forget her ornaments, or a bride her attire? Yet my people have forgotten me days without number:* Or instead of ordering political affairs in subserviency to the purity of the church, the State has moulded the church according to political interest and the popular inclination, Amos iv. 4, 5. *Come to Bethel, and transgress; at Gilgal multiply transgression; and bring your sacrifices every morning, and your tithes after three years. And offer a sacrifice of thanksgiving with leaven, and proclaim and publish the free offerings: for this liketh you, O ye children of Israel, saith the Lord God.*

Whatever we may say of the kindness of Providence at the Revolution; however much regard we must express for those eminently godly ministers whose lives and labours then edified the church; yet when we consider the proceedings of the church in her courts of judicature, we must acknowledge the truth of the following observations.

1. The church made no suitable remonstrances against the evils of the civil rulers; but submitted to their impositions. Happy to find outward circumstances now so much changed for the better, professors thought it improper and unseasonable to find fault with the arrangements made by the civil autho-

rity. When the fears and alarms we have been long harraffed with, are over, we are too apt to give our-ourfelves to unwatchfulnefs and indolent repofe. As foon as the church of Scotland was relieved from oppreffion at the Revolution, fhe feems to have fallen infenfibly into a great degree of that fin of Ifrael which the prophet reproves, Micah vi. 16. *The ftatutes of Omri are kept, and all the works of the houfe of Ahab, and ye walk in their counfels.* The people of this generation have little or no impreffion of the heinoufnefs of public evils, or of compliances with the wicked ordinances of magiftrates; but the Lord fhews us the ruin that follows upon fuch compliances in the following words: *That I fhould make thee a defolation, and the inhabitants thereof an hiffing.*

2. THE church took no due care to vindicate our covenanted reformation from the indignities that had been done to it in the great apoftacy of the two preceding reigns. There was no particular acknowledgment, by the church-judicatures, of the feveral fteps by which our fathers declined from that reformation: no exprefs or fuitable condemnation of thofe enfnaring bonds, oaths and declarations, which had been framed in the preceding reigns for annulling our folemn covenants; and which had occafioned great fufferings to the witneffes of Jefus: nor any particular act paffed by the General Affembly for the neceffary purpofe of vindicating the alone headfhip of Chrift over the church, and the church's intrinfic power; truths which had been fo recently trampled on with heaven-daring contempt. Far from inflicting due cenfure on any for being concerned in the grievous apoftacy from our covenanted reformation, the judicatures did not fcruple to receive into communion the indulged minifters, and even fome who had been of the Epifcopal denomination: the indulged minifters, who had meanly fubmitted to

preach under such limitations, both with respect to the matter and manner of their preaching, as a tyrannical and malignant prince thought proper to impose. Thus, at the Revolution, the church of Scotland was, by no means, duly concerned to make an impartial inquiry into the grounds of the Lord's controversy, not to purge out the old leaven; things so necessary to be done that without them there never was, nor ever will be any thorough reformation.

3. THE church neglected, at the Revolution, to take proper steps toward the revival of national covenanting. Considering to what an uncommon height all ranks of men had carried their perfidy toward the Most High, it was unquestionably the duty of the church to acknowledge the breach of her covenant with the Lord, and to avow her return to him as explicitely and solemnly as she had ever done. But the judicatures did not so much as pass any particular act for the purpose of asserting the obligation of our covenants on these lands; or even the morality of what our fathers had done in entering into such engagements. The passing of such an act might have prepared the way for national covenanting. Surely it was wrong to treat with so much neglect the public covenant-relation to the Lord, into which, thro' his good hand upon our godly progenitors, he had graciously brought the isles of the sea.

4. TESTIMONIES against these neglects were much disregarded. The above-mentioned paper of Mr. Shields was read in a committee, which, having passed a severe censure upon it, refused to lay it before the assembly. Other petitions and representations were treated in the same manner. Various instances of the like tyrannical treatment of petitioners, by the committees and commissions of the General Assembly, have occurred since that time; particularly in the years 1731 and 1732. From these well known transactions it may easily be inferred: That in the state of the church of Scotland after the revolution, there

was a grievous departure from our covenanted reformation, since the facts on which these testimonies proceeded, (facts which could not be denied even while recent) were so many instances of such departure: And that the state of the church of Scotland after the revolution was that of a backsliding, not of a reforming church. We do not speak of particular members, or particular parts; but of the whole body of the church; of her judicatures, especially the supreme. We do not speak of particular acts of assembly, (for several of these, passed since the revolution, have been very commendable) but of the disposition manifested in the general course of judicial proceedings, toward that purity and agreeableness to the word which the church had attained in what is called our covenanting period.

THUS the church aggravated the errors of her conduct, by disregarding the testimonies that were given against those errors. This greatly heightened the Lord's controversy with the land, Hosea xi. 7. *My people are bent to backsliding from me: though they called them to the Most High, none at all would exalt him.*

ON the whole, it seems very plain, that both church and state were, at this time, chargeable with neglecting our covenanted reformation. It was in direct opposition to it, that the state imposed, and the church accepted, an Erastian settlement of religion. And though they removed some real evils, and did several things really commendable; yet those evils were not removed as contrary, nor these good things done as agreeable, to our covenanted reformation. All that the Lord's right hand wrought for us in the above-mentioned period, and the obligations of our solemn covenants were either despised, or forgotten, or at least, no way suitably regarded by church and state.

WE may be ready to apologize for our fore-fathers at the revolution, considering them as men liable to the ordinary weaknesses of our nature. Sudden and surprising events, like the revolution, commonly fill the human mind with such a confusion of hopes, fears and anxieties as render it incapable, for a time, of calm reasoning and deliberation

Indeed we have no reason to think, that, in their situation, we ourselves would have acted more faithfully than they did: And were we drawing the character of any individual who had a share in these wrong managements at the Revolution, charity would lead us to admit every excuse or alleviation with which the circumstances of the case, or the general tenor of his principles and behaviour should furnish us. But we are speaking of public measures, not of private characters: We are inquiring, whether the proceedings of church and state were right or wrong. Here it behoves us to guard against palliating any thing really sinful, as ever we would avoid the curse pronounced against those who call evil good, and good evil: We must bring the proceedings in question to the test of the word, and try, whether church and state improved the opportunity providence had given them, as they ought? whether they endeavoured to hold fast whatever conformity to the word had been already attained in these lands? whether they were duly concerned to wipe off all the reproaches that had been cast on Zion's king, on his cause and interest? Whether their measures were such as evidenced a sincere desire to make progress in reformation? Whether, in fine, they chearfully complied with the Lord's call to return to him? or whether they treated it with neglect and opposition?

We have insisted the more largely on the manner of settling religion at the Revolution, as the evils of it may justly be accounted the root of all those corruptions which are now grown to such a height in the church of Scotland. It is only the Erastianism and worldly policy which prevailed in the Revolution Settlement, that have ever since been operating with increasing strength, in patronages, in the civil magistrate's absolute and authoritative appointment of fast days, and in other instances of incroachment on the church's freedom and independence. Then were admitted into the church a set of corrupt, time-serving office bearers who had accepted of indulgences and been guilty of base compliances with the open apostacy in the two preceding reigns: The successors of whom, increasing ever since, have now become the ruling party, or rather, (as, in the communion of the establishment, there is no regular opposition to them on the principles of our covenanted reformation) their leaven has now leavened the whole lump. That enmity against a faithful testimony for the truth, (which immediately after the Revolution was manifested by the judicatures disregarding petitions and representations) grew stronger by degrees, till it came to such a pitch that ministers were no longer allowed to have protests marked in the records of the Assembly, but were prosecuted in a vexatious manner, for testifying in their doctrine against the public corruptions; and at last when they would not submit to be censured for what they judged their duty, they were suspended and cast out of communion. In fine, the revolution church having admitted to her communion a great many persons of the most jarring principles, formed a body of very heterogeneous parts, and had evidently in her constitution the seeds of all the secessions and divisions that have since taken place among her members.

Thus, we have reason to say of those who profess to bear testimony against the present corruptions of the established church of Scotland, while they approve the manner of its establishment at the Revolution; that they condemn in the effect the same thing which they justify in the cause: They are too much like those of whom the prophet complains, Lam. ii. 14. *Thy prophets have seen vain and foolish things for thee; and they have not discovered thine iniquity, to turn away thy captivity; but have seen for thee false burdens and causes of banishment.*

ESSAY V.

Of the Church's Toleration of any thing sinful.

THE term *Church* is frequently to be understood as comprehending all that are called out of the world *lying in wickedness* to the fellowship of Christ; all that are saved and set apart to the service of God, Eph. v. 25, 26. *Christ loved the church and gave himself for it: that he might sanctify and cleanse it with the washing of water by the word, that he might present it to himself a glorious church.* Hence it is called the spouse of Christ, his spiritual temple, his body. This church, being made up of his friends only, manifests or makes herself visible by observing his commands, John xv. 14. *Ye are my friends, if ye do whatsoever I command you.*

INDEED, the real enemies of Christ may pay him an external homage, and appear to be church-members: nevertheless, the true end and design of such homage as prescribed by Christ, is to distinguish his real friends from his real enemies; and those only are true church-members whose external homage corresponds to that end and design; others are liars and impostors, Rom. x. 6. *They are not all Israel which are of Israel: neither because they are the seed of Abraham, are they children,* 1 John ii. 19. *They went out from us; but they were not of us.* Traitors may wear the badges of loyal subjects: but these badges were never designed for traitors†.

---

† A church ought, no doubt, to proceed upon visible evidences in judging particular persons to be duly qualified church members; and in consequence of such a judgment, they must be reckoned church-members with respect to all the purposes of external society.

THE enemies of Chrift can no more be reckoned true church-members for being among them, than tares can be reckoned wheat for growing together with it, Matth. xiii. 24,—30. A number of the enemies of Chrift agreeing together for fome carnal ends to make a fair profeffion of his name, might, from that profeffion, bear the denomination of *his church;* but in truth, they would only be *a fynagogue of Satan.* Rev. ii. 9. *I know the blafphemy of them who fay they are Jews, and are not, but are the fynagogue of Satan.*

SOCIETY, however, as an inftance of obedience to the commands of Chrift, is one principal way of rendering our church-memberfhip vifible, Heb. x. 25. *Not forfaking the affembling of yourfelves together, as the manner of fome is.* 2 Theff. v. 11. *Wherefore comfort yourfelves together and edify one another, even as alfo ye do.* Acts ii. 42. *They continued ftedfaftly in the apoftles doctrine and fellowfhip, and in breaking of bread, and in prayer.* It is a fociety in fpiritual exercifes and in fpiritual privileges, that is here meant.

BUT we are very much limited in the enjoyment of fociety: it cannot have place but in proportion as nearnefs of fituation, acquaintance, fimilarity of principles and views, give occafion to focial inter-

---

But it is plain, that the ordinances and proceedings of a church, agreeable to the word and warranted by the authority of an invifible king and head, have an immediate refpect to an invifible kingdom in the hearts of men, for the erection of it in thofe who are to be church-members, and for the advancement of it in thofe who are fuch already: So that in the cafe of mere nominal Chriftians, thefe ordinances and proceedings may juftly be faid to want what is properly their object in church members. Hence the abfurdity of any affociation of men imagining that, when by carnal policy they increafe their numbers, they are therefore contributing to the increafe of the church of Chrift: Hence, too, the importance of the fcriptural ordinances and the fcriptural proceedings of a church of Chrift to vital and practical religion; all fuch ordinances and proceedings having an immediate refpect to, and an appointed influence upon, the invifible kingdom of God in the heart: Finally, hence no fociety can pofitively allow the contempt of fuch ordinances or proceedings without injury to practical religion. Whatoever is contrary to thofe ordinances and proceedings, being contrary to found doctrine, is likewife fo *to the power of godlinefs.*

course. Hence as it is impossible for all the members of the church of Christ, scattered over the whole world, to hold fellowship immediately and habitually with one another in a visible church-state; it is necessary that they form themselves into various distinct societies for the worship of God and for their mutual edification. These societies are called *Churches*, Acts xv. 41. *He went through Syria and Cilicia confirming the churches.* Rom. xvi. 16. *The churches of Christ salute you.* Such were the churches of Corinth, of Ephesus, of Galatia, of Thessalonica, of Philippi and of Colosse.

It is abundantly clear, that every church, in this sense of the term, should be constituted according to the pattern which Christ hath given us in his word. She should consider herself as in the same relation to Christ with his church or mystical body at large, and as under the same obligations to endeavour after conformity to him in all things. Hence the apostle Paul so often speaks to particular churches in terms that are properly applicable to the church invisible: *Feed*, says he to the Ephesian elders, *the church of God which he hath purchased with his own blood. I am confident*, says he to the Philippians, *of this very thing, that he who hath begun a good work in you will perform it until the day of Jesus Christ.* The more exactly a particular church is conformed to the pattern of the word, her members have the better opportunity of evidencing by their fellowship with her, that they indeed belong to Christ's mystical body. This is an end so important, that where it is not in some degree answered, the proper design of a visible church is utterly lost.

The question which we now propose to consider is this: Whether a church of the kind just now mentioned, may tolerate in her members the practice or profession of any thing she herself acknowledges to be sinful? *Any thing*, we say, whether, comparatively considered, it is of greater or of less importance; whether it has been or is still controverted among Christians: if it be really sinful and acknowledged by a church to be so; it is with regard to that church, what is here meant by *any thing sinful*, as being opposite to some of the truths and duties known and professed by that church; for the attainments of other churches are out of the question.

WHEN a church condemns any thing judicially, she is justly considered as holding it to be sinful; sinful either in itself, or on acount of some offensive circumstances attending it. We have a remarkable instance of this kind in the Acts of the apostles, fifteenth chapter. As the proceedings of the synod at Jerusalem are an excellent pattern for the imitation of all future synods; so, in what is said of the obligation of their decrees upon the churches, we have proper instruction as to the regard that is due to the synodical decisions that are consonant to the mind of the Holy Ghost speaking in the scriptures. These decrees are called a burden laid upon the church, Acts xv. 28. *For it seemed good to the Holy Ghost and to us, to lay upon you no greater burden than those necessary things.* We cannot suppose a person would have been admitted a member of the church of Antioch, who should have refused to take upon him the common burden of the church. Besides no person in that church could reject those decrees without being in some degree liable to the charge, which the synod brought against the Judaizing teachers, of *troubling the church and subverting souls.*

IT is not our present design to determine the degree of censure to be passed upon persons who are chargeable with what is meant in the question by *any thing sinful*. That subject may be considered afterward. We may only observe, that a church may justly be considered as tolerating what she herself owns to be sinful, if persons openly chargeable with it, and who give no evidences of being sorry for it or of desiring to forsake it, are habitually admitted to the most sacred pledges of her communion.

It is a dictate of scripture and of reason, that the discipline of a church ought to correspond with her doctrine. If she allows in her terms of communion the same thing which, in her public instructions, she acknowledges to be sinful; what does she but destroy in one way what she builds in another? Hence if a church ought, according to the Lord's express injunction, to teach her members to *observe all things whatsoever Christ hath commanded us;* she ought likewise, to make the observance of all those things as far as the visible church-state will permit, the general term of her communion; and consequently she ought not to tolerate in her members any thing in particular that she acknowledges to be contrary to Christ's command, or, in other words, to be sinful. Thus, as the practice of a church member ought to be according to his knowledge, so the discipline of a church ought to be according to her doctrine.

It is inconsistent with that watchful care which the church ought to exercise over her members, to suffer sin upon any of them, or positively to tolerate any evil in them, whether with respect to principle or practice. The duty of the church to each of her members is, in this particular, the same as that of one individual to another, Lev. xix. 16. *Thou shalt not hate thy brother in thy heart: thou shalt in any wise rebuke thy brother, and not suffer sin upon him.*

The toleration, in question, is inconsistent with the good order of any society; and therefore is contrary to the general rule, *Let all things be done decently and in order.* Suppose a particular practice is determined by any society to be wrong and utterly inconsistent with the design of its erection; to admit persons into such a society, while they are openly chargeable with that very practice, would be the destruction of policy and good order. Now, when a church declares any thing to be sinful, she declares it to be, on the matter, inconsistent with the great purpose she was designed for, with her testimony against the enemies of Christ, with that universal holiness which is her honourable and heavenly characteristic, Ezek. xliii. 12, *This is the law of the house; upon the top of the mountain, the whole limit thereof round about shall be most holy. Behold, this is the law of the house.* It is therefore utterly against the law, the appointed order of the house, for any church to allow her members in what she herself acknowledges to be sinful.

This toleration is likewise contrary to the remarkable analogy between the case of the visible church and that of the particular believer. The believer is one who *hates every false way:* however weak or defective, he must not, even for a moment, give positive allowance to any sin. Nothing, indeed, is more plainly or more necessarily implied in the character of a believer than this; that he maintains a constant opposition to whatever he accounts sinful, and belonging to the old man or the kingdom of Satan. And though the opposition may sometimes be faint, or seem greatly overpowered, yet it is out of character for the Christian to drop it altogether, even in a single instance. It is no less unbecoming a church of Christ, so far to give up her opposition to any thing she acknowledges to be sinful, as to allow it openly and expresly in her members. The public character of the church in all in her proceedings, ought to be, at once, a counterpart, an example, and a help to the real Christian. Every particular church, constituted agreeably to the word, consists of such as are, or at least acknowledge they ought to be, saints or members of Christ's mystical body: and therefore though some other things may belong to the description of a church than what belongs to that of the Christian; yet we should not have any thing to say of the former *contradictory* to what we say of the latter. But that would be the case, were we to assert that a church may tolerate in her members, what no Christian can allow in his practice.

The toleration we speak of, is inconsistent with the due maintenance of a testimony for truth: which appears whether we consider whom this toleration admits to church-communion, or the truths and duties which are thereby disregarded. For, if a church admits to her communion one person who obstinately rejects something which she herself acknowledges to be a truth or a duty of God's word, she cannot consistently refuse admittance in the same way to ten, to twenty, to a hundred, to a thousand, or any number that may apply to her for that purpose. Hence that whole church may soon come to be made up of those who obstinately reject such a truth or duty; and who instead of holding, trample upon a testimony for it. And then, if we consider the intimate connection among the truths and duties of Christianity, not only as bearing the stamp of the same authority, but as they are mutually supported by and dependent on each other; it will appear, that, if a church allows her members in a positive rejection of any thing that she herself acknowledges to be a truth or a duty of God's word, she will soon extend her allowance, and her members their rejection to other truths and duties: because the same reason that was deemed sufficient for such a toleration in the case of one truth or duty, will be found also sufficient in the case of others. Besides, if reasons drawn from the external circumstances of the church, or from the characters of particular persons are allowed to overbalance the authority of Christ in one instance, they will soon be allowed to do so in more. Thus, through the powerful tendency of depraved nature to backsliding, a relaxation of discipline, or a church's suffering her members to neglect *any* thing which Christ hath committed to her trust, being once wilfuly and deliberately begun, will, in the ordinary course of things, continue on the increase, till her laxness arrive at such a pitch that she shall not retain the least appearance of faithfulness to her trust in any respect whatsoever.

K k

Indeed, seeing church-members have no joint participation of their spiritual privileges, nor joint exercise of religious duties, or, in other words, they do not walk as church-members at all, but in so far as they are *of one heart and one way:* it is plain that they bear no suitable testimony in their united capacity against any thing sinful, but in so far as they are unanimous in their opposition to it as such. Hence the apostle gives that solemn caveat against diversity of judgment among church-members, 1 Cor. i. 10. *I beseech you brethren, by the name of our Lord Jesus Christ, that ye all speak the same thing; and that there be no divisions among you; but that ye be perfectly joined together in the same mind and in the same judgment.* For a church to admit to her communion persons who avowedly approve and practise what she herself condemns as sinful, is to invite the very thing which the apostle here solemnly charges her to guard against.

Farther, This toleration is contrary to all such texts of scripture as warrant separation from corrupt churches and disorderly walkers, 2 Cor. vi. 17. *Wherefore come out from among them, and be ye separate saith the Lord, and touch not the unclean thing: and I will receive you.* 2 Thess. iii. 6. *Now we command you, brethren, in the name of our Lord Jesus Christ, that ye withdraw yourselves from every brother that walketh disorderly.* If we ought not to continue our fellowship with persons that walk disorderly, we ought much less to receive such into our fellowship. Surely it is as necessary to endeavour to keep infection out of the house; as to leave it after it is infected. But the toleration in question says, that endeavour is needless. Besides, the duty of a church and of particular persons in this matter is reciprocal: for it is no less incumbent on a church to withdraw from corrupt persons, than for persons to withdraw from a corrupt church.

Object. 1. " Would you then have a church re-
" quire perfection in her members."

Answ. It is only meant, that she should not tolerate or *suffer sin upon them*. As her pastors must not shun to *declare the whole counsel of God;* so she must not shun to testify against and censure whatever is opposite to that counsel. Indeed her members are far from being perfect: they are spiritually diseased, like others; only while others remain insensible of their miserable condition, they profess to be convinced of it, and to want a cure. Hence the church, if she acts the part of a wise and good physician, and aims at a thorough cure, will endeavour to examine every symptom, and to spare no part of the disorder: She will not be guided by fair but deceitful appearances, or by the inclinations of her patients, but by the grand, infallible dispensatory of heaven, the Bible.

Object. 2. " It is enough, if a church oblige " her members to the essential truths and duties of " Christianity; she need not be so strict with regard " to circumstantials."

Answ. Surely, the very circumstantials of Christianity, like the filings of gold, are precious; they should not be thrown away, but carefully gathered up and preserved. And pray, how may the circumstantial truths of the Bible be known from the essential?

" The circumstantial are such as we may be ig" norant of, or deny, without endangering our sal" vation."

Obvious enough indeed! but the question still recurs, how may these be distinguished from others?

This answer is not only unsatisfactory, but it is insnaring, as it seems to insinuate that the evil of error lies *only* in the danger to which it exposes our souls, and not in its opposition to the authority of God speaking in the word: and thus the idol of depraved nature, Self, under the refined pretext of concern for our everlasting salvation, is made the rule and reason of our faith in divine truth: for, upon this supposition, the evil of rejecting divine truth is deemed less or greater according as self is endangered by the rejection†. But it is unworthy of reasonable creatures, who should *do all for the glory of God*, to make self their end and aim. Self is a very doubtful rule; self, we mean, as a principle of man's corrupted nature. It is peculiarly doubtful in the present case; as we are far from being competent judges of the comparative importance of divine truths; and as one principal danger is here entirely overlooked, that of *making God a liar*.

THE truth is, we should estimate the danger of any error rather by the degree of evidence which, in the case of that error, is rejected or despised, than by our notions about the superior value and importance of one truth compared to another, John iii. 19. *This is the condemnation, that light is come into the world, and men loved darkness rather than light, because their deeds are evil:* Compared with verse 23. *No man receiveth his testimony.* Our danger lies not merely in rejecting such truths as we think of great importance to our salvation; but in our loving darkness rather than light; which light is God's testimony. It is not said our condemnation is, loving errors more than some of the most important truths revealed in the word; but the expression is general; our condemnation is the not receiving of God's testimony; the whole of which is represented to us under the notion of light in opposition to darkness. Hence it is plain, that our rejection of any one truth belonging to what is here called, *the light that is come into the world,* or to the divine testimony in the word, is so

---

† A concern for our salvation, subordinate to the glory of God, is our indispensible duty; but, separated from a single regard to the glory of God, it is an abomination. We are to receive the word, in the first place, on account of its divine authority, or *as the word of God*; we are to receive it, in the second place, *that we may be saved:* The primary ground and reason of faith is, not that such truths are connected with our salvation, but that they bear the stamp of *Thus saith the Lord.*

dangerous that it may be our condemnation. It is, indeed, undeniable, that, in religion, there are truths of more importance than others: but as there is no rule laid down in the word for fixing precisely the degrees of their importance, it seems to be the only certain as well as scriptural way of estimating the evil of error, to consider the degree of light and evidence (including both external and internal evidence, both outward instruction and inward conviction) to which the error stands opposed*.

On this principle, it is, indeed, still evident, that there is greater guilt, for the most part, in the denial of the more important truths of Christianity, on account of the greater degree of light and evidence with which they are attended. At the same time, supposing there are two points of divine truth which, considered in themselves, appear to be, one of greater, the other of less importance: the evil of denying the latter in some circumstances, may be more aggravated than that of denying the former in other circumstances.

Thus the errors of those Judaizing teachers who were for bringing the Christians at Antioch under the yoke of circumcision, seem to have been far more blameable, than the mistaken apprehensions of the disciples, while they followed Christ in the days of his flesh, with respect to the nature and necessity of his death and resurrection; though it is plain, that the truth about the death and resurrecti-

---

* The following passage of an eminent writer in the Deistical controversy is very opposite to the loose manner in which many speak of what they call the *circumstantials* of Christianity: "As it is one of the peculiar weaknesses of human nature, when, upon a comparison of two things, one is found of greater importance than the other, to consider this other as of scarce any importance at all: it is highly necessary that we remind ourselves, how great presumption it is, to make light of any institution of divine appointment; that our obligations to obey all God's commands whatever, are absolute and indispensable; and that commands merely positive, admitted to be from him, lay us under a moral obligation to obey them: moral in the strictest and most proper sense." *Butler's Analogy.*

on of Chrift, is, in many respects, of more importance than the truth about the freedom of Christians from the yoke of circumcision. But here was the difference: the disciples were weak and ignorant; but they did not set themselves against the truth, like the Judaizing teachers, to the troubling of the church and the subverting of souls.

OBJECT. 3. "It seems better for the church to "leave many things indifferent: it is enough that "her members walk honestly according to the light "of their conscience."

ANSW. The church ought to leave a thing indifferent, if the law of God leaves it so. Nor ought she to declare a thing sin or duty, for any other reason whatsoever, than this; because either the thing itself, or the necessary consequences of it, are plainly commanded or plainly forbidden by the law of Christ; for the business of the church is not to make laws, but to publish those of Christ.

WITH respect to persons acting according to the light of their consciences, it is, at best, only one part of holiness, namely, sincerity: and however excellent it is, other parts of holiness are also necessary; such as, an humbling sense of our sinfulness and misery, the saving knowledge of God in Christ, reliance on the Spirit of grace, watchfulness, spiritual strength and stedfastness, liveliness and activity in the way of the Lord. Thus, though sincerity is essentially necessary in church-members, they ought to have other qualifications than sincerity.

IT is true, conscience is God's deputy in the soul, declaring in his name one thing to be duty, and another to be sin: soothing with its approbation, if we comply with the former; and denouncing vengeance and fiery indignation, if we commit the latter. For a person to act contrary to the dictates of conscience, is to rebel against and contemn the authority of God; whose voice the person either hears or thinks he hears in the remonstrances of conscience. But this, like the other faculties and operations of the soul, is now corrupted; and though it still speaks in the name of God, and shews much of the law not yet blotted out of the heart; yet it is, in many instances, weak, mistaken or defiled. 1 Cor. viii. 7. *Howbeit, there is not in every man that knowledge*, or a well conformed conscience, *for some with conscience of the idol unto this hour eat it as a thing offered unto an idol*, that is, they consider their doing so as rendering them partakers of idolatry, and yet they do not abstain from it; *and their conscience being weak is defiled.* As the whole man is defiled with sin, the conscience is so in particular, Tit. i. 15. *To them that are defiled and unbelieving is nothing pure, but even their mind and conscience are defiled.* Here it is plain the defilement *of them that believe not*, and *of their mind* is sin; and we have no reason to put any other interpretation upon the epithet *defiled* as here applied to the conscience, than what we put upon it as applied to *them that believe not* and to *their mind.* But what is it for the conscience to be defiled with sin? Is it to accuse of sin and condemn on account of it? No, for that is only its duty: But surely the conscience is defiled, when it calls evil good, and good evil.

THERE is not any thing, indeed, in which the great degree of man's corruption more signally appears than in this; that the conscience itself is drawn over to the side of wickedness. Hence our Lord says, Matth. vi. 23. *If the light which is in thee be darkness, how great is that darkness!*

SURE no one will deny that conscience is liable to error, if he considers, that it is no other than the mind of man as exercised in judging of sin and duty, and viewing the consequences of right and wrong conduct. A small acquaintance with scripture and with human nature will be sufficient to convince us that men are continually forming false judgments, on those subjects.

But to speak more directly to the objection, the rule it insinuates for the admission of persons to the communion of a church may well be rejected for this reason; that it is impracticable. A church may know in some measure, the agreement between a person's profession and his outward practice; because both the one and the other may, alike, be subjected to her examination. But in order to know whether these be agreeable to the person's conscience, the church must find means to bring that secret principle, without the help of either words or actions, under a judicial review. But can she indeed enter the person's mind, observe the moral lights as they rise, mark each conviction wrought by the word and Spirit of God, and hear the warnings of conscience before they are put into words? We can perceive the agreement or disagreement between two extremes only in so far as we know the extremes themselves. But here the church has not the least knowledge of the one, that is, the person's conscience; otherwise than as it is uniformly manifested by the other, that is, the person's conversation.

OBJECT. 4. "It seems warrantable from the xiv. chapter of the epistle to the Romans, for a church to receive persons that differ from her in some of their opinions and practices."

ANSW. It is very unlikely, that Paul who shewed on all occasions such a concern to preserve the peace and purity of the church; who so earnestly exhorted the Thessalonians to *withdraw from every brother that walketh disorderly;* who warned the Ephesian elders to beware of ravenous wolves that would *creep in among them, not sparing the flock;* who wished to have them cut off that troubled the church of the Galatians; who withstood Peter to the face when he took part with those Judaizing teachers that were such enemies to the liberty wherewith Christ hath made us free; we say, it is very unlikely that this faithful and zealous apostle would direct the church of Christ at Rome to receive into her bosom such as were open and avowed despisers of any thing that she herself acknowledged to be a command of Christ. Hear what a solemn charge he gives to this very church: *I beseech you, brethren, mark them who cause divisions and offences contrary to the doctrine which ye have learned; and avoid them.* But who are they whom a church must consider as the causers of such divisions and offences? Those, undoubtedly, who in the eyes of that church, openly and obstinately despise any commandment of the Lord. Surely, then, the apostle would never advise the Romans to receive such into their communion.

The case concerning which the apostle here gives directions, was shortly this: Some persons who had been probably either of Jewish extraction or proselytes, having professed their faith in Christ, continued still to observe many of the usages of the ceremonial law; they abstained from certain sorts of meat; they kept certain days, such as, those of Pentecost and of the Passover. These persons had expressed their desire of being admitted into the association of Christians at Rome. They were ignorant indeed, but they wanted to grow in grace and in the saving knowledge of our Lord Jesus Christ: they indeed still thought it their duty to observe some parts of the ceremonial law; but they were, by no means, enemies to Christian liberty; they sought an opportunity of being farther instructed in it. The apostle directs the Romans to receive these persons into their communion; and shews how respectfully and charitably church-members ought to behave toward them, and they again, toward fellow-church-members. It is obvious, that these persons, meek humble, teachable, desirous of getting free from their prejudices in respect of which they were rather weak than wicked, were directly the reverse of those Judaizing teachers, troublers of the church and subverters of souls, against whom the apostle cautions the Philippians in these words: *Beware of evil workers, beware of dogs, beware of the concision.*

It is necessary to enquire more particularly, what those things were, the practice of which in these weak and unexperienced church-members was to be borne with. Those usages may be considered in two lights:

First, They were things that God expresly commanded under the Old Testament. The person of whom the apostle is here speaking, was convinced of this; but he was not so much enlightened in the knowledge of the New-dispensation as to see that these things were already abrogated. We need not wonder that this was the case with private church-members, when even the apostle Peter was so much stumbled at some of the privileges of the New-dispensation, Acts x. 14. Gal. ii. 11. How great was the difference between the regard these Christians had for the usages which bore the stamp of divine authority, and that superstitious attachment to certain modes of religious worship, for which no other warrant can even be pretended than the invention and authority of men? Hence the apostle says in verse 6th of this chapter, *He that regardeth the day, regardeth it to the Lord*, that is, he is influenced by the divine authority of the Old Testament precept enjoining the observation of such a day: and on the other hand, *He that regardeth not the day, to the Lord doth he not regard it*, that is, he likewise is influenced by the divine authority of the New Testament revealing our freedom from the burden of ceremonial observances. To the same purpose the apostle adds, *He that eateth, eateth to the Lord, and giveth God thanks; and he that eateth not, to the Lord he eateth not, and he giveth God thanks.* The import of this thanksgiving is, that the one as well as the other aimed at the glory of God in what he did. But sure it is only so far as a person is swayed by a regard to God's authority that he can be said to aim at his glory in what he does; especially so to aim at it as to be worthy of the apostolic approbation. But it may be asked, how it came about that the same principle of regard to God's authority could lead some to do, and others not to do, the same things? This was owing to a peculiar circumstance of that period: the Lord saw meet that the ceremonial, which was his own law, should die gradually and be buried honourably; and that his people should get, by degrees, from under the yoke of the Old Testament, to enjoy the glorious liberty of the New. Hence the apostle represents the old dispensation, not as removed at once by an instantaneous introduction of the new, but as *decaying, waxing old and ready to vanish away*. The Lord was pleased to bear with the weakness of his people in their attachment to some of the ancient ceremonies; while they were not so fully instructed in the reasons of the abrogation of them as he designed they should be afterward by the epistle to the Hebrews and other books of the New Testament not then published; while the observation of the Old Testament worship was not rendered impracticable by the destruction of Jerusalem and the temple; and while they did not seek justification by a scrupulous adherence to the law of Moses, putting it in the place of Christ and his righteousness. Thus the Lord did not condemn them; and what are we, that we should censure them with severity? The synod of the apostles and elders of which we read in Acts xv. instead of condemning them, made a decree for preventing the Gentile converts from giving them offence. Should it still be urged, that if it was right to observe these ceremonies, then the omission of them must have been sinful: We answer, that though these usages may be considered as having been enjoined by divine authority; they also admit, as they were observed by some Christians at this time, of another consideration: viz.

SECONDLY, That they were of an indifferent nature; that is, they were things which Christians were neither expresly commanded, nor expresly forbidden; things which they were or were not, to practise according to the measure of their light, and of their acquaintance with the nature and privileges of the New Testament dispensation. The observation of the ceremonial law, even under the Mosaic œconomy, depended upon the circumstances of time and place: circumcision was discontinued the forty years that the children of Israel sojourned in the wilderness: No sacrifices were offered during the seventy years of the Babylonish captivity. Thus compared to the superior and perpetual obligation of the moral law, the obligation of the ceremonial, even when in its highest vigour, may be said to have been only occasional, circumstantial, and subject to change. Immediately after the death and resurrection of Christ, it became indifferent; that is, the church could no longer require her members to observe it, except in so far as it was necessary for the exercise of charity toward weak brethren. Still, however, the Lord would have it honoured as his own law; nor might any one cast it off till he was so much enlightened in the knowledge of the New Testament dispensation, as to see the Lord's warrant for doing so. To be so much enlightened was far from being, at this time, the general attainment of church-members, especially of those who had been accustomed to the use of the ceremonial law, it being the Lord's usual way to carry on his work by degrees. Hence he did not permit the church at once to declare the observance of the ancient institutions unlawful, lest very many, not being duly enlightened in the knowledge of the new-dispensation, should have been tempted to trample upon the authority of God, by their ignorant manner of casting off those institutions. The church, therefore, was in the right to leave many of them indifferent. Hence the apostle says, *To him that esteemeth any thing to be unclean, to him it is unclean. The kingdom of God is not meat and drink, but righteousness and peace and joy in the Holy Ghost. For he that in these things serveth*

Chrift, is acceptable to God and approved of men. Had the ufages the apoftle here fpeaks of, been contrary to any command of God, furely perfons could not be faid to have ferved Chrift in them; and inftead of being acceptable to God, and approved of men, they would have been defpifers of the divine authority, and in the fight of men tranfgreffors of the law. The indifferent nature of thefe ufages appears, too, from the reafon which the apoftle affigns for prohibiting church-members from the open contempt and difregard of them; which is, that fuch contempt and difregard would offend weaker fellow-church-members. *All things indeed are pure; but it is evil for that man who eateth with offence. It is good neither to eat flefh, nor to drink wine, nor any thing whereby thy brother ftumbleth, or is offended, or is made weak.* We cannot better define an indifferent thing than by faying, That it is a thing which becomes wrong whenever it becomes offenfive. We cannot fay that of any thing which God hath exprefly commanded or forbidden.

What we have faid may help us to underftand feveral exhortations in this chapter. *Him that is weak receive, but not to doubtful difputations.* This does not fay, that we fhould not defend the truth by difputing againft error: God's bleffing has often made difputation ufeful to his people: It is recommended to us by the example of Stephen, of Paul, and of our Lord Jefus himfelf. But the difputation againft which the apoftle here warns the Romans, was doubtful; it was difputation which neceffarily began and ended in doubt; as neither he who condemned his brother for regarding the ceremonial ufages, nor he who condemned his brother for the neglect of them, had any plain declaration of God's word on his fide. Befides, difputation at an unfeafonable time, and in an unfuitable manner, tends to difcourage and offend weak church-members, and to fill them ftill more with doubt and perplexity. Again, the apoftle fays, *Let every one be fully perfuaded in his own mind.*

This does not mean that a person should be very confident and obstinate in his opinion, whatever it is. That is only self conceit; it is what the Lord strictly prohibits even with respect to things that seem to be in themselves indifferent, Deut. xii. 8. *Ye shall not do after all the things that we do here this day, every one whatsoever is right in his own eyes.* A person who does whatsoever is *right in his own eyes*, or in modern language, according to his conscience, is but a poor character in the Bible. But the intent of this exhortation, is, that our consciences ought to be well informed of the mind and will of God as to whatever we do; and particularly, that a due respect should be paid to the authority of God in regarding or not regarding the usages of the ceremonial law. The apostle explains his meaning by his own example in verse 14. *I know, and I am persuaded by the Lord Jesus, that there is nothing unclean of itself.* Farther, the apostle says, *Who art thou that judgest another? To his own master he standeth or falleth.* We must not understand this as a warrant to overlook the conduct of our brother, or to neglect reproving him for his offensive behaviour. It was the language of Cain, *Am I my brother's keeper?* We must not only teach, but also admonish and reprove one another. We must not with-hold what the Psalmist calls *a kindness, and precious ointment that shall not break the head.* This caveat, therefore, must be understood as levelled against that evil which our Lord condemns, Mat. vii. 1. *Judge not, lest ye be judged;* against either thinking or speaking uncharitably of the person or state of our brother, especially on account of a diversity of opinion and practice as to indifferent things. Once more the apostle says, *Hast thou faith? have it to thyself.* It does not follow from this, that we should not make a profession of our faith for the edifying of the church; which would be contrary to the exhortation in verse 19. *Follow the things wherewith one may edify another;* and in Heb. x. 13. *Let us hold fast the profession of our faith without wavering.*

The apostle's meaning is this: if a church-member has strong faith, he may enjoy the comfort of it before God, and bring forth the genuine fruits of it in holiness of heart and life; but he should not insult over his weak brethren, nor do any thing that may prove offensive or stumbling to them.

We have dwelt the longer on this chapter, not only because it is often quoted on the subject of church-communion, and often perverted; but also because it is a passage of scripture that is peculiarly useful for the direction of the church with regard to the receiving of such persons and the estimation of such things as the apostle here speaks of. Things that the church, in her representative or collective capacity, has never determined and cannot clearly determine from scripture to be sin or duty, may justly be considered in the same light as the meats and days here mentioned: and as to the matter of admission to the fellowship of a particular church, such things, whatever individuals may think of them, are still to be held indifferent: that is, neither the omission nor the performance of them should be any bar to church-communion. Besides even with respect to such things as the church has determined to be sin or duty, persons should not be utterly rejected for their ignorance of some of them, provided they are such persons as *the weak in the faith* toward whom the apostle exhort the Romans to behave with so much tenderness and charity. Among those who apply for admission to the fellowship of any church, she ought certainly to make a difference between the weak and the wicked; between the teachable and the obstinate; between the ignorant and those who contradict and blaspheme; between those who love the light and lament their want of it, and those who hate it because their deeds are evil.

Object. 5, " Every church ought to imitate
" Christ her head: he holds communion with his
" people notwithstanding much remaining corrupti-

"on: Who would partake of his fellowship, were he to exclude from it all that are chargeable with any thing he has declared to be sinful?"

Answ. We own, the communion of the saints with Christ, and their communion with a particular church may be compared together, in such respects as the following: Those who have communion with Christ are such as make it the study and business of their lives, to keep his commands, 1 John ii. 3. *Hereby do we know that we know him*, or have union and fellowship with him, *if we keep his commandments*. So it is only those whom a church judgeth to be such that she ought to admit to her fellowship. He chastises his people when they wander from his way, by various rods; particularly, by depriving them of the comfortable sense of their communion with him, Psal. lxxxix. 30, 32. *If his children forsake my law, and walk not in my judgments,—then will I visit their transgression with the rod, and their iniquity with stripes*. In like manner, a church ought to censure her members when she sees them go astray.

But still it does not necessarily follow that whoever has real communion with Christ must have likewise actual communion with a particular church; for in some respects there is no comparison between the one and the other. The communion of Christ and that of a particular church cannot be compared in respect of necessity. The latter is indeed one of the appointed means of our sanctification; but the former belongs to the very essence of our sanctification. A person may be sanctified by the fellowship he has with Christ in his word and in prayer, though he should never have an opportunity of joining himself to any particular church. It is necessary for Christ to hold real communion with his people at all times, in their worst as well as in their best cases. Thus *he preserves their souls in life*, even when the overflowing of some corruption renders them rather hurtful than edifying to fellow church-members. He takes care of them even while in the hands of their enemies; restraining these enemies, and over-ruling all their deceit and violence to his own glory. Such was his gracious presence with the ark while in the hands of the Philistines, that instead of destroying it, they were obliged to do it honour. Thus Christ was with Peter to support his faith, even when Satan was permitted to sift him as wheat. Farther, the communion of the saints with Christ and their communion with a particular church cannot be compared with one another in respect of the evidence on which they proceed. Christ, as *he knows what is in man*, deals immediately with the hearts of his people; but the church can only deal with their outward profession and their outward practice. As he discerns the naughtiness of a church-member under the fairest external appearances; so, too, the reality of grace, even where the church can see nothing but evil; and such evil as appears to render him unfit for her communion. It is plain, therefore, that, in some respects, we cannot draw a strict parallel between a person's invisible communion with Christ and his visible communion with a particular church. Indeed the communion of poor sinners with Christ is a mystery of incomparable grace and sovereignty. When a particular church receives a person into her communion, it is with this view; that such a person may be useful to her as well as that she may be so to him. But in our communion with Christ, he alone is profitable to us, not we to him; if we are enabled to make him any returns of service and of gratitude, he is himself the author and the finisher of them. *He works all our works in us.* We dare not hold communion with disorderly brethren, because being evil already, we grow worse by evil communications: But Christ may well invite them to communion with him; because he is able to render them meet for it; he *sanctifies them wholly.*

SINCE a church's positive allowance of any thing in the practice or profession of her members which is acknowledged by herself to be sinful, appears contrary to the ends that are common to the church with other societies; and still more so to those that are peculiar to herself: it may be useful to observe the progress and the effects of such toleration in various churches.

The most flagrant instance of it is in the church of Rome. After the fourth century, as her corruptions increased, that course of public humiliation, which, as it was at first practised in the church, was only designed to evidence the repentance of public offenders, came at length to be considered as a proper commutation for offences and for crimes. When the pretensions and abuses of clerical power were carried to a great height, then the church pretended that it belonged to her alone to regulate those commutations. In consequence of that, the Pope and his council decreed various alterations with respect to them; as, that money should be accepted instead of those humiliating appearances formerly in use: In order to give weight and authority to such absolutions, they represented them as the same, or inseparably connected with those of heaven: having gone thus far, it was not difficult to go a step farther; they offered not only pardon for the past, but indulgence for future crimes: And that they might not seem to have undertaken what was beyond the compass of their power, they pretended to have discovered a treasure of merit in the church; a treasure consisting of the works of supererrogation performed by innumerable reputed saints, together with the infinite merits of Christ. Then was a certain price put upon every crime; and a member of the church of Rome, on paying a sum of money, had all the allowance his spiritual guides could give him, to persist in the practice of the greatest villanies. No wonder that so enormous an abuse was among the first things that occasioned that concurrence of wonderful events which distinguished the æra of the Reformation,

Nor have the reformed churches themselves been duly careful to keep clear of this evil. Thus if we take a view of the church of England; what with the inconsistency between her superstitious modes of worship and her testimony against the church of Rome; what with the custom of administring the Lord's Supper in order to qualify persons for civil offices; what with her dependance on the state, and her obsequious compliances with it; what, in fine, with her total neglect of church discipline, (the penalties imposed on offenders by the bishop's courts being rather a persecution of the members of civil society than the exercise of spiritual discipline on church-members as such) the church of England is deeply chargeable with this evil.

The church of England and the church of Scotland have public articles and confessions of faith directly pointed against the tenets that go under the names of Arianism, Socinianism and Arminianism: but where is the person who is now kept from their communion on account of those dangerous errors?

The opinions laid before the assembly for the judgment of that court, in the processes of Messrs. Simson and Campbel, are plainly contrary to the acknowledged principles of the church of Scotland; and yet how those offenders were screened from due censure, is well known. Nothing can be more contrary to her established order and rules of discipline, than for a clergyman to be intruded into the ministry of a reclaiming congregation: And yet how many such clergymen are in her communion?

It is lamented by the serious part of those who are still in the communion of the church of Scotland as well as by others, that, in admitting persons to her sealing ordinances, there is daily less attention paid even to such things as are allowed by Christians in general to be sinful and immoral.

Nor are those who profess to have withdrawn

from the establishment in Scotland on account of its corruptions, free from blame in this matter.

For example; those who call themselves, *The Presbytery of Relief*, because they are said to relieve the Christian people from the oppressive execution of the law of patronages, declare, by their profession of the presbyterian religion, that whatever is contrary to it, particularly Episcopacy and Independency, is to be held sinful: and yet, by a determination of their clergy*, they invite such as are openly chargeable with those evils, to participate in the most sacred pledges of their communion.

With respect to another set of dissenters from the Establishment, their practice in opposition to their brethren; such as their neglecting to set about public covenanting at present, their justification of the religious clause in some burgess oaths, their censuring various passages in the Judicial Act and Testimony; is, at least, plainly an allowance of what is determined to be sinful in public deeds which, by their own confession, they themselves have passed; deeds which they have never yet thought proper to repeal; and therefore deeds, under the authority and obligation of which they are standing to this day †.

---

* See a copy of this determination in pages 30, 31, 32. of a late valuable publication, entitled, *The Relief Scheme considered*.

† The public deeds here meant, are these: The Act, declaration and testimony, published in 1737; The Act of the Associate Presbytery for renewing our solemn covenants in a way and manner agreeable to our situation and circumstances in this period, passed in 1743; and the act of the Associate Synod against swearing the religious clause in some Burgess Oaths, passed in 1746. The Brethren of whom we here speak, pretend to find *errors and mistakes* in the first of these acts: They deem the second, in contradiction to its title, *unseasonable and disagreeable to our present circumstances*: The *manner*, they say, in which the Synod passed the third was *rash* and *unfair*: Some of them are traduced as having the worst *effects*; as raising *doubts* in the minds of many persons; and as encouraging a spirit of *pride*, of *self-conceit* and *animosity*. One should think that any act justly liable to these charges ought, in reason, to be repealed; and yet, however amazingly preposterous it may seem, some of these very charges have been offered as an apology for not repealing one of the acts abovementioned.

WITH respect to another body of dissenters who refuse to acknowledge the present civil government in Britain, we may observe, That their principles on this head, considered as in opposition to the principles of those who are endeavouring as well as they, to testify against every thing in the civil constitution or administration that is really evil, or contrary to our covenanted reformation, must imply a disapprobation of all the public justice and all the preservation of peace and good order we have by means of the civil magistrate: principles which are not only unwarrantable; but which never can be carried into practice, unless we either take arms against civil society, or forsake it. This is an instance of a church declaring something to be sinful in which she must either indulge her members, or oblige them, as the apostle says in another case, *to go out of the world.* This indulgence is dangerous as having a tendency to the relaxation of discipline: and so much the more, that occasions daily occur, such as the paying of taxes and the summoning of persons to appear before civil courts of judicature; which can hardly fail to be attended with such compliances as, according to those principles, are doubtful at least, if not evidently sinful.

UPON the whole, when a church opposes the truth as maintained by another church; when she ceases to endeavour after more conformity to the word of God; when she is satisfied with her attainments and values herself upon them; we have reason to conclude she is in a backsliding state; a state which is not only characterized, but in a great measure constituted by this unscriptural toleration.

ESSAY VI.

Of the Constitution of the Associate Synod.

ON this head, we would only offer some answer to the two following questions: The first is, Whether that body of ministers and elders which met in Mr. Gib's house the next morning after the breach, (of which we have given some account) had a right to act as a court of Christ? The other is, Whether the denomination of the Associate Synod belonged to that body?

With regard to the first we may observe, that if several persons regularly called and ordained to the office of the holy ministry meet together in order to exercise the authority which Christ hath given them for the edification of the church, taking their warrant and encouragement from his word, Matth. xviii. 20. *When two or three are gathered together in my name, there am I in the midst of them;* if the general scope or tenor of their proceedings be such as gives some good evidence that they are sincerely aiming at the glory of Christ, and the advancement of the church's peace and purity; if they are not in any stated opposition to the truth or testimony of Jesus as held by another society, (for we must not set up altars by God's altars, nor weaken the hands of those who are truly bearing witness for Christ) if these things are found in any body of ecclesiastical office-bearers, what should hinder us from accounting it a court of Christ?

As for the above-mentioned ministers, it was never heard that even their enemies objected to the validity of their call and ordination to the sacred office. And whatever may have been wrong in particular instances, the general tendency of their proceedings to the revival of our covenanted reformation seems very evident. To demonstrate this, we might enter into a detail of their transactions; but that does not seem necessary, the character here given to their proceedings being such as those who are the least acquainted with them, will hardly offer to deny; a character indeed that will not much recommend them to the fashionable part of this generation. They have published several acts on behalf of the purity of presbyterian discipline and government; on the behalf of public covenanting as a moral duty, and proper to be set about at present: and charity, which thinketh no evil, will acknowledge that, whatever errors some may suppose them chargeable with, they have endeavoured, in the general tenor of their conduct, to preserve an entire consistency with those acts. And, alas! what is the greatest attainment of either societies or individuals in the present state of imperfection, but endeavouring to do well? The most successful are those who are most taken up in acknowledging and lamenting their mistakes and failings, looking, at the same time, that they may be set right by the word and Spirit of Christ.

AFTER all, if they were stating themselves in opposition to any point of the testimony of Christ as held by those of another profession, it would be much against them; it would go a great way to destroy their pretensions to the authority of a court of Christ. The purest church may walk contrary to the truth in particular instances: but the case here supposed is the fixed opposition of a corrupted to a pure profession: and we own that Christ will never give the stamp of his authority to that opposition; and that where it becomes the characteristick of a society to such a degree, as to have the ruling influence in its proceedings; that society, so far as this is the case, may justly be considered as destitute of the authority of the Lord Christ, who says, *He that gathereth not with me, scattereth:* It is obvious, that he will never lend his authority for the purpose of scattering, or opposing his cause and testimony.

This charge, however, of being in a stated opposition to any part of the present truth or testimony of Christ, has very seldom been brought against the judicatures of the Secession. Some, indeed, have insinuated the charge. How well they have supported it by attempting to find faults and historical mistakes in the judicial testimony and other deeds of the associate presbytery and the associate synod, must be determined by candid examination. Those, however, who have any discernment of the necessity of the Secession-testimony as levelled against the various steps of defection, since the year 1649, from our covenanted reformation, cannot well refuse to acknowledge the Associate Synod as a court of Christ: for, admitting that the Secession-testimony is according to the word; admitting that the constitution of the synod is not against any point of that testimony, held by some other society; but is in defence of the whole in opposition to many enemies of it; one should think there is no reason to doubt of the synod being a court of Christ, having a right to act authoritatively in his name: for it is undoubtedly a court of Christ the constitution of which is grounded upon an adherence to the testimony of Christ.

It now remains that we enquire whether that body of Seceders which, for the sake of distinction, we have already called the Associate Synod, or the defenders of the religious clause of some Burgess Oaths, have the better right to that title?

It will easily be allowed, that a court, or indeed any society may retain its title, as long as, generally speaking, it holds the principles and pursues the ends, which gave occasion to the title. Bodies of men, have, indeed, often continued to go under the same names after the original principles and ends of their affociation were loft. Thus though the Roman fenate, (meaning a free and independent branch of the legiflature) was no more after the ufurpation of Julius Cæfar, yet the title continued to be given to an affembly which was only the echo of the Emperor's will and pleafure. Thus Great Britain may have a parliament and yet want, what every true Briton underftands by that word, a guardian of the rights and liberties of the people. In this way, defigning and ambitious men put fuch titles on their projects and undertakings, as are beft calculated to deceive the unthinking populace into a favourable opinion of thefe projects and undertakings, and to divert the attention from their real nature and tendency. It is a common artifice, and yet almoft every day we fee it, in fome degree, fuccefsful. The fcripture (which indeed fupplies armour againft every evil) warns us againft this abufe of language, telling us of fome *who fay they are Jews and are not, but are the fynagogue of Satan.* Hence when we enquire after the affociate fynod, let us guard againft taking up with the name where the principles and the ends of its inftitution are forfaken. Surely the diftinguifhing principles of its inftitution, in due fubordination to the fcriptures of truth, were no other than thofe expreffed in the Judicial Teftimony and fworn to in the bond for the renovation of our covenants: and the great end of its inftitution was the maintenance and prefervation of thofe principles.

Now, there are two bodies of ecclefiaftical officebearers, each of which calls itfelf, The Affociate Synod. To which of them does the title juftly belong? To that body which has made a violent oppofition to fome important parts of the Judicial Teftimony, and which difapproves of engaging in the above-mentioned bond; or to that which is never blamed for any thing fo much as for abiding by the testimony and the bond, even to a fault? It seems to be abundantly clear, which of these two bodies is the Associate Synod, on the supposition that we are to seek it where the the Secession Testimony, as it was stated by the Associate Presbytery, directs us. This is, at length, rather a matter of fact than a matter of reasoning.

With regard to the accidents which took place at the breach, let us for a moment, suppose the worst: let us suppose that the members of the synod took some irregular steps; that they broke through some common forms: are we to conclude that, on account of a transient act not quite agreeable to ordinary forms, their constitution was overturned, tho' they were, as much as ever, holding fast the testimony on which their constitution was founded? Few societies would exist during the course of a single year, were they to be dissolved by every act that is irregular. The truth is, the members of synod had a right from the Lord Jesus the great head of the church, a right prior and superior to all those forms which human prudence has devised for preserving decency and order; a right which no accident could deprive them of; to come together as providence gave opportunity, to form themselves into a court of Christ, and in that capacity, to exhibit and maintain the testimony they had solemnly espoused.

When we examine into the propriety of their conduct, we should consider that nothing is more absurd than to confound the constitution of the synod with any particular place of meeting, or with any particular number of members; or to suppose that the constitution of the synod is affected by any accident or violence which might occasion an alteration in these respects. The constitution of the synod may be preserved, in any place where it is convenient to meet, by two or three or any greater number: and if their meeting is broke up by any unexpected accident, they may seize the first opportunity of coming together again, and proceed to act as a court of Christ, for the edification of the church without ever once supposing that their constitution was infringed. The reason is, that the members of a presbytery, synod, or any other court of Christ, derive their warrant and authority to meet, not from their former meetings, but immediately from his word; his word which respects each of their meetings alike, and independently of any connection with the rest; for he still says to his servants on every such occasion, *Where two or three are gathered together in my name, there am I in the midst of them.*

CONSIDERING the synod's constitution in this light, can we reasonably suppose that it was any way injured, because it removed from a place where the freedom of its procedings was violently controuled; or because it consisted of twenty-three members only, who zealously opposed a question, the affirmative of which, though it overturned their constitution as a witnessing court of judgment, was carried against them by twenty? It is true, these twenty considered themselves as the majority: in order to make up which majority, they annexed to their number, contrary to all the rules of procedure in courts of judicature, such as were silent on the question. But supposing (as the twenty-three members who met in Mr. Gib's house believed) that the advocates for the lawfulness of the religious clause of some burgess oaths, by their obstinate adherence to the affirmative of the above-mentioned question, had forsaken the constitution of the Associate Synod, (a constitution which consisted entirely in an adherence to a testimony for our covenanted reformation); surely in that case, it was necessary for these twenty-three members, if they were heartily concerned to preserve the synod's constitution inviolate, to leave a place where those who had forsaken that testimony, were assuming an uncontrouled superiority. They were evidencing the most genuine regard for the constitution of the Synod, when they forsook those who had forsaken that constitution.

On the whole, since the synod held the same testimony, and contended for the same covenanted work of reformation after as before the breach, its constitution appears to have suffered no alteration from what happened on that mournful occasion.

ESSAY VII.

Of the Church's power to inflict Censures.

SOCIETY cannot well subsist without government: nor will the ends of government be attained if it has not the power, both of bestowing privileges and of inflicting punishments. The church, being a society instituted by the Lord Christ, cannot once be supposed to be without government, or any of the requisites of government. The glory of his wisdom and of his goodness, makes the supposition absurd. Accordingly governments are mentioned among the benefits that the Lord bestowed upon the church, 1 Cor. xii. 28. *God hath set some in the church, first apostles, secondarily prophets, thirdly, teachers, after that miracles, then gifts of healing, helps, governments, diversities of tongues.* Some of these particulars indeed, were extraordinary, and continued only for a time in the church; but no body will consider *governments* which are common to societies of every kind, as belonging to this class. We cannot suppose that the apostle means civil magistracy, since these governments, as is plainly the case with the other things here mentioned, are immediately given to the church by her great head, as tokens of peculiar favour, whereas magistracy is a common privilege which providence grants to mankind at large. The names and exhortations that are given to ministers and to church-members are such as plainly intimate the relation between those who govern and those who are subject to government, Acts xx. 28. *Take heed unto yourselves, and to all the flock over which the Holy Ghost hath made you overseers, to feed the church of God, which he hath purchased with his own blood.* 1 Thess. v. 12. *We beseech you brethren, to know them who labour among you, and are over you in the Lord and admonish you.* Heb. xiii. 6. *Remember them who have the rule over you, who have spoken to you the word of God.* Ver. 17. *Obey them that have the rule rule over you, and submit yourselves, for they watch for your souls, as they that must give account: that they may do it with joy, and not with grief.* The greek word translated *those that have the rule over you,* is a name, says Beza, very remote from the claims of ambition, while it secures very great authority to faithful ministers. Pontius Pilate's highest title was a word that comes from the same verb. The term is employed by Stephen, in Acts vii. 10. to describe Joseph as next in authority to the king of Egypt. Nay the same word is used in Matth. ii. 6. to denote our Lord's supreme authority over his people. We must allow then, that there is a right of governing vested in the pastors of the church; a power or authority which the Lord hath given them for edification, and not for destruction. This is meant by the keys with which the apostles, and in them all the succeeding ministers of the word, were entrusted. In saying to Peter, Matth. xvi. 19. *And I will give thee the keys of the kingdom of heaven,* our Lord shews him how much the grace of God would be manifested in his case. The Father had revealed Christ to him in a saving manner: by which revelation he was enabled to make a faithful confession of Christ as the Son of the living God. And on this confession, or rather on Christ who is called a rock, 1 Cor. x. 4. as exhibited in this confession, was the church to be so built that the gates of hell were never to prevail against her. Peter was likewise to be honoured with the full power of an apostle of the Lamb. But we have no reason to suppose, with the church of Rome, that the keys here mentioned were given to Peter exclusively of the rest of the apostles.

There is no appearance afterward, of Peter being poſſeſt of any other office-powers than his fellow-apoſtles. Nay, preciſely the ſame explication of the keys which is here addreſſed to Peter is addreſſed to all the apoſtles equally, in Matth. xviii. 18. *Verily, I ſay unto you, whatſoever ye ſhall bind on earth ſhall be bound in heaven, and whatſoever ye ſhall looſe on earth, ſhall be looſed in heaven.* So much, by the way, concerning the popiſh blaſphemy which would make Peter the rock on which the church is built, in direct oppoſition to the determination of the Holy Ghoſt, 1 Cor. iii. 11. *Other foundation can no man lay than that is laid, which is Jeſus Chriſt*; and which would give Peter a lordly dominion over his brethren in direct contrariety to the expreſs charge which our Lord gave the diſciples, Luke xxii. 25, 26. *And he ſaid unto them, The kings of the Gentiles exerciſe lordſhip over them: and they that exerciſe authority upon them are called benefactors.*

We have ſtill farther evidence that the keys in queſtion include a right to govern. Theſe keys were primarily given by the Father to Chriſt as mediator and head of the church; from whom the office-bearers of the church have them to be inſtrumentally or miniſterially exerciſed for her benefit. Now, the keys that were committed to Chriſt were thoſe of government, as appears from Iſa. xxii. 22. *And the key of David will I lay upon his ſhoulders:* (equivalent to the expreſſion Iſa. ix. 6. *The government ſhall be upon his ſhoulder*). *So he ſhall open, and none ſhall ſhut; and he ſhall ſhut and none ſhall open:* compared with Rev. i. 18. *I am he that liveth, and was dead; and behold, I am alive for evermore, amen; and have the keys of hell and of death.* Theſe keys are among the gifts which the exalted Redeemer received for men, even for the rebellious, that God the Lord might dwell among them, Pſal. lxviii. 18. and which he gives to the church for her edification, Eph. iv. 7, 8, 11. Hence he ſays to his diſciples after his reſurrection, John xx. 21. 23. *As my Father hath sent me, even so send I you;* As if he had said, The keys which I received from the Father as his honorary servant, I commit to you, who are in like manner, my servants, as I am the Father's.

These keys are to be exercised by the pastors and rulers of the church meeting together in Christ's name, or by what the apostle calls a presbytery or eldership, 1 Tim. iv. 14. *Neglect not the gift that is in thee, which was given thee by prophecy, with the laying on of the hands of the presbytery.* It may be admitted as a maxim, that we should set about every duty as well in a social as in an individual capacity, unless (as in personal self-examination) there is something in the nature of the duty which makes it impracticable for a society as such to perform it. But no body will say that there is any thing in the nature of the keys of government which Christ has committed to the office-bearers of his house, that forbids the social exercise of them: Reason and the history of mankind recommend it, declaring that in the multitude of counsellors there is safety: the scriptures warrant it. In Matth. xviii. 15,—18, the judicative power before which the case of an offence between two brethren is directed to be laid, is called the church, η' εκκλησια;* a word that has no meaning at all, if it does not signify a society greater or less; a

---

* This name was borrowed from the Greeks, as being descriptive of the followers of Christ, who are *called out* of the world lying in wickedness; as serving to distinguish them from the Jews who chose to be called *the synagogue*; and, in fine, as being very familiar to the Gentiles who were to compose the greatest part of God's people. Besides there is something popular and engaging in this appellation; because it was used among the Greeks to denote a multitude of people assembled, regularly indeed, and according to law, but consisting of citizens of various ranks and situations in life, not excluding the lowest. Hence it was an appellation highly proper for the church of Christ; of which the apostle says in 1 Corinth. i. 26. *Ye see your calling, brethren, how that not many wise men after the flesh, not many mighty, not many noble are called.* As to the authority of the *ecclesia* or assemblies of the people in the ancient Greek Republics, it was very great; the laws were made, magistrates elected, peace and war resolved on, by the suffrage of those assemblies.

word that, the critics agree, is used in the best Greek writers for an assembly that has the power of judging and determining causes; a word that, in this passage, stands connected with such circumstances as naturally lead us to understand it of some lawful judicature: for why is it so expresly required that what passes between the two parties, should be established in the mouth of, at least, two or three witnesses, but that there may be sufficient evidence for the church to proceed upon, according to the rule of judicial procedure in Numb. xxxv. 30. and Deut. xviii. 6.? It seems to be abundantly clear, who are meant by the church, from the 18th verse. If any should object to our Lord's injunction, that perhaps the sentence of the church would be as much disregarded as the remonstrances of the offended brother had been: Our Lord answers, Whoever the offender may be, it is at his peril, if he disregards the sentence of the church. For, adds he, *Verily I say unto you*, to you whom I mean by the church, to you my apostles, and in general to you, faithful office-bearers of my house unto the end of the world, *Whatsoever ye shall bind on earth shall be bound in heaven, and whatsoever ye shall loose on earth, shall be loosed in heaven.* Nor need you be discouraged from the exercise of the discipline and government that I have ordained, by the smallness of your number; for *Again, I say unto you, that if two of you* (the least number that can be said to pass a judicial deed) *shall agree on earth as touching any thing they shall ask, it shall be done for them of my Father.* By the church, then, we are here to understand a number of ecclesiastical office-bearers come together, and agreeing to exercise the keys of government and discipline which the Lord hath committed to them. The eldership is called the church, " either because a prin-
" cipal part is put for the whole, the elders distin-
" guished from the people being here called the
" church, in like manner as the people distinguished

"from the elders are called the church, in Acts xx. 28. or becauſe in every matter of importance; their determinations are accompanied with the knowledge and conſent of the church †." *Acts* xv 22. *Then it pleaſed the apoſtles and elders with the whole church.*

Thus in the rule here laid down for our procedure againſt an offending brother, it is plainly intimated that the office-bearers, whom the Lord Chriſt has appointed in his houſe, ought to exerciſe the government committed to them, in a joint capacity. Conformable to this rule is the example of the apoſtles, and other miniſters of the word contemporary with the apoſtles. It belongs to the government of the church to ſend forth paſtors and teachers, and to aſſign them particular provinces that their labours and their talents may be properly deſtributed for the moſt extenſive benefit to the church of Chriſt. We have an example of the joint exerciſe of this branch of church-government in Acts xiii. 1, 2, 3. *Now, there were in the church that was at Antioch, certain prophets and teachers, both Barnabas and Simeon who was called Niger, and Lucius of Cyrene, and Manaen (who was brought up with Herod the tetrarch) and Saul. Now, as they were miniſtring to the Lord and faſting, the Holy Ghoſt ſaid, Separate me Barnabas and Saul for the work to which I have called them. Then having faſted and prayed, and laid their hands on them, they ſent them away.* Here is a joint exerciſe of the powers which our Lord had granted to Simeon, Lucius and Manaen in ſending away Barnabas and Saul, or, as the word απολυσαν imports, in looſing them from any engagements they were under to make a longer ſtay at Antioch; a pattern for the church's imitation to the end of the world. It is true, this was done in compliance with an immediate intimation of the mind of the Holy Ghoſt. The extraordinary manner of this intimation was ſuitable to the

---

† Gilleſpie's Aaron's rod bloſſoming, page 406.

state of the new-testament church before the model of her constitution as delineated in the word, was compleated. But the intimation itself corresponds to that guidance which a court of Christ, in every step of its procedure, ought still to look for from his word and Spirit. The Lord could easily have removed Barnabas and Saul from Antioch as he did Philip from the Ethiopian Eunuch, or in some other way, by an immediate interposition of his providence; but he rather chose to order the matter so as to give the church an example of the joint exercise of ministerial authority; ministerial authority, for the imposition of hands which was used in sending them away was an usual token of such authority, 1 Tim. iv. 14. and v. 22. 2 Tim. i. 6.

We have a remarkable example of the keys which our Lord committed to the office-bearers of his church in the fifteenth chapter of the Acts. Certain teachers from Jerusalem, taught the brethren at Antioch, that except they were circumcised after the manner of Moses, they could not be saved. This tenet having occasioned much disputation, it was determined that Barnabas and Paul with some others should go up to Jerusalem to the apostles about this matter. They arrived at Jerusalem. The apostles and elders came together to enquire into the affair. The cause is opened: The members of the assembly reason upon it; they compare word and providence, as the courts of Christ, while they act in character, do still: they come to a determination; which, for its judicial authority, is called *a decree of the apostles and elders which were at Jerusalem*, and *a necessary burden laid upon the churches*; which, for its importance, put an end to a doctrinal controversy, directed the practice of church-members, and, upon the matter, censured the Judaizing teachers, as *troublers of the church and subverters of souls*.

The apostle, writing to the Corinthians, gives us a very clear warrant for the joint exercise of those powers of binding and loosing which Christ has committed as an important trust to the office bearers of the church. He shews us how the church of Corinth was to set about excommunicating the incestuous person, in 1 Cor. v. 3, 4, 5. *For I verily as absent in the body but present in spirit, have judged already as though I were present concerning him that hath done this deed; In the name of our Lord Jesus Christ, to deliver such an one to Satan for the destruction of the flesh that the spirit may be saved in the day of the Lord Jesus:* With this we may compare the apostle's direction for the absolution of the criminal upon his repentance, in 2 Cor. ii. 5, 6, 7, 8. *But if any have caused grief, he hath not grieved me, but in part: that I may not overcharge you all. Sufficient to such a man is this punishment, which was inflicted of many. So that contrariwise, ye ought rather to forgive him, and comfort him, lest perhaps such a one should be swallowed up with overmuch sorrow. Wherefore I beseech you, that you would confirm your love toward him.* On this case we would make the two following observations.

The first is, That the apostle here injoins the church of Corinth to do something in an authoritative manner for the purging out of the old leaven. The sentence *(that such an one should be delivered over to Satan,* whatever may be the meaning of it) is very decisive and strongly implies a power and authority in those who passed it, over the person who was the object of it. And then that spiritual authority which belongs to church courts was no less apparent in the manner in which the awful sentence was to be passed; it was to be passed *in the name and by the power of the Lord Jesus Christ.* Besides, the absolution or removal of censure which the apostle directed the Corinthians to grant the person upon his repentance, was an authoritative absolution. *I beseech you,* says he, *to confirm your love toward him.*

The Greek word here translated *to confirm*†, signifies to ratify by public authority, to declare something as a judicial deed. Thus the church of Corinth was now called upon to exert that authority which the Lord had given her.

THE second observation is, That there was, in this case, a joint exercise of that authority. The sentence of excommunication was to be pronounced when the people *were gathered together*, by those, no doubt, to whom our Lord confided the powers of binding and loosing, that is, by the office-bearers of the church appointed in his word. The apostle says, *the punishment or censure was inflicted of many*, or (it should rather be read) *of the many*, of the presbytery, or company of elders in whose hands the government was placed. Thus a spiritual authority was exercised in this case; exercised not by one, but by the many.

Of the nature of Church Censures.

WE have seen that Christ has appointed a government in his church and in whose hand he has placed that government. We are now to speak of a very important branch of it; namely censures, or ecclesiastical punishments.

SINCE the entrance of sin, every society as well as every individual is liable to disorder: nor is the church exempted from the common lot. Nay, considering that the church bears the image of Christ, and that Satan, the world and the flesh are engaged in perpetual war against it; considering that the tares and the wheat grow up together in it, and its professed members are often in reality of the world, lying in wickedness; considering, too, that the church is

---

† The verb κυρόω comes from κυρος *authority*, and is used by good writers to signify the ratifying of public deeds.

yet in a state of childhood and weakness; when we think of these things, we will not wonder that there are disorders in the church. Hence the necessity of censures as a remedy against these disorders. What cannot be cured must be cut off. The old leaven must be purged out; for a little leaven leaveneth the whole lump. This holy discipline is one way in which the church is to evidence her love to Christ, to his truths and cause, and in which she is to maintain her testimony against the contrary evils. How severely is the church of Pergamos reproved for her negligence in this particular? Rev. ii. 12, 14, 16. *To the angel of the church in Pergamos, write these things saith he who hath the sharp sword with two edges.—But I have a few things against thee, because thou hast there them that hold the doctrine of Balaam.—Repent or else I will come unto thee quickly, and will fight against them with the sword of my wrath.*

THE censures of the church must be spiritual: *for her weapons are not carnal but mighty through God.* They do not produce their effect by bodily pain, but by persuasion.—Hence it is a maxim with regard to church censures that they should never be corporal punishments: to be whipt, or to be fined in a sum of money are, by no means what the church as a spiritual society ought to seek—credible evidences of gospel repentance. Submission to censures is not expiatory but evidential; we mean, church-members are by no means, like the papists with their penances, to look upon their undergoing the reproofs and corrections of the church as any ransom or atonement for their sins; but as manifesting their faith in the great atonement of our Lord Jesus Christ, an attonement to which nothing can be added for all the sins of all true church-members as well as manifesting a godly sorrow for sin, and a sincere purpose through grace of new obedience.

THESE censures are not inflicted by the authority of men, of kings or emperors, but by the authority of him who, unseen by a blinded world, is the great head of the church, ruling in her, and taking particular notice how his laws and inſtitutions are obſerved. The only rule according to which theſe cenſures are to be adminiſtered, is the word. Miniſters and elders, as far as they obtain mercy to be faithful, are ſwayed in every proceſs of cenſure, by a ſingle regard to the law and the teſtimony, guarding againſt the influence of pride, paſſion, prejudice, and worldly policy : for theſe are quite unſuitable to the nature of that kingdom which is not of this world. It is only the conformity of cenſures to the word that can encourage us to aſk or expect the bleſſing of Chriſt on them ; the word from which they derive all their uſe and efficacy, they being, in fact, no other than a particular application of the word as the rod of Chriſt's ſtrength in the hand of the church. As the general grounds of cenſure are moral and the ſame under both the old and the new-Teſtament diſpenſations, ſo the cenſures themſelves are the ſame. When our Lord erected the new-Teſtament-church, he did not inſtitute any new cenſures; but when the love of Chriſt was placed more fully in the view of his people by his actual humiliation and obedience unto death, even the death of the croſs, ſo that he had occaſion to give them the old precept to love one another under the engaging form of a new-commandment ; then he ſaw it proper to give them inſtructions ſuitable to that new commandment, with reſpect to their behaviour toward their brethren in the important article of church cenſure. Hence the obſervance of the rule that our Lord lays down in Matth. xviii. for our dealing with an offending brother, is the only way, in the ſuppoſed caſe, of expreſſing affectionate regard and genuine friendſhip. How ſhall we account for men's oppoſition to a precept evidently dictated by the moſt amiable generoſity, otherwiſe than by ſuppoſing that as they are little in the practice, ſo they have loſt the knowledge of real friendship, and that they are naturally *hateful and hating one another?* But the believer whose heart the Lord has purified by faith, is enabled to the faithful discharge of this as well as of every other duty. 1 Pet. i. 22. *Seeing ye have purified your souls in obeying the truth through the Spirit, unto unfeigned love of the brethren; so that ye love one another with a pure heart fervently.*

Of the Censures previous to Excommunication.

THE degrees of church censure are such as these; Admonition*, rebuke, suspension and excommunication. The first of these supposes that the person has been overtaken in a fault, or is in danger of being so, without implying any charge of either past or present obstinacy; for admonition is not adequate censure where obstinacy is in the case. There is more frequent accasion for admonition both private and presbyterial than for any other censure; and it is mentioned as a part of the ordinary work of church rulers, 1 Thess v. 12. *We beseech you, brethren; to know them which labour among you, and are over you in the Lord, and admonish you.*

WITH regard to rebuke, it implies a degree of obstinacy in the person rebuked, as it supposes admonition, doctrinally at least, has been used in his case, without effect, 1 Tim. v. 20. *Them that sin,* †

---

* Mr. Gillespie objects to the propriety of calling even Presbyterial Admonition a censure. He says it is only " a degree toward "censure. Admonition," adds he, " does not exclude from any " church privilege: nor is it a binding, since it does not require a " a subsequent loosing." It is true, admonition when fallen in with, ends the process; but that is equally the case with rebuke. There seems to be no impropriety in calling (for it is only about a name that we have any reason to differ from that acute and scriptural writer) admonition a censure, so far as it implies a charge of something faulty in the person admonished. Aaron's rod blossoming, page 478.

† *Sinning* in scripture is often put for making a constant practice of sin, or persisting obstinately in it, as in 1 John iii. 6. John viii. 34.

that is, who go on in sin notwithstanding the admonitions that have been given them, *rebuke before all*.

Suspension from sealing ordinances implies a greater degree of obstinacy. Suspension supposes that the person's obstinacy is or has been carried so far that the church sees cause to debar him for a time from her solemn ordinances, not having as yet sufficient evidence of his reformation to judge him disposed or fit to enjoy the fellowship of the saints.

We have this censure exemplified under the Old Testament in the instance of keeping persons from holy ordinances on account of ceremonial pollution. Thus the unclean were kept back from making any offering in the temple in Jehoiada's time, 2 Chron. xxiii. 19. *And he set porters at the gates of the house of the Lord, that none which was unclean in any thing should enter in.* If the breach of a ceremonial law thus precluded them from partaking of a holy ordinance; how much more would a breach of the moral law do so? The Lord severely reproves the priests for their neglect of this censure by which a difference is made between the holy and the profane, Ezek. xxii. 26. *Her priests have violated my law, and have profaned my holy things: they have put no difference between the holy and profane; neither have they shewed difference between the unclean and the clean, and have hid their eyes from my Sabbaths, and I am profaned among them.*

Christ has given solemn ordinances to the new-testament-church, the profanation of which is to be guarded against as carefully as was that of the ordinances under the old testament. Such ordinances are baptism and the Lord's supper. The terms upon which persons are to be admitted to baptism for themselves and children, are faith and repentance, Acts ii. 28. *Then Peter said unto them, repent and be baptized every one of you in the name of Jesus Christ, for the remission of sins.* Chap. viii. 36, 37. *The eunuch said, see, here is water; what doth hinder me to be baptized? And Philip said, if thou believest with all thine heart, thou mayest.*

WITH regard to the Lord's Supper, none are warranted to partake of it without examining themselves; and therefore it must be profaned, if persons are admitted who appear to be utterly void either of capacity or of disposition to set about that exercise, 1 Cor. xii. 28. *But let a man examine himself, and SO let him eat of that bread, and drink of that cup. For he that eateth and drinketh unworthily, eateth and drinketh damnation to himself, not discerning the Lord's body.* Hence the grosly ignorant, or those who are known to refuse to let go some grievous sin, or some grievous error, cannot, in the judgment of charity, be deemed, (though we may think well of their state) in a proper frame for an impartial self-examination, nor of consequence, for partaking of the Lord's supper. For the office-bearers of the church to neglect keeping back the ignorant and the disorderly from the sacraments, is to forget our Lord's prohibition, Matth. vii. 6. *Give not that which is holy unto dogs, neither cast ye your pearls before swine;* and the apostle's solemn charge, 2 Thess. iii. 6. *Now we command you, brethren, in the name of the Lord Jesus Christ, that ye withdraw yourselves from every brother that walketh disorderly, and not after the tradition which he received of us.* By such neglect they expose themselves to the danger the apostle warns them of, 1 Tim. v. 2. *Be not partaker of other men's sins, keep thyself pure;* compared with 2 John ii. *For he that biddeth him God speed is partaker of his evil deeds:* Surely, for an office-bearer of the church to admit persons to sealing ordinances, while he sees them engaged in any sinful course, is to bid them God speed.

WE have only one thing more to observe with regard to suspension, which is, that when the grounds upon which a person is kept back from sealing ordinances, are disputed; and having been brought before a presbyterial court, are by that court, deemed sufficient, the suspension of the person is then judicially declared, which declaring has been called *the less excommunication.*

Of Excommunication.

WE are now to consider excommunication properly so called; the highest censure that the church inflicts. It differs from suspension as exclusion from some of the privileges of the state differs from banishment: For the excommunicated person is considered as cast out of the church, as a heathen man and a publican, as externally at least, in the power of Satan, the prince of this world. A church-member is one called out of the world, that is, out of Satan's territories. But many that are so called, go on frowardly in the way of their own heart: when this frowardness breaks out into an explicit and obstinate rebellion against the laws of Christ's kingdom, it becomes necessary for the church to send the rebellious person back to the world to experience something of the tyranny of his old master, and something of the misery of his wretched subjects; that when the person is come to himself, he may, like the prodigal, be sensible of his folly, and may be brought to return in the way of acknowledging his iniquity, saying, *Father, I have sinned against heaven and before thee, and am no more worthy to be called thy Son.*

Of the use of this Censure under the Old Testament.

THE Church had the ordinance of excommunication under the Old Testament.

This appears to be sometimes meant by *the cutting off from the people or congregation of Israel,* which we read of so frequently in the law of Moses. This cutting off was a public deed, that the whole congregation of Israel might be instructed and admonished, Levit. xvii. 4, 5. where after an offender is appointed to be cut off, the intention of this punishment is expressed in these words; *To the end that the children of Israel may bring their sacrifices which they offer in the open fields, even that they may bring them unto the Lord, unto the door of the tabernacle of the congregation, unto the priest, and offer them for peace offerings unto the Lord.*

This expression is sometimes used to signify the deposing of one from the priesthood, 1 Sam. ii. 33. *And the man of thine, I shall not cut off from mine altar:* Sometimes divorcement, so in Deut. xxiv. 1. a bill of divorce is called *Sepher Cherithuth,* a book or writ of cutting off. There seems to be a real distinction between cutting off from the people or congregation of Israel, and cutting off from the land as in Zeph. i. 3. where it must be understood of cutting off by death.

Many of the laws inforced by this penalty are of a religious nature, laws the execution of which belonged to the church; such as that against forbearing to keep the passover, Numb. ix. 13. and that against any one partaking of the peace-offering while he was under the ceremonial uncleanness, Lev. viii. 20, 21. Now though cutting off, when annexed to laws the breach of which was punishable by the state might signify natural death, or perhaps banishment; yet we cannot understand it so, when it is annexed to laws the breach of which was punishable by the church alone, because it is not competent to the church, a spiritual society, to take away one's natural life, or to deprive one of his natural rights.

Farther, what was the consequence of this cutting off? to suppose that the Israelites were to be put to death for every offence for which they were threatened with cutting off would multiply their capital crimes beyond all the bounds of credibility: to suppose the law of Moses made every person liable to death, who happened to compound ointment or perfume like those of the tabernacle, or to taste the fat or the blood, or to neglect the sprinkling of the water of separation after having touched any thing that the ceremonial institutions called unclean; to suppose the laws of Moses made these and the like things capital crimes; would be to suppose them, like those of Draco, written in blood. But there is no reason for such a supposition. We have not a single instance, in the history of the Old Testament, of death being inflicted on any of these accounts. Besides, it is observable that according to Levit. vii. 21. he who touched an unclean thing, and so presumed to eat of the flesh of the sacrifice of the peace offerings, was liable (without any exemption on account of the circumstance of ignorance) to be cut off from his people. And in the 2d and 3d verses of the 5th chapter, a person is supposed in like manner to have touched an unclean thing; but it is hidden from him: Now, if we only suppose (which is probable enough) that the person, while his defilement is hidden from him, eats of the peace-offering, the latter case will plainly coincide with the former. But we have an expiatory offering prescribed for the latter case, ver. 6, 7, 8, 9, 10. Hence cutting off appears to have been a censure of the church; since in this instance at least, it was to be prevented by an expiatory offering, an ordinance of the church: for no such ordinance can be supposed to stop the course of justice in the state; though it may well be supposed to prevent an ecclesiastical censure.

We should likewise consider that this cutting off is oftener than once alluded to in the New Testament, where freeing the church from unprofitable members is treated of. In 1 Cor. v. where the apostle speaks of casting out the incestuous person, it is evident he had the institution of the passover in his eye. He calls Christ our passover who is sacrificed for us. He alludes to the strict charge that was given the Israelites, that when they were keeping the passover, there should be no leaven found in their houses, when he says, *Purge out the old leaven, that ye may be a new lump.* In like manner, when he says, *Put away from among yourselves that wicked person,* he seems to allude to the penalty annexed to the prohibition of leaven: Exod. xii. 15. *Whosoever eateth leavened bread from the first day until the seventh day, that soul shall be cut off from Israel.* Besides, in Gal. v. 12. (where it is evident from the connection that freeing the church from hurtful members is meant) the apostle, adopting the language of the Old Testament, expresses his desire to have some Judaizing teachers that troubled the church *cut off.*

But further, to shew that the Old Testament church had this ordinance of excommunication, we may take notice of the remarkable example of it in Ezra. x. 8. *They made a proclamation that whosoever would not come to Jerusalem within three days, according to the counsel of the princes and of the elders, all his substance should be forfeited, and himself separated from the congregation of those that had been carried away.* In this proclamation the wilful neglect of coming up to Jerusalem for the purposes intimated in the preceding verses of the chapter, is considered as an injury both to the church and to the state. For the injury to the latter, their goods were to be confiscated; for the injury to the former themselves were to be excommunicated, or separated from the congregation of those that had been carried away. We need not be surprized to observe the proceedings of the Jewish church and of the Jewish state, concur and second one another, since it is obvious that, wherever as in Israel, church and state have the same individuals for their members, such concurrence may (and must) frequently happen without prejudicing the independency and distinction of the one from the other.

The Jews were often blamed for misapplying this censure. Now, when a thing is, in any instance, said to be abused, the lawful use of it is established by that assertion; for when the use of a thing is not admitted, we do not say, it is abused, but we say, it ought not to be. The following instances, then, of the unjust exercise of excommunication clearly intimate that there was a lawful use of it in the Jewish church, Isa. lxvi. 5. *Hear the word of the Lord, ye that tremble at his word, your brethren that hated you, that cast you out for my name's sake, said, Let the Lord be glorified: but he shall appear to your joy, and they shall be ashamed.* That a church-censure is meant by the casting out here appears, *first*, from the appellation of *brethren* which is given to those who inflicted the censure; the common appellation of church members; Psal. lxxxiii. 1. Matth. xxiiii. 8. The rulers of the church are to consider themselves as brethren to their fellow-church-members; and never more so, than when they go about the highest acts of that authority which our Lord Jesus Christ has vested in them. There is no such worldly superiority as has place in civil society, to be assumed by any in the administration of the ordinances of Christ. As to any authority given to office-bearers in such matters, it is to be regarded only as the authority of Christ administring the government of his church by their instrumentality according to his word. And *secondly*, This casting out must be understood of a church censure, because the professed, immediate end of it is wholly religious: *They cast you out for my name's sake, and said, Let the Lord be glorified.* Thus the casting out here meant seems to be excommunication. The excommunication of the blind man, John ix. is expressed by the same phrase: *They cast him out.*

That was done in consequence of a decree of the assembly of the Pharisees, *that whosoever should confess Jesus to be Christ should be put out of the synagogue*: a censure which was undoubtedly ecclesiastical as it consisted in exclusion from a worshipping assembly. Thus we see that excommunication, or casting out of the synagogue, while our Lord tabernacled on earth, was commonly practised in the Jewish church. Surely had it been a mere human invention, the faithful and true Witness could never have suffered it to pass unnoticed or unreproved.

As our Lord's disciples, who had been always members of the Jewish church, would, no doubt, be accustomed to have an awful sense of the condition of persons under excommunication; so we may reasonably suppose that nothing would be more shocking to them than to be threatened with that censure: This, however, they were to meet with in the course wherein they were engaged, of witnessing for Christ. That this peculiarly heavy trial might not come on them unawares, our Lord takes care to warn them of it, John xvi. 1, 2. *These things have I spoken unto you that you should not be offended. They shall put you out of the synagogues;* that is, they shall excommunicate you. Luke vi. 22. *Blessed are ye, when men shall hate, and when they shall separate you from their company, and shall reproach you, and cast out your name as evil for the Son of man's sake.* The import of the Greek word rendered *they shall be separate*, says Beza, is, *they shall cast you out of the synagogues:* They shall separate you, like the leper, from their congregation.

Of the use of this Censure under the New Testament.

UNDER the New Testament, this censure, as we hinted before, continues the same; our Lord only directs the use and application of it, agreeably to the new dispensation, in Matth. xviii. 15, 16, 17. *Moreover, if thy brother shall trespass against thee, go and tell him his fault between thee and him alone: if he shall hear thee, thou hast gained thy brother. But if he will not hear thee, then take with thee one or two more, that in the mouth of two or three witnesses every word may be established. And if he shall neglect to hear them, tell it unto the church: But if he neglect to hear the church, let him be unto thee an heathen man and a publican.*

We have already endeavoured to shew that *the church* here means a company of ecclesiastical office-bearers acting in a judicative capacity. We would now only offer two observations on the passage.

The first is, That the fault or trespass here mentioned, is to be understood of any thing which may justly offend the conscience of a fellow-church-member, and which, consequently, may be a ground of church censure. The fault is not here considered merely as prejudicial to the person or outward estate of a brother; for private faults of this kind, when neither a good conscience, nor the interest of the church are concerned, should rather be passed over in silence than told to the church. Besides, were it merely a fault of this kind, all that a brother could aim at or obtain by dealing with the offender, would be the reparation of his loss: Thus he might gain money or an accession to his estate. But the object our Lord would have us aim at, is the gaining of our brother, the winning of his soul †. It is apparent, therefore, that this fault is such a one as affects the conscience; it may be a fault that no way hurts the person or interest of the offended brother. A church-member is offended, in the language of the New Testament, who observes any thing sinful in the conduct of a fellow-church-member, Rom. xvi. 21. *It is good neither to eat flesh, nor to drink wine, nor any thing whereby thy brother stumbleth, or is offended, or is made weak.* 2 Cor. vi. 3. *Giving no offence in any thing, that the ministry be not blamed.*

THE second observation is, That the censure implied in the words, *He shall be unto thee an heathen man and a publican,* is the highest church censure.

WE have already endeavoured to shew that there is an exertion of judicial authority in this case. Now we want only to know what is here pointed out as the effect of that exertion in these words, *Let him be unto thee as a heathen man and a publican.* Under the term *heathen* the Jews comprehended all who did not belong to their church and commonwealth; or who were without, as the apostle speaks, 1 Cor. v. 12. He gives us a remarkable description of the heathen in Eph. ii. 12. *At that time ye were without Christ, being aliens from the commonwealth of Israel, and strangers from the covenants of promise, having no hope, and without God in the world.* Surely, if this is the character of a heathen, we need not say any thing further to shew that the church inflicts the highest censure on a person, when she accounts him a heathen. As to the publican, it was a character held in the greatest detestation among the Jews, both from their impatience of the Roman yoke, which the Publicans as they collected the taxes, made them daily feel; and likewise because the bulk of those who engaged in such an odious employment, were infamous in

---

† The zeal of true friendship, which we ought to evidence for the recovery of a brother that is overtaken in a fault is strongly expressed in the original word here used, which signifies not merely to tell him his fault, but to use every argument to convince him of it.

their morals: Hence, in the evangelists, they are constantly ranked with the vilest of mankind: a Pharisee, it seems, could hardly mention a Publican without hinting that he was a great sinner, Matth. ix. 11. *And when the Pharisees saw it, they said unto his disciples, why eateth your master with Publicans and sinners?* Surely the church cannot inflict a higher censure than this, which puts a person on a level not only with the heathen, but with those who are worse than the heathen; who are visibly lost to all propriety of conduct.

Our Lord is here directing the behaviour of each particular church-member toward an offending brother; for it is his usual way to bring his word home to the cases and consciences of particular persons. The duty of the New-testament-church in the case of one refusing to hear it, was clear even from the practice under the Old Testament; but particular persons are apt to evade the obligation of duties, while they are only considered with respect to the church in general. It is on this account that Christ does not say, let him be unto the church, but *let him be unto thee*. It is plain however, that the church is included: In the first place, because the reason of the offending brother being accounted a heathen and a publican, that is, neglecting to hear the church, is much stronger and more immediate with regard to the church itself, than with regard to any of its members. If an offending brother is to be a heathen and a publican to a church-member, because he will not hear the church; much more should he be so to the church itself. In the second place, because one cannot justly esteem a fellow-church-member a heathen, unless he is actually *cast out;* that is visibly deprived of the privileges of the church of Christ. But those only are so deprived whom the church esteems heathens and publicans.

We may now go on to consider the charge which the apostle gives the Corinthians with regard to the inceſtuous perſon, 1 Cor. v. 5. *to deliver ſuch a one to Satan for the deſtruction of the fleſh, that the Spirit may be ſaved in the day of the Lord.* Interpreters have underſtood this paſſage either of a miracle, or of the higheſt church cenſure. That the latter is meant, and not the former, appears from theſe conſiderations.

Our Lord's rule in Matth. xviii. for proceeding againſt an offender, as far as it regards the public procedure of the church, is applicable to this caſe: So that to deliver one to Satan is to account him a heathen and a publican. Why, ſays Beza, ſhould we go to Chryſoſtom, when we may learn from Chriſt himſelf what it is for the church to deliver an obſtinate offender to Satan?

Let us conſider the circumſtances of this delivering to Satan. The Corinthians are directed to ſet about it in the apoſtle's abſence, Ver. 3. *For I verily as abſent in body, but preſent in ſpirit, have judged already,* &c. But the apoſtles were always preſent when they wrought miracles: for they wrought none by proxy, as the apoſtle, ſuppoſing that he was to have wrought one, muſt have done in this caſe: for the cenſure was to be inflicted by the Corinthians, and not by the apoſtle. He, indeed, under the immediate direction of the Spirit, determined what was the duty of the Corinthians in this matter. He does not ſay that he would himſelf purge out *the old leaven;* but he exhorts the Corinthians to purge it out; particularly by putting away that wicked perſon. When the Corinthians were gathered together, this cenſure was to be inflicted of many, ver. 4 and 2 Cor. ii. 6. We have already endeavoured to ſhew that the elders of the church of Corinth, acted jointly, on this occaſion. But there was no reaſon for ſuch a concurrence of many with the apoſtle, had he been propoſing to work a miracle.

The ſame thing is meant by delivering the perſon to Satan as by taking him away, in ver. 2. as by purging out the old leaven in ver. 7, as by putting away the wicked person in ver. 13. Surely the church can do these things without a miracle.

To what end did the apostles work miracles? For the confirmation of their doctrine and extraordinary divine mission. But the immediate end of the person here being delivered to Satan was *for the destruction of the flesh*, of that depraved nature, that old man which the apostle speaks of crucifying and putting to death, *that the spirit*, the poor soul united to the second Adam, and become a new creature, may be saved in the day of the Lord. The immediate end of the apostles, miracles—which was to confirm the facts they witnessed, concerning the life, death, resurrection and ascension of the Lord Jesus, and likewise to confirm their own extraordinary mission,—was peculiar to the period of the first propagation of those facts, and of the continuance of that mission. But the end of this censure is the salvation of the soul, the common end of all those ordinary means and ordinances which Christ has appointed the church to observe till he come again. Where the end aimed at by any means is ordinary, we should not without necessity, suppose the means themselves to be extraordinary, or miraculous. Hence it appears that this delivering to Satan is not miraculous but ordinary, and to be practised by the church as occasion requires, since the end of it is common to all the ordinary means and ordinances of the church.

We have another passage where so great a censure is represented in the same terms, as having been used for an end suited to all times and circumstances of the church, 1 Tim. i. 20. *I have delivered Hymeneus and Alexander to Satan, that they may learn not to blaspheme.* It is always the church's concern that her members who have fallen into error, may learn not to blaspheme.

Some have taken the *destruction of the flesh*, for some grievous bodily torture such as Satan brought upon Job. But besides that *the destruction of the flesh* never can be restrained to mean such torture only; it is inseparably connected with the salvation of the Spirit in the day of the Lord Jesus; which cannot be said of any bodily affliction, as it may, of what the apostle calls the crucifixion of the old man. In fine, since the Holy Ghost foresaw that cases like this, in which the censure of *delivering to Satan* was directed to be inflicted, would frequently occur in the Christian church, and the effect intended by it, which was the casting out of a dangerous member, would often be indispensably necessary; it is highly improbable, on the one hand, that he would order a miracle to be wrought for a purpose which might have been as well effected by an ordinary mean; and on the other, we have good reason to believe that, in this remarkable instance, he meant to set a fair example for the church of Christ to follow in similar cases.

We shall only take notice of another passage of scripture. It is in Gal. v. 11. *I would that they were even cut off who trouble you.* Here the apostle has in his eye those Judaizing teachers who had so far drawn away the Galatians from the doctrine of justification by faith in Christ to a legal regard for the ceremonial institutions, that the apostle upbraids them in these very severe terms, *O foolish Galatians, who hath bewitched you that you should not obey the truth, before whose eyes Jesus Christ hath been evidently set forth crucified among you?*

I would that they were cut off. To be excommunicated was, in the language of the synagogue, to be cut off.

It is observable, indeed, that the apostle does not directly enjoin the Galatians to cut them off; he only expresses his desire that it were done. But this manner of expression no way takes off from the obligation the Galatians were under to set about censuring these troublers: it only implies that something hindered them from setting about it at that time.

But whence did such hindrance arise? Was it from the number of the offenders, or from the nature of what was laid to their charge? There is no appearance that the hindrance was from either of these causes: if it had been from either of them, we cannot see how the apostle could have entertained such a desire. The truth is, the Galatian church had been so far bewitched by the arts of these corrupt teachers, that she was now almost utterly disabled from exercising against them these powers that Christ had given her: she had not herself, as yet, got free from that heresy, on account of which these corrupt teachers were to be excommunicated.

Having thus reviewed some of the warrants for excommunication, we may now endeavour to give some scriptural answer to the following questions.

Quest. What are the immediate grounds on which the sentence of excommunication proceeds?

Answ. They are such as these:

1. Something commonly known to be in the principle or practice of a church-member, which is inconsistent with his character as a church-member. Excommunication evidently supposes that inconsistency, because it declares that the person, continuing in his present course, cannot now be considered as bearing the character of a church-member. The inconsistent principle or practice must be commonly known; because excommunication being a public deed, the ground of it should be public, 1 Tim. i. 19, 20. *Holding faith and a good conscience; which some having put away, concerning faith have made shipwreck: Of whom is Hymeneus and Alexander: whom I have delivered unto Satan, that they may learn not to blaspheme.* 1 Cor. v. 1. *It is reported commonly that there is fornication among you, and such fornication as is not so much as named among the Gentiles, that one should have his father's wife.*

2. An evil of an infectious nature, that troubles and corrupts other church-members; for the incura-

bly diftempered part of the body muft be cut off, to the end that the reft of it may be preferved found. 2 Tim. ii. 16, 17, 18. *They will increafe unto more and more ungodlinefs: and their word will eat as doth a canker: of whom is Hymeneus and Philetus, who concerning the truth have erred, faying the refurrection is paft already; and overthrow the faith of fome.*— Compared with 1 Tim. i. 20. Gal. v. 12. *I would they were even cut off, who trouble you.* 1 Cor. v. 1. *Your glorying is not good: know ye not that a little leaven, leaveneth the whole lump.*

3. An evil which, if fpared, muft prove ruining or at leaft extremely hazardous to the perfon on whom the cenfure is inflicted. The church ought to go about excommunication in pity to the offender. Gentle methods ought, no doubt, to be tried in the firft place, and the iffue of them expected with patience and long-fuffering. But when it fufficiently appears that gentle methods fail of fuccefs, fevere ones muft not be neglected; the latter as well as the former bearing the ftamp of divine authority, and defigned for the recovery of backfliding church-members. It is plain that the end of the whole procefs in Matth. xviii. 15, 16, 17, 18. is the gaining of the offender; which fuppofes that he was in great danger from his obftinacy in the offence. In like manner, excommunication was to be inflicted on the inceftuous perfon, 1 Cor. v. 5. *For the deftruction of the flefh, that the fpirit might be faved in the day of the Lord;* which implied that his falvation appeared to be in hazard through the prevailing of the flefh.— The cafe of fome perfons may be fo dangerous, as to require fuch violence to be ufed for their prefervation as the church ufes in excommunication, Jude 23. *And others fave with fear, pulling them out of the fire.*

4. The aggravation of all thefe circumftances by obftinacy. Obftinacy is undoubtedly the moft immediate and rational ground of excommunication, as

the necessary effect of it is, that neither the church can be of any use to the person, nor the person to the church: and indeed what other is excommunication, than a solemn judicial declaration, that the person's behaviour has brought matters to so sad an extremity? for of what use can the church be to him, when he will not hear it? and of what use can he be to the church, while he is disposed rather to weaken than to help it? In short, by obstinacy the person, as it were, excommunicates himself, as by rebellion one throws himself out of the civil society against which he takes arms. So that, in this case, the church's highest censure is only a judicial declaration of the heinous guilt and dangerous consequence of what the person himself does, Matth. xviii. 27. *But if he neglect to hear the church, let him be unto thee as an heathen man and a publican.* Titus iii. 10. *A man that is an heretick, after the first and second admonition, reject.*

In fine, since excommunication, wherever it is justly inflicted, supposes the offence which is the occasion of it, to be in the extreme; for nothing but necessity can justify the use of the last remedy.—Hence there will hardly occur an instance of lawful excommunication which does not proceed upon all the above-mentioned grounds: upon one or two of them chiefly and more expresly; upon the rest implicitly at least, and by evident consequence.—Only it may be observed, that as what was at first a small offence may, through continued obstinacy, become, at last, a very proper ground of excommunication; so even great offences can hardly be considered as a ground of the highest censure without obstinacy †; for how is it reasonable to excommunicate

---

† The following quotation from some answers to the questions proposed by the king to the General Assembly in 1597, which answers Mr. Calderwood calls judicious, may well be considered as agreeable to the principles of the church of Scotland in that reforming period: "There can be no greater cause of excommunication "than a proud, contumacious heart, that will not hear God's voice "in his kirk; and no crime incurreth the censure of excommunication without contumacy." Calderwood's History, p. 392.

a person who already gives proper evidence that *he hears the church*, and that he has *learned not to blaspheme?* If the limb bids fair to be healed, a humane physician will not think of amputation. We may grant however, that a crime may be so atrocious in its nature, and so rapid in its infection, that the honour of Christ and the safety of the church may require, that excommunication should be immediately inflicted upon the conviction of the offender, even before the church can have sufficient evidence, whether the person is or is not obstinate after conviction. The usefulness of excommunication, like that of the noble act of Phinehas, may lie much in its infliction being without any delay. Such was the *Summary excommunication* under which the Corinthians were directed to lay the incestuous person. The leaven was ready to leaven the whole lump: it was therefore necessary that the remedy should be immediately applied.

QUEST, 2. If a person of whose state we have formed a judgment of charity, is justly excommunicated; are we bound to reverse that judgment of charity in consequence of his excommunication?

ANSW. We are not in every case.

1. Because we know from scripture, that the Lord sometimes permits, for holy and wise ends, the power of sin to break forth openly in the conduct of some of his own people: that he chastises them for one sin by suffering them to fall into another; as in consequence of denying Christ, Peter was left to curse and swear: and, lastly, that the spiritual eyes of the Lord's people being holden so that they cannot see, they may be very obstinate in a sinful course; as David was in his purpose of numbering the people in opposition to the remonstrances of Joab; nor does the scripture determine this obstinacy to a longer or shorter time. Suppose David had been excommunicated (as on supposition of obstinacy he justly might) for his transgression in the matter of Uriah, we cannot suppose that such as were intimately acquainted with him in the days of his youth, when he tended

his father's flock; when, as is generally thought, he penned the 119th pfalm; when he flew the lion and the bear, and conquered the giant of Gath; would have been obliged, in confequence of his excommunication, to look upon themfelves as utterly deceived by all the regular and uniform evidences of religion that they had feen about him.

2. Excommunication and the judgment of charity proceed upon widely different grounds. The ground of excommunication is a charge of one or more offences obftinately perfifted in; a charge which is confined to thefe offences, abftracting from all other parts of the perfon's character or conduct. The perfon, according to our Lord's rule in Matth. xviii. is to be excommunicated for neglecting to hear the admonitions of the church with regard to the trefpafs committed againft his brother mentioned in ver. 15. There is not a fyllable about the offender in any other refpect. The fame obfervation holds with regard to the cafe of the inceftuous perfon, of Hymeneus and Alexander. Indeed, it is contrary to all the rules of judicial procedure, to condemn a perfon in any other refpect, than that of the crime for which he is tried.

But as to the judgment of charity, it has the fulleft range: it does not proceed upon two or three inftances; but upon whatever knowledge we have of the perfon, of his regard to both tables of the law, in the general courfe of his life. The judgment of charity is formed upon an univerfal furvey, as far as our knowledge extends, of the perfon's behaviour in public and in private, with refpect to God, his neighbour, and himfelf.

The church, in a procefs of cenfure, confiders the fault that the perfon is accufed of, with relation to the difpofition of mind that he difcovers, either to juftify or condemn it. But it is far otherwife with charity; it confiders the fault with refpect to the general tenor of the perfon's conduct; and when it finds a prevailing regard to the law of God in the latter, it freely forgives the former; for *charity covereth a multitude of sins.*

THE judgment of the church, then, in passing the sentence of excommunication, is not inconsistent with the judgment of charity: but they have different objects.

THE former is a judgment concerning the demerit of a fault: of a fault considered, as the church considers every fault, in connection with the disposition of mind that the person discovers toward it: this judgment is like the sentence of a civil judge, determining the punishment due to any particular crime, according to law.

THE latter, again, is a judgment concerning the general character and behaviour of a person; importing that they are commendable on the whole, and becoming the gospel; a judgment this, which is far from supposing that the person may not be chargeable with faults which may occasion church-censure. The judgment of charity is like the general esteem and affectionate regard that one may retain, upon good grounds, for a friend, even when he must own that that friend has been justly condemned, in a particular instance, by the laws of his country.

ON the whole, it seems evident, that excommunication does not necessarily overthrow our judgment of charity. And tho' the church, regarding singly the person's obstinate persisting in a trespass, may justly pronounce him, in respect of such obstinacy, a heathen man and a publican; though we are bound to evidence our approbation of such a sentence as accompanied with the authority of the Lord Christ, by behaving toward the person agreeably to it, giving him no countenance in his contumacy; lastly, though all this may occasion the deduction of some grains of that evidence in his favour on which our judgment of charity was founded; yet when we take an enlarged view of his life and character, we may see a sufficient degree of evidence remaining in his favour, to warrant our looking upon him, in our private judgment, as a Christian indeed, as having the root of the matter in him; however with respect to the affair in which he is become obnoxious to the censure of the church, we must acknowledge that he has gone astray like a lost sheep. But the Lord will seek and find those that are his own; though, it must be acknowledged, that the time, the occasions, and, in a great measure, the way of their recovery, are to us impenetrable secrets.

QUEST. How far may church members deal with with an excommunicated for his recovery?

ANSW. It is true, church-members are not to have any such dealings with him as may be construed into a countenancing of his obstinacy: They are to be particularly careful in this respect; that they may not be partakers of other mens sins, 1 Cor. v. 11. *But now I have written unto you, not to keep company, if any man that is called a brother be a fornicator, or covetous, or an idolator, or a railer, or a drunkard, or an extortioner; with such an one, no not to eat.* 2 Thess. iii. 14. *And if any man obey not our word by this epistle, note that man, and have no company with him, that he may be ashamed.* What follows in the last mentioned place will serve to direct our conduct toward the excommunicated; *yet count him not as an enemy; but admonish him as a brother.* We should use every argument to deter him from persisting in his obstinacy; and to invite him back to the communion of the church, and to the enjoyment of her privileges. We should give every proper evidence, as opportunity offers, that we love his person, while we hate his vices. If we ought to pray for persons in bodily affliction, much more ought we to pray for one labouring under a violent spiritual disease: and if we should seek and hope that God will glorify himself by working deliverance in the one case; much more should we seek and hope that he will do so in the other.

QUEST. Is an excommunicated to be looked upon as without the visible church?

ANSW. It is a plain fact, that he is cast out of the particular church or association of which he was a member: and if the sentence is just, he should be excluded from all other Christian associations: and besides, though every sin persisted in, exposes a man to the greatest hazard; that does so especially, in which the person goes on in opposition to the solemn and judicial warnings of the church of Christ. The sentence being ratified in heaven, the person has nothing to expect in a course of rebellion against it, but manifold tokens of God's anger. But if, by being without the visible church, is meant that, because a person in respect of a particular instance of contumacy, is to be deemed a heathen man and a publican, we must therefore cease to regard him in the general character of a Christian; we must give up all hopes of his salvation, (which, to be sure, is no where to be obtained but in the church of Christ); we must no more entertain a judgment of charity concerning him; we confess that, in this sense, it is by no means necessary to consider an excommunicated as without the church: nay, such a view of his case, however warrantable it may appear from his perversion of this ordinance, is quite contrary to the gracious nature and salutary design of it, as it was appointed by Christ.

QUEST. Should a church proceed to excommunicate offenders, even though their number, their character, or the nature of the offence be such; that, humanly speaking, so high a censure would have no agreeable consequences?

ANSW. It is true, a particular church, as we have observed in the case of the Galatians, may not always have that degree of purity, faithfulness and vigour which is necessary for the adequate application of the censures: she cannot, in this matter, go beyond her measure; that is, her exactness in the infliction of censures must, in the nature of the thing, hold proportion to the degree of her knowledge and profession. The truth is, the caution our Lord directs church-members to observe in reproving one another, should likewise be observed by every particular church in censuring her members, Mat. vii. 5. *First, cast out the beam out of thine own eye, and then shalt thou see clearly to cast the mote out of thy brother's eye.* This weakness of a particular church, this defect of purity, or of unanimity seems to be what some pious and eminent writers have had in their eye, when they speak against proceeding to the higher censures against the offences of a multitude; as tending rather to destruction than to edification. Thus the Galatians were so deeply infected with the erroneous doctrine of the judaizing teachers, that the apostle does not command them to be immediately cut off or excommunicated.

On the other hand, so far as the faithful in any church are unanimous and resolute to hold the testimony of Christ; they are warranted to withstand all that oppose them, as Paul did Peter on a particular occasion, to the face; they may admonish, reprove, rebuke, and according to the opposition they meet with, having no respect of persons, on account either of their number, or their high reputation, they may proceed to greater degrees of censure. *For every tongue that riseth against Zion, in judgment she shall condemn.*

Of the History of Excommunication.

SUCH is the wickedness of many, and the weakness of all, that no church could ever subsist long without a reformation: now, it is one of the first and most necessary steps of reformation to cast out obstinate offenders. We have a very early example of it in the ejection of Cain. The Lord said to him; *A fugitive and a vagabond shalt thou be on the earth:* that is, since thou hast given so manifest an evidence of thy unbelief, hypocrisy and rebellion against my authority in the murder of thy brother; thou shalt no more associate with my people, nor partake of the privileges of their sacred communion. After Cain was cast out, or, as the scripture expresses it, *had gone out from the presence of the Lord*, the church of God was preserved in the family of Seth; whose descendants on account of their pure profession of the truth, and in opposition to the cursed Cainites, are called *sons of God;* till, in the time of Noah, professors mingling with the profane, *all flesh*, at length *corrupted their way*, and provoked the Lord to bring on the universal deluge. Only Noah and his family, and in it the church of God were saved from destruction. Small as the number then was of church-members, it was not long before scandal broke out among them. The impiety of Ham discovered itself in his undutiful conduct toward his father, Gen. ix. 22. It was a crime against the clearest dictates of reason and the light of nature, being contrary to the reverence of children for their parents, which is the foundation of all the good order and just subordination that has place in society. It therefore behoved Noah to curse Ham or to cast him out of the family or church of God. Canaan, indeed, is mentioned as the immediate object of the curse, either because being Ham's youngest son, he was the delight of his father; or because he was a witness and approver of his father's crime; or because he was to be the first of Ham's family who should depart from the church and the pure worship of God; or because it would comfort and encourage the Israelites, when they understood that the war they had to carry on against the Canaanites in order to their possession and enjoyment of the promised land, was with a people who were long before devoted to servitude and to destruction. In pronouncing this curse, Noah may be considered in two lights: In the first place, he was a prophet. Hence he for-told that Canaan should be *a servant of servants unto his brethren.* In this respect the curse terminated on Canaan. In the second place, as he was the head, so he was the priest of his family, and at that time the overseer of the whole church of God upon earth. He was a preacher of righteousness, and he offered sacrifices in the name of his family. On account of of this character, we may consider the curse of Canaan as an infliction of censure upon his father. Ham could not be cursed in his family and posterity without being excommunicated from the church of God; such a curse being directly contrary to the promise which respects all church-members as such indiscriminately; the promise which is to their children as well as to themselves.

The law of Moses is plain with respect to excommunication, as it directed the Israelites to separate from their congregation such as were ceremonially or morally unclean. Thus the leper was to dwell alone; his habitation was to be without the camp. When the law pronounces any person unclean or guilty, or one that shall bear his iniquity, it is to be understood as a direction concerning his exclusion from the congregation of the Lord, either for a longer or a shorter time. We have already enquired into the import of cutting off considered as an ecclesiastical censure.

The first degree of excommunication among the Jews was called *Niddui* or separation from the assembly of the church. By this censure the person was forbidden to approach within four cubits of his nearest relations. He continued under the sentence for thirty days: and if he did not give proper evidences of repentance in that time, it was prolonged to sixty days, and sometimes, though seldom, to ninety. If it did not appear after all, that the person had repented, a heavier censure was then inflicted. The Jewish writers mention twenty four crimes as the grounds of this censure; among which are the following: Despising a Rabbin, a master, or a teacher even after his death; calling one's neighbour a slave; selling one's land to a Christian or a Gentile; bearing witness against an Israelite in a Christian court; making the blind fall. This censure corresponded to the suspension in use among Presbyterians, by which offenders are kept back from the Lord's table.

The second degree of excommunication was called *Cherem*, by which the person was cast out of the synagogue with curses and comminations, taken from Deut. xxviii. and other places of scripture. A person so excommunicated, was in the language of the New Testament, one excluded from the synagogue: It is true, he was allowed to attend the public means of instruction in the temple; but then it was in such a way as declared his state of separation from the rest of the worshipping assembly. Thus when others entered into the temple by a gate on the right hand, the excommunicated entered by a gate on the left. His fellow-church members were prohibited from all intercourse with him in common life. This excommunication could not be inflicted but by an assembly consisting, at least, of ten men. This corresponds to the greater excommunication of Presbyterians; and how far it is warranted by scripture has been already shewn.

The third and last degree of excommunication was called *Shammatha*. Some derive the word from *Shammah* to exclude or separate: and therefore it is sometimes used to denote the first degree of excommunication. Others derive it from *Shamma* the Lord and *Atha* he hath come; that is, (putting the preterite for the future) he will most certainly come: This is equivalent to the word used in 1 Cor. xvi. 22. *If any man love not the Lord Jesus Christ, let him be Anathema Maranatha.* A Syriack word compounded of *Maran* the Lord and *Atha* he hath come. The excommunication of Alexander the copper-smith seems to have been of this kind; 2 Tim. iv. 14. and that of the city of Meroz, Judg. v. 23. Indeed, it does not seem to be so properly a church-censure as an extraordinary denunciation of the divine vengeance against such as are altogether given up of God. It was like a sentence of perpetual banishment, as it cut off all hopes from the excommunicated of ever being restored to the communion of the church. It is contrary in this respect to the nature of the ordinances which Christ hath appointed for the ordinary use of his church: which ordinances, however fatal they may prove to his enemies who rebel against, and abuse them, yet as to their primary and proper intention, are all gracious and salutary.

THE godly discipline of the primitive church *the restoration of which,* says the English liturgy, *is much to be wished)* seems to have been exercised with a considerable degree of purity during the first and second century. About the middle of the second century, a controversy arose between the eastern and the western churches about the time of observing Easter: The churches of the east were for observing it with the Jews on the fourteenth day of the moon; those of the west, on the day of our Lord's resurrection. A vain and foolish controversy, as the ancient historian Socrates justly observes, since there is no command of God for observing Easter at all. Victor the bishop of Rome, entered so warmly into the contest, that, in zeal for the western practice, he precipitately excommunicated Polycrates and the Asiatic churches. This was done in the year 195. Many were offended at the rashness of the Roman bishop, particularly Irenæus bishop of Lyons who reproved him severely for it. The papists, however, endeavour to defend the conduct of Victor; and consider this excommunication as an evidence that he was head of the Asiatic churches, and consequently that he was their universal bishop. But protestant writers justly deny the consequence: For in that age it was not always by superiors that persons were excommunicated; it was often by equals, and by such as claimed no superiority over the excommunicated. Thus Cyprian excommunicated Novatian the Roman Presbyter; John Patriarch of Antioch excommunicated Pope Liberius. Nay, there are not wanting instances of persons being excommunicated by their inferiors: thus in the year 513, Severus bishop of Antioch was excommunicated and deposed by two bishops who were subordinate to him, Cosmas of Epiphany and Severian of Arethusa. And indeed why may not the church of Christ employ this censure against any one who by his errors and offences openly endeavours to hurt her, whether his rank in life be higher or lower? Surely her discipline should be exercised without respect of persons.

Excommunication, says a historian writing of the second century, was now no other than a separation or casting out of communion; without any such damnation, or such curses with the extinguishing of candles or the ringing of bells, as are now in use with the church of Rome. This like all the other ordinances of Christ, is liable to many abuses and corruptions.

In the first place, It is often misapplied; as it was by those who are spoken of in Isa. lxvi. 5. *Hear the word of the Lord, ye who tremble at his word: Your brethren who hated you, that cast you out for my name's sake, said, Let the Lord be glorified: but he shall appear to your joy, and they shall be ashamed.* So it was by the Pharisees, John ix. 22. *The Jews had agreed that, if any man did confess that he was Christ, he should be put out of the synagogue.* It is indeed the manner of corrupt churches, to harden themselves in their evil course, and to endeavour to discourage the faithful witnesses by the abuse of ecclesiastical censures.

In the second place, The power of excommunication has often been exercised with a rigour altogether contrary to the gracious nature and design of that spiritual discipline which Christ hath appointed in his word. This abuse of excommunication naturally attends the misapplication of it. For as there is nothing in the ordinance itself to gratify the cruel and persecuting spirit of injustice; so, for that end, it has been often found necessary to add to it, or substitute in the room of it, some hard penances, dire anathemas, fines, outlawries, imprisonments, and other severities of the like nature. Besides, when Christianity became fashionable, and the church was filled with worldly men, ecclesiastical officers themselves being now become worldly, began to distrust the efficacy of those mild and spiritual censures appointed by our Lord Jesus Christ, (censures which indeed are suitable to, and have their proper effect on believers and spiritual men only) and they found something more severe and terror-striking necessary to restrain the promiscuous multitude which had then got into the churches.

The fathers even of the third century carried their severity very far. When a person was excommunicated they appointed him to continue in that state sometimes for three, sometimes for seven years, and sometimes for life. Those who relapsed a second time into the same crime were cast out, never to be readmitted. Such were the first fruits of men's carnal wisdom pretending to improve upon the institutions of Christ.

How the bishop of Rome, aiming at universal monarchy over the church, abused excommunication, employing it as an instrument of tyranny against all who opposed his usurpations; overturning the order of civil society by dissolving the relation between magistrates and their subjects; laying whole kingdoms under interdicts; and passing sentence upon individuals, and sometimes upon whole classes of men, determining their eternal state (thus incroaching on the incommunicable prerogative of the judge of all the earth) is well known to every one who takes a view of the history of Europe from the sixth to the end of the sixteenth century.

The manner of excommunication in the church of England favours more of the Popish than of the Protestant religion. As soon as an English bishop certifies an excommuuication, a writ is issued from the chancery directing the sheriff to take the body of the person excommunicated, and imprison him till he has made satisfaction to the church. In consequence of this sentence the person becomes an out-law; he is disabled from sueing any one in an action at law, from being a witness, and from every other judicial act. Such a procedure suits well with a church which is a creature of the state; but is utterly reprobated in *the kingdom which is not of this world.*

The cause or occasion of excommuuication in the Protestant churches has not only been such crimes as are contrary to the light of nature; but also such offences obstinately persisted in, as were plainly subversive of the truth and testimony of Christ held by those churches. Thus in 1580, when the church of Scotland was contending against the usurpations of Episcopacy, the General Assembly ordained the bishops to desist from preaching, from the administration of the sacraments, and from every other part of the pastoral office; till they should receive admission anew from the General Assembly: and if they should be found disobedient to this act, the sentence of excommunication was after due admonition to be executed against them†. Thus in 1586, Mr. Patrick Adamson was excommunicated for usurping the function of a bishop against the ordinance of the kirk and to the slander of the ministry; for displaying a banner against the whole good order and government of the kirk; and especially for his notorious impugning the settled order of the General Assemblies and Presbyteries grounded upon the word‡.

† Calderwood's history, page 90.

‡ Item, page 200. It is true, this sentence was reversed soon after: but that was owing, as Mr. Calderwood speaks, *to the fear and flattery of a court working upon weak and inconsiderate ministers,* page 212.

Thus had the Judaizing teachers at Antioch whom the Synod of Jerusalem, branded as *troublers of the church and subverters of souls,* made an obstinate opposition to the charitable compromise between the Jewish and Gentile converts; might not that venerable court have cut them off, as the apostle Paul wished to be done in the case of those that troubled the churches of Galatia?

Few events with respect to religion for many years past, have been so much the subject of controversy, of reproach and of commendation, as the censures which were passed above thirty years ago, on some ministers of the Secession for their obstinate attachment to the religious clause in some burgess oaths.

We shall conclude this essay with remarks on two sorts of objections to that excommunication.

First, Some object to it in the following strain: " It is contrary to the Spirit of Christianity to deal " much in excommunications. The Burgher mini- " sters had done nothing to deserve so heavy a cen- " sure: All the crime they could be charged with, " was, That they mistook the meaning of an oath. " They were eminent ministers and holy men: it was " therefore a horrid profanation to deliver them up " to the devil. As these censures were cruel and un- " just, so they were without effect: These ministers " preached; they lived and died as well as if no such " censures had ever been passed."

It is obvious, that this common-place declamation is directly contrary to what we have already advanced as the doctrine of the scriptures with respect to excommunication. From which we may deduce this truth: " That in every case in which a " church is in a capacity to exercise the power of dis- " cipline committed to her by Christ, and in which " she has the grounds to proceed upon, laid down " in scripture for excommunication, she may war- " rantably pass that censure without respect of persons " and without fear of consequences." We have endeavoured to shew that excommunication is altogether suitable to the mild spirit of Christianity; that the Associate Synod, having preserved its constitution inviolate, had a right to exercise its judicial authority in the infliction of censures, as well as in other instances; and that, in the circumstances of the Secession from the church of Scotland, it is a very aggravated offence to take or to justify the taking of the religious clause in some Burgess Oaths.

In the second place, Others argue against the excommunication of the brethren in a very different strain: "We are convinced, say they, of the un-
"lawfulness of swearing the religious clause in some
"Burgess Oaths: We are satisfied as to the consti-
"tution of the Associate Synod: We have no doubt
"as to the authority of that court to exercise the dis-
"cipline of the church. But still we cannot see the
"propriety or expediency of proceeding so quickly,
"as was done, to lay the brethren under the greater
"excommunication. We fear there was too much
"passion and alienation of heart on both sides for a
"proper use of those means, such as joint prayer and
"mutual conference, which are previously neces-
"sary in order to that awful censure. Besides the
"neglect of those previous means with which we
"fear both parties were in some degree chargeable,
"we apprehend that the convulsed state of the church
"at that time, required lenity, and rendered it un-
"seasonable to come to extremity."

People ought to be at liberty to express their opinions (provided they do so with candour) on particular steps of ecclesiastical administration; the steps, we mean, which cannot be considered as belonging to the system of principles which is denominated, *The Secession Testimony;* which are not reckoned among the terms of communion; and which are of that sort of public measures, that a society must allow a diversity of opinion concerning them, otherwise either sincerity or social union would be at an end: Hence though we cannot give a decisive answer to these objections, we may offer an observation or two on the subject.

In the first place, It deserves our consideration, supposing the grounds of any sentence of excommunication to be sufficient according to the word of God, how far the validity of that sentence is affected by the manner in which it is passed. Were every degree of passion, prejudice, or other unsuitable disposition that church officers are liable to, or discover in the exercise of spiritual discipline, to render it null and void; there would be no lawful exercise of it at all. It is no certain proof that a person is in an error, that he delivers his opinion in a passionate and disagreeable manner. Though his manner is wrong, his matter may be right. There is no just reasoning from the one to the other. Thus we may grant there was much wrong in the manner of proceeding against the brethren, and yet maintain that the sentence is valid and obligatory upon them.

In the second place, If we ask, When is excommunication expedient? It will be answered, when it tends to edification and not to destruction: but the question still recurs, when is it for edification? Is it when it increases the number of visible church-members? No, for in our times, the faithful exercise and wholesome severity of church-discipline never fails to diminish their number. Is it when it is evidently necessary for the promoting of holiness and of peace among church-members? But this can be determined no otherwise than by examining how far it serves to promote the stedfastness and purity of the church in her profession of the truth as it is in Jesus; for that is the true scriptural way of edifying her members in peace and holiness: The seed of Christ *keep the commandments of God in the way of having the testimony of Jesus,* Rev. xii. 17.

We need not say any thing here concerning the importance of the grounds upon which the excommunication proceeded. We have only to observe, that if these grounds were of real importance, the more trivial they were in the eyes of the world, and even in the eyes of many church-members, the excommunication was the more necessary: the reason is, that it is one principal end of excommunication to impress church-members with a suitable sense of the particular evil which is the cause of it †.

† The ground of this censure was the same with that on which the Associate Synod had maintained its constitution at the breach, and asserted its right to exercise the government and discipline of the church. How can we suppose that the same ground was sufficient to warrant the exercise of church discipline in general, but insufficient to warrant the exercise of it in a particular instance? We speak of the ground of the excommunication, abstracting from the manner of proceeding upon that ground.

It is said, that the brethren desired conference with some members of the Associate Synod, as a mean of healing the breach that had taken place. But before we can justly blame those members for not complying, we should examine what sort of conference was required: whether it was a conference about falling from the testimony which had been given against some Burgess Oaths; or about giving up the the lawfulness of the constitution of the Associate Synod. A free people should not once allow themselves to hear a proposal which appears to call their liberty in question; much less are Christians to suffer themselves to be tampered with to forsake the Lord's way in which they *walk at liberty*. The ministers, therefore, did right in rejecting the proposed question, if it was to proceed upon an allowance of the religious clause of some Burgess Oaths or upon the nullity of the Associate Synod: But if it was to proceed upon neither of these; but was merely in order to bring about a better understanding between the parties; the proposal should have been accepted.

ESSAY VIII.

Of the Religious Character of the Times.

THE principal religious characters of the present age seem to be, the fashionable Deist, the Temporizer, the selfish Devotee, the Waverer, and the serious but desponding Christian.

I. THE *Deists*. They own the being of GOD, but deny the divine authority of the scriptures, or that the Bible teaches the only way in which a sinner can be saved. The causes of the plentiful growth of Deists, seem to be the following.

1. IGNORANCE. Such as reject Christianity without having read the Bible with attention, or without having attained any distinct knowledge of its doctrines; such as think no credit is due to the bible because some of the facts have been represented as contradictory to one another, or set in a ridiculous light; such as have satisfied themselves with considering these parts only which appeared the most liable to exception without ever having taken, or seriously endeavoured to take, a connected view of the whole: all these are Deists from ignorance.

2. PRIDE. Those who, accounting their own reason and virtue sufficient to direct their steps and secure their happiness, see no need of a revelation for these purposes; who reject revelation because it is not communicated to as many as they think pro-

per, because the ancient heathens or modern Indians are ignorant of it; who will not yield their assent to the doctrines of it, because they are doctrines which reason could never discover, and when discovered, which it never can account for; who, in fine, reject the bible, because it exposes the weakness and depravity of human nature: all these are Deists from pride.

3. Vicious habits and dispositions in general. Those who think some other plan of morality more conducive to the happiness of man than that which is laid down in the scriptures; who imagine the spiritual exercises and enjoyments recommended by the bible, are vain or unattainable; who fancy there is no need of any other guide in morals than their own taste, or feelings; who would rather have the scriptures false than their own depraved inclinations mortified; who condemn the bible, because the bible condemns them: all these are Deists, for the sake of their vicious habits and dispositions.

To these causes of infidelity, besides, what is the root of them all, the natural enmity of man's heart against the purity of the scriptures, we may add, the works of some elegant writers, and the example of the greater part of those who pique themselves on the superiority of their taste, their politeness, or their high rank. We do not think that infidelity in itself, is favourable to genius or to good taste; for it is truth alone that gives vigour to the one or stability to the other. Sensible of this, such writers on the side of infidelity as are any way remarkable for these qualities, have always taken care, in the first place, to acquire a reputation by illustrating some useful truths, which are indeed perfectly agreeable to Christianity; but which they have attempted, by oblique reflections or by satyrical hints, to contrast with some part of Christianity.

It is another cause of the prevalence of Deism in the present age, that many who are called Christians, do not receive the truths and ordinances of the bible as from God: they confider them as harmlefs things belonging to the religion of their country; but they cannot fee it any way neceffary to adhere very ftrictly to them, or to engage in the zealous defence of them. They do not mean, for their part, *to fuffer for the caufe of Chrift.* It is enough for them to hold a kind of fyftem of natural religion, which they have framed for themfelves. Accordingly they are left to amufe themfelves with their miferable fchemes of religion, while God, in his righteous judgment, fuffers them to become more and more blind to the evidences of Chriftianity.

The general prevalence, and the open avowal of Deifm prefage the approach of our national ruin. The Sadducees, as one juftly obferves, never became very numerous among the Jews, till a little before their final deftruction.

IT was a fine fummer morning, when Lorenzo took a turn with his friend Lælius in fome gardens, which had been laid out with the greateft tafte, and which, in this feafon, afforded the higheft regale of beauty and fragrance to the fenfes. They walked until they came to an eminence where they had a full profpect of Lorenzo's eftate; on which he began to congratulate himfelf and entertain his friend with an account of the improvements he had made, the profits he had reaped or expected to reap, and the refined pleafures which, he faid, he tafted: "Thefe, "thefe are folid enjoyments: thefe are elegant fatis- "factions." Lælius, thinking he was too much tranfported with fuch tranfitory things, and that he was too much like the covetous wretch who faid to himfelf, *Soul, take thine eafe, thou haft goods laid up for many years,* could not forbear interrupting his reverie, and fuggefting a plain, but faithful and friendly admonition in the following manner.

LÆLIUS. You seem then, Lorenzo, to place your happiness in the gaieties of life, and in the solid enjoyment, as you term it, of a plentiful fortune; yet in the moments of reflection, you must think how uncertain this happiness is; how quickly it may be interrupted, by the spleen, by sickness, by a thousand accidents; and, when you die, how unavoidably it must be ravished from you for ever.

LORENZO. My conduct has ever been such, that I have nothing to reproach myself with: it has been my greatest pleasure to do good to my fellow-creatures.

LÆL. Have you, indeed, taken an impartial view of your past life? On the strictest enquiry, have you found that you never entertained a thought, nor spoke a word, nor did an action dishonourable to God, or contrary to his law? If you are guilty in a single instance, God may justly be displeased with you for that instance. This being the case, if you do not consider it, you shew a disregard and contempt of the injured honour of that INFINITE BEING, on whom you depend for every breath you draw, and who is able to punish you in such a manner and in such a degree as is far beyond all your present conceptions.

LOR. The supreme being is daily loading me with his favours: he gives me all things richly to enjoy: as he is now, so will he prove in a future state, my friend.

LÆL. Nothing is more essential to our idea of God than this; That he is one who delights in virtue or in righteousness. Hence his favour is annexed to virtue, and his hatred to vice: which hatred must be according to the degree of its object. But how common is it to see the man of distinguished wickedness arrayed in scarlet, and faring sumptuously every day; while he who is virtuous, or at least far less vicious, is clothed in rags and oppressed with poverty: a convincing proof, that it is, by no means, in-proportion to the abundance and variety of a person's outward enjoyments, that he shares in the favour of God. The supreme Disposer of human affairs is often seen to indulge a great degree of prosperity to those very states which he has doomed to a sudden and signal destruction: witness Carthage, Tyre, Babylon. History affords examples without number. In like manner, a person may be all his days in affluent circumstances, and yet not be certain but that, in a future scene, he may appear to have been all along an object of God's displeasure. Even in the ordinary course of providence, we cannot certainly conclude from our prosperity to day, that we shall be prosperous to-morrow: far less can we infer from the kindness of providence in this life, that we shall not be miserable in the life to come.

Lor. It seems most reasonable to conceive of God as a mild and benevolent Being, who wants his creatures to be happy: sure then he does not observe all our faults with extreme severity.

Læl. Let us try to consider the matter impartially. You will grant that God has appointed laws to the moral as well as to the natural world. A law suiting a reasonable creature must have rewards and punishments annexed to it. Now the same goodness of God that prescribed these laws, that delights in the obedience given to them, that desires in rational creatures the perfection and the happiness with which that obedience is connected; even that very goodness must see to the execution of these laws; must be averse from viewing the disobedience of these creatures; and must, at least, withhold every mark of favour from the disobedient. Consider, Lorenzo, that his favour is our life, and to experience the loss of it, must be as death. Besides, we see a great deal of misery actually taking place among mankind. It is inconsistent with all that we understand of God's wisdom and power, to suppose that this or any other thing takes place against his will. Whatever misery, therefore, we ourselves or our fellow-creatures endure, we may be certain, that neither the appointment nor the infliction of it is inconsistent with the goodness of God.

Lor. The miseries of the present life are only for the chastisement and correction of mankind.

Læl. Be it so; yet the fact shews one thing incontestibly, *i. e.* That there are reasons which may make it agreeable to the goodness of God, to inflict punishment: you have mentioned one of these reasons: but for any thing we know, there may be others of equal or of greater importance: others which, for any thing nature can say with certainty, may render it necessary that we should be punished at last in a manner of which we have no example in the present state.

Lor. Your reasoning is rather too metaphysical.

Læl. It is an argument of the depravity of human nature, and of our indispensible need of a divine revelation, that men are so much indisposed to give any serious or suitable attention to subjects which a small reflection may convince them, are, at least, very likely to prove of everlasting consequence. Indeed, they might attain to certainty in matters of religion, by a far less degree of diligence and application of mind than what they often bestow on philosophical trifling and ingenious amusement.

Lor. The modes of religion are various: the substance of it is the same in all ages and in all countries. I am of the same opinion with the poet:

For modes of faith let graceless zealots fight;
His can't be wrong whose life is in the right.

Læl. But when may one's life be justly said to be in the right?

Lor. When he does to others as he would be done by; when he assists or instructs them; when he acknowledges and corrects the faults himself may have fallen into.

IæL. But is it no part of a good life to have a chief regard to God who gave us our being and all our enjoyments? The benefits that men receive from one another lay them under obligations to do good to one another. But what are all these obligations compared to those we are under to him who is the *God of our life and the length of our days.* Trust me, Lorenzo, unbiassed reason will pronounce your life entirely in the wrong, unless you are habitually remembering God; unless you fear and love him; unless you seek the knowledge of his will, walk according to it, and do all you can to make others esteem him. Hence we see the truth of what the poet says concerning a person's faith,

His can't be wrong whose life is in the right;
taking one's *life* here to signify our inward disposition as well as our outward behaviour; our regard to God as well as to man: for if one's life, so understood, is in the right, it must not proceed from a wrong, but from a right faith; that is, from just views of God as well as a proper concern for our neighbour's welfare; views, by the way, which we have not heard that any of mankind ever obtained otherwise than by that revelation which we have in the scriptures. Besides, when we speak of what is acceptable to God, our secret principles and motives impenetrable to our fellow-creatures, are vastly more to be attended to than our overt actions: the first thing to be enquired, is, whether we are actuated by the love of God, by a willing submission of heart to his authority, by a single regard to his glory? and then, Whether our hearts are free from hatred, envy, vain-glory, or any other inordinate affection toward our neighbour? Whether we love our neighbour for God's sake? If we are deficient in these or the like internal principles of action, it is a poor vain imagination for us to think our life right before God, *who searcheth the heart.*

As to your observation, that the different modes of religion are, in substance, all the same; how far the various forms of superstition in different ages and countries may be resolved into the same general principles, might be a subject of curious and not unprofitable enquiry: but without any elaborate disquisition, it is plain that Christianity is essentially different from all other religions, and even from natural religion itself.

LOR. You surprize me, Lælius;—Christianity seems, indeed, to be more refined and free from superstition than the religion of the ancient Greeks and Romans, or that of the Mahometans; but, by the confession of many eminent writers on the side of Christianity, it is only an improvement on natural religion.

LÆL. Christianity is not contradictory to pure Theism or natural religion, as it certainly is to idolatry and superstition. But Christianity discovers much concerning God and concerning the way of salvation from sin, which is far beyond the sphere of what is commonly called natural religion. That religion never taught any thing like the doctrine of God manifesting himself, and communicating his favours to poor sinners by a Mediator, who is himself the Most High God. To a mere moral philosopher nothing can appear more absurd than this proposition; *That God is in Christ reconciling the world to himself, not imputing their trespasses to them.* Neither Socrates, nor Plato, nor Aristotle was known to use such language. The philosopher would have but an obscure notion of *God reconciling the world to himself*: he might conjecture that it was a strange, out-of-the-way expression for *reclaiming mankind from vice.* But when he came to read, *not imputing their trespasses to them*, he would be apt to ask, whether it were not downright nonsense? For to whom should a person's own trespasses be imputed but to himself? At best, he must look upon it as a paradoxical, harsh and improper phraseology for a very plain idea, that of *pardoning sin, or forbearing to punish it;* though still he would think *pardoning* the world but a very poor way of *reclaiming* it. Above all, the very first words of the sentence, *God is in Christ*, would absolutely puzzle and confound him. He would not be able to conceive how God can be in Christ; or how God, by being in Christ, reconciles the world to himself. Indeed, Lorenzo, the duties that are most commonly inculcated in the new Testament are utterly unintelligible on the supposition that they are, in substance, no other than what we are informed of by natural religion; such as these; *Putting on Christ, receiving him, walking in him, praying in the Spirit, putting off the old man, eating the flesh and drinking the blood of the Son of God.* Were Christianity materially the same with natural religion, men might attain a sufficient knowledge of it by the diligent use of their natural faculties without any special or supernatural illumination. But this is contrary to the scripture itself, 1 Cor. xi. 14. *The natural man receiveth not the things of the Spirit of God, they are foolishness to him, neither can he know them, because they are spiritually discerned.* Mat. xiii. 11. *It is given to you,* said Christ to his disciples, *to know the mysteries of the kingdom of heaven, but to them it is not given.* Mat. xvi. 17. *Jesus answered and said unto him, Blessed art thou Simon Bar-jona, for flesh and blood* (an expression denoting whatever naturally and essentially belongs to man) *hath not revealed it to thee, but my Father who is in heaven.*

FARTHER, Lorenzo, Christianity affords a vastly more glorious display of the divine perfections than the religion of nature. That religion says, God is so just that he will give every one his due. But, says Christianity, He is so just, that rather than let the sins of those whom he had determined to save, pass with impunity, he chose to make his own Son suffer for their sins; for *it pleased the Lord to bruise him, to put him to grief, and to make his soul an offering for sin.* The religion of nature says, God is so true, that he never will deceive his creatures: but Christianity declares, that God is so true and faithful, that rather than one jot or tittle of his word should fail, he would not spare the Son of his love, but made him sin and a curse though he knew no sin, that the scriptures might be fulfilled. In the same manner, we might go on to shew how much superior the testimony of revelation is to that of nature with respect to the other perfections of the divine nature.

Lor. You speak so mystically that I cannot understand you.

Læl. I endeavour to be plain. Take heed, Lorenzo, lest, while you seem not to understand revelation, you be, in reality despising it. You are at least a Theist; you believe a God: Consider that you cannot shew a greater contempt of him than by rejecting the only revelation he has given to mankind.

Lor. I have heard of a great many systems of religion; each of which, according to its votaries, came down from heaven; while some find their account in propagating pious frauds.

Læl. Do you mean the systems of the ancient philosophers? They ascribed their pretended wisdom, not to the kindness of heaven, but to their own industry and penetration. So well did they succeed in exposing the vanity and absurdity of one another's systems, that the perusal of all their writings would only serve to convince us that they were all in the wrong. Besides, there was never a philosophical system so much adapted to the capacities and situations of the bulk of mankind, as in any age or country to become the popular belief. Do you mean the systems of the Bonzes in China or of the Magi in Persia? These claim no other original than the authority of Fohi or Zoroaster: nor do we learn that Zoroaster or of Fohi pretended to be favoured with any divine revelations: they enjoined their observances on their followers in their own names only. Or do you mean the system of Mahomet? Consider the life of Mahomet: Consider his manner of propagating his religion: review the trivial conceits, the inconsistencies, and the palpable falsehoods of his Koran; and then say, whether Mahometanism will bear a comparison with the religion of the Bible. Besides, by acknowledging the authority of our JESUS as a prophet, Mahomet has for ever overthrown his own. Or farther, with some wits of modern days, would you prefer the traditions of the untutored Indians, who expect at their death to be wafted to certain green islands where they shall sit under the shady trees and drink wine out of the skulls of their enemies; and as they have no idea of rational society, their dogs shall bear them company?—But why should we insist? Know you a composition that bears such evident marks of a divine original as the scriptures? Or while it speaks in the name of the only living and true God who created heaven and earth, carries such conviction of its truth to the conscience?

FALSE religions become ridiculous, but Christianity becomes more venerable by the progress of true knowledge. Every science attests the superior excellence of the Bible. For example, geography gives its testimony to the accuracy of scripture narration by shewing how exactly it corresponds to the true situation of places: Ancient history, where it is not plainly fabulous or inconsistent with itself, agrees with that of the Old and New Testament; while modern history verifies what is there foretold. Natural philosophy shews how justly the system of the universe or the productions of the earth are alluded to or described in scripture. In fine, true criticism points out the propriety, the majestic simplicity, the native elegance, and pathetic energy of the inspired writings †.

† The classical writers of antient Greece and Rome, as might be expected from the time in which they lived and from the subjects of which they treat, mention many of the facts recorded in scripture, and throw light upon many passages of it by the view they give us of the political state of nations, of antient languages, customs and

With regard to persons finding their account in promoting particular systems of religion, it may be sufficient to observe that it was not Christianity itself, but the abuses and corruptions of it that ever served the purposes of avarice and ambition. Read the Bible, and you cannot fail to see how unjust it is to blame Christianity for the pride, for the aspiring or interested views of too many priests and prelates.

Lor. I am perplexed with the different readings of the Old and New Testament; with the different opinions as to the degree of inspiration under which the sacred penmen wrote; and with the different interpretations of many passages.

Læl. The spots in the sun's bright orb hinder him not from communicating light and heat to the world: Nor will the variations of different copies of the scriptures hinder them from being profitable for doctrine, for reproof, for correction and instruction in righteousness. None of the leading and distinguishing truths of Christianity depend upon a word, but are fully displayed and frequently repeated through the whole Bible: so that we can be at no loss to find them in the most incorrect copies and in the worst translations. No body questions whether Homer's genius and knowledge of human nature appear in the Iliad and the Odessey; or Virgil's judgment and delicacy of taste in the Georgics and the Eneid; though the variations in the reading of those poems are incomparably greater and more numerous than the variations in the reading of the scriptures. And shall we suppose that a few blunders of a transcriber of the Old and New Testament may hinder us from discerning the authority, holiness, wisdom, power and mercy of God so peculiarly displayed in the sacred pages? Surely, the character of God is more uniformly and strongly marked in his word, than the

manners. It is, therefore, a remarkable dispensation of Providence that so many of their productions have been preserved, and in almost every civilized country, are accounted the standards of taste and of elegant composition.

characters of Homer and of Virgil in their poems. Indeed, there is no comparison; for the manner of expression or of arrangement is almost all that characterises the poets; whereas God's word is characterised by the great and glorious things that it reveals. Farther, the same wisdom and goodness of God that bestowed this revelation on mankind, we may assure ourselves, will take care, by a special providence, to preserve it in such purity as is necessary to make it answer the end for which it was bestowed. Hence we have good reason to believe, not only that the various readings are few and mostly immaterial; but likewise that, in every instance, the true reading is preserved somewhere, and may be found out by a careful collation of copies, by attending to the scope and connection, by observing the analogy of faith, and by the use of other means.

As to the degree in which the penmen of scripture were inspired, it is sufficient for us to believe that the matter which they spoke and wrote, as they were moved by the Holy Ghost, was only what was necessary to constitute the perfect rule of the church's faith and practice; and that they expressed that matter, under the same infallible guidance, by the fittest words which the language they wrote in could supply them with. How far the Holy Spirit made use of the particular natural geniuses of the penmen in those divine compositions is rather a matter of curiosity than of importance or edification.

Why are you stumbled at the misinterpretation of the scriptures? The works of creation and the ways of providence are often misinterpreted as well as the scriptures; so that this, like too many of the objections of Deism, will serve the cause of Atheism as well. Turn away your attention from jarring interpretations of the scriptures to the scriptures themselves: there you may find such plain passages as he that runs may read and understand. And if you seek in earnest to increase in this which is the best kind of knowledge, you will by degrees obtain more and more satisfaction as to the meaning of passages that are more obscure. Then instead of being stumbled at the various interpretations of authors, you will be enabled to make a proper use of them.

Lor. It is not improbable, but that God may be delighted with the various manners of worshipping him which divide the world.

Læl. The love of variety is ownig to the imperfection of our nature. Wanting satisfaction in our selves, we look for it in other things: missing it in one of these things, we seek it in another: disappointed in our expectation from that, we have recourse to a third, and so on without end. Carried to excess, this passion is exceedingly hurtful: it is a levity of temper which unfits one for any useful employment or any laudable pursuit: a passion, surely, never to be ascribed to the supreme Being who is necessarily happy in the contemplation of his own perfections.

As we know not what is acceptable to God, unless he teach us; as both the manner and matter of our worship should express our regard to his supreme authority; so it is most reasonable to believe that he hath himself appointed the manner in which he is to be worshipped. If this be the case, then worshipping God in any other way than he has appointed, instead of doing him acceptable service, must be a transgression of his law; and a transgression so much the more aggravated that it is committed under the pretext of paying him homage. And shall we consider the supreme Being as delighted with the variety of ways in which his creatures trample on his law and commit rebellion?

Lor. Our religion is for the most part no other thing than the prejudice of education.

Læl. What then? Do you mean that it is a sufficient reason for dropping our religion, that we have been taught it in our infancy? This can be no re son against Christianity, or indeed, against any thing at all, being a circumstance compatible alike with truth and with falsehood. The word prejudice may be applied to any opinion whether true or false which we are led to entertain without rational conviction. The real errors in which we are educated are always prejudices as long as we adhere to them; because we relinquish them as soon as we begin to reason right about them. On the other hand, even the truths in which we are educated may be called prejudices while we are ignorant of the reasons of them; but they become our genuine principles when those reasons are discerned. Properly speaking, prejudices respect the manner in which persons assent to propositions, not the propositions themselves.

Lor. I am confounded whenever I turn my thoughts to the subject of religion: I am apt to say with Cato, that—Shadows, clouds, and darkness rest upon it.

Læl. The reason why most people find so little satisfaction in their enquiries concerning religion is that they set about them with levity of mind. Religion will never do for an amusement: It is a vastly more agreeable recreation to play at nine-pins, than to read our modern theories and natural histories of religion. If ever you would have any solid, satisfying views of religion, you must look upon yourself as a poor and miserable creature; you must have a felt conviction that none of the creatures, neither the necessaries nor the conveniences of life, nor your personal qualities, nor your friends and relations can help and relieve you; but God Almighty can: he can easily make himself known to you as your refuge and your portion. The great, the tremendous question is, Whether he *will* do so or not? The scriptures alone, (I declare it without the least hesitation) in proportion as you discern more clearly the internal evidence of their divine authority; and as you become more acquainted with the *great things of*

God's law; the scriptures will give you an answer more and more satisfying, clear and comfortable.

CONSIDER yourself as in the sight and presence of God who knows the heart, and who is in a little to be your judge; and then ask your own heart the important question, whether you have diligently perused the scriptures; and having fairly examined the external and especially the internal evidence of their divine authority; whether you are satisfied in your conscience that there is nothing at all in it? Ask your own heart, whether you are absolutely sure that the account given in scripture, of the entrance of sin among mankind, of the present deplorable state of human nature, and of the manifestation of God's holiness and mercy in the salvation of sinners by a divine Redeemer, be all a cunningly devised fable?

OBSERVE the present state of the world; search antient and modern history, and see whether the characters of men and the course of providence be not a continued fulfilment of the scriptures. Compare, especially, the history of the church with the description of her lot in the Bible. Consider whether the same Almighty hand that made and that preserves the world, be not manifest in the erection, in the propagation, in the defence, and in the various deliverances of the church.

SERIOUSLY consider the testimony of many thousands (which could not be refused in any civil matter) concerning their experience of God manifesting himself to them and holding communion with them according to and by means of the scriptures. You cannot reasonably call them dishonest, without direct and positive evidence in opposition to their testimony: but such evidence it is impossible to produce. It would be rash and absurd in the extreme to say they were only persons of a weak or disordered judgment. Besides, they had the best opportunity of judging, whether living in the faith of the scriptures, or living in unbelief be the best and the most comfortable kind of life; becaufe they had tried both; which no infidel ever did.

It is common with infidels to confider religion only with refpect to the enjoyment of the prefent life, and to like or diflike it as it appears to fuit or to be inconfiftent with temporal profpects and pleafures. On the contrary, when you fet about enquiring what religion you fhall embrace, I would have you annihilate the prefent life, which in this enquiry can only ferve to prejudice or pervert your judgment; and confider yourfelf as on the point of being called before God's awful tribunal; on the point of entering into an eternal and unchangeable ftate. It is true, godlinefs is for our prefent comfort; but in order to our knowledge of this, it is firft neceffary to know that it has the promife of the life which is to come.

Make trial of Chriftianity. You are often propofing your doubts and difficulties to your fellow creatures: you fhould rather be employed in feeking to know God *your maker who giveth fongs in the night*: he alone can give you a fatisfactory folution of thofe doubts and difficulties; and therefore if you fincerely want it, apply to him for it: and try to come to him as the fcripture directs, making mention of Chrift's name. Say to him that you have heard that he has devifed a method of glorifying all the perfections of his nature by fhewing mercy to fuch finners as you are, by pardoning and faving them through a Mediator: Cry to him that he would make you underftand this wonderful method; and that he would fhine in your heart to give you the light of the knowledge of the glory of God in the face of Jefus Chrift. Try immediately to truft in this Saviour according to the knowledge you have of him, and that knowledge will increafe.

II. The *Temporizers*. They are always of that religious perfwafion which is the moft agreeable to their connections, which they have been educated in, or which is fashionable in the age or country wherein they live. They are chiefly of three sorts.

1. THE slothful or dissipated temporizers. Persons who, from the love of ease, are averse to all enquiries concerning religion; whose time is so much engrossed by business or amusements that they have none left for thinking deliberately of religious concerns; who find the duties of religion inconsistent with their favourite pursuits or their favourite pleasures; who instead of aiming at or desiring perfection in holiness, would have only so much of it as is absolutely necessary to evidence them to be in a state of grace; who, in their choice of a religious profession, are sure to fix on that which is likely to be the least attended with trouble or inconveniency; all these are temporizers from indolence and dissipation. Being *slothful*, they are not *followers of them who through faith and patience inherit the promises.*

2. THE covetous and and aspiring temporizers. Persons who are apprehensive that a strict adherence to the ways of religion would be utterly inconsistent with their views of rising in the world; who *make haste to be rich*, and find religion would be an obstacle in their way; who having formed a plan for making a fortune or for obtaining preferment, resolve to heed nothing that would divert them from the prosecution of it; who study to appear either lukewarm or zealous about the matters of God, as lukewarmness or zeal bids fairest to recommend them to the wealthy and the great; all these are temporizers from interested and ambitious views. Of this sort was Demas, who *forsook Paul, having loved the present world.*

3. THE cowardly temporizers. Persons who would not, for a world, be reckoned either more or less religious than their neighbours; who are as much afraid of being accounted strict professors as of being accounted abandoned profligates; who have not the resolution to abide by a religious profession, unless the world countenance them in it; who dread the

wrath of man more than the wrath of God, and love the praise of man more than the praise of God; who incessantly frighten themselves and others with terrible representations of the losses and hardships they are likely to suffer in adhering to the cause of Christ and a good conscience; who talk a great deal about prudence as the first of human virtues, by which they mean the art of keeping well with the world; and a great deal about moderation, by which they mean a disposition to forbear being pointed or explicit in a religious profession before its avowed enemies; in fine, who have some conviction of the truth, but suppress that conviction so far as to neglect endeavouring to glorify God by an open profession of it: all these are *Temporizers* from that *fear of man which bringeth a snare*. Such was Nicodemus who came to our Saviour by night.

Timothy had been a fashionable Temporizer. He possessed many valuable talents; but it was chiefly his complaisance and the art he had of accommodating himself to the humour of the great, which induced a man of quality to appoint him governour to his eldest son. Timothy had been a considerable time in that situation, when he was brought under deep impressions of his sin and danger. His concern for *the great salvation* made him indifferent to his former worldly pursuits. The sense he had of the *exceeding sinfulness of sin*, constrained him to reprove it, even when the reproof was contrary to the maxims of worldly prudence. The Spirit of God had shewn him the vanity of man's wisdom as to matters of religion in so strong a light, that now he could not bear human devices in the worship of God: On that account, he thought proper to withdraw from the church of England; and excused himself from attending his pupil, as usual, on the Sabbath. In consequence of such a revolution in his sentiments and conduct, he declined gradually in the favour of his patron; who at last, took an opportunity to tell him,

That as he intended to send his son to a boarding school, he had no farther occasion for his service; but should be happy to see him at his house as often as ⸺⸺. A day or two after, Timothy met with Lysander an old acquaintance: who having been acquainted with what had happened, accosted him in this manner.

Lys. So, it seems, you have been turned out of your place for refusing to conform to the church of England. It was a meer whim, Timothy. You might have been as good a Christian among the Episcopalians as among the Presbyterians. The prudent part of the world will call you a fool; and men of moderation and liberality of sentiment, a fanatic.

Tim. I had withdrawn from the church of England for reasons which I was convinced were clearly contained in the scriptures of truth: and I am still under the same conviction. How then, consistently with a due regard to the scriptures as the word of God, can I return to the communion of the church of England?

Lys. I hope, I esteem the scriptures as much as any man: but I would not contend so much for circumstantials as *for judgment, mercy and faith*, which our Saviour calls *the weightier matters of the law.*

Tim. The passage itself you refer to affords a convincing argument for a sacred and inviolable regard to what you call *circumstantials* as well as to the weightier matters: for our Lord adds, *These ought ye to have done, and not to leave the other undone.* From which it appears, that our Lord did not find fault with the Pharisees for their exactness in observing the *ceremonial law*, but for the want of a due regard to God's authority in observing it; which they evidenced by their neglect of the most important duties of morality.

Why, Lysander, did you turn off your steward Fungosus? Was he dishonest?

Lys. No.

Tim. Did he ufe his fellow-fervants ill?

Lys. No.

Tim. Did he grow inattentive to his bufinefs?

Lys. No; but he would never follow my directions in any thing. It is true, the fellow was very ingenious, and executed his own plans dextroufly; but I could never make him execute mine. Indeed he had fuch a fpirit of contradiction as no merit in other refpects could render fufferable.

Tim. Are we poor infignificant mortals apt to be in fuch anger with our inferiors, when they happen to crofs our inclination? And fhall not the Lord of heaven and earth be much more difpleafed, if in any inftance, we difregard his will revealed to us in the fcriptures? But we are guilty of fuch difregard whenever we pretend to worfhip him by other means than what he has appointed in his word. *In vain*, fays our Lord, *do ye worfhip me, teaching for doctrines the commandments of men.* Vain worfhip is a profanation of God's name: Vain worfhip brings the curfe inftead of the bleffing on its obfervers.

Lys. You know our Saviour himfelf was in communion with the eftablifhed church of the Jews, and ufed to join in their public worfhip. Perhaps the liturgy which the Jews then made ufe of was as exceptionable as the Englifh liturgy. We are fure the Jews were, at that time, exceedingly corrupt.

Tim. We have no account in the New Teftament of any public liturgy among the Jews. As to the Talmud and other compofitions of the Jewifh Rabbins, however ufeful they may be for preferving fome of their national cuftoms or opinions, little redit. is otherwife due to them with refpect to hiftorical facts.

As our Lord fet us a perfect example of every duty, fo particularly of a faithful teftimony againft the evils of our times. With what wholefome feverity did he expofe the reigning vices of the Pharifees; their pride, their hypocrify, their covetoufnefs and extortion? He never neglected an opportunity of tendering suitable reproof: When he was at meat in the house of a Pharisee, he faithfully reproved his entertainer for his pride and self conceit, Luke vii. 36,——47. When he was in the family of Lazarus which had so distinguished a share of his affection, we find him dealing plainly with Martha as to the excess of her care and anxiety about the things of the world, Luke x. 41. When Peter, from a mistaken tenderness, expressed himself against the sufferings of his beloved Lord, he received this terrible rebuke, *Get thee behind me, Satan; thou favourest not the things that are of God, but the things that are of men*†.

We are sure our Lord would never countenance in his practice those evils against which he cried so loudly in his doctrine. He was *holy, harmless, undefiled and separated from sinners.* He never practised any of their unwritten traditions: he and his followers openly distinguished themselves from all the sects into which the Jews were divided at that time. If we find him often in the synagogues or in the temple, it was because these were places of public concourse where he had an opportunity to preach the gospel to the people. Another reason for his attendance in the temple was, that he might perform such parts of Old Testament-service as were appropriated to that holy place.

Lys. Our Saviour instead of approving a secession from the scribes and Pharisees, exhorted the disciples to hear their instructions, Matth. xxiii. 3.

Tim. Our Lord could never be inconsistent with himself. But in Matth. xvi. he charges his disciples to *beware of the doctrine of the Pharisees.* In Matth.

---

† This is perhaps the severest reproof our Lord ever administred to any of his faithful followers. And whence was his severity on this occasion? Was it because his heart was so much set upon finishing the work that was necessary for the salvation of sinners that nothing was so offensive to him as the least opposition to it? An evidence of the greatness of Christ's love to poor sinners. A caveat against unbelief.

xv. he calls them *blind, leaders of the blind*. He says, they would not *suffer those that were entering into the kingdom of heaven, to go in*. They made their proselytes *twofold more the children of hell than themselves*. It seems plain, therefore, that our Lord considered them as false teachers whose *instructions caused to err from the words of knowledge*. This passage must therefore be so understood as to consist with a testimony against the corrupt doctrine as well as against the corrupt practices of the Scribes and Pharisees. But the people are here exhorted to observe and do whatsoever the Scribes and Pharisees enjoined as publishers and interpreters of the divine law, and, particularly, as members of the *Sanhedrin* or the council of seventy; who might well be said *to sit in Moses seat*, since according to God's immediate direction, they were originally ordained by Moses to share with him the burden of judging the causes of Israel. In this view, our Lord tells his hearers, that the instructions which the Scribes and Pharisees delivered agreeable to the word of God and to the original design of their office, should be carefully attended to, nor should offence be taken at any of them for the contrary practices of the Scribes and Pharisees.

Lys. You are too rigid: you must make allowances for the weakness and the variety of men's understandings and tempers.

Tim. In those instances where a person or a church has not, as yet, attained to the knowledge of the truth, or is only ignorant or misinformed, or is sincerely struggling against some evil not yet overcome; in such cases we ought to entertain sentiments of charity and forbearance: we are indeed to testify plainly and particularly against every real evil; but in the above mentioned cases, we are to encourage rather than condemn the church and the individual; we are to encourage them to proceed in reformation. On the other hand, when there appears much contempt of the truth, with the aggravation of apostacy from it, and of obstinacy and enmity against it, a sharper manner of reproof becomes necessary; we must withstand such opposers to the face; we must withdraw ourselves from them; such *tongues* as thus *rise up against Zion, she must condemn.*

Christians can tell, as matter of experience, that there is not any thing more usually accompanied with the sensible hiding of the Lord's face and with his sharp rebukes, than the wilful neglect of opportunities of reproving sin, or of testifying against error: and no wonder; since it is so peculiarly nauseous to Christ for church-members to be of such a lukewarm temper, *neither cold nor hot*, as to be indifferent to the indignities that are done to him: it makes him threaten to *spue them out of his mouth.*

Lys. It seems to be the part of a wise man to comply with the humour of the times in some things, that he may procure attention to his instructions in other things of more importance. So did Socrates and Plato, and Pythagoras, who conformed to the established worship of their country, though, it is probable, they were sensible of its absurdities. Even the apostle Paul *became all things to all men.*

Tim. The false prudence or policy of the world may suggest, That we may do evil that good may come; That the end may sanctify, or at least excuse unlawful means. But the bible, by which Christians are to regulate their conduct, knows no such maxims. Christians are expresly forbidden *to follow a multitude to do* any *evil.* It is at their peril if they deny Christ's name in any respect, or on any account.

The representation you have given of some celebrated philosophers is little to their advantage. They were, it seems, poor cowardly wretches, who durst not utter a syllable against what they knew to be a system of the grossest lies that were ever imposed upon the credulity of mankind: for such, if they had any knowledge of the true God, must have been their views of the religion of their country. They were as cruel as cowardly; otherwise how could they have remained silent spectators of the delusions which they saw mankind under, with regard to points of so much consequence to their happiness as the being of God and the right manner of worshipping him. Sure, one honest man that endeavours to make an upright stand for truth in opposition to the tide of fashion and vulgar prejudice, deserves far better of society, than a thousand such pusillanimous philosophers.

A WITNESS of Christ, however, should guard against giving any unnecessary offence; he may study to be agreeable without being unfaithful: *Be courteous*, is a divine command, as well as *be stedfast in the faith*. We are to shew out of a good conversation our works *in meekness of wisdom*. There are certain prepossessions in favour of particular indifferent customs of a country; and certain innocent peculiarities of temper and demeanour, which it would be a morose peevishness rather than any necessary zeal for the truth to insist on people's relinquishing. It was in such respects as these, that Paul *became all things to all men;* but as to any point in which the cause of Christ or of his truth was really concerned, never man was more steady or more determined than was this apostle.

YES, Lysander, let us detest the character of him who deliberately *sells the truth;* who, at the call of interest or of worldly favour, tramples on conscience and the honour of God. On the other hand, let us contemplate as a pattern for our imitation, such a character as that of the seraph Abdiel in Milton:

Among the faithless, faithful only he:
Among innumerable false, unmov'd,
Unshaken, unseduc'd, unterrify'd,
His loyalty he kept, his love, his zeal.
Nor number, nor example, with him wrought
To swerve from truth, or change his constant mind
Though single.

Let us follow them who have been *faithful unto death*. Let us follow Chrift efpecially; whofe ardent zeal for the houfe of God *did eat him up;* who *fet his face like a flint* to accomplifh our falvation in his *obedience unto death, even the death of the crofs*. How hard are our heart that can refift the influence of fuch an example, and of *love that paffeth knowledge!*

III. The *Selfifh Devotees*. A perfon of this character pretends to be fo much taken up with heart-religion that he has no leifure for attending to external or pofitive inftitutions. He thinks all queftions about the outward order and government of the church quite needlefs. With him it is a matter of mere indifference what profeffion a perfon makes, provided his heart be right, which, in his opinion, is equally the cafe with devout Chriftians of all denominations.

Some of this character are very talkative about religion: others are againft uttering a fyllable on that fubject; for, fay they, when we fhew our religious knowledge, we feed our vanity. But they all agree in defpifing what they call outward forms.

Among the caufes or occafions of this devotional extravagance, we may reckon the following:

1. The offence that fome have taken at the abufes of the outward forms of religion. When they faw men cover their fchemes of ambition with the pretext of zeal for the external ordinances of religion, they were tempted to confider thefe ordinances as always connected with evil defigns. Having feen them made fubfervient to the purpofes of vice, they no longer thought they could be fo to thofe of virtue and true piety.

2. The want of proper views of God's authority in thofe ordinances; and of the connection between the due obfervance of them and our partaking of fpiritual bleffings. No one that ever attained fuch views of thofe inftitutions, can altogether lofe his e-

steem of them. But it is no wonder to see one disregard them, who never sought more in attending on them, than merely to amuse himself with the external part or what is exhibited to the carnal eye. Besides, in our day, when iniquity abounds, ordinances are little accompanied with visible effects; a providential dispensation whereby men harden themselves in the disregard of them.

3. CONSIDERING the innate corruption of human nature, we cannot help ascribing this strange devotional contempt of God's ordinances, to pride. Persons must have a very high notion of their attainments in religion, when they think they can do well enough without those outward helps which are so necessary to other Christians. To be sure, they must be soaring (in their own conceit) to wonderful heights in the divine life, when they pretend to be devout in some other way than by using the ordinary means of God's appointment. Indeed, some of them have carried their extravagant pretensions so high, that they have actually boasted of being already perfect.

IF it be asked, Where are these Devotees to be found? Perhaps among the Quakers, or the followers of Madam Guion?‡ We answer, not among them only. Are there not many called Presbyterians, and other Protestants, who, in place of contending for the purity of the external institutions of Christ, regard a testimony against the corruptions of them with the coldest indifference? Do they not defend that indifference by alledging that such a testimony is of little importance to the religion of the heart? And yet is it not plain, that if these ordinances themselves are of importance to practical godliness, a testimony on their behalf must be so too? Since on the one hand, it is only while we endeavour to observe the institutions of Christ according to his word, that we can warrantably expect his blessing on them: and

---

‡ She gave rise to Quietism in France. She preached up, says Voltaire, the tranquillity of the soul, the annihilation of all its faculties, and inward worship.

since, on the other hand, Satan and man's depraved nature are ever at work to corrupt those institutions; it is plain, that the due observance of them and our profiting by them, must be very closely connected with a testimony on their behalf. We heartily approve of the sentiments which devout people of this description express with respect to the difficulty and importance of heart-religion: we only mean that they are guilty of inconsistency and of abuse, when they set these sentiments in opposition to the profession of the truth, and an open adherence to the cause of Christ.

VERUS having been enlightened to discern the spiritual beauty of our Lord's institutions, desired to adhere closely even to such of them as were the most generally neglected or despised. One day returning from a considerable journey which he had taken in order to have an opportunity of joining in public worship with some people who he understood were testifying against various corruptions of divine ordinances, he happened to meet with Simplicius. Simplicius had religion at heart: but he could not, he said, enter into the views of his friend with respect to the importance of circumstantials. I am afraid, continued he, you are too anxious about your testimony; your outward forms, and the purity of your profession. These things divert your attention, Verus, from the exercises of the heart.

VERUS. Does a merchant's exactness in executing the commissions of his correspondents abroad, argue inattention to his business at home?

SIM. Quite the reverse: for these correspondents make him such returns as enable him to deal to a far greater extent than ever before.

VER. In like manner, though a particular ordinance may not appear so closely connected with the case of our souls as some others; yet, Simplicius, if we observe that ordinance from a single regard to the divine authority, we shall find it more to our spiritual advantage than a great many selfish endeavours to better our case. Keeping the words of Christ is the way to have communion with him, John xiv. 23. *He that is liberal* in this respect, *shall be made fat*, Prov. xi. 25. If we would be *kept from the hour of temptation*, we should be careful to *keep the word of Christ's patience*, Rev. iii. 10. But what think you of a servant who cares not for obeying his master's commands, unless they be nearly connected with his own interest?

SIM. He may be said to serve himself rather than his master.

VER. How provoking, then, to the Lord of heaven and earth is that selfishness which leads us to dispute his commands, because they do not seem to contribute so much to our comfort or our interest as we could wish! A reverence of the divine authority should make us have respect to all God's commandments, *If I am a master, where is my fear, saith the Lord of hosts?*

SIM. Surely this is a chief command, *Keep the heart with all diligence.*

VER. True, Simplicius; and we should be careful to keep the heart by watching against a cold indifference to any of God's truths or institutions: for as we are affected toward these, he accounts us affected toward himself.

SIM. I have often observed, that persons who are very rigid adherents to what they call scripture-forms of worship and church-government, are very remarkable for pride and self-conceit.

VER. Consider, Simplicius, that various principles enter into the composition of every human character; and many different motives may occasion the same appearances of temper and behaviour. Hence when we lay the blame of what is wrong in a person's character or conduct upon any religious opinion which he seems to entertain, we would know, either from the nature and tendency of the opinion itself, or from proper evidence of the fact, that it actually is the cause of that wrong: if we find it to be the cause, we are likewise to examine the degree in which it is so: and farther still, whether the person has just views of it; or whether he does not pervert it.

But with respect to the character of those who endeavour after an exact observance of the institutions of Christ, allow me, Simplicius, to ask you a question. Suppose two persons are the patients of the same physician: the one follows the physician's prescription in every part of it as exactly as he can: the other observes only as much as he thinks essential. Say, now, which of the two distrusts himself, and confides in the honour and ability of the physician? Which of the two discovers the least pride and self-conceit?

Sim. He undoubtedly who endeavours to follow the whole of the prescription. But your outward forms of religion are so much controverted, that—

Ver. It will not follow that they are either right or wrong, frivolous or important. That a proposition has been the subject of much disputation is merely an accidental circumstance which argues neither its truth nor its falsehood, but only that men have had different apprehensions concerning it. Should this be deemed a sufficient reason for rejecting any thing in religion, we may reject the whole of it; and not only religion, but the first principles of reason and the testimony of our external senses; all which have been controverted. It is, therefore, a mere vulgar prejudice against the institutions of Christ, that they have been the subject of disputation. It is unworthy a man of sense to give over the search of truth or of excellence, merely because others have been unable to find it, or unwilling to acknowledge it. It is unworthy a man of candour to say that either persons or things should have no friends or adherents, only because they happen to have many enemies.

SIM. Though these outward observances might be highly proper in the infant state of the church, they seem now to be antiquated and of no more use. We who have the advantage of the new Testament, are to *worship God*, not with outward forms, but *in spirit and in truth*.

VER. The observances, indeed, of the old Testament that respected the coming of Christ *to put away sin by the sacrifice of himself* as a future event, are now no more necessary, when Christ the substance of them has actually appeared, and finished the work that was given him to do. But of all the other ordinances that God hath appointed in his word, there is not one which we are not indispensably bound to observe, or which will not continue obligatory on the church till the end of time. We are indeed to worship God *in spirit*, without those carnal ordinances which were in use before the coming of Christ; *and in truth*, as having the substance and reality of the ancient figures clearly revealed to us; so that we may behold the glory of the Lord with open face, the veil of Mosaic institutions being drawn aside. But our freedom from the yoke of the ceremonial law, does not lessen our obligation to glorify God in our *bodies* as well as in our *spirits* by a careful observance of the few positive institutions which our Lord has left us. The authority of a lawgiver should not be the less but the more regarded, that it is exerted with gentleness and moderation. It is remarkable that the Lord hath connected his blessing with the external observance of his ordinances much in the same manner in the new Testament as he had done in the old. He said in the old Testament, *In all places where I record my name, I will come unto thee, and I will bless thee*: he says in the new, *Where two or three are gathered together in my name, there am I in the midst of them.*

Sim. If we have the inward sentiments of true piety; if the love of God and universal goodwill to mankind reign in our hearts; we need be no more anxious about the form of our religion than about the cut of our cloaths.

Ver. Rather say, If we have the true love of God shed abroad in our hearts by the Holy Ghost, we will not, for the whole world, give our deliberate consent to the breach of one of God's commands, however trivial the matter of it, (like the eating of the fruit of a certain tree which was the matter of the first positive precept ever given to mankind) may appear to the eye of sense and reason. If we have a true, heart-felt love of mankind, we must be in pain, whenever we see them incur the displeasure of the Almighty, by persisting in the breach of even one of the least of his commands; and especially when we see them casting off any of those institutions, with the observance of which he has been pleased to connect his blessing.

The bible knows nothing of that heart-religion which does not manifest itself in suitable actions. It is vain for a person to pretend that he has the principle of faith, if he does not shew it by good works; that he loves his neighbour, if he neglect to relieve his necessities; that he believes with the heart unto righteousness, if he is no way concerned to make confession with the mouth unto salvation; that he loves Christ, if he is ashamed to keep the word of his patience; or, in fine, that he is willing to *stand with the Lamb on mount Zion, having his Father's name*, both in the heart and in the hand, if he still refuses to have it, *written in his forehead.*

Beware, then, Simplicius, of estimating the duty of obeying a divine command by the judgment that carnal sense and reason pass upon the matter of it: if at any time, you are apt to lose sight of the importance of any scriptural duty, you need not, like the leprous nobleman of Assyria, when the prophet bade him go wash in Jordan, perplex yourself with much reasoning about the matter of such a duty: you need not apply to this or the other subtile casuist: you have free access to the infinite Lawgiver himself; go to him as your God and Father in Christ, and cry, that he would shew you his authority, his majesty, sovereignty, wisdom, holiness, love and faithfulness in such a precept, according to his word. *the meek will he guide in judgment, the meek will he teach his way.*

IV. THE *Waverers.* These profess to be enquiring after the truth, but they never find it. One may fitly address them in the words of Elijah to the people of Israel, *How long halt ye between two opinions? If the Lord be God, follow him: but if Baal, then follow him.* Why are many at such a loss? Is it because the revelation which God hath given us is obscure and hard to be understood? By no means; for though there is enough in the scriptures to exercise the most elevated understanding, they are calculated in the best manner to instruct the meanest.— They have milk for babes, as well as meat for strong men. But the following are some of the causes or occasions of this wavering:

1. Men's conceit of their own wisdom. Wavering or doubting implies a consciousness of ignorance; how then does it spring from self-conceit? When persons come to the study of the scriptures, full of themselves, with all their prejudices strong about them, it may well be said of them that hearing they do not hear, and seeing they do not perceive, and reading they do not learn. It is only the humble and the simple-minded who attain to certainty and establishment in divine truth, according to the scripture, Matth. xi. 15. *At that time Jesus answered and said, I thank thee, O Father, Lord of heaven and earth, because thou hast hid these things from the wise and prudent, and hast revealed them to babes.* 1 Cor. iii. 18.

Let no man deceive himself: if any man seemeth to be wise in this world, let him become a fool that he may be wise.

2. Duplicity. James i. 8. *A double-minded man is unstable in all his ways.* The affections, leading different ways, never fail to bias the understanding; and we need not wonder if we are not certain of truths to which we have an aversion; or if we waver, where we have no inclination to be fixed.

3. Want of experience of the spiritual favour and sanctifying efficacy of divine truth. Such experience, while it produces a more permanent conviction than the clearest reasoning, engages the affections, and makes persons be rooted and grounded in the love of the truth. How directly opposite to the character of which we speak, was that of the saints recorded in scripture! to whose taste the word was *sweeter than the honey dropping from the comb, and who esteemed it more than their necessary food.* If at any time they were tempted to waver, they set themselves, through the mercy of God upholding them, to resist the temptation: and whenever they felt any disposition to slacken their resistance, or to fall in with the temptation, they said, *This is mine infirmity:* Nor would they allow themselves any rest, till in the way of going to God's sanctuary and in the diligent use of appointed means, they were, through God's blessing, delivered, and brought to a thorough establishment in the very truth about which they had been tempted to waver. See remarkable examples of this in the 73d and 77th psalms. Whence was it that they were so resolute in holding fast the truth? The reason was, they had experienced the saving, sanctifying power of it in their hearts; they received it as the word of God that wrought in them effectually. It is owing to the want of this experience that wavering or doubting of the truth abounds so much in our day.

4. The neglecting to view divine truths as connected with the person of Christ; that most important connection whence they derive all their saving efficacy. The whole of revelation is either concerning the wonderful constitution of the person of Christ, concerning the doing, suffering, and glory of his person, concerning the benefits to be enjoyed in union to his person, or in fine, concerning the duties by which we express our regard to his person, Eph. iv. 20, 21. *But ye have not so learned Christ; if so be, that ye have heard him, and have been taught by him, as the truth is in Jesus.*

5. A great many occurrences or incidents are laid hold of as pretences for wavering: such as the disputes about matters of religion, the eminent men and their plausible reasoning on both sides of a question, the adherents to opposite religious tenets being equally virtuous or equally immoral.

The prevalence of this character in the reformed churches seems to be one principal cause of the present decline of religion in them, and indeed threatens their utter ruin. They not only shew no disposition to make any farther advances in reformation, but have lost all resolution to hold fast what they attained. Hence they allow in their communion such as deny and are not ashamed to ridicule the leading principles of the reformation.

EUSTATHIUS and Polysephus were intimate friends. Their conversation often turned on religion. Eustathius, though ready to acknowledge that his proficiency in the knowledge of divine truth was very little, considering the advantages he enjoyed, was firmly persuaded of many doctrines which he had learned from the scriptures, and which he found the Holy Spirit made use of as the appointed means of our sanctification. Polysephus, on the contrary, having taken up many of his religious opinions from the conversation of the gay and the fashionable part of the world, was not convinced of the neceſſity of a well-grounded aſſurance in matters of religion, and with regard to the moſt part of them, looked upon it as of no conſequence what a perſon aſſented to, or what he denied.

Eustathius and Polyſephus happened one day to meet at the houſe of their common friend. They found that they had come from the ſame village but by different roads. Upon which Polyſephus took occaſion to obſerve, That people's different perſuaſions, if attended with a virtuous life, would iſſue alike in the heavenly happineſs.

Eus. Whatever you mean by a virtuous life, I am ſure there are opinions that tend to lead us away both from holineſs and from heaven. Errors are among thoſe evil thoughts which proceeding out of the heart. defile the man. The apoſtle lays it down as the conſequence of an error concerning the reſurrection of the dead, *That our faith would be vain, and we would be ſtill in our ſins.* If the truth make us free from ſin, then error muſt tend to bring or keep us under the power of it. Indeed, it is a principle of common ſenſe, that we cannot ſhew any due regard to a character which we take to be ſomething altogether different from what it really is. But what elſe is our obedience than the regard we ſhew to the God of ſalvation, as he is revealed in the ſcriptures of truth?

Pol. I am often at a loſs when I conſider the fair pretences of the different parties which now divide the Chriſtian world.

Eus. From the very beginning there were wolves in ſheep's clothing that got into the flock of Chriſt, *not ſparing it.* Theſe occaſioned diviſions and offences even in the firſt ages of the Chriſtian church. Many of theſe diſcovered themſelves in broaching opinions which were a diſgrace as well to reaſon as to Chriſtianity: ſuch were the Gnoſtics and the Manichees. Afterward, when the rulers of the world began to favour the Christian church, the dominion of some aspiring ecclesiastics grew by degrees to such a pitch, that at length, it had all the marks and characters of the *man of sin and son of perdition, who opposeth and exalteth himself above all that is called God, or that is worshipped ; so that he, as God, sitteth in the temple of God, shewing himself that he is God.* The greater part of what was called the Christian world submitting themselves to this dominion, the faithful few who endeavoured to adhere to the simplicity of the truth as it is in Jesus, were obliged to separate themselves from the majority. The world, therefore, called them sometimes Lollards, sometimes Wickliffites, sometimes Hussites ; for it always reckoned them odious and contemptible. At last, by the instrumentality of Luther and other preachers of the everlasting gospel, *the tenth part of the city fell,* and that glorious event, the reformation from Popery, was brought about. Then whole provinces and kingdoms took the name of Protestants, and flocked to the banner of Christ's testimony against Popery. But even in these protestant countries, the devil was at no loss for instruments to corrupt or to oppose the church of God. Protestant princes were led to gratify their ambition at the church's expence. The restraints that those princes put upon the consciences of their subjects, and the liberty they took to mould the Protestant churches to their taste and inclination, induced many of the faithful to maintain their Christian freedom and the purity of gospel-ordinances by testifying against the constitution of these churches, and, at last, by separating from them. The princes, impatient of being thwarted in their schemes by these dissenters, tried, at first, to suppress them by coercive methods ; but finding the attempt utterly unsuccessful, they discovered that they would gain their political ends much better by toleration. Thus providence, at last, having granted to dissenters, from national establishments, outward peace and prosperity, they became numerous, and in a great measure fashionable; they were *of the world* as well as *in it.* Then the minds of men took a new turn: formerly they acquired reputation and made their fortunes by paying their court to kings and to their ministers, and by conforming to the established religion; but now they attain the same worldly objects by other means more adapted to a cultivated state of society; by forming systems of theology, by address, by eloquence, by their pretensions to superior sanctity and wisdom; and, in fine, by all the arts proper for procuring followers and making parties. But a dutiful regard to God's authority in his word is as plainly different from the levity, the vain curiosity and the affected singularity which prevail with sectarists, as from the mean complaisance, the implicit faith and blind obedience with which the dictates of popes and princes, in matters of religion, have been received. Those *who heap up to themselves teachers having itching ears,* and *those who receive the mark of the beast,* are both condemned by the scripture.

Pol. When I see a set of people distinguished by the purity and simplicity of their manners, I am apt to think their principles not so bad as their enemies represent them.

Eus. I wish to disapprove as much as any one of exaggerating the faults or errors of any set of men, as being a thing both uncharitable and unjust. But if you mean, that when we hear some sectarists applauded by all the world as exceedingly virtuous, we are merely on that account to conclude that their opinions, however unscriptural we have reason to think them, are innocent and unblameable: I am afraid your test for judging of religious principles will prove a very false one. In the first place, View them closer. What seems beautiful to the superficial eye, is often discovered by a severer scrutiny to be full of deformity. Enquire whether they have an impartial regard to the whole of God's law; to the first as well as to the second table of it: whether they be men of prayer as well as men of honour: whether they are spiritually minded: whether they are not much disposed to justify themselves and to despise others: whether they do not make more mention of their own righteousness than of Christ's: and whether they do not pay more attention to the devices of men than to the ordinances of God: Sins in these and the like respects, however much the world may make light of them, are peculiarly heinous in the sight of God. Indeed *what is highly esteemed among men is abomination to the Lord.* And then supposing there are many things in their outward deportment amiable or praise-worthy, should not these things be rather ascribed to the principle of honour, to the natural dictates of conscience, to some valuable truths which they still retain, than to their false and dangerous opinions.

Poly. But does not our Lord lay it down as the rule whereby we may know false teachers, *By their fruits ye shall know them?*

Eust. Yes, Polysephus; but then you must understand by these fruits whatever is contrary to *the power of godliness.* Though a doctrine may not *sensibly* lead us to such irregularities of outward conduct as may expose us to the censure of the world; yet if it has a native tendency to increase our unbelief of God's word, or to lessen our regard to him as our God and Redeemer; to make us less grieved for sin, or less spiritually minded; we may be sure that that doctrine is not from God. Our Lord having *cautioned* his disciples against those false teachers who, though inwardly *ravening wolves,* would come to them *in sheep's clothing;* adds, *Ye shall know them by their fruits:* that is, they will discover themselves to spiritual discerners (who can well distinguish the voice of Christ from that of strangers) by their proper fruits; by their *instructions that cause to err from the words of knowledge;* by their influence and example tending to corrupt the church, and to divide her members from the testimony of Christ, and from one another in him; and in fine, by their words and actions being habitually contrary to the law and the testimony. We are not, however, to conclude that these false teachers will always be reputed immoral in their lives: On the contrary, their coming *in sheep's clothing* intimates that the smoothness of their external behaviour would procure them a fair and unblemished reputation. The truth is, the whole of God's law is evidently designed to promote the happiness of men: and though they are so much blinded by the corruption of nature as not to see this tendency in many parts of the law, in those especially which are more spiritual and refined; yet there are other parts of it in which this tendency is so visible and striking that self love leads them to study some outward conformity to such parts in their own conduct, and to commend it in the conduct of others. Now, false teachers may carry their morality thus far (which is all that is necessary to gain the applause of the world) consistently enough with their endeavours against the purity of the truths and ordinances of Christ. Hence we hear so many encomiums on the Quakers, the Glassites and other daring blasphemers of the institutions of Christ in our day.

POLY. You should not give people uncharitable names: When persons become positive as to the truth of their religious opinions, they pass the harshest censures on such as cannot see things in the same light. In my mind, uncertainty with moderation is better than such ungoverned zeal.

EUST. Uncharitableness, I think, may be defined, the hatred of our neighbour, or at least, the want of due love to him, manifested in a disposition to condemn him without sufficient evidence of guilt, or to put a bad construction on what may admit of a good one. But it is no hatred of our brother, but an instance of real friendship, to inform him of any thing that is wrong in his principles or practice, laying open its sinful nature and pernicious consequences in order to make him relinquish it. It would, no doubt, be uncharitable to charge one with erroneous opinions without sufficient evidence, from his own confession or otherwise, of his holding them. But if the opinions that one proclaims and glories in, are plainly unscriptural, it is our duty, it is true charity to reprove him and warn others by declaring such opinions to be, what they really are, unscriptural.

POLY. But it may be, he is in the right, and your own opinions, not his, are unscriptural.

EUST. Then I am chargeable with rashness and mistake. But I speak of the connection between a certain knowledge of our brother's error and the duty of testifying against it. In which case, our testimony and admonition may, through the Lord's blessing, *turn one from the error of his way and save his soul from death.*

IT would be very absurd for one who had neglected to give his friend good counsel in a case where it was plainly necessary, to justify the neglect by the general principle, that there is a possibility of mistaking the nature and consequences of human actions. It is equally unreasonable to neglect declaring the truth, or warning others against error for this general reason, that we may be wrong in our views of both. Indeed, if this reasoning, *that because men may be and frequently are mistaken, we must not suppose ourselves to be certain of any thing in particular, nor act as if we were so,* be once admitted; then our acquaintance with history and even our knowledge of the common affairs of life, whether acquired by our own experience or by the testimony of others, will be of little or no use.

POLY. But does not too much confidence of the truth of our opinions hinder us from an impartial examination of them. A little scepticism seems more favourable to free inquiry.

Eust. Yes, Polysephus; there is a rational scepticism which is highly commendable: for never will we be sensible where evidence is, unless we be sensible where it is not. If we doubt of a proposition, we should have a reason for doubting of it. That reason being entirely removed, we cannot rationally doubt any longer: we are certain of it. That certainty, being sincere, not pretended; being real, not imaginary, instead of being shaken by the freest enquiry, is more firmly established.

With respect to opinions in general, certainty is the end we aim at in our enquiries concerning them. But surely it is unreasonable to suppose that a partial attainment of our end will discourage us from using the means. Success will rather animate our endeavours. It is well known, that there is nothing in mathematical science that so much engages persons to prosecute it, as the certainty with which it is attended.

Christians, indeed, are often anxious to avoid the hearing of false teachers or the reading of erroneous books; but this does not proceed from an unwillingness to have their principles thoroughly examined: these they know will abide the severest scrutiny: But knowing they have a depraved nature susceptible of bad impressions, they are justly afraid of having the affections alienated from the truth; the affections which would bias the understanding, and hinder it from discerning the evidence of divine truth. The evidence of divine truth, they know, cannot be overturned, but then they may lose sight of it. Thus a mathematician's fear that he may forget the demonstration of a proposition in Euclid, is very different from a fear that the demonstration itself may prove a sophism.

Poly. Enthusiasts pretend a great deal of certainty with regard to what all but themselves see to be extravagant fancies.

Eust. In my mind, it is for want of that satisfaction which the certainty of divine truth affords, that persons are led to take up with vain imaginations, and become Enthusiasts. Hence a solid and full persuasion of the truth as it is in Jesus is the only never-failing preservative against enthusiasm.

If a proposition is evidently founded on some plain text, and is agreeable to the general tenor of scripture; if its tendency is the same with that of the gracious revelation which God hath given us, to give all glory to God, and to exclude the boasting of the creature; the truth of such a proposition, where the authority of the scripture is duly regarded, cannot reasonably be called in question. But whatever use an Enthusiast seems to make of the letter and sometimes of the doctrine of scripture, his assent to any proposition is chiefly influenced by some favourite but ungrounded imagination, to which he thinks it agreeable; by the strong impressions that it makes upon him; by the hopes and the joys which it inspires. An Enthusiast cannot bring himself to examine impartially the opinions on which his hopes and joys are founded, for this plain reason; that it is for the sake of his hopes and joys that he entertains those opinions*. On the contrary, the Christian is anxious to know whether his opinions be according to the scriptures, because it is on account of their agreeableness to the scriptures that he holds them. Besides the Enthusiast is wholly intent upon some particular part of religion to the neglect of other parts†: and what he thus doats on is most commonly some imagination or invention of his own: But the Christian's believing adherence to any truth or duty of God's word, instead of leading him, like the Enthusiast's fond attachment, to neglect other truths

---

* When the heathen philosopher said, "That if the belief of of the souls immortality was a delusion, it was so agreeable a one that he wished to continue in it;" he spoke like an Enthusiast.

† This is a remarkable trait in the character of an Enthusiast: If he is much in devotional exercises, he makes little account of the duty that he owes to his neighbour. He talks much of his transporting joy, while he discovers little concern for the body of sin.

or duties, never fails to increase his uniform and universal regard for them.

POLY. If I prosecute my enquiries, I am afraid I shall be continually changing my religious persuasion: on the other hand, it is dangerous to continue in an error.

EUST. Go on, by all means, Polysephus, in your enquiries. As you advance, the truths you already know will be known more perfectly: every step you take will throw new light upon them: every difficulty or objection, when removed, will strengthen your conviction. Every prejudice and every error you get rid of, will contribute to your establishment in the truth. Only let your enquiries be directed by the scripture, influenced by the love of the truth as it is in Jesus, and accompanied with earnest prayers to God, saying, *What I know not teach thou me.* Distrusting yourself, look up to God for the spirit of wisdom and revelation in the knowledge of Christ. Yes, Polysephus push your enquiries as far as the means and opportunities afforded by Providence permit you. Shake off the restraints of custom, of authority whether ancient or modern. Pay no regard to names or parties. Receive the truth wherever you can find it. As in practice Christians ought to fear nothing but sin; so in matters of faith they should fear nothing but error.

POLY. The reasoning of one party seems very plausible, till another party comes and exposes the vanity of it.

EUST. What conclusion do you draw from that? That a pearl is no better than a glass toy, or a piece of pure gold than a counterfeit? I have read a story of two Knights who met at a pillar which had the same inscription on two sides: " Sure," said the one Knight as he read it on the side next him, " he " must have been a gallant hero, and defender of in- " nocence who is the subject of this golden inscrip- " tion." " No doubt," said the other, reading it on the opposite side; " but I beg leave to correct a "mistake; the inscription is in silver." They maintained their several assertions with inflexible perseverance, till each of them thought himself bound by all the laws of honour and of knighthood, to lift his arms against so unreasonable an opponent. They were preparing for the combat, when an honest traveller happening to come up, enquired the cause. Both parties being heard, the traveller desired them only to observe that on the one side of the pillar the inscription was in gold; on the other it was in silver. Thus partial views may occasion many controversies; in which case persons may be blameable for inattention, for sloth and negligence, for rashness in asserting more than they know, and in supposing they are acquainted with the whole of the subject, while they are acquainted only with a part. But how much more blameable or rather criminal is the artful Sophister who is resolved to try all methods fair and unfair to maintain some preconceived opinion or the peculiarities of his party. In the first place, he states the question in so ambiguous a manner that the reader or hearer is apt to confound it with something quite distinct from it. In the next place, he tries to connect his darling tenet with some popular topic on which he expatiates a great deal, in order both to catch the attention of the public, and to prevent the weakness of his arguments from being observed. Then he addresses the passions and prejudices of his readers or hearers, which he knows are much more attended to by the bulk of mankind, than candid reasoning. If any difficulty occur, he neglects it, misrepresents it, or treats it with contempt. If he is writing or speaking against any particular opponent, he never scruples to pervert his words to a meaning the farthest imaginable from what was plainly intended. He neglects that part of his opponent's reasoning on which he knows the greatest stress is laid; and imputes to him consequences which are drawn, not from his declared principles, but from an invidious construction of them, or from unguarded and unconnected expressions. These, not to mention many grosser methods, such as lies, calumny and detraction, are to be held in abhorrence by every honest man, as well as by every sincere enquirer after truth.

The sincere and modest enquirer after truth! Where is he to be found, who is in love with truth for its own sake; especially with divine truth for the sake of its infinitely glorious Revealer: who labours to separate from the subject of his enquiry whatever does not belong to it, that his conceptions of it may be clear and distinct: who wants to mark precisely where knowledge and certainty end, where ignorance and conjecture begin: who is willing to receive instruction from every quarter, from the learned and the unlearned, from friends and foes: who rejoices whenever truth is victorious, though he should himself be vanquished: who is critical, but too enlarged and elevated in his views to be nice; modest without timidity, and bold without insolence?

In fine, Polysephus, the maxims of politicians may be discovered to be false, and the theories of philosophers to be chimerical; but the truths of the Bible and the peculiar doctrines of Christianity will only become more illustrious for every attempt against them; and they shall continue to shine with increasing splendor, till he who is the truth, shall himself appear to the everlasting confusion of all his enemies.

Poly. I have a great aversion to the character of your *witnesses*. They are generally fierce bigots: morose and gloomy in their manner of living, they affect to abhor every gaiety and every polite amusement. At the same time, they are often deficient in that purity of morals, which alone can compensate for their sour and unsociable humour.

Eust. What is this hateful thing you call a Bigot? Is it one who is positive in his opinion without reason? Then a witness for the truth as it is in Jesus is no bigot: becauſe he has the weightieſt of all reaſons for what he adheres to, even the authority of God's word. Is it one who contends for trifles, as if they were matters of the utmoſt importance? Then the faithful witneſs for the truths of Chriſt is no bigot: becauſe we never can prize thoſe truths too much; we are to buy them and not to ſell them. Compared to them, all thoſe tranſitory advantages for which politicians debate and armies engage, are but the toys of children. Is it one who is exceſſively zealous for ſome favourite point which he reckons truth, while he diſregards other things of equal or greater conſequence? Then the witneſs of Chriſt is no bigot; for he has an univerſal regard to the doctrines and the commands of Chriſt: the authority of Chriſt engages him to eſteem them all. Is it one diſpoſed to propagate his religious tenets by fire and ſword? Then the witneſs of Chriſt is no bigot: Knowing that *the wrath of man worketh not the righteouſneſs of God*, he endeavours to *ſhew out of a good converſation, his works in meekneſs of wiſdom.* His chief aim is to be like the Lord Jeſus who is *meek and lowly in heart. The weapons of his warfare are not carnal, but mighty through God to the pulling down of ſtrong holds.* If he is called to an account for his religious principles, *he is ready to give a reaſon of the hope that is in him with meekneſs and fear.* Is it one who hates any farther diſcoveries of the truth, and deſpiſes the means of better information? Then the witneſs of Chriſt is by no means a bigot: He is one who loves the light: he wants to learn more and more of him who is the great Revealer of ſecrets. He deſires, like Mary, to ſit at his feet and hear his words. Inſtead of being proud of his wiſdom, he acknowledges himſelf a fool, and comes to Chriſt that he may be made truly wiſe.

With reſpect to what you ſay about moroſeneſs, it is far from belonging to the character of a witneſs of Chriſt as it is delineated in the Bible; which is the only view in which we plead for that character. It is a maxim with such a one, that *a merry heart doth good like a medicine.* He knows that *the ways of wisdom are ways of pleasantness, and all her paths are peace.* He has a conscientious regard to the precept, *rejoice evermore.*

It is true, that, though they have a relish for the enjoyments of life, they are careful about two things: In the first place that they be lawful; that they be neither sinful in themselves, nor incentives to any thing sinful. Hence they abstain from many fashionable amusements; such as, games of chance, theatrical entertainments, promiscuous dancings, and the like. Whoever has read the apologies of the primitive Christians, must know that their testimony against these things was much the same with that of the witnesses of Christ at this day†.

In the next place, They do not place their happiness in outward enjoyments or possessions. *The Lord is their refuge and portion in the land of the living.* Hence it ill becomes them to be elated with worldly prosperity, or much cast down with worldly losses and disappointments. But what though they have no taste for the jovial madness and riotous excess of the sons of dissipation? They endeavour after evenness of temper, solid peace of mind, and the possession of themselves, in the only way in which these blessings can ever be obtained; in the only way that

---

† The reproaches that are now cast upon the witnesses of Christ, are much the same that the Heathens used to throw out against the primitive Christians. Vos vero, says Cæcilius pleading the cause of heathenism in the Octavius of Minutius Felix, suspensi atque solliciti, honestis voluptatibus abstinetis: non spectacula visitis, non pompis interestis; convivia publica absque vobis; —— pallidi, trepidi estis.

The same elegant author, vindicating the Christians on this head, represents the public shows of his time in a manner that will apply very well to those of our own. Nos igitur qui moribus et pudore censemur, merito malis voluptatibus et pompis vestris et spectaculis adstinemus, quorum —— noxia blandimenta damnamus. Nunc enim mimus vel exponit adulteria, vel monstrat: nunc enervis histrio amorem, dum fingit, infligit. Idem simulatis doloribus, lacrymas vestras vanis gestibus et nutibus provocat.

God hath appointed; that is, by a believing improvement of Chriſt for all the purpoſes of wiſdom, righteouſneſs, ſanctification and redemption; by rejoicing in Chriſt Jeſus, having no confidence in the fleſh.

On the one hand, our Lord Chriſt regards the world as his enemy in its prevailing cuſtoms, its favourite pleaſures and purſuits; and therefore ſays to his followers, *Be ye not conformed to the world*. On the other hand, the men of the world, full of enmity againſt him, avoid the acquaintance of his profeſſed followers; and are prone to condemn, without knowing them. It is true, though the view they have taken of them has been diſtant and ſuperficial, yet they have obſerved two things with regard to them: *one* is their profeſſed relation to Chriſt: *the other* is, the contrariety of their taſte, of their ſentiments and of the general tenor of their conduct, to their own. Theſe two things are enough to make the world hate them.

As to what is really immoral in the converſation of ſome profeſſed witneſſes for the truth, I have no apology to offer: it muſt be acknowledged and lamented with ſhame and confuſion of face. One thing however is obvious, that it is wrong to draw a concluſion from ſuch particular inſtances againſt the character in general of witneſſes for Chriſt; ſince thoſe inſtances are plainly deviations from this character; and ſince it is unjuſt to impute the faults of ſome individuals to the whole body with which they ſtand connected. Though the offences of thoſe profeſſing a ſtrict adherence to the truths of Chriſt are numerous and heinous and deeply aggravated; as depraved nature is the ſame in them as in others; as the devil and the world, from the mortal hatred they bear them, are ſure to reſerve for them, the moſt violent aſſaults or the moſt refined and ſubtle methods of temptation; and as their irregularities contraſted with the ſpotleſs purity of their evangelical profeſſion, appear greatly the more glaring and enormous: yet after all, we have reason to think the charges that the world brings against them would be considerably diminished, were we to deduct whatever has been added to their real offences by calumny and slander; whatever, in the case of others, men would ascribe to the unavoidable weakness of human nature; whatever exaggerating representations some have given of particular faults in order to bring down to their level a character which, their conscience testifies, is, in general, far superior to their own.

The truth is, all the evil with which the men of the world reproach the witnesses of Jesus, is little to what they see in themselves. They know the plague of their own heart: they readily acknowledge themselves the chief of sinners. Were you to compliment them on their piety and virtue, they would reject the fulsome flattery: "We are only poor sinners," would they say; "and as no *outcasts ready to perish* " were ever in greater need of salvation, we seek it " through our Lord Jesus Christ: and our quar- " rel with the world is this, that they neglect the " great salvation, and refuse to give God the glory " of it."—Whence is the sorrow which the world ignorantly calls melancholy and morofeness? Why are they so oft in the house of mourning, and walk softly all their years in the bitterness of their soul? Why is there a mixture of sadness in all their mirth? And why rises the sigh from the bottom of their heart even in the moments of transporting joy? The true reason is, they groan under the burden of a depraved nature: its deceitful workings and deplorable effects are matter of hourly lamentation.

Poly. Uncertainty as to religious opinions seems to do little harm.

Eust. It is dishonourable to God: it reflects upon that revelation which he hath given us, as if it were so obscure and doubtful as to be unfit to answer its end. Nay, if we do not believe God's record, that is, if we are not certain of it, the apostle John assures us, we *make the God* of truth *a liar*. We can have no experience of the sweetness or saving efficacy of divine truth, unless we are assured of it. While you willingly or indolently harbour any uncertainty of divine truth, you are apt to give it up altogether: you are an easy prey to every seducer. You must stand upon sure ground, if you would not be drawn away with the error of the wicked.

There seems to be no religious duty or spiritual exercise but what is hindered by wavering. One who allows himself in it, cannot read or hear the word with profit, because he does not mix it with faith; that is, with a full perswasion of the truth, Heb. iv. 2. He cannot pray, acceptably, for we are to *ask in faith nothing wavering; for he that wavereth is like a wave of the sea, driven with the wind and tossed*, James i. 6. He cannot receive the sacraments aright; because the very end of them is to confirm our faith, and deliver us from wavering. Finally, if we would hold fast our profession, we must study to get free from wavering, Heb. x. 23.

Poly. I am discouraged by the levity of my temper which disposes me much to wavering, and by the difficulties which must be surmounted before one come at the certain knowledge of divine truths.

Eust. You should, therefore, despair of attaining the saving knowledge of divine truth by your own endeavours meerly. Come to Christ who is *the great prophet whom the Lord our God hath raised up unto us*. Look to him for all that effectual teaching which is imported in such promises as these: *They shall be all taught of God; They shall all know me from the least even to the greatest; I will teach thee to profit*. Trust in him as the Wonderful Counsellor for the accomplishment of these promises, and you shall not be disappointed nor ashamed.

Be not offended at the manner of Christ's school. The first lesson you have to learn is very humbling and mortifying to proud nature; it is concerning your own ignorance and unworthiness. And then he teaches much by experience: he may probably bring you through fire and water in order to teach you some important lesson thoroughly. As he led the Israelites forty years in the wilderness and humbled them, that they might know what was in their heart, and might learn that *man liveth not by bread alone, but by every word proceeding out of the mouth of the Lord,* Deut. viii. 2, 3. Be not discouraged, however; the more you know of our Lord's way of teaching, you will see the more of his wisdom, his kindness and condescension in it. They are but strangers to him, who think him an austere or hard master.

Be much in prayer. *If any man lack wisdom, let him ask it of God who giveth to all liberally and upbraideth none; and it shall be given him.* Ask the Spirit, Luke xi. 13. He is our guide into divine truth. Look to the Lord that he may establish and keep you. It is grace that establishes the heart, Heb. xiii.

V. The sincere but desponding Christian. Persons of this character love Christ, and have communion with him in his ordinances. Hence the good of the church which is his body, is the chief object of their concern. But on taking a survey of the present state of religion, they are apt to indulge themselves in such a plaintive strain as the following.

"Alas," says one of them, "the work of Christ
" in my soul seems to make no progress. I am very
" much under the feet of my enemies. The Lord
" is dishonoured: I have little or no strength for
" spiritual exercises, for the mortification of sin, or
" for walking in newness of life. It is long since I
" had any comfortable experience of the Lord lift-
" ing up the light of his countenance upon me; and
" now I am apt to call in question the reality of for-
" mer experiences. Still I desire to wait on him in

"his ordinances; but I generally find he has *with-*
"*drawn himself.* Such being my own case, I need
"the less wonder at the mournful things in the pub-
"lic state of religion. Yet I must lament these things.
"I dare not, I cannot seek or expect my own deli-
"verance, but in the way of seeking and expecting
"the deliverance of the church of God. The great
"things that God wrought for his church in Britain
"and Ireland are not only forgotten but burried; and
"all the grave stones which the force of human laws,
"the arts of sophistry, or the malevolence of slan-
"der could roll, are accumulated upon the Lord's
"work. We have turned what was the glory of
"these lands, their covenant-relation to the Lord,
"into shame. Our civil constitution as it compre-
"hends the ecclesiastical supremacy, and is blended
"with the establishment of Prelacy, the ruling prin-
"ciples and manners of the times, say, there is no
"such relation. And yet while this relation is deni-
"ed, and we persist in a course of open, heaven-da-
"ing perjury, we cannot reasonably look for a refor-
"mation. Surely the first step toward our returning
"to the Lord with the whole heart, will be a full
"and free acknowledgment of our treachery. But
"before we can be brought to that, there must be
"such a revolution in the sentiments and opinions,
"in the public and private conduct of all ranks in
"these lands, as we can hardly expect in the ordi-
"nary course of Providence. Besides, men are form-
"ing to themselves new schemes of religion with e-
"ven fair and plausible pretences of reformation, in
"avowed contempt of that which we are bound to
"by our solemn covenants. And they seem to pro-
"sper in their way; while many serious Christians
"are drawn over to their side. Our Lord does not
"now plead his cause by giving such remarkable
"checks to the opposers of his work, or such remark-
"able countenance to the professed friends of it,
"as he was wont to do in former times. Alas!

"these professed friends are grown too much like the church of Laodicea, lukewarm, neither cold nor hot; and therefore our Lord threatens to spue them out of his mouth. Nay, he seems to have begun the execution of his threatening in the awful spiritual judgments that abound among us. There is a great restraint of the Holy Spirit; and we are under a great prevalence of Atheism, unbelief, carnality and sinful conformity to the world. The glory is departed from our Israel."

This, to be sure, is a most deplorable case; and he must have a heart void of sensibility to all that regards the glory of God or the welfare of his church, who is not affected with it. But still an unbelieving despondency is quite unjustifiable. We are indispensibly bound *to judge him faithful who hath promised,* even when providence wears the gloomiest aspect, and appears the most to contradict the promise. Like Abraham, *against hope* we are to believe *in hope.* We must endeavour to do so as ever we would not wish to be chargeable with the crime of *making* the *God* of truth *a liar.* It was the approved exercise of all the saints recorded in scripture, particularly of that illustrious group of them in the eleventh of the epistle to the Hebrews, to trust the divine word in opposition to all appearances. Two things are always at the bottom of this desponding frame of Spirit.

The first is, a disposition to think of the church, as if it were to be supported and advanced by the same worldly means that are used to support and advance a civil society, and that without those external supports, it must be ruined. On the contrary, we are to consider the church as a building the carrying on of which is in Christ's hands; for he *shall build the temple of the Lord, and shall bear the glory:* We are to consider it as the fruit of the travail of his soul; the production and gathering of which cannot possibly fail, being altogether the work of the wisdom, power, mercy and faithfulness of God: We are to consider it as the body of Christ, which by his infinite care and love, is in as perfect safety (so faith beholds it) amidst all his enemies on earth, as the huhuman nature of his wonderful person, far, far as it is beyond their reach in heaven.

The other thing is rashness in determining, that the Lord is not at all accomplishing his promise, because he is not doing so to our carnal apprehensions and limited views. Jacob was in this unbelieving haste when he said, *All these things are against me.* What political sagacity could have discerned the advancement of Joseph in his state of slavery and imprisonment? Who would have thought that God was accomplishing the most glorious of all his works in humiliation and sufferings of Christ, in the reproaches, the temptations, the mocking, scourging, buffeting, crowning with thorns, the wrath of God, and the cursed death which he endured?

As these desponding apprehensions have a tendency to relax our endeavours for the advancement of Christ's kingdom; so they are too often used as a pretext or excuse for the neglect of such endeavours. The language of spiritual sloth is like that of one who came to the ruler of the synagogue from his house; *Thy daughter is dead, trouble not the Master.*

It is indeed our duty to mourn for the grounds of the Lord's controversy with us. But unbelieving despondency unfits us for the exercise; since it hardens the heart by leading us to entertain dishonourable suspicions of God as if he would not, or could not accomplish his promise. Unbelieving despondency is only grieved for the Lord's righteous procedure against a sinning people; but gospel-humiliation is a kindly sorrow of heart for the sin and rebellion which have been the cause of such awful procedure. Unbelieving despondency leads us to murmur at the ways of God, and to excuse our own conduct; on the contrary, true humiliation of soul leads us to

C c c

justify God and condemn ourselves. This despondency, therefore, however it may put on the mask of humility, is, at bottom, the most intolerable pride and rebellion.

So much with regard to the spirit of despondency in general; we may now consider some of the particulars complained of.

In reply to all these particulars we may observe, that it is the Lord's usual way to suffer his work both in persons and in churches, to be brought very low, even to the very brink of utter destruction, at least in their apprehension, that his revival of it may be the more conspicuous; that he may appear in his glory. Another reason why he suffers it to be so, is, that his people, deprived of all carnal means and of every sensible support, may be shut up to a single dependence on the God of their salvation, on that unseen hand which hath wrought such wonders, and is ever working for the church's deliverance. In the promise, the tribulation of the church is infallibly connected with her deliverance; and the apparent extreme of the former with the most glorious instances of the latter; a connection which believed and duly improved, would give us *meat out of the eater, and sweetness out of the strong.*

We need not wonder that very fair and plausible schemes are formed in opposition to the testimony of Christ; and some of the Lord's people themselves are led away by them, as the apostle Peter was oftener than once, to oppose the work of God. Many and various are the devices of Satan: He leads the men of the world to an open and direct opposition to the cause of Christ; but he has more refined methods of drawing even the godly to oppose it in some respect or another. The Lord himself permits it to be so, that the church may see the necessity of having a single regard to the law and the testimony; to shew her members that they are not to call any man master in the matters of God, however great his usefulness or his attainments in godliness; to incite Christians to more diligence in studying the testimony of Christ; for as many of the properties of gold are discovered by comparing it with such metals as are likest it in appearance; so we may attain a more accurate knowledge of the cause of Christ or the word of his patience by comparing it with the schemes of religion which bear the nearest resemblance to it. In fine, the Lord permits it to be so in order to shew Christians what hazard they run, while in this world, of being corrupted both in principle and practice. The most eminent saint may soon be led astray, if he grow careless and unwatchful.

We have great cause to lament the abounding of spiritual judgments: these are far more unequivocal evidences of God's wrath against a people than any outward calamities. Few, indeed, have any sight or sense of them; but they are only so much the more fatal. Well may we wish, with the prophet, that *our head were waters, and our eyes a fountain of tears*, to mourn the sore spiritual judgments that lie upon this generation. Only in such exercise, we should guard against two errors. One is charging God foolishly, as if he were to be blamed for these judgments: the procuring cause of all the hiding of his face, of our unprofitable attendance on ordinances, of our hearts being hardened from his fear, and of our being left to err from his way, is wholly with ourselves, not with God: For he says to us, *The Lord is with you, while ye are with him; and if ye seek him, he will be found of you: but if ye forsake him, he will forsake you.* We have ourselves only to blame for the restraint of the Holy Spirit, Micah ii. 7. *O thou that art named the house of Jacob, is the Spirit of the Lord straitened? Are these his doings? Do not my words do good to him that walketh uprightly?* The other error which we should study to avoid, is, unthankfulness for what kindness the Lord still continues to shew his people. We have his word and ordinances; and we may well believe they have their effects, however little observed: for *wherever he makes name be recorded, he will come* unto his people, *and bless them.* While he favours us with the pure preaching of the word and the administration of his ordinances, some will *be born in Zion;* some will be edified; Christians may want a very comfortable sense of the Lord's presence, but still his hand will lead them and support them. Perhaps indeed they know it not now; but they shall know hereafter. O how much reason have believers to be thankful for what light and conviction, for what strength, refreshment and establishment the Lord affords them by means of his word, even while they are saying, *Verily, thou art a God that hidest thyself, O God of Israel, the Saviour!*

It is true, The church of Christ is no more appropriated to any particular kingdom or corner of the world: She is not represented in scripture as stationary, but as sojourning from place to place: So that the Lord may soon remove his candlestick out of its place, and no one has ground to assure himself of its continuance for any particular space of time. We may only observe, that these lands of Britain and Ireland have been particularly honoured, not only in the eminent degree to which reformation has been carried in them; but in regard of the express and formal manner in which the Lord condescended to take them into covenant-relation with himself. It is true, the Jews were highly honoured in this respect, and yet they have been cut off. Nay, the Lord's anger seems to burn with peculiar intenseness against those who having entered into covenant with him, are obstinate in departing from him: if they will not be *his people,* according to their solemn engagement, he will make them *no people.* The political constitution of the Jews was destroyed almost at the same time with their ecclesiastical: when they ceased to be the church of God, they ceased to be a nation. We are assured, however, that the dispersed remains of them shall yet be *turned to the Lord*. They are still preserved distinct from all the nations among whom they are scattered for this, among other important ends, that their conversion may be the more conspicuous. In like manner, though these lands should depart still farther from the Lord, and though he should be provoked to make them a desolation; yet after all such dreadful calamities, when we shall be brought to know the Lord, we may look for a revival of his work: *He will bring a third part thro' the fire, and will refine them as silver is refined, and will try them as gold is tried; they shall call on his name, and he will hear them: he will say, it is my people; and they shall say, the Lord is my God.* When the Lord's time comes, all the opposition to his work from prejudices, from the most deep-rooted opinions, from civil laws and constitutions, will prove no more than flax before the devouring flame. It is, indeed, affecting to think of the calamities that are likely to take place before so glorious a revolution: but it will comfort the heart of a real Christian to consider that even the calamities of Britain and Ireland, will be over-ruled to the advancement of Christ's kingdom; that they bear the most threatening aspect on the enemies of his work in these lands; and may be somehow an occasion of the spreading of the gospel to the remotest climes and to the most barbarous nations.

F I N I S.

INDEX.

A

ABEL's profession, Page 100.
Abraham, the church's profession from him to Moses, 105——112. Of the Lord's covenant with him, 106—108. Of his profession, 108, 109.
Accommodation of our covenants to our present circumstances, 263.
Adam, Of the church's profession from him to Abraham, 99——105.
Admonition, 324.
Antioch, a dispute among the church-members of, determined at Jerusalem, 189, 190.
Ariminum in Italy a council at, 191.
Arius's heresy, 190.
Asa, the covenanting in his time, 143—145.
Associate Presbytery, formed, 33. their entering into the bond for renewing our covenants, 256. their act concerning covenanting, 263, 264.
Athanasius, 192.
Augsburg, a diet of the empire held there, 197, 198.

B

Babylonish captivity, advantageous to the church, 155.
Baptismal engagements how to be understood, 60, 61.
Bohemia, the brethren and sisters of, 194.
Breach of covenant an aggravated sin, 79, 80.
Burgess Oaths, on the controversy concerning the religious clause of, 5——26.

C

Calvin's agreement with the church of Zurich, 199, 200.
Campbel Mr. his tenets, 32.
Censures, the church's power to inflict them, 313——321. nature of them, 321—324.

Ceremonial laws, 118.
Ceremonies, not commanded of God, no way like covenanting, 63, 64.
Cerinthus 187.
Character of Covenanters, 62, 63.
Charles Vth. his opposition to the reformed religion, 196, 197.
Charles I. struggles between him and the Scots, 214——221.
Christianity different from all other religions, 366, 367. how we should enquire into the evidences of it, 373, 374.
Church, how the word is used in scripture, 279, 281, 316, 317.
Church-communion, the nature of, 281—286. when that of a particular church may be departed from, 22, 23, 24.
Concordate, 199.
Confessions of the Protestant churches, 200.
Confessions of faith, how ratified at the revolution, 268, 271.
Congregation. when the Scots reformers were so called, 203.
Constantinople a council held at, 192.
Constitution of the Associate Synod, 312, 313.
Covenant how the word is used in scripture, 168, 169.
Covenanting, characteristics of it, 46——62, how distinguished from the sacraments, 57—63, *History* of it, 96, 97, 98—265
Creeds of the ancient churches. 180,--192.

D

Deism, the causes of it, 359—361.
Delivering up to Satan, the meaning of in the New Testament, 336, 337.
Despondency of Christians, 410.
Devotional selfishness, 384, 385.
Dort, the Synod of, 201.

E

Ebion's heresy, 187.
Education the prejudices of it, 372, 373.
Ends of covenanting, 81, 82.
Enos, the state of the church at his death, 100, 101.
Enthusiasm, 100, 181.
Egypt, 56, 91.
Erasmus, a saying of, 195.
Eutyches's heresy, 193.
Essentials and circumstantials, 287.
Examples, the use of those in scripture, 180, 181; of those in church history, 187.
Excommunication, 327. under the Old Testament, 327——332. under the new, 333——339. grounds of it, 339——342. consistent with charity, 342—345. history of it, 347——358.
Ezra, the covenanting in his time, 257, 258.

F

Fathers severe in the exercise of church discipline, 353.
France, a bond entered into by the Protestant church of, 201, 202.

G

Gibeonites, their league with Joshua, 69. 70. obligation of it analogous to that of covenanting, 70, 71, 72.

H

Ham excommunicated by Noah, 349.
Herem, 350.
Hezekiah's covenanting, 147—150.
High commission, the court of, 213.
Hussites, 174.

I

James I. 212—214.
Idolatry, 128, 129.
Jehoash the covenanting in his time, 145, 146.
Jewish state, 120——130. and church 130—132.
Independents, overturned the reformation in England, 232, their toleration, 247, 248.
Indulgences popish, 302.
Joshua's renewal of the covenant, 140, 141.
Josiah, the covenanting in his time, 151——154.
Ireland covenanting in, 234
Isaac and Jacob the covenant renewed with, 111. profession of the latter. 111, 112.
Judicial laws, 1119.

K

Kings of Israel useful to the church, 142, 143. in what characters many of them acted, 148, 149.

L

Law, why the Lord's revelation to Moses so called, 114. how it is to be considered as it was given by Moses, 115—117. of the nature and different kinds of the laws of Moses, 118—120.
Leith besieged, 206, the last bond at, 207.
Liberty contended for in the reformation of Scotland, 202, and in the covenanting of the three kingdoms, 215.
Lollards, 194.
Lorain, the house of, 202.

M

Marrow of Modern Divinity condemned by the Gen. Assembly, 32.
Martyrs for our covenanted reformation, 244.
Mary Queen of Scots, 208, 209.
Monuments of idolatry destroyed, 203, 204.
Moral nature of covenanting, 174——177.
Moses, Of the Lord's revelation to, 113.
Murray earl of, 209.

N

Nations may join in covenanting, 65, 66, 172.
Nehemiah, covenanting in his time, 159——161.
New Testament dispensation, the characteristics of, 167——174.
Noah's covenant, 101—103. his profession, 104, 105.

O

Oath, the important nature of it, 13. religious oaths imposed by civil societies, 5.
Obligations from covenanting 67. the extent of them, 68——80. those of our covenants recognised in the bond of the Associate Presbytery, 253.
Occasional duties, 84, 85. occasion of public covenanting, 83——96. at present, 264.
Offences given to Christians, 14.
Old Testament, its uses and obligations, 161——167.

P

Perth a treaty at, 204, 205.
Practice of a duty having been long neglected no reason for omitting it, 158, 159.
Presbyterial exercise of church power, 316——321.
Profession of religion, 18, 19.
Progress in reformation how to be endeavoured, 41, 42.
Promise, why the revelation made to Abraham so called, 107, 108, 114.
Protestants, the rise of that appellation, 197.
Public resolutioners, 39, 229, 230.

Q

Queen Regent under the influence of the house of Loraine, 202. Her opposition to the reformers, 203——207.

R

Rebuke, 234.
Rechabites, 74, 75.
Reformation, the difficulties of, 195.

Renewing of the covenant which the Israelites had entered into at Sinai, 139, 140.
Renovation of our covenants in the Secession, 237.
Representation necessary in some religious duties, 68. and in covenanting, 74, 75.
Revolution, the advantages of it, 266, how misimproved, 267——278.

S

Sacraments, why baptism and the Lord's supper called so, 59, 60.
Samosatenus's heresy, 189.
Secession testimony, 27, 45. its rise and progress, 30—33. matter of it not new, 34, 35. explained in three particulars, 35——40.
Shammatha, 325, 326.
Signs were in place of history in the Patriarchal age, 110.
Simson Mr. his tenets, 32.
Sinai, the transaction at, 115, 116, 117, 133, 134.
Smalcaldic league, 198, 199.
Solemn league and covenant, 230——236. defended, 237——254.

T

Temporizer the character of, 375, 376, 377.
Testimony of the church, the nature of, 28, 29.
Tumult occasioned by the imposition of the English Liturgy, 216.

U

United provinces, 200.

V

Valens and Ursacius two artful opposers of the Nicene Creed, 191, 192.
Variety in religion, 372.
Vowing, a characteristic of covenanting, 52, 53.

W

Waldenses and Wickliffites, 188, 189.
Worms, a diet of the empire held at, 196.

Z

Zeno, the emperor's henoticon, 192, 193.

ERRATA.

Page 36. line. dele *go forth and.* P. 49. l. 5. for *languages* read *language.* Page 55. l. 4. dele *the purport of.* P. 268. l. 15. for *act that* read *act of that.* P. 363. l. 23. for *natural* read *material.* P. 368. l. 34 and 35. for *Fohi* read *Fo.*

www.ingramcontent.com/pod-product-compliance
Lightning Source LLC
Chambersburg PA
CBHW030544300426
44111CB00009B/851